Advancing the Power of Learning Analytics and Big Data in Education

Ana Azevedo
CEOS:PP, ISCAP, Polytechnic of Porto, Portugal

José Manuel Azevedo
CEOS:PP, ISCAP, Polytechnic of Porto, Portugal

James Onohuome Uhomoibhi
Ulster University, UK

Ebba Ossiannilsson
International Council for Open and Distance Education (ICDE), Norway & European Distance and e-Learning Network (EDEN), UK & Swedish Association for Distance Education (SADE), Sweden

A volume in the Advances in Educational Technologies and Instructional Design (AETID) Book Series

IGI Global
PUBLISHER of TIMELY KNOWLEDGE

Published in the United States of America by
IGI Global
Information Science Reference (an imprint of IGI Global)
701 E. Chocolate Avenue
Hershey PA, USA 17033
Tel: 717-533-8845
Fax: 717-533-8661
E-mail: cust@igi-global.com
Web site: http://www.igi-global.com

Library of Congress Cataloging-in-Publication Data

Names: Azevedo, Ana, editor. | Azevedo, Jose Manuel, DATE editor. | Uhomoibhi, J. O., editor. | Ossiannilsson, Ebba, DATE editor.
Title: Advancing the power of learning analytics and big data in education / Ana Azevedo, Jose Manuel Azevedo, James Onohuome Uhomoibhi, Ebba Siv Ingegärd Ossiannilsson, editors.
Description: Hershey, PA : Information Science Reference, an imprint of IGI Global, [2021] | Includes bibliographical references and index. | Summary: "This book reports on the role and impact of learning analytics training and development in education, investigating how various stakeholders are engaged in the design, deployment and assessment of successful and sustainable learning analytics"-- Provided by publisher.
Identifiers: LCCN 2020036951 (print) | LCCN 2020036952 (ebook) | ISBN 9781799871033 (hardcover) | ISBN 9781799885658 (softcover) | ISBN 9781799871040 (ebook)
Subjects: LCSH: Educational technology--Research--Methodology. | Education--Data processing. | Computer-assisted instruction.
Classification: LCC LB1028.3 .A35527 2021 (print) | LCC LB1028.3 (ebook) | DDC 371.33--dc23
LC record available at https://lccn.loc.gov/2020036951
LC ebook record available at https://lccn.loc.gov/2020036952

This book is published in the IGI Global book series Advances in Educational Technologies and Instructional Design (AETID) (ISSN: 2326-8905; eISSN: 2326-8913)

British Cataloguing in Publication Data
A Cataloguing in Publication record for this book is available from the British Library.

All work contributed to this book is new, previously-unpublished material.
The views expressed in this book are those of the authors, but not necessarily of the publisher.

For electronic access to this publication, please contact: eresources@igi-global.com.

Advances in Educational Technologies and Instructional Design (AETID) Book Series

ISSN:2326-8905
EISSN:2326-8913

Editor-in-Chief: Lawrence A. Tomei, Robert Morris University, USA

MISSION

Education has undergone, and continues to undergo, immense changes in the way it is enacted and distributed to both child and adult learners. In modern education, the traditional classroom learning experience has evolved to include technological resources and to provide online classroom opportunities to students of all ages regardless of their geographical locations. From distance education, Massive-Open-Online-Courses (MOOCs), and electronic tablets in the classroom, technology is now an integral part of learning and is also affecting the way educators communicate information to students.

The **Advances in Educational Technologies & Instructional Design (AETID) Book Series** explores new research and theories for facilitating learning and improving educational performance utilizing technological processes and resources. The series examines technologies that can be integrated into K-12 classrooms to improve skills and learning abilities in all subjects including STEM education and language learning. Additionally, it studies the emergence of fully online classrooms for young and adult learners alike, and the communication and accountability challenges that can arise. Trending topics that are covered include adaptive learning, game-based learning, virtual school environments, and social media effects. School administrators, educators, academicians, researchers, and students will find this series to be an excellent resource for the effective design and implementation of learning technologies in their classes.

COVERAGE

- Hybrid Learning
- Educational Telecommunications
- Adaptive Learning
- Collaboration Tools
- Instructional Design Models
- Higher Education Technologies
- Instructional Design
- Virtual School Environments
- Bring-Your-Own-Device
- Online Media in Classrooms

IGI Global is currently accepting manuscripts for publication within this series. To submit a proposal for a volume in this series, please contact our Acquisition Editors at Acquisitions@igi-global.com or visit: http://www.igi-global.com/publish/.

The Advances in Educational Technologies and Instructional Design (AETID) Book Series (ISSN 2326-8905) is published by IGI Global, 701 E. Chocolate Avenue, Hershey, PA 17033-1240, USA, www.igi-global.com. This series is composed of titles available for purchase individually; each title is edited to be contextually exclusive from any other title within the series. For pricing and ordering information please visit http://www.igi-global.com/book-series/advances-educational-technologies-instructional-design/73678. Postmaster: Send all address changes to above address.

Titles in this Series

For a list of additional titles in this series, please visit: http://www.igi-global.com/book-series/

Applying Universal Design for Learning Across Disciplines Case Studies on Implementation
Frederic Fovet (Royal Roads University, Canada)
Information Science Reference • © 2021 • 335pp • H/C (ISBN: 9781799871064) • US $195.00

Advancing Online Course Design and Pedagogy for the 21st Century Learning Environment
Daniel Chatham (Middlebury Institute of International Studies at Monterey, USA)
Information Science Reference • © 2021 • 382pp • H/C (ISBN: 9781799855989) • US $195.00

Affordances and Constraints of Mobile Phone Use in English Language Arts Classrooms
Clarice M. Moran (Appalachian State University, USA)
Information Science Reference • © 2021 • 229pp • H/C (ISBN: 9781799858058) • US $175.00

Examining an Operational Approach to Teaching Probability
Alessio Drivet (Geogebra Institute of Turin, Italy)
Information Science Reference • © 2021 • 369pp • H/C (ISBN: 9781799838715) • US $195.00

4C-ID Model and Cognitive Approaches to Instructional Design and Technology Emerging Research and Opportunities
Guilhermina Maria Lobato Ferreira de Miranda (Instituto de Educação, Universidade de Lisboa, Portugal) Manuel Joaquim Henriques Rafael (Universidade de Lisboa, Portugal) Mário Marcelino Luis de Melo (UI, DEF, Instituto de Educação, Universidade de Lisboa, Portugal) Joana Martinho de Almeida Costa Pardal (Instituto Universitário de Lisboa (ISCTE-IUL), ISTAR, Portugal) and Thiago Bessa Pontes (Universidade Federal do Cariri, Brazil)
Information Science Reference • © 2021 • 243pp • H/C (ISBN: 9781799840961) • US $175.00

IGI Global
PUBLISHER of TIMELY KNOWLEDGE

701 East Chocolate Avenue, Hershey, PA 17033, USA
Tel: 717-533-8845 x100 • Fax: 717-533-8661
E-Mail: cust@igi-global.com • www.igi-global.com

Table of Contents

Section 2
Organizational Issues

Section 3
Application Cases

Detailed Table of Contents

This chapter describes how a public university has met the challenge of changing inside the educational culture and preparing its teachers to manage online teaching-learning processes using learning analytics to contribute to the design, evaluation, and improvement of SMOOC. From the results obtained with a survey answered by the teachers, a twenty-hour class SMOOC was developed that focuses on instrumental aspects of digital technological resources in the teaching and learning contexts, as well as in the pedagogical issues, which concern the appropriate use of digital technologies. The findings of this research demonstrate that the SMOOC has been able to meet the teacher training needs, which are changing the way they work since remote education has been the viable alternative to guarantee the functioning of the university in the coronavirus pandemic period. However, it is believed that the knowledge that teachers are acquiring will contribute to changes in professional practice even post-pandemic.

Despite the idea that learning is individual, the YouTube channel has been examined to explain how learning is controlled in social networks. What kind of mechanism does the YouTube channel, which deeply influences the education world, work with and what does this structure tell the educators? What do data such as the number of views and comments on YouTube mean? Also, what kind of a model can be established between the video proposition system and our individual and social learning? This study has been prepared to shed light on the questions mentioned.

The meaning of the term "big data" can be inferred by its name itself (i.e., the collection of large structured or unstructured data sets). In addition to their huge quantity, these data sets are so complex that they cannot be analyzed in any way

Preface

This book provides the researcher and professional, policy makers and interested practitioner with an easily understood introduction, insight, tools, techniques and current state of developments in the field of Big data and learning analytics. This is a field, which has seen phenomenal changes that continue to impact education, governments and society.

Big Data and Learning Analytics topic of growing interest in the research communities. INFORMS defines analytics as the scientific process of transforming data into insights with the goal of making better decisions. Since the field of analytics is in the area of decision support systems, it has a wide range of applications. One important application relates to the educational environment where the three types of analytics, namely descriptive, predictive and prescriptive, are used.

Learning analytics can also be explained as the measurement, collection, analysis, and reporting of data about learners and their contexts in order to understand and optimize learning and the environments in which it occurs. The growth of online learning since the 1990s, particularly in higher education, has contributed to the evolution of Learning Analytics as student data can be captured and made available for analysis. When learners use an LMS, social media, or similar online tools, their clicks, navigation patterns, time spent on an assignment, social networking, information flow, and concept development can be tracked through discussion. The rapid development of Massive Open Online Courses (MOOCs) provides additional data for researchers to evaluate teaching and learning in online environments.

Big Data is hugely relevant today. Big data analytics accelerates the speed at which research work is done. One such example is the decoding of DNA strings which now takes minutes to accomplish leading to faster creation of cures and ability to predict trends of diseases. Big Data is changing the world and is heavily used in security, health, science, retail and finance.

Learning Analytics, as a field, has several disciplinary roots. While the fields of artificial intelligence (AI), statistical analysis, machine learning, and business intelligence provide an additional narrative, the most important historical roots of analytics are those directly related to human interaction and the educational system. More specifically, the history of Learning Analytics is closely linked to the development of four Social Sciences' fields that have converged over time. These fields pursued and still pursue four goals:

1. *Definition of Learner*, in order to cover the need of defining and understanding a learner.
2. *Knowledge trace*, addressing how to trace or map the knowledge that occurs during the learning process.
3. *Learning efficiency and personalization*, which refers to how to make learning more efficient and personal by means of technology.
4. *Learner – content comparison*, in order to improve learning by comparing the learner's level of knowledge with the actual content that needs to master

Four models are recognized and used for Learning analytics. They include

- Learning Analytics as a prediction
- Learning Analytics as a generic design framework
- Learning Analytics as data-driven decision making
- Learning Analytics as an application of analytics

Nowadays, the term Learning Analytics is used in the context of using analytics in e-Learning environments. Learning Analytics is widely used to improve quality. It utilizes data about students and their activities to provide better understanding and improve student learning.

The use of LMS where student activities are easily accessible has promoted the use of Learning Analytics to understand the journey of students during the learning process and help them improve during this process. Proficient use of Learning Analytics can help students become aware of their progress, allowing them to take control of their own learning. Another important application of Learning Analytics relates to the detection of situations where students drop out of the course prematurely, which is an important problem in eLearning environments.

Relevant topics related to Learning Analytics include, which was also given in the call, but are not limited to:

- Pedagogical and Educational Perspectives
- Techniques and methods for Learning Analytics
- Impact of Learning Analytics
- Feedback for students
- Software for Learning Analytics
- Adaptive Learning

- Learning Metrics
- Ethical and legal issues
- Analytics in e-assessment applications
- Educational Mining
- Virtual and Remote Experiments Based Learning
- Learning in Mixed Environments
- Innovative learning Spaces
- Quality related issues based on Learning Analytics
- Others considered relevant to this area

The target audience for this book are primarily teachers, professionals in the area of Learning Analytics, senior managers, researchers, academicians, practitioners, and graduate students. As the use of Learning Analytics can be related to the four different frameworks: generic design, prediction, data-driven design and applications there can be a variety of diverse stakeholders.

A lot has changed in education. Although it can be said that learning analytics has been part of teaching and learning since the beginning of education, in the current digital age, there is exponential growth of data that brings with it the potential to analyse the trends in order to determine possible actors for the improvement of learning and teaching success. Today the challenge lies not in gaining access but in the determination of which data are significant and why they are so.

The primary goal of this book is to provide insight into the use of Big Data and Learning Analytics. This is a highly topical and important subject that deserves reflection, and this book is an excellent opportunity to do so. The book aims to:

- Report on the role and impact of big data and learning analytics training and development in education.
- Accept research contributions that report on how different stakeholders are involved in the design, deployment and evaluation of successful and sustainable big data and learning analytics. These contributions may be theoretical, methodological, empirical, and technical in nature.

Factors influencing Learning Analytics and Big Data would include for example (i) human factors in learning analytics systems, (ii) geographical factors (physical and virtual), (iii) technical/technological factors, (iv) analytical tools, and (v) ethical and legal factors of the use of Learning Analytics.

The 11 chapters in this book are organized in four sections

- Section 1: Background and Literature Review (3 chapters)
- Section 2: Organizational Issues (3 chapters)

- Section 3: Application Cases (3 chapters)
- Section 4: Some Technological Issues (2 chapters)

Chapter 1 presents and examines the current state of learning analytics by providing a synthesis review based on the combination of activity theory and pedagogy. It contributes to the understanding on how to combine Activity theory and pedagogical strategies as an analysis framework. The chapter analyzes Learning Analytics applications in several scenarios within seven components: subject, objective, community, tools, rules, division of labor and outcomes. In addition, it addresses that a variety of stakeholders, have their needs for Learning Analytics. Combining AT and pedagogical strategies as an analysis framework, this chapter analyzes LAs application scenarios in seven components: subject, objective, community, tools, rules, division of labor and outcomes. It concludes that with learning applications, teachers and students are main subjects; knowledge mastery is a common object; researchers and administrators play important role; that learning analytics integrate with multiple assessments; behaviorism, cognitivism and constructivism embodied at different degrees and that measurements of learning analytics application are diverse.

Chapter 2 reports on the opportunities for adopting open research data in learning analytics. It discusses some of the progress that the Learning Analytics community has made in shifting towards open practices, and it addresses the barriers that researchers in this discipline have to face. In addition, the chapter addresses the relevance of Open Research Data. It shows that in Learning Analytics though, it seems that data are not sufficiently published and re-used. The barriers are evaluated, the causes are investigated, some potential ways forward are considered.

Chapter 3 is on reflections on adaptive learning analytics. It draws on the individualized nature of learning analytics which provides more effective learning experience and opportunities to explain the concepts. It shows adaptive learning analytics, as a subset of learning analytics provides content to provide learners with more effective and adaptive learning opportunities resulting in accurate individualized learning.

Chapter 4 deals with ethics in predictive analytics using an empirical case study on students perceptions in a Northern Irish university. The chapter contributes strongly to the increased privacy and ethical issues related to Learning Analytics, and it especially address how students perceive the way ethical issues are related to Predictive Learning Analytics (PLA) in the light of sensitive data harvesting practices. To date few very few empirical studies have been done on this subject. This chapter identifies three distinct classes of students based on their assumptions. They include (1) Naïve and Trusting, (2) Cautious and Compromising, and (3) Enlightened and Demanding, focusing only on the issue of informed consent. It goes further to support the need for predictive learning analytics researchers to recognize this and to educate all types of students in issues related to ethics.

Chapter 5 proposes an overview on the use of Learning Analytics (LA) and Educational Data Mining (EDM) in addressing issues related to its uses and applications in higher education. It is important as it provides significant answers to how both LA and EDM can advance Higher education from a large scale, big data educational research perspective. Various tasks and applications already in existence in EDM and LA in higher education are provided and categorised based on their purposes, uses and impacts on various stakeholders. Implications for ethics and privacy in using EDM and LA in higher education are considered.

Chapter 6 encapsulates the framework of learning analytics by considering the practice of gaining universal values based on learning analytics framework. Leisure activities and practices of students in learning outcomes based on the role of learning analytics framework are evaluated. Students are seen to feel the value of practice-based activities and they become satisfied in their leisure times with different activities. In-Service training is reported to be essential for teachers to develop the practice of leisure education.

Chapter 7 deals with learning analytics in the monitoring of learning processes with focus on 3D educational collaborative virtual environments. It presents a framework that tries to extend the collaborative three-dimensional virtual environments for educational by integrating a LA tool aimed at helping teachers to be able to monitor and evaluate students' learning in these types of environment. The chapter provided a comprehensive analysis of learning analytics tools, the design and in-depth evaluation of user-centred framework for identification of possible patterns of students.

Chapter 8 is about learning analytics as a tool for planning, evaluation and improvement of a SMOOC for teacher development in higher education. Using the case of Brazil, it describes how a Public University has met the challenge of changing internal educational culture and preparing its teachers to manage online teaching-learning processes using learning analytics to contribute to the design, evaluation, and improvement of SMOOC, which is shown to meet the training needs of teachers in unprecedented times of the coronavirus pandemic. It is project that the knowledge and skills which teachers are acquiring will contribute to changes in professional practice post-pandemic

Chapter 9 takes a look at social learning analytics by examining and reporting on how learning is done on YouTube. Although learning is mainly an individual process, the chapter explains how learning is controlled in social networks and provides insight into the mechanisms are adopted, what they are, how they influence the education world and they are measured and applied. Such factors as number of views of a channel and comments made are considered. All of these are important as they shed light on how we learn on YouTube.

Chapter 10 begins by defining big data, explaining the need and usefulness in education, research, business and society. The importance of big data and their relevance, usefulness and methods of handling them or knowledge extraction are investigated and reported. The chapter also examines characteristics of big data and cloud computing as a tool that provides a platform for computation of the massive amount of data and its storage.

Chapter 11 examines and reports on educational data mining (EDM) used to discover knowledge from educational and academic databases for decision making in educational and academic systems. chapter addresses educational data mining (EDM) which is useful in many different areas including identifying at risk students, identifying priority learning needs for different groups of students, increasing graduation rates, effectively assessing institutional performance, maximizing campus resources, and optimizing subject curriculum renewal. The importance of this chapter stems from the fact that the techniques and applications presented and discussed provide insight and clear-cut ideas for educational data mining and research work.

Big data and learning analytics have the power to transform education, educational research and society. Governments, businesses, and researchers are only now beginning to realize and appreciate the potential that big data and learning analytics offer in informing policy ideas, contributing to the development of new educational tools and innovative ways of conducting research as well as improving lives of individuals and organizations in society. The various chapters explore current state-of-the-art of Big data and learning analytics, examining them and their implications for education and schooling for today and the future.

This book, with contributions from all authors, makes an important contribution to the study, knowledge, and application of Learning Analytics. The chapters have both theoretical and practical implications within their fields. The rise and extent of open online learning and the shift of education to online and distance learning due to the pandemic COVID -19 there are many important and crucial lessons for what to call the new normal, the next normal, the best normal, for whom and why. In addition, the rise and scale of Massive Open Online Courses (MOOC) during the Learning Analytics pandemic will provide very important information for the future of education that relates to all of the now recognized four frameworks. All the major MOOCS providers such as COURSERA, EDx, FutureLearn, Miranda and SWYAM have reported this scale and increase. For example, COURSERA reported back in July 2020 that more than 1.6 million learners worldwide benefit from the contributions of Coursera partners. They also provide free access to over 3,600 online courses from leading universities and companies. Learning analytics are in this respect incredible useful to achieve valuable insights in respect of its four domains' and to make predictions for the futures of education, not at least from the learners perspectives, to learn to know the learners.

Big data and learning analytics have impacts on teachers and policy makers, students, data itself and systems. They influence decision making for teachers and policy makers as they engage in monitoring and reporting. They influence students, their own data and own learning as they engage in reflective practice, deduction of personal feedback and use of personal analytics for improvement of own learning. The influence on data we consider the research questions posed and the potential of the data generated. In the case of systems, their use make it possible for systems to be able to adapt, be automated and be informed of change.

We wish to express our special gratitude to all authors and reviewers for their kind cooperation and contributions in making the publication of this book a success. We also thank members of the publishing team at IGI Global for their kind advice and help in producing this book.

Ana Azevedo
CEOS:PP, ISCAP, Polytechnic of Porto, Portugal

José Manuel Azevedo
CEOS:PP, ISCAP, Polytechnic of Porto, Portugal

James Onohuome Uhomoibhi
Ulster University, UK

Ebba Ossiannilsson
International Council for Open and Distance Education (ICDE), Norway & European Distance and e-Learning Network (EDEN), UK & Swedish Association for Distance Education (SADE), Sweden

Acknowledgment

To all the authors of the chapters, and to all the reviewers: we feel very much grateful with their collaboration with this project; without their work this could be not possible.

To all the members of the Publishing team at IGI: we are very much grateful for their help, expert support, and guidance.

Last but not the least, this book is dedicated to our respective families.

Section 1
Background and Literature Review

Chapter 1
Current State of Learning Analytics:
A Synthesis Review Based on the Combination of Activity Theory and Pedagogy

Wenting Sun
Humboldt University of Berlin, Germany

Niels Pinkwart
Humboldt University of Berlin, Germany

Tongji Li
Tongji University, China

ABSTRACT

Applying learning analytics (LAs) to actual teaching scenarios is a huge challenge. One of the problems that is required to be solved is how to combine LAs with pedagogy. Activity theory (AT) provides a conceptional tool for social human activities including objects and tools. Combining AT and pedagogical strategies as an analysis framework, this chapter analyzes LA application scenarios in seven components: subject, objective, community, tools, rules, division of labor, and outcomes. And learning theories present an in-depth analysis of rules. Conclusion shows in the LA application: teachers and students are main subjects; knowledge mastery is a common object; researchers and administrators play important roles while teachers have no specific teaching guidance to follow; presentation strategies of content are abundant; LAs integrate with multiple assessments; behaviorism, cognitivism, and constructivism embodied at different degrees; measurement of LAs application are diverse; not only learners, but characteristics of tasks need to be further studied.

DOI: 10.4018/978-1-7998-7103-3.ch001

INTRODUCTION

Learning analytics (LAs) has penetrated into modern learning activities. The Horizon Report 2011 putted LAs in the list of four to five years widespread adoption educational technologies (New Media Consortium, 2011), whereas LAs become a common part of the educational technologies in the Horizon Report 2020 (Educause Publications, 2020). As an integral part of the education system, LAs affords tools for studying learning behaviors of students, strengthening adaptive or personalized learning and improving potential learning efficiency. LAs plays useful roles in the effective usage of educational big data and the construction of ubiquitous learning environment. On the other hand, the development of LAs demands the combination of learning behaviors, pedagogic strategies and educational decision-making process.

However, as a long-existed human activity, involving new tools into education's normal operation is complicated. The application of LAs follows certain rules and patterns. For instance, the RAPID outcome mapping approach (ROMA) engages LAs in the institution community of stakeholders (Macfadyen et al., 2014). A generic framework for LAs offered by Greller and Drachsler (2012) incorporates LAs with learning activities and pedagogic strategies. A preliminary model of pedagogical learning analytics intervention design focus on addressing questions about how to directly impact instruction and learning activities using LAs (Wise, 2014). It could be seen from the above, stakeholders, pedagogies and learning process are what should be concerned when integrating LAs into a given education context. Those involved factors try to find their own places in education activities, which is a group human activity carefully designed with purpose, result orientation, and clear division of labor. In this way, Activity theory (AT) offers a general analysis framework. Based on Vygotsky's foundational work, the third generation of AT proposed by Engeström (1987/2015) try to address questions of diversity and to understand the interaction between different perspectives. The third-generation of AT framework consists of seven basic factors: subject, object, rules, tools, community, division of labor and outcomes. The interaction between those factors in the framework makes a conceptional tool available for the application of LAs in the education context which considers the dynamic interactivity among stakeholders, tools, pedagogy, objects and outcomes. In order to better understand the integration of LAs with learning and teaching process, this study applies AT to analyze the involved subject, objects, community, LA tools and pedagogy strategies in LAs application context.

BACKGROUND

Learning Analytics (LAs)

There are many different definitions of the term, Learning analytics (LAs). LAK'11 conference (2011) defines LAs as "the measurement, collection, analysis and reporting of data about learners and their contexts, for purposes of understanding and optimizing learning and the environments in which it occurs" (https://tekri.athabascau.ca/analytics/). Ifenthaler and Widanapathirana (2014) emphasize the real-time nature of the whole process of LAs in order to better benefit stakeholders and the integration of LAs into the learning and teaching process. There are overlaps among those definitions: LAs aims at establishing a virtuous circle between teaching and learning process in education environments. This means LAs should concern personalized learning and pedagogic strategies.

LAs require support of pedagogies to be integrated into educational context. Greller and Drachsler (2012) pointed out that pedagogies ought to be keep in mind when education data turn learning goals to learners' performance and suggested a model of learning analytics and pedagogy. LAs is regarded as a part of the teaching and learning practice process in a given educational context, to improve the effectiveness of teacher intervention as a basis (Wise, 2014; Persico & Pozzi, 2015). Koehler et al. (2007) putted forward a technological pedagogical content knowledge (TPCK) model conjoining three interacting components of content, pedagogy and technology in teaching knowledge. Further, Angeli and Valanides (2009) extend this model in details.

However, many articles still find the shortage of pedagogy in LAs. New Media Consortium (2011) mentioned that to better utilize the strength of LAs in educational environments, relevant personnel are required to construct association between technology and teaching methods. Ferguson (2012) discussed that the development of LAs short of pedagogy theories. Bakharia et al. (2015) noticed that the critical challenge of LAs is how to utilize available LA tools and data to support teaching process.

Although more and more attention has been paid to the combination of LAs and pedagogies, focused on the combination of LAs and actual teaching situations (Wise, 2014; Koh et al., 2016), the literature in this area still need to be expanded (Tempelaar et al., 2015). Further, the published articles do not specifically clarify how the collected data promotes and connects the learning analysis process (Ferguson & Clow, 2017). Thence, this chapter explores how LAs as mediation tools serves teaching and learning process in current LAs application contexts.

Pedagogy

The unified definition of pedagogy is difficult to recognize. According to Alexander (2008), "Pedagogy is the act of teaching together with its attendant discourse of educational theories, values, evidence and justifications" (p.47). Shulman (1987) said, "general pedagogical knowledge, with special reference to those broad principles and strategies of classroom management and organization that appear to transcend subject matter" (p.8). Tan and Koh (2017) discussed, "Pedagogy is concerned with the specific and cumulative relationships and interactions among learners, educators, the content, and the environment" (p.4). The relationship between teaching and learning deepen the understanding of pedagogy (Loughran, 2013). Pedagogy is more a kind of tacit knowledge, which closely related to learning process.

Learning and teaching are inseparable. The theories of pedagogy require the conjoined effort of learning theories (Tan & Koh, 2017). And optimizing learning necessitates the founding that knowing how learning happen and how to support learning, for which learning analytics plays powerful supporting roles (Ferguson, 2012). Considering the relationships between pedagogy and learning, this chapter not only study the pedagogical strategies in the LAs using context but also learning theories behind it.

Activity Theory (AT)

AT feeds a useful systematic structure for analyzing the usage of tools in social context (Stevenson, 2008). There have been some articles using AT to analyze the combination of tools and pedagogies in educational activities (Stevenson, 2008; Joyes, 2006). But they are still a minority, and the entire teaching activity is not regarded as an activity, lacking the integration of pedagogies, learning theories and tools. AT try to integrate two directions, organizations, history on the one hand and actions, situations on the other hand (Engeström, 1987/2015). Similarly, it is essential for pedagogy to overcome this kind of split. National education policies, regulations and schools-level's education measures impact the pedagogical strategies teachers choose, while teachers further take interventions to students learning process considering specific education situation. Found on the distinction between activity and actions, the explanatory possibility of AT requisite the concrete analysis of data (Engeström, 1987/2015). Specifically, education activities consist of stakeholders' actions, like teachers' actions, students' actions and so on, for which the collected data in LAs support the interpretation materials. Therefore, this chapter combines AT with pedagogy as an analysis framework for the currently LAs usage scenarios.

THEORY FOUNDATION

This section integrates pedagogical strategies and AT to form the analysis framework and proposes questions which this chapter aims to solve. Besides, learning theories combined with pedagogies offer coding reference for later literature analysis.

Pedagogy and AT

Ciavarelli (2002) referred pedagogy as "the art of effective teaching" (p. 697) and concretize it with few questions. From those questions, pedagogical strategies are further derived (AbuSneineh & Zairi, 2010).

In addition to original three components (subject, object and tools), Engeström (1987/2015) expended AT by adding another 4 components: rules, community, division of labor, outcomes.

Combined with the above pedagogical strategies (AbuSneineh & Zairi, 2010), this chapter reinterprets the seven elements of AT to analyze the learning environment using LAs as tool:

Subject: mainly refers to users of the tool or target group of the tool, involving the characteristics of learners or the characteristics of teachers;

Object: what the subject wants to achieve through the tools. Sometimes there are two levels of meanings, one referring to the goal when the tool itself is designed, another referring to the goal which users of the tool own;

Tools: the LA tools employed in the learning process or specific algorithm of the LA tools;

Community: other related stakeholders along with the subject, referring to the human context of the activity, a school group or institution;

Rules: more related to pedagogy, mainly involving two aspects, showing three contents. The first is content-related, such as the discipline context involved in learning activity, the organization of content, the presentation or delivery strategy of content. Specific examples are model to display learning content, interaction helps to solve the difficulties of knowledge, to present the problem first or read the material first. The second is related to assessment, such as the conducted time and test methods. The third is the learning theory thoughts embodied by the first two;

Division of labor: the roles of subjects and communities involved in specific learning activities. Mainly, the roles of teachers, students, and tools in the entire learning activities, which has a certain overlap with the "object";

Outcomes: the positive and negative impact on users or the application scope of the tool.

This chapter aims to analyze the current status of LA tools with pedagogies by clustering them into AT framework. Based on the AT combined pedagogy strategies, the following six questions guide the review:

Question One: Who is the major subject of the LA tools using context impacted by pedagogies?

Question Two: Which objects appeared in the LA tools using context?

Question Three: What are the common types of LA tools in the learning context impacted by pedagogies?

Question Four: Which stakeholders are considered in the community besides subject and what division of labor are they taken?

Question Five: What content organization, assessment strategies and learning theories reveals in the LAs using context has been investigated?

Question Six: What interpretation can LA tools provide to help students understand their own learning process or help teachers guide their own teaching process?

Question Seven: What kind of outcomes of the LAs using have been investigated?

Pedagogy and Learning Theories

Learning theories is able to be applied as principles to guide specific pedagogical strategies. In an attempt to understand LAs and pedagogies more deeply and to make better use of LAs serving the entire large learning environment, learning theories is a part of this chapter, which is embodied behind the pedagogies.

The learning theory analysis structure of this chapter refers to the structure of learning theories and related pedagogies proposed by Ertmer and Newby (1993), as shown in the table 1, considering behaviorism, cognitivism and constructivism. The information of connectivism is based on another article written by Siemens (2005).

RESEARCH METHODOLOGY

There are five main stages to conduct the chapter, including combining learning theories and pedagogical strategies with AT framework, searching literature to collect data, reviewing and selecting the key articles, coding and synthesizing the results, reporting the review.

Thousands of papers on LAs has appeared in recent years. For that reason and topics relevance, two main international conferences and one academic database were selected, including Learning Analytics and Knowledge conference proceedings (LAK, main conference in this research field), Educational Data Mining conference proceedings (EDM, main conference in this research field) and Web of Science (WOS, a comprehensive citation database). The time frame of the search was in the last two years (2018-2019).

Table 1. Learning theories and pedagogies

Learning Theories	Behaviorism	Cognitivism	Constructivism	Connectivism
Learners' Characteristic	•Individual, reactive to the learning condition.	• Individual, active in the learning process.	• Individual, active in the learning process.	• Individual. • Organization. • Database.
Instruction or Design Goals	• Discrimination. •Generalizations. • Associations. • Chaining.	• Meaning made between new content and existed knowledge. • Learning strategies.	• Experience about authentic, relevant contexts. • How to construct meaning and update this construction.	• Know where to find knowledge needed besides know-how and know-what.
Content Presentation Strategies	• Prompts using. • Practice sequence.	• Hierarchical analysis of knowledge.	• Realistic settings. • Tasks relevant to students' experience.	• Connected specialized nodes or information sources.
Assessment	• Pre-assessment. • Behavioral objectives. • Criterion-conferenced assessment.	• Pre-assessment. • Knowledge memorized in an organized, meaningful manner.	• How effective learners solve authentic problems.	• Ability to synthesize and recognize connections and patterns.
Primary Concerns	• Make associations between stimulus and response.	• How information processed by the mind.	• Learners build personal interpretations of the world.	• Cycle of knowledge development to keep learners remain current in their field.
Pedagogical Strategies	• Reinforcement. • Tangible rewards. • Instructional cues. • Practice (e.g. error-trial).	• Advance organizers. • Hierarchical relationships. • Matrices. • Concept mapping.	•Apprenticeships. • PBL (Problem-Based learning). • Social negotiation. • Presentation of multiple perspectives.	• Social networks.
Application Learning Context	• Mastery learning. • Basic skills in structured knowledge domains.	• More complex cognitive processes. • Basic skills in relatively structured knowledge domains.	• Complex topics, thinking in a given content area as an expert user.	• Management and relationship. • Personal knowledge management in relation to organizational knowledge management. • Design of learning environments.

Source: (Ertmer & Newby, 1993; Siemens, 2005)

Considering the research goals towards the pedagogy of LAs, at the stage of key articles selecting, inclusion and exclusion criteria were conducted, as shown in the table 2.

Table 2. Include and Exclude criteria

Include	Exclude
• Articles using LA tools to give feedback scaffolding or instruction (e.g. exercise and courses recommendation).	• Articles only predict learners' performance (e.g. engagement, efficacy) without feedback or instructional intervention.
• Articles contain stakeholders, division of labor or decision making using LA tools.	• Simple demonstration, introduction or only conception of LA tools (esp. in conferences).
• Data from 2018 to 2019, LAK, EDM and WOS.	• Experience description articles (e.g. key lessons learnt).

In WOS, the search strategy was: "learn* analytic*" as key words for topic search, "article or proceedings paper" as document types. Except the proceedings of LAK18-19 and EDM18-19 (453 articles), 393 articles yielded (search day is 2020.06.09).

After two rounds of screenings, one is title and abstract analysis, and another is full text analysis, 38 articles were considered as more related to the research goals.

Coding Categories

These coding categories were synthesized from previous articles and each of these categories was then separated into sub-categories based on AT, pedagogical strategies and learning theories. None of the sub-categories were totally exclusive with each other, which means that there are some overlaps in the coding.

RESULTS

Subject

LAs emphasizes the data of students' learning process. These data are not only the focus of students themselves, but also teachers, curriculum designers, and education policy makers. In this chapter, attention has been paid to the combination of specific pedagogical strategies and LAs.

In general, the LA users are diverse, including K-12, undergraduates, masters, formal and informal education, students, teachers, management staff in formal education and instruction designers.

When target users are students, different characteristics are concerned. Vijh et al. (2019) considered K-6 learner's ability estimate, e.g. question difficulty, learners' response times. Vainas et al. (2019) paid more attention to K-12 students' learning history, offline exercise metadata and online student-exercises features. Adult learners' individual characteristics such as profile overview, projects, and course history were what Abhinav et al. (2018) concerned. Backenköhler et al. (2018) focused on learners' course profile in University like age, nationality, sex, course of studies, course type and lecturer. The collection of these data is to partially solve the cold start problem in recommendation systems and establish a learner model for personalized use of LA tools.

Some LA tools have already selected specific learning goals when they are designed, so they are specific in who is the target user, e.g. foreign language vocabulary learners (Hasnine et al., 2019; Abou-Khalil et al., 2018; Whitehill & Movellan, 2018), foreign language translation learner (Sunahase et al., 2019). Some LA tools have higher requirements for learners. The tool appeared in the research of Vieira et al. (2018) required freshmen students basic high school level science knowledge and good English-speaking skills.

Moreover, the target users can be teachers or instruction designers. The LA tools deliver instruction designers reference data to stimulate the growth of learners' goal setting ability (Tran et al., 2018) and help teachers become instruction designers (Davis et al., 2019). Helping teachers better manage, handle the gap between teaching goals and the actual situation of learners is another advantage that LAs take (Misfeldt et al., 2019; Wiley et al., 2019).

The subject could be more than one kind of group. Combing teachers and students in the LAs using process, the display of students' learning state improve the accuracy of personal feedback from teachers (Lim et al., 2018; Azcona et al., 2018; Quigley, 2018; Kaw et al., 2019) and support assessment of the learning (Dasgupta et al., 2019). Directly connecting students, academic leads and school management staff better simulate the achieving of teaching goals (Bucic et al., 2018)

Object

The main purpose of LAs is to assist students learn more efficiently, for which there are different specific goals.

One major of the LA tools is to promote knowledge mastery as a practice assistant, eps. concept learning (Phua et al., 2019; Vijh et al., 2019; Ai et al., 2019; Vainas et al., 2019; Whitehill & Movellan, 2018; Mittelmeier et al., 2018; Meegahapola &

Thilakarathne, 2019). Besides personal learning content and exercise recommendation according to the actual learning status of learners (Vijh et al., 2019; Hoppenbrouwers et al., 2019; Azcona et al., 2018; Sunahase et al., 2019; Meng et al., 2019; Rosen et al., 2019), test or demonstrate one skill of students is also possible provided by LAs (Broisin & Hérouard, 2019). In addition to recommendation from machine, learners can receive feedback from teachers. Through LA tools, the interactions between learners and the reflection of learners to knowledge applying are gathered, which gives teachers chances to consider effective intervention (Lim et al., 2018; Quigley, 2018; Davis et al., 2019; Lucas et al., 2019; Kaw et al., 2019; Wiley et al., 2019). What's more, learners can ask help from peers or teachers about topics after schools (Khachan & Özmen, 2018).

Furthermore, LAs present new forms of materials attracting learners' attention. Learners get customized learning content in English writing through comparative analysis between learners' essay and standard corpus (Hilliard, 2019). The connection of geolocation information and learning history puts learners in learning contexts which reminding them what has been learned in right place (Hasnine et al., 2019; Abou-Khalil et al., 2018). The comparison materials between Lewis structure and space-filling model facilitate students deal with perceptual-fluency problems in chemical molecules learning (Sen et al., 2018). A simulated trip by using VR technology can induce learners into an authentic task (Fung et al., 2019).

LA tools aid learners and teachers select, manage and monitor their learning or teaching goals. A flexible adjustment of teaching content can be conducted through an objective comparison tool between teaching goals and national curriculum standards (Misfeldt et al., 2019). As teaching reflection tools, LA tools assist teachers to determine which instruction strategy is beneficial to the realization of teaching goals (Wu et al., 2019).

While teachers own their objects from institutions, students lack of self-regulation skills to select their own goals or courses. Based on similarity group and learners' history, a short list of recommended courses or some interested learning content is a solution proposed by LA tools (Polyzou et al., 2019; Backenköhler et al., 2018; Abhinav et al., 2018). Also, self-regulation skills can be improved with the assistance of LA tools (McKenna et al., 2019; Flanagan et al., 2019; Tran et al., 2018).

Some LA tools demonstrates the ability to help set learning environments in which learners' complex problem-solving skills improved, like engineering design courses (Dasgupta et al., 2019; Vieira et al., 2018; Mio et al., 2019), marketing-based decision courses (Bucic et al., 2018) or game design courses (Richard & Giri, 2019).

Tools

In the selected articles, LA tools involved are recommendation systems, learning analytics dashboard (LAD), feedback systems and communication systems.

The recommendation systems afford many kinds of materials. The major recommended content are exercises, like adaptive learning mathematics platform (Phua et al., 2019), Intelligent Practice System (Ai et al., 2019) and E-gostky (Vainas et al., 2019). Then the second is learning content recommendation. AntConc supports personalized corpus for English writing learning (Hilliard, 2019). EMERGO toolkit (Mio et al., 2019) and edu2VR (Fung et al., 2019) give new visual learning content. Course recommendation is another part. Scholars Walk (Polyzou et al., 2019) and LeCoRe (Abhinav et al., 2018) are course recommendation system using different algorithms.

About LAD, McKenna et al. (2019) combined a Python-based application and visual-form LAs to show personalized retrieval practice activities. Goal Arrow demonstrated national curriculum standards, teaching goals and evaluation of lessons (Misfeldt et al., 2019). EcoSurvey is a digital modeling tool, which displays the interactions when students model (Quigley, 2018). Some LAs keep a tool community to integrate the existing knowledge maps to model learning behaviors (Flanagan et al., 2019).

There are some other kinds of LAs. For example, OnTask is an LA-based feedback system, which have the ability to support blended courses (Lim et al., 2018). IMSSAP is communication tools to help students get helps about some topics after school (Khachan & Özmen, 2018).

Division of Labor

According to different users, initiators of the tool, and whether teacher's guidance is essential during the use process, this chapter analyzes the division of labor of the selected articles. Some LAs emphasize the important role of teachers, while other LAs usage scenarios include not only teachers and students, but also other management staff.

Firstly, some LA tools are used by students and initiated by themselves, esp. in informal language learning (Hasnine et al., 2019; Abou-Khalil et al., 2018). Adult learners prefer self-regulation learning with the assistance of LA tools (Abhinav et al., 2018; Sen et al., 2018; Tran et al., 2018). The students' using tools can also be initiated by teachers. Teachers direct and adjust lectures, students learn by themselves following prompts (Hilliard, 2019; Flanagan et al., 2019; Ai et al., 2019).

Students are not alone using LA tools. There are some chances for them to get guidance or helps from teachers. K-6 students have relatively low self-regulation skills, and online learning requires the supervision and minor from teachers to guide them in general directions and specific skills (Vijh et al., 2019). In problem-based learning, students are driven by problem with little prior knowledge. Teachers take good roles to help and promote students' learning (Wu et al., 2019). That is also true in computer courses (Broisin & Hérouard, 2019).

Then, besides students, teachers are another major subject of LA tools. Referring national curriculum standards, Goal Arrow platform displays teachers' object, resources and evaluation of the lesson, which makes teachers a flexible planner in day to day classroom (Misfeldt et al., 2019). Using LA tools to find central topics discussion within forums, teachers become topic miners (Davis et al., 2019). With valuable near-time insight into how their students are conceptualizing targeted lesson concepts, LA tools turn teachers into effective dynamic learning behavior analyst (Wiley et al., 2019).

LA tools increase the possibility of teachers to become a course designer. For instance, teachers propose a learning challenge first. In the next design stage, teachers have many choices, like choose a blended learning context and metrics, providing contextualized feedback (Lim et al., 2018); give formative feedback to help understanding when students make modeling (Quigley, 2018); or work with other institutions to help students design a game (Richard & Giri, 2019).

Not only in the using of LA tools, teachers make efforts to the designing process of LA tools further. In the design of personalized learning path recommendation system, experienced teachers help determine the difficulty and relationship of each knowledge and generate the relevant values of knowledge model (Meng et al., 2019).

School administrative staff and researchers are important role in the LAs using context. Administrative staff assist teachers in launching LA applications (McKenna et al., 2019) or grant ethical approval for the using (Mio et al., 2019). Sometimes tutorial services and study advisors give feedback on content and design through LA tools (Hoppenbrouwers et al., 2019). Researchers are familiar with LA tools. They explain the function to learners clearly (Phua et al., 2019), gather students' opinions (Azcona et al., 2018), work together with teachers to design the learning unit and assessment (Dasgupta et al., 2019), add lessons to initiate topic discussion (Khachan & Özmen, 2018) and consider the assigned levels of students (Sunahase et al., 2019). In some online learning, instructional design team have a powerful effect on learners from knowledge components to assessment scope (Rosen et al., 2019).

Rules

This part is divided into three subparts, content, assessment and learning theories, which is the main information about pedagogical strategies.

Content

Single discipline and interdisciplinary both are the concerns of LA tools.

From a single discipline vision, LAs appear more often in STEM (science, technology, engineer and mathematics) courses. For example, primary school mathematics (Meng et al., 2019; Ai et al., 2019); high school mathematics (Phua et al., 2019); biology classroom in middle and high school (Quigley, 2018); K-12 physics (Wiley et al., 2019). When turn to university, more disciplines involved. Problem-solving skills in mathematical competences (Hoppenbrouwers et al., 2019), numerical methods course for mechanical engineers (Kaw et al., 2019), traditional Chinese medical (Wu et al., 2019), clinical practice for pharmacy (Lucas et al., 2019), biological sciences courses (Lim et al., 2018), marketing course (Bucic et al., 2018), computer science courses (Azcona et al., 2018; Broisin & Hérouard, 2019), information science (Flanagan et al., 2019). There are some for adult learners, such as chemistry (Sen et al., 2018). Most of single discipline LA tools focus on the learning of knowledge framework, imitating traditional teaching methods, as recommendation systems of personalized learning content and exercises content. In addition, there are single-discipline LA tools that focus on personal experiences of teaching content, increasing learners' interest and involvement. EMERGO toolkit designs an online scenario to support scenario-based learning interactive (Mio et al., 2019). Edu2VR is a web-based VR online platform to simulate a field trip to an overseas site (Fung et al., 2019).

Language learning is a frequent research area of LA tools in humanism and social science field. For instance, foreign language vocabulary learning (Hasnine et al., 2019; Abou-Khalil et al., 2018), language translations learning (Sunahase et al., 2019).

Whole discipline involved learning system is similar to collecting different single disciples into one system. For instance, Korean partner's tablet-based education system in K-6 (Vijh et al., 2019). Whole discipline involved LA tools not only concern students' concept mastery, but also arrange management platform for teachers teaching goals (Misfeldt et al., 2019) and course recommendation for students (Polyzou et al., 2019; Backenköhler et al., 2018; Abhinav et al., 2018).

Interdisciplinary LA tools appears more often in STEM design course and the learning context where study items are divided by work fields for adult learners. The objects of this learning environment are more related to ability development (Tran et al., 2018), to assessing students' experimentation strategies in an engineering design challenge (Vieira et al., 2018), to suppling opportunities of computational thinking (Richard & Giri, 2019) and improving content-discover ability (Tran et al., 2018).

Assessment

In terms of execution time, assessment can be divided into pre-assessment, formative assessment and post-assessment. Knowledge mastery LA tools have a pre-assessment to locate the level of knowledge mastery where the learner at. The main method used for this pre-test is knowledge quiz (Hasnine et al., 2019; Flanagan et al., 2019). Dynamic and formative assessment update students' personal data faster, and improve the speed and accuracy of teachers' feedback (Quigley, 2018). According to learners' dynamic Zone of Proximal Development (ZPD) detection, learning materials are recommended more flexibly (Vainas et al., 2019). Post-assessment test students' mastery of learning content (Wiley et al., 2019), reinforce concept learning as learning materials (Phua et al., 2019; Kaw et al., 2019) and provide analyzable data for learners' next stage of learning recommendation (Vijh et al., 2019).

The testing methods are diverse, including quiz, coding analysis, peer assessment, modeling. Many test methods are combined. For example, coding analysis of group discussion content and personal speech content (Wu et al., 2019), completion of model in class and program analysis in the process of learner modeling (Vieira et al., 2018), workshops combined with multi-period quiz (Lim et al., 2018), the combination of qualification test and peer assessment (Sunahase et al., 2019), the completion of the model in class and the test of knowledge points before and after class (Dasgupta et al., 2019), game design completion in classroom and case analysis after-class (Richard & Giri, 2019).

Some assessment materials are utilized as learning content, such as personalized Retrieval Practice Activities (RPAs) (McKenna et al., 2019), error-trial practice in writing courses (Hilliard, 2019), Bash language learning in computer science courses (Broisin & Hérouard, 2019), reflective writing in clinical experiences and ePortfolio maintained (Lucas et al., 2019).

In more complexed application of assessment, there are Problem-Based Learning (PBL) (Mittelmeier et al., 2018) and Scenario-Based Learning (SBL) (Mio et al., 2019), which places learners in a context to deal with real-word problems.

Learning Theories

Most LA tools and their application refer to more than one kind of learning theories. Behaviorism, cognitivism and constructivism are all involved at varying degrees. This section analyzes the subsequent learning theories from the aspects of assessment, content and exercises recommendation, learning content presentation strategy, and course recommendation.

The usage of pre-test or dynamic process test in different LA application scenarios may reflect different learning theories. The behaviorist-based LAs focuses on reinforcement and error-trail practice (Broisin & Hérouard, 2019; Whitehill & Movellan, 2018). The cognitivism-based LA tools regards pre-test as advance organizers, and uses hierarchical relationships of knowledge to strengthen the connection between the knowledge points that learners have mastered and not yet mastered. Those strategies are common in LAs using. Knowledge and concept mapping develop learners' knowledge management capabilities while improve their knowledge mastery (Flanagan et al., 2019). Advance organizer strategy combined with knowledge mapping assistant students in dealing with design challenges (Meng et al., 2019). Sometimes, advance organizer appears more than once as dynamic assessment (Vainas et al., 2019).

Blooms' taxonomy especially applying and analysis are emphasized in cognitivism-based LA tools. Goal Arrow enrich teachers' ability to analyzing teaching objectives (Misfeldt et al., 2019). LAD presents examples for students to analysis their individual strengths, weaknesses, and subsequent choice in learning (Hoppenbrouwers et al., 2019). Visual representation of personalized Retrieval Practice Activities (RPAs) gives students a chance to reflect their own searching behavior and increase self-regulation skills (McKenna et al., 2019).

The more diverse the object is, the more learning theories are revealed and more types of LAs are used. For example, a marketing course in the study of Bucic et al. (2018) have three key learning goals, including knowledge concepts learning, values delivery and develop decision-making skills, which using three LA tools besides Moodle, reflecting cognitivism and constructivism. Even connectivism is reflected in using multiple databases to build relationships and extract effective information with aims at recommends learning opportunities (Abhinav et al., 2018).

The learning content and exercises recommendation LA tools mainly refer to cognitivism and behaviorism. The combination of those two learning theories boosts the mastery of knowledge points, especially memory, to cope with tests, like adaptive learning mathematics platform in high school (Phua et al., 2019), Korean partner's tablet-based educational system in K-6 (Vijh et al., 2019) and Intelligent Practice System (IPS) in K-5 math curriculum (Ai et al., 2019). Likewise, there are combinations of constructivism and behaviorism, such as using peer assessment to increase practice of language interaction (Sunahase et al., 2019).

Constructivism focuses on learners' personal experience and real problem-solving learning. Constructivism-based LAs support concept mastery too. For instance, the building of relationship between learners' personal data storage and real-time geolocation strengthens learners' personal meaning of materials when learn vocabulary (Hasnine et al., 2019), a storyboard in one online engineering scenario reinforce personal meaning in task solving (Mio et al., 2019). A VR field trip presents students first-hand learning materials (Fung et al., 2019).

Learning content presentation strategies reveal learning theories too. Real-world learning scene materials construct relevant objects and help learners quickly find learning content when facing real-world problems (Tran et al., 2018), which expresses the combination of constructivism (personal meaning materials in authentic task) and cognitivism (hierarchical relationships of knowledge). Cognitivism (hierarchical relationships of knowledge) and constructivism (PBL, group discussion) are often combined in STEM design courses, like studies of Richard and Giri (2019), Dasgupta et al. (2019) and Vieira et al. (2018).

What's more, course recommendation systems reflect different learning theories. Scholars Walk (Polyzou et al., 2019) mainly embodies constructivism, combing learner's personal course history (personal meaning materials), data of older students (a kind of group discussion), and discussion with teachers. In contrast, the personalized recommendation graph of courses of Backenköhler et al. (2018) reflects cognitivism, using the hierarchical relationship between curriculum knowledge and the interrelationship between curriculum and individual learning history.

In general, error-trial practice of behaviorism, hierarchical relationships of knowledge and advanced organizer strategy of cognitivism, and ZPD, group discussion and authentic tasks of constructivism are used frequently. Among them, ZPD can be seen in almost every LAs usage scenario because of its in-depth understanding of individual learning status.

Community

Most of the LAs in the selected articles applied in school, which are expressed in the subject section in details. some are applied in informal learning environment, forums or companies. In details, Learning Log Navigator in the study of Hasnine et al. (2019) recommend foreign language vocabulary when learners travel. N-gram-based graphs are employed in forums to find central topics (Davis et al., 2019). Through learners' profile, Learning & Development team within Accenture developed LeCoRe to recommend learning information for adults (Abhinav et al., 2018). IBM Watson Natural Language Understanding is used to extract learning objectives on web helping self-learning at a pharmaceutical company (Tran et al., 2018).

Outcomes

Both formal and informal education systems have an existing teaching and learning systems. LAs, as new tools, has certain obstacles when integrating with education system. Therefore, the evaluation criteria for LAs use is necessary to be diverse. Here are some evaluation criteria found in the selected articles:

Whether the system can run. For instance, Flanagan et al. (2019) conducted a preliminary experiment of a knowledge map portal. N-gram-based graphs can be used at scale to find central topics within discussion (Davis et al., 2019).

Test of the effectiveness of recommendation system. Whether the accuracy and diversity of a learning path recommendation system can be verified (Meng et al., 2019)? Whether the analysis results can be understood (Wiley et al., 2019; Polyzou et al., 2019)? Whether the stored learning objectives are useful for instruction design (Tran et al., 2018)? How about the accuracy of the assessment and the necessity of other materials as supplement (Vieira et al., 2018)?

Number of people voluntarily using LA tools, such as over 1700 learners from over thirty-nationalities (Hasnine et al., 2019).

User acceptance of LAs. Customize learning materials is a specific learning content, which learners have a positive attitude towards (Hilliard, 2019). When students' effort is able to be seen by themselves, students are more willing to accept the tool (Khachan & Özmen, 2018). A LAD showing individual strengths and weaknesses has good usability scores (Hoppenbrouwers et al., 2019). Encouragement feedback get more appreciation from students (Lim et al., 2018). Receptiveness are reported in VR teaching content (Fung et al., 2019) and SBL (Mio et al., 2019) regardless of the students' performance level.

Impact on learning performance. According to students' mastery of knowledge, targeted exercises are recommended by LAs. When assessment method is similar quiz about the mastery of knowledge points, this kind of LAs tool generally has a positive impact on learners' scores, like a Korean partner's table-based education system in K-6 online learning (Vijh et al., 2019) and a power system engineering course (Meegahapola & Thilakarathne, 2019) in university.

DISCUSSION

LAs is a kind of student-centered design, even if the target users are teachers or policy makers. The main purpose is to continuously cultivate learners' self-regulation learning ability so that they can adapt to the changes in surrounding living environment during their growth. That is partly reason for many LA tools to collect learners' personal data.

Teachers play important roles in the design, use, and testing of LA tools. The literature selected shows that according to the comparison of learner's personal knowledge mastery and the discipline knowledge structure, learning content and subsequent exercises are recommended by LA tools utilizing a certain algorithm (Hasnine et al., 2019; Vijh et al., 2019; Ai et al., 2019; Vainas et al., 2019). However, in some key judgments, it is up to teachers based their own experience. Such as judgment of the degree of difficulty of knowledge points (Meng et al., 2019), code analysis of students' personal learning path and learning process collected by LAs (Vieira et al., 2018; Wu et al., 2019;), estimation of the growth of learners' certain high-level problem-solving ability, quickly and pertinently guide learners in the modeling process combining knowledge with problems to be solved (Quigley, 2018; Wiley et al., 2019; Vieira et al., 2018; Richard & Giri, 2019).

In higher education, the role of teaching is gradually weakening, whereas design philosophy of curriculum designers, the collection of personal data of learners and the use of LA tools are closer related (Rosen et al., 2019; Hoppenbrouwers et al., 2019; Davis et al., 2019; Abhinav et al., 2018; Tran et al., 2018). Among adult learners, the relationship between designers and learners is much closer. Adult learners need use knowledge in a certain field to solve real-world problems. The existing knowledge framework may not offer solutions. Therefore, designers need collect information to form a reference solution for a certain type of problem. For instance, Tran et al. (2018) used natural language understanding to extract learning objects from real word data on banking industry and pharmaceutical company, which is useful for instruction designers in course packages created.

Most LA tools has not provided teachers with guidelines for pedagogical strategies. Teachers still use tools based on their teaching experience. The reasons for that may in two aspects. On the one hand, the complexity of teaching situations hinders the predictability of LA application scenarios. On the other hand, LA tools already have their own functional expectations during the design process, such as knowledge mastery (Phua et al., 2019; Vijh et al., 2019; Ai et al., 2019), teacher-student communication (Khachan & Özmen, 2018), and course recommendation (Abhinav et al., 2018; Polyzou et al., 2019). Therefore, it is depended on teachers who select the LA tools to be used in specific teaching scenarios according to their specific teaching goals and the pedagogies which they think is reasonable. Besides, LAs using activities of novice teachers affect their intention to LAs using, whereas intention to LAs using affects how well teachers utilize LA tools and assist researchers to improve LA tools (Jonassen & Rohrer-Murphy, 1999). Teachers need more opportunities to try to integrate and adjust LAs into daily classrooms.

Collaboration of researchers. Teaching goals, learning goals, and learner characteristics are complex and diverse, so that LA tools are required to be modified in line with various specific teaching scenarios. To this end, an important step is the later operation of LA tools. Researchers and designers ought to maintain continuous contact with users. This measure can not only heighten the utilization efficiency of LA tools and a good user experience, but also further obtain learning context data providing big data for the development of other LA tools in the level of application scenario.

As an explanation of learning behaviors, learning theories are embodied in the whole process of LAs design and application. Although not clearly shown, learning theories are revealed through further analysis. Most learning activities are inseparable from the support of the three learning theories, behaviorism, cognitivism and constructivism.

Which learning theories are chosen as the basis of instruction, mainly related to tasks and learners. Specially, whether learners own the required knowledge level when tasks need to solve. Then considering the specific conditions of tasks and learners, different instruction strategies are chosen, like behavioral strategies to facilitate basic knowledge about "what", cognitive approach to connect cognition relationship among rules applying in similar tasks about "how", or constructivist strategies to deal with authentic questions about "reflection" (Ertmer & Newby, 1993). This requires the support of big data and LAs tools in order to more comprehensively analyze the degree of matching between learners' personal situation and tasks' requirement.

Tasks also need to be further analyzed to classify problem types, e.g. well-structured questions and ill-structured questions. Different types of problems require different skills, which means own different objects and goals, leading to different corresponding activities. Then the following specific actions, operations and the tools chosen to interact with activities will be different either (Jonassen & Rohrer-Murphy, 1999).

The selected literature does not show the collection and analysis of learners' emotion data by LA tools. This does not mean that there is no learning emotional LAs. For example, Chen et al. (2019) uses a Fitbit 1-like tracking tool to collect emotional states of parents and children's interaction in math problems and Wampfler et al. (2019) analyzes affective states from learners' handwriting data in math tasks. But those are a later period reflection tool and cannot provide information to assist interventions, which are not satisfied the requirement about LAs and pedagogies of this chapter.

CONCLUSION

This chapter takes the application of pedagogies in LA application scenarios as research questions, and combines seven components of AT with pedagogical strategies to form an analysis framework, for which 38 articles were selected from 846 articles. With the increase of users' knowledge level, more and more attention has been paid to the improvement of learners' self-regulation learning ability and the help to solve real-world problems in LAs design and using. Different LA tools reflect different learning theories, but three learning theories including behaviorism, cognitivism and constructivism are more or less involved to a certain extent.

Some learning theories have been around for long period of time. In new era, it is necessary to revisit these learning theories, paying more attention to the connection between context and learners. The advantages of LAs own potentials to help learning theories further develop in new era. Saving and analyzing learners' personal data and external learning environment data, LAs makes learning theories-based instructions more personalized and contextual, and increases the chances of converting learning theories into instruction practices.

Activity and goals support each other (Jonassen & Rohrer-Murphy, 1999). The low efficiency of some learning activities needs consider the specific situation of learners. From the cognitive perspectives, when design instructions there are two aspects to consider: whether the learner's knowledge level meets the task resolution situation and whether the division of the task's structure is reasonable. In the same situation, different questions can be asked and set. Different sets of skills are required for different kinds of questions, which means different forms of instructions are needed (Jonassen, 2010).

However, questions need to leave some space for learners to manipulate, increasing personal meanings for learners (Jonassen & Rohrer-Murphy, 1999). This construction requires joint efforts of more stakeholders. Working with researchers boosts the effective application of LAs, and increases the scope of education big data. Cooperation with policy makers expand the application of LAs and reduce the barriers to communication with peer LA users. Teachers are more experienced in dividing the difficulty level of problems and whether it is suitable for learners' personal situation. Researchers can provide teachers with more help in the operating mechanism of LAs and learning theories. In addition, some LAs have their own objectives. But whether those are related to the users' goals needs further discussion.

This chapter only discusses some teaching application scenarios of LAs from a static perspective. But teaching activities are dynamically developing. To further analyze the process of learners using LAs to complete the learning process and the far-reaching impact of the use of LAs on the community of learning, a combination of quantitative research and qualitative research, synchronic research and diachronic research is needed. In addition, academic emotion is closely related to self-regulation learning. Academic emotion and self-regulation learning in LAs also call for more attention.

ACKNOWLEDGMENT

The appreciation is given to Dr. Nguyen-Thinh Le of Humboldt University zu Berlin for his instant feedbacks about this research.

REFERENCES

Abhinav, K., Subramanian, V., Dubey, A., Bhat, P., & Venkat, A. D. (2018). LeCoRe: a framework for modeling learner's preference. In *Proceedings of the Eleventh International Conference on Educational Data Mining (EDM' 18).* International Educational Data Mining Society.

Abou-Khalil, V., Flanagan, B., & Ogata, H. (2018). Learning false friends across contexts. In *Proceedings of the Eighth International Conference on Learning Analytics & Knowledge (LAK' 18).* Society for Learning Analytics Research.

AbuSneineh, W., & Zairi, M. (2010). An evaluation framework for E-learning effectiveness in the Arab World. International Encyclopedia of Education, 521–535. doi:10.1016/B978-0-08-044894-7.01708-5

Ai, F., Chen, Y., Guo, Y., Zhao, Y., Wang, Z., & Fu, G. (2019). Concept-aware deep knowledge tracing and exercise recommendation in an online learning system. In *Proceedings of the Twelfth International Conference on Educational Data Mining (EDM' 19).* International Educational Data Mining Society.

Alexander, R. (2008). *Essays on pedagogy*. Routledge.

Angeli, C., & Valanides, N. (2009). Epistemological and methodological issues for the conceptualization, development, and assessment of ICT–TPCK: Advances in technological pedagogical content knowledge (TPCK). *Computers & Education, 52*(1), 154–168. doi:10.1016/j.compedu.2008.07.006

Azcona, D., Hsiao, I.-H., & Smeaton, A. (2018). PredictCS: personalizing programming learning by leveraging learning analytics. In *Proceedings of the Eighth International Conference on Learning Analytics & Knowledge (LAK' 18).* Society for Learning Analytics Research.

Backenköhler, M., Scherzinger, F., Singla, A., & Wolf, V. (2018). Data-driven approach towards a personalized curriculum. In *Proceedings of the Eleventh International Conference on Educational Data Mining (EDM' 18).* International Educational Data Mining Society.

Bakharia, A., Corrin, L., De Barba, P., Kennedy, G., Gašević, D., Mulder, R., . . . Lockyer, L. (2016, April). A conceptual framework linking learning design with learning analytics. In *Proceedings of the Sixth International Conference on Learning Analytics & Knowledge (LAK' 16).* Society for Learning Analytics Research.

Broisin, J., & Hérouard, C. (2019). Design and evaluation of a semantic indicator for automatically supporting programming learning. In *Proceedings of the Twelfth International Conference on Educational Data Mining (EDM' 19).* International Educational Data Mining Society.

Bucic, T., Vigentini, L., & King, M. E. (2018). Juggling system and data streams to personalize feedback: the case of a large first year course. In *Proceedings of the Eighth International Conference on Learning Analytics & Knowledge (LAK' 18).* Society for Learning Analytics Research.

Chen, L., Gjekmarkaj, E., & Dubrawski, A. (2019). Parent as a Companion for Solving Challenging Math Problems: Insights from Multi-modal Observational Data. In *Proceedings of the Twelfth International Conference on Educational Data Mining (EDM' 19).* International Educational Data Mining Society.

Ciavarelli, A. (2003). *Assessing the Quality of Online Instruction: Integrating Instructional Quality and Web Usability Assessments.* https://files.eric.ed.gov/fulltext/ED480084.pdf

Dasgupta, C., Magana, A. J., & Vieira, C. (2019). Investigating the affordances of a CAD enabled learning environment for promoting integrated STEM learning. *Computers & Education, 129*, 122–142. doi:10.1016/j.compedu.2018.10.014

Davis, G. M., Wang, C., & Yuan, C. (2019). N-gram graphs for topic extraction in educational forums. In *Proceedings of the Twelfth International Conference on Educational Data Mining (EDM' 19).* International Educational Data Mining Society.

Educause Publications. (2020). *2020 Educause horizon report (teaching and learning edition).* Author.

Engeström, Y. (2015). *Learning by expanding: An activity-theoretical approach to developmental research* (2nd ed.). Cambridge University Press. (Original work published 1987)

Ertmer, P. A., & Newby, T. J. (1993). Behaviorism, cognitivism, constructivism: Comparing critical features from an instructional design perspective. *Performance Improvement Quarterly, 6*(4), 50–72. doi:10.1111/j.1937-8327.1993.tb00605.x

Ferguson, R. (2012). Learning analytics: Drivers, developments and challenges. *International Journal of Technology Enhanced Learning, 4*(5-6), 304–317. doi:10.1504/IJTEL.2012.051816

Ferguson, R., & Clow, D. (2017, March). Where is the evidence? A call to action for learning analytics. In *Proceedings of the Seventh International Conference on Learning Analytics & Knowledge (LAK' 17)*. Society for Learning Analytics Research.

Flanagan, B., Majumdar, R., Akçapınar, G., Wang, J., & Ogata, H. (2019). Knowledge map creation for modeling learning behaviors in digital learning environments. In *Proceedings of the Ninth International Conference on Learning Analytics & Knowledge (LAK' 19)*. Society for Learning Analytics Research.

Fung, F. M., Choo, W. Y., Ardisara, A., Zimmermann, C. D., Watts, S., Koscielniak, T., Blanc, E., Coumoul, X., & Dumke, R. (2019). Applying a virtual reality platform in environmental chemistry education to conduct a field trip to an overseas site. *Journal of Chemical Education, 96*(2), 382–386. doi:10.1021/acs.jchemed.8b00728

Greller, W., & Drachsler, H. (2012). Translating learning into numbers: A generic framework for learning analytics. *Journal of Educational Technology & Society, 15*(3), 42–57.

Hasnine, M. N., Ogata, H., Akcapinar, G., Mouri, K., & Uosaki, N. (2019). Learning analytics to share and reuse authentic learning experiences in a seamless learning environment. In *Proceedings of the Ninth International Conference on Learning Analytics & Knowledge (LAK' 19)*. Society for Learning Analytics Research.

Hilliard, A. (2019). Developing an English learner corpus for materials creation and evaluation. In *Proceedings of the Ninth International Conference on Learning Analytics & Knowledge (LAK' 19)*. Society for Learning Analytics Research.

Hoppenbrouwers, N., Broos, T., & Laet, T. D. (2019). Less (context) is more? Evaluation of a positioning test feedback dashboard for aspiring students. In *Proceedings of the Ninth International Conference on Learning Analytics & Knowledge (LAK' 19)*. Society for Learning Analytics Research.

Ifenthaler, D., & Widanapathirana, C. (2014). Development and validation of a learning analytics framework: Two case studies using support vector machines. *Technology. Knowledge & Learning, 19*(1-2), 221–240. doi:10.100710758-014-9226-4

Jonassen, D. H. (2010). *Learning to solve problems: A handbook for designing problem-solving learning environments*. Routledge. doi:10.4324/9780203847527

Joyes, G. (2006). An activity theory approach to the exploration of tutors' perceptions of effective online pedagogy. In *Proceedings of the 23rd Annual Conference of the Australasian Society for Computers in Learning in Tertiary Education (Ascilite): Who's learning? Whose technology*. Sydney University Press.

Kaw, A., Clark, R., Delgado, E., & Abate, N. (2019). Analyzing the use of adaptive learning in a flipped classroom for preclass learning. *Computer Applications in Engineering Education, 27*(3), 663–678. doi:10.1002/cae.22106

Khachan, A. M., & Özmen, A. (2019). IMSSAP: After-school interactive mobile learning student support application. *Computer Applications in Engineering Education, 27*(3), 543–552. doi:10.1002/cae.22096

Koehler, M. J., Mishra, P., & Yahya, K. (2007). Tracing the development of teacher knowledge in a design seminar: Integrating content, pedagogy and technology. *Computers & Education, 49*(3), 740–762. doi:10.1016/j.compedu.2005.11.012

Koh, E., Shibani, A., Tan, J. P. L., & Hong, H. (2016, April). A pedagogical framework for learning analytics in collaborative inquiry tasks: An example from a teamwork competency awareness program. In *Proceedings of the Sixth International Conference on Learning Analytics & Knowledge (LAK' 16)*. Society for Learning Analytics Research.

Lim, L., Gentili, S., Pardo, A., Dawson, S., & Gašević, D. (2018). Combining technology and human intelligence to provide feedback and learning support using OnTask. In *Proceedings of the Eighth International Conference on Learning Analytics & Knowledge (LAK' 18)*. Society for Learning Analytics Research.

Loughran, J. (2013). Pedagogy: Making sense of the complex relationship between teaching and learning. *Curriculum Inquiry, 43*(1), 118–141. doi:10.1111/curi.12003

Lucas, C., Gibson, A., & Shum, S. B. (2019). Pharmacy students' utilization of an online tool for immediate formative feedback on reflective writing tasks. *American Journal of Pharmaceutical Education, 83*(6), 6800. doi:10.5688/ajpe6800 PMID:31507274

Macfadyen, L. P., Dawson, S., Pardo, A., & Gaševic, D. (2014). Embracing big data in complex educational systems: The learning analytics imperative and the policy challenge. *Research & Practice in Assessment, 9*, 17–28.

McKenna, K., Folkestad, J. E., & Moraes, M. C. (2019). Reflections of visual form learning analytics: spaced retrieval practice activity. In *Proceedings of the Ninth International Conference on Learning Analytics & Knowledge (LAK' 19)*. Society for Learning Analytics Research.

Meegahapola, L. G., & Thilakarathne, C. (2019). Dynamic learner-assisted interactive learning tools for power systems engineering courses. *Institute of Electrical and Electronics Engineers (IEEE) Transactions on Education, 62*(2), 149–156. doi:10.1109/TE.2018.2889621

Meng, L., Zhang, M., Zhang, W., & Shi, X. (2019). Personalized learning path recommendation based on knowledge structure. In *Proceedings of the Ninth International Conference on Learning Analytics & Knowledge (LAK' 19)*. Society for Learning Analytics Research.

Mio, C., Ventura-Medina, E., & João, E. (2019). Scenario-based eLearning to promote active learning in large cohorts: Students' perspective. *Computer Applications in Engineering Education, 27*(4), 894–909. doi:10.1002/cae.22123

Misfeldt, M., Allsopp, B. B., Dreyøe, J., & Tamborg, A. L. (2019). Learning objectives and curriculum standards as multimodal analytics in learning platforms. In *Proceedings of the Ninth International Conference on Learning Analytics & Knowledge (LAK' 19)*. Society for Learning Analytics Research.

Mittelmeier, J., Rienties, B., Tempelaar, D., Hillaire, G., & Whitelock, D. (2018). The influence of internationalised versus local content on online intercultural collaboration in groups: A randomised control trial study in a statistics course. *Computers & Education, 118*, 82–95. doi:10.1016/j.compedu.2017.11.003

New Media Consortium (NMC). (2011). *The 2011 Horizon Report*. Author.

Persico, D., & Pozzi, F. (2015). Informing learning design with learning analytics to improve teacher inquiry. *British Journal of Educational Technology, 46*(2), 230–248. doi:10.1111/bjet.12207

Phua, J. Y. C., Yeo, E. M. Y., & Ng, S. J. Y. (2019). Understanding teaching and learning practices of online adaptive mathematics tutoring platform. In *Proceedings of the Ninth International Conference on Learning Analytics & Knowledge (LAK' 19)*. Society for Learning Analytics Research.

Polyzou, A., Nikolakopoulos, A. N., & Karypis, G. (2019). Scholars Walk: a markov chain framework for course recommendation. In *Proceedings of the Twelfth International Conference on Educational Data Mining (EDM' 19)*. International Educational Data Mining Society.

Quigley, D. (2018). A learning analytics approach to scaffolding scientific modeling in the classroom. In *Proceedings of the Eighth International Conference on Learning Analytics & Knowledge (LAK' 18)*. Society for Learning Analytics Research.

Richard, G. T., & Giri, S. (2019). Digital and physical fabrication as multimodal learning: Understanding youth computational thinking when making integrated systems through bidirectionally responsive design. *ACM Transactions on Computing Education, 19*(3), 1–35. doi:10.1145/3243138

Rosen, Y., Lopez, G., Rushkin, I., Ang, A., Tingley, D., Munson, L., Rubin, R., & Weber, G. (2019). The effects of adaptive learning in a Massive Open Online Course on learners' skill development. In *Proceedings of the Ninth International Conference on Learning Analytics & Knowledge (LAK' 19)*. Society for Learning Analytics Research.

Sen, A., Patel, P., Rau, M. A., Mason, B., Nowak, R., Rogers, T. T., & Zhu, X. (2018). Machine beats human at sequencing visuals for perceptual-fluency practice. In *Proceedings of the Eleventh International Conference on Educational Data Mining (EDM' 18)*. International Educational Data Mining Society.

Shulman, L. (1987). Knowledge and teaching: Foundations of the new reform. *Harvard Educational Review*, *57*(1), 1–23. doi:10.17763/haer.57.1.j463w79r56455411

Siemens, G. (2005). Connectivism: A Learning Theory for the Digital Age. *International Journal of Instructional Technology and Distance Learning, 2*. http://www.itdl.org/Journal/Jan_05/article01.htm

Stevenson, I. (2008). Tool, tutor, environment or resource: Exploring metaphors for digital technology and pedagogy using activity theory. *Computers & Education*, *51*(2), 836–853. doi:10.1016/j.compedu.2007.09.001

Sunahase, T., Baba, Y., & Kashima, H. (2019). Probabilistic modeling of peer correction and peer assessment. In *Proceedings of the Twelfth International Conference on Educational Data Mining (EDM' 19)*. International Educational Data Mining Society.

Tan, J. P. L., & Koh, E. (2017). Situating learning analytics pedagogically: Towards an ecological lens. *Learning: Research and Practice*, *3*(1), 1–11. doi:10.1080/23735082.2017.1305661

Tempelaar, D. T., Rienties, B., & Giesbers, B. (2015). In search for the most informative data for feedback generation: Learning analytics in a data-rich context. *Computers in Human Behavior*, *47*, 157–167. doi:10.1016/j.chb.2014.05.038

Tran, K.-N., Lau, J. H., Contractor, D., Gupta, U., Sengupta, B., Butler, C. J., & Mohania, M. (2018). Document chunking and learning objective generation for instruction design. In *Proceedings of the Eleventh International Conference on Educational Data Mining (EDM' 18)*. International Educational Data Mining Society.

Vainas, O., Ben-David, Y., Gilad-Bachrach, R., Ronen, M., Bar-Ilan, O., & Shillo, R. (2019). Staying in the zone: sequencing content in classrooms based on the zone of proximal development. In *Proceedings of the Twelfth International Conference on Educational Data Mining (EDM' 19)*. International Educational Data Mining Society.

Vieira, C., Seah, Y. Y., & Magana, A. J. (2018). Students' experimentation strategies in design: Is process data enough. *Computer Applications in Engineering Education, 26*(5), 1903–1914. doi:10.1002/cae.22025

Vijh, U. P., Verhagen, J., Phillips, W., & An, J. (2019). Empowering tutors with big-data learning analytics. In *Proceedings of the Ninth International Conference on Learning Analytics & Knowledge (LAK' 19)*. Society for Learning Analytics Research.

Wampfler, R., Klingler, S., Solenthaler, B., Schinazi, V., & Gross, M. (2019). Affective State Prediction in a Mobile Setting using Wearable Biometric Sensors and Stylus. In *Proceedings of the Twelfth International Conference on Educational Data Mining (EDM' 19)*. International Educational Data Mining Society.

Whitehill, J., & Movellan, J. (2017). Approximately optimal teaching of approximately optimal learners. *Institute of Electrical and Electronics Engineers (IEEE). Transactions on Learning Technologies, 11*(2), 152–164. doi:10.1109/TLT.2017.2692761

Wiley, K. J., Bradford, A., Pardos, Z., & Linn, M. C. (2019). Beyond autoscoring: extracting conceptual connections from essays for classroom instruction. In *Proceedings of the Twelfth International Conference on Educational Data Mining (EDM' 19)*. International Educational Data Mining Society.

Wise, A. F. (2014, March). Designing pedagogical interventions to support student use of learning analytics. In *Proceedings of the Fourth International Conference on Learning Analytics & Knowledge (LAK' 14)*. Society for Learning Analytics Research.

Wu, B., Du, F., & Hu, Y. (2019). PBL Discourse analysis in ill-constructive field based on ENA – A case study of Chinese medicine education. In *Proceedings of the Ninth International Conference on Learning Analytics & Knowledge (LAK' 19)*. Society for Learning Analytics Research.

ADDITIONAL READING

Engeström, Y. (2015). *Learning by expanding: An activity-theoretical approach to developmental research* (2nd ed.). Cambridge University Press. (Original work published 1987)

Jonassen, D. H. (2010). *Learning to solve problems: A handbook for designing problem-solving learning environments*. Routledge. doi:10.4324/9780203847527

Lockyer, L., Heathcote, E., & Dawson, S. (2013). Informing pedagogical action: Aligning learning analytics with learning design. *The American Behavioral Scientist*, *57*(10), 1439–1459. doi:10.1177/0002764213479367

Macfadyen, L. P., Dawson, S., Pardo, A., & Gašević, D. (2014). Embracing big data in complex educational systems: The learning analytics imperative and the policy challenge. *Research & Practice in Assessment*, *9*, 17–28.

Price, M., Handley, K., Millar, J., & O'donovan, B. (2010). Feedback: All that effort, but what is the effect? *Assessment & Evaluation in Higher Education*, *35*(3), 277–289. doi:10.1080/02602930903541007

Shin, N., Jonassen, D. H., & McGee, S. (2003). Predictors of well-structured and ill-structured problem solving in an astronomy simulation. *Journal of Research in Science Teaching*, *40*(1), 6–33. doi:10.1002/tea.10058

KEY TERMS AND DEFINITIONS

Division of Labor: The roles of subjects and communities involved in specific learning activities.

Learning Analytics: Learning analytics aims at establishing a virtuous circle between teaching and learning process in the education environment through the analysis of student-centered data according to certain algorithm.

Object: What the subject what to achieve through the tools using. Sometimes have two level of meanings, referring to the goal when the tool itself is designed, and users of the tool also have their own goals.

Outcomes: The positive and negative impact on users or the application scope of the tool.

Pedagogies: A kind of tacit knowledge, closely related to learning process as instructions to implement effective teaching. The aim of pedagogy is to promote learner develop self-regulation skills.

Rules: In this chapter a term related to pedagogy, mainly involving two aspects, showing three contents: content (the organization of the content, the presentation or delivery strategy of the content), assessment, learning theory thoughts embodied the first two.

Subject: Users of tools or target group of tools, involving the characteristics of the target group.

Chapter 2
Opportunities for Adopting Open Research Data in Learning Analytics

Katarzyna Biernacka
https://orcid.org/0000-0002-6363-0064
Humboldt University of Berlin, Germany

Niels Pinkwart
Humboldt University of Berlin, Germany

ABSTRACT

The relevance of open research data is already acknowledged in many disciplines. Demanded by publishers, funders, and research institutions, the number of published research data increases every day. In learning analytics though, it seems that data are not sufficiently published and re-used. This chapter discusses some of the progress that the learning analytics community has made in shifting towards open practices, and it addresses the barriers that researchers in this discipline have to face. As an introduction, the movement and the term open science is explained. The importance of its principles is demonstrated before the main focus is put on open data. The main emphasis though lies in the question, Why are the advantages of publishing research data not capitalized on in the field of learning analytics? What are the barriers? The authors evaluate them, investigate their causes, and consider some potential ways for development in the future in the form of a toolkit and guidelines.

DOI: 10.4018/978-1-7998-7103-3.ch002

INTRODUCTION

The movement to publish datasets has been growing for some time now. Research institutions, funders, a growing number of publishers, and even the research communities themselves, promote the publication of research data (DCC (Digital Curation Centre); Deutsche Forschungsgemeinschaft, 2019; European Commission, 2016; L. Jones, Grant, & Hrynaszkiewicz, 2019; Kim, 2019). Although the benefits of sharing data are already known (Heather A. Piwowar & Vision, 2013), Learning Analytics data has still held back. One of the reasons for this could be the large amount of personal data collected by the Learning Analytics systems. The strict data protection regulations and the anonymization procedures seem to prevent scientists from sharing their data, or at least make it more difficult (Biernacka, & Pinkwart, 2020).

The Humboldt-Elsevier Advanced Data and Text Centre (HEADT Centre)[1] has set itself the goal of exploring the various facets of research integrity. The EU General Data Protection Regulation (GDPR) plays an important role for research integrity, as do the legal regulations of other countries and regions. One of the central topics of the initiative is therefore to investigate the legal regulations as an aspect of research integrity. The answer varies across disciplines and it is especially relevant when research data includes personal data. The degree of data protection, however, may interfere with transparency, which is a key value of research integrity. The goal of this research project is to investigate the conflict between publication of research data and the issues of privacy, and to identify and test solutions, considering both differences between disciplines and between cultural perspectives.

In this chapter the authors explore the handling of Learning Analytics research data with a focus on the publication process. It begins with a comprehensive introduction into the movement of Open Science, and then proceeds to the topic of Open Research Data. This foundation is necessary to understand the difficult situation in the field of Learning Analytics regarding this movement. The chapter continues with a look at the barriers of publishing research data in Learning Analytics, based on studies conducted in Germany, Peru, India and China. In the final part of the chapter, the authors intend to provide guidance to scientists in Learning Analytics. Furthermore, the authors offer possible practical solutions for the publication of research data in this discipline. The chapter ends with a conclusion.

BACKGROUND

What is Open Science?

The literature has not yet agreed on a definition of Open Science, as different actors within the scientific process have different ideas on what should be opened up. The most used and cited definition though, is the informal one from Nielsen (Gezelter, 2011): "Open science is the idea that scientific knowledge of all kinds should be openly shared as early as is practical in the discovery process." Vicente-Saez and Martinez-Fuentes (2018) define it as "(…) transparent and accessible knowledge that is shared and developed through collaborative networks". In general, Open Science means opening up the research by making all of its outcomes publicly available with the goal of dissemination and re-use of knowledge for a better world. Open Science is thus a welfare-enhancing phenomenon that enables transparent, accessible, shared, collaborative and rapid public disclosure of new knowledge.

The openness, as a key principle of Open Science, creates new opportunities for researchers, decision makers, platform programmers and operators, publishers and the general public (Fecher & Friesike, 2014; Open Science and Research Intitiative, 2014). For each of these stakeholders the term Open Science has a different meaning and concerns different areas. There is often a confusion between the principles, practices, outcomes or processes regarding Open Science. Therefore, it was decided on a taxonomy, including nine terms used at a first instance: Open Access, Open Data, Open Reproducible Research, Open Science Definition, Open Science Evaluation, Open Science Guidelines, Open Science Policies, Open Science Projects and Open Science Tools (see *Figure 1*) (Pontika, Knoth, Cancellieri, & Pearce, 2015).

Fecher and Friesike (2014) decided to structure the discourse by proposing five Open Science schools of thought: the infrastructure school, the public school, the measurement school, the democratic school and the pragmatic school. Between these schools there is no clear cut, they can share some ontological principles. *Table 1* shows the central ideas of each school.

Table 1. Open Science Schools of Thoughts (Fecher & Friesike, 2014)

School of thought	Central idea
Infrastructure	Develop openly available platforms, tools and services for efficient research
Public	Encourage the public to collaborate in research through citizen science, and make science more understandable and accessible for the public
Pragmatic	Open up the scientific process and increase the effectiveness of research and knowledge dissemination
Democratic	Make knowledge freely accessible to everyone
Measurement	Find new standards for the determination of scientific impact

Figure 1. Open Science Taxonomy
Source: (Pontika et al., 2015)

The infrastructure school concerns, as the name already says, the technical infrastructure. The advocates of this school emphasize that openly available platforms, tools and services are needed for efficient research. They see Open Science as a technological challenge to enable research on a bigger, wider scale. The infrastructure is a key element in all the subsequent school of thoughts: repositories, collaborative writing tools or storage.

The public school encourages the public to collaborate in research. The advocates of this school argue that science needs to be accessible and comprehensible for a broader public and interested non-experts. The research process can be made open and accessible, the audience can participate in the research process or just observe/follow it. A very well-known example for this stream is Citizen Science (Catlin-Groves, 2012; Irwin, 1995), e.g. zooniverse.org, which enables everyone to take part in real research in many different disciplines. This stream is possible through the new technologies that have arisen since Web 2.0. Alternatively, the researchers can open their results to the public in more comprehensible way than in the common scientific article. Examples of science communication in the context of this tenet of the public school are (micro)blogs (Ebner & Maurer, 2008), articles in non-scientific journals or talks, e.g. TEDTalks (TED, 2020).

The pragmatic school wants to make research and knowledge dissemination more efficient in optimizing the research process, e.g. opening the scientific value chain, including external knowledge or allowing collaboration through online tools.

Nielsen (2012) shows on the example of the Polymath Project[2] how science can shift from closed to collaborative. Experts from different institutions and countries can work together using an online tool, e.g. Wiki.

The democratic school of Open Science focuses on the accessibility of research products, in particular on the free access to research publications and research data. Thus, the two main streams emerging from the democratic school are Open Access and Open Data. In this section the authors will focus on Open Access, Open (Research) Data will be highlighted in the next section.

Open Access to research publications – in particular peer-reviewed journal articles - means the "free availability on the public internet, permitting any users to read, download, copy, distribute, print, search, or link to the full texts of these articles, crawl them for indexing, pass them as data to software, or use them for any other lawful purpose, without financial, legal, or technical barriers other than those inseparable from gaining access to the internet itself. The only constraint on reproduction and distribution, and the only role for copyright in this domain, should be to give authors control over the integrity of their work and the right to be properly acknowledged and cited" (Chan et al., 2002). This term was established by the Open Access Budapest Initiative[3] in 2002.

Since then, Open Access has grown in importance and a variety of full Open Access journals have been launched, e.g. PLOS. Still there has been a resistance to publish in these journals, as the subscription-based journals retained the highest impact factor and this measurement is still important for the evaluation of the scientific impact, and therefore for the reputation of the researchers. One of the solutions for this problem is the publication of unpublished works on preprints servers, e.g. arXiv[4] of PeerJ Preprints[5]. In some domains, computer science and physics among others, this practice is already well established (Gentil-Beccot, Mele, & Brooks, 2009; Larivière et al., 2013). The benefits of submitting unpublished work to a preprint server include, free and fast dissemination and citeability. For the latter case DOIs are assigned, which gives a time stamp to the preprint, which can be important for priority claims too.

Another solution to the problem of impact factors is encompassed by the measurement school which aims to find new standards for the determination of scientific impact. Rentier (2016) successfully draws the comparison between social processes to achieve prestige, and peer review. He shows that heredity, courtship or clubbing can also occur in the latter case. This could be prevented e.g. with Open Peer-Reviews by also making this process more transparent. The value of a scientific publication is currently defined by the reputation of the journal or collection in which it is published (Journal Impact Factor) and not by the quality of the article itself. According to this school of thought, an alternative and faster impact measurement that includes new forms of publication is needed. The umbrella term for this new impact measurements is altmetrics (Priem, Taraborelli, Groth, & Neylon, 2010). Altmetrics include tweets, blog discussions, bookmarks (e.g. on Mendeley or any research network), HTML views, citations and use in public APIs across platforms to gather data with open scripts and algorithms. According to the manifesto of Priem et al. (2010), altmetrics are great for measuring impact in this diverse scholarly ecosystem, tracking impact outside the academy, impact of influential but uncited works, and impact from sources that aren't peer-reviewed. Altmetrics expand the idea of what scientific impact nowadays consists of (see *Figure 2*).

Figure 2. Four ways to measure the impact of an article
Source: Priem et al. (2010) licensed under the Creative Commons CC BY-SA license

A different perspective to look at Open Science is throughout the research lifecycle (see Figure 3). From there, five main aspects of Open Science may be identified: Open Data, Open Methodology, Open Access (Open Paper), Open Peer-Review (Open Evaluation) and Open Source (Open Code). Additionally, as an important part of research: Open Educational Resources. In the next section the focus will be on Open Data.

The Push to Open Research Data

In the past, data was rarely public. There can be several reasons for this, but one of the most important was certainly the medium: paper is not a good data storage medium. The digital world has now opened up new possibilities and thus the call for open data. The change of technology has made data collection, storage, and sharing more feasible and the movement has been driven by increasing amount of data sharing policies and mandates from research funders and journals.2014)

Figure 3. Opening up of the research process
Source: Based on European Commission (2014)

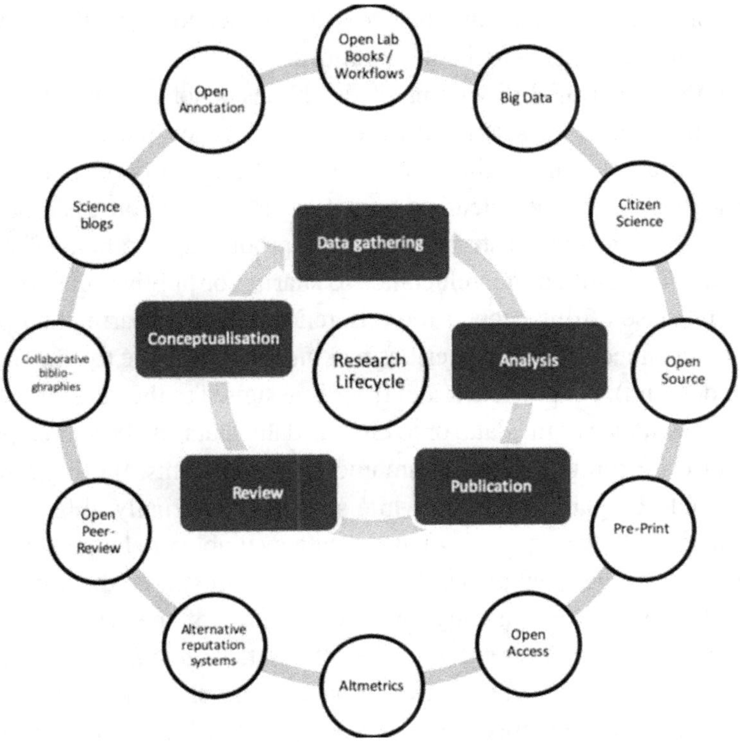

Open Data as one of the tenets of the democratic school of Open Science promotes the equal right to access knowledge – in this case to access data. The definition of "openness" is based on the Open Definition: "Open means anyone can freely access, use, modify, and share for any purpose (subject, at most, to requirements that preserve provenance and openness)." (Open Knowledge Foundation, 2015) and more specific: "Open data and content can be freely used, modified, and shared by anyone for any purpose" (Open Knowledge Foundation, 2015). This means that data has to be interoperable and give researchers the ability to interoperate - or intermix - different datasets (Open Knowledge Foundation, 2013). This type of data disclosure also makes it possible to create more transparency in science. Here we speak of Open Research Data.

Research transparency was already put into focus by government leaders and funders, to rebuild the trust in science. In 2011 the UK House of Commons Science and Technology Committee examined research integrity and the peer review process and concluded that "Access to data is fundamental if researchers are to reproduce and thereby verify results that are reported in the literature" (House of Commons

Science and Technology Committee, 2011). Frauds, such as those highlighted in a discussion of reproducibility issues by Ince (2011) can be avoided. The early publication of research data can thus help to reduce misconduct, facilitate replication, and support further research and collaborations.

Yet still, the data availability in many disciplines is not a common practice. For many years the quality of scientific work was judged on the conclusions drawn from the data, rather than on the data itself. This led to a poor understanding of data management along the scientists (e.g. missing descriptions, bad preservation of the data) and a general mistrust in the data produced by others. The concerns about data quality resulted in a reluctance to sharing or publishing research data.

For the purpose of this chapter the difference between sharing and publishing should be determined. *Sharing* describes making data available to other researchers (mostly on demand). No persistent identifier is assigned to the data, and it's hard to verify the provenience of the data, or to cite the data. Data can be shared personally, via repositories or through other communications platforms. Putting resources on a website would be public sharing, while sharing it internally with collaborators – private sharing. However, simply having data available or shared is not of much use. It is not guaranteed that data put on a website will still be there in 3 years. To raise overall research transparency, the transparency of the whole data creation process is needed. In the latter case, when the data is *published*, it should fulfil four criteria: it should be available, documented, citable and validated (Kratz & Strasser, 2014)[6]. To meet these criteria, it is important to document the research data extensively and to provide them with (subject-specific) metadata. This increases the traceability and findability of the research work among the peers. The next step is to choose a suitable, subject-specific repository that is relevant to the community[7]. In order to make the research data available and citable over the long-term, it is important to assign a persistent identifier to the data. Most often, the repository assigns a Digital Object Identifier[8] (DOI) at this point. This makes the research data uniquely referenceable. The biggest hurdle to overcome is the data validation. It is difficult to decide what criteria can be used to evaluate the quality of research data, in particular because it can be distinguished between technical and scientific evaluation (Callaghan et al., 2012).

Besides the governments and funders, various institutions already demand data accessibility (publication) too. ALLEA (2017, p. 6) – All European Academies – requires in the European Code of Conduct for Research Integrity, that "Researchers, research institutions and organisations ensure access to data is as open as possible, as closed as necessary, and where appropriate in line with the FAIR Principles (Findable, Accessible, Interoperable and Re-usable) for data management" and "Researchers, research institution and organisations provide transparency about how to access or make use of their data and research materials". The FAIR Principles were published in 2016 (Wilkinson et al., 2016) and are intended to act as guideline for enhancing the re-usability of data. Besides to the requirements for findability, accessibility and the assignment of persistent identifiers (see criteria for published data as above mentioned), interoperability is also important here. The data should be available in such a way that it can be exchanged, interpreted and integrated with other data sets (re-used).

Not all published data is FAIR data by definition, and not all FAIR data is open though. In order to open the data in the sense of Open Science is to minimize the *usability* restrictions. The minimum requirement of Open Data is to have open terms of use (open licenses). The most frequently used licenses for research data are the Creative Commons[9]. Care should be taken to ensure that the re-use conditions are as "open as possible and as closed as necessary" (ALLEA, 2017, p. 6). Of the seven licenses they offer, three are in line with Open Science: CC0, CC BY and CC BY-SA. The other four are too restrictive.

To achieve greater openness of data, paywalls have to be avoided and machine-readable, non-proprietary formats and open standards used. This higher degree of openness is, where FAIR data meets and overlap Open Data.

In this chapter the authors focus on these research data that fulfil the ideas of published and open research data that meet the FAIR Principles. In the following sections, the Open Research Data[10] in Learning Analytics will be considered.

Advantages of Publishing Research Data

As already shown in the section about Open Data, informal data sharing still seems to be much more common in many disciplines than formal publication of research data (either on a repository or as a data paper). Even though there is evidence that publication of data leads to more citations (Gleditsch, Metelits, & Strand, 2003; Peng, 2011; Pienta, Alter, & Lyle, 2010; Heather A. Piwowar & Vision, 2013), researchers still seem unconvinced.

In addition, many projects are financed by third-party funds - whether from public or private funding agencies. The publication of the data, which is now increasingly demanded by the funders (Colavizza, Hrynaszkiewicz, Staden, Whitaker, & McGillivray, 2019; European Commission, 2016), can at this point also be seen as an investment in one's own reputation. The time spent on proper management, documentation, and the publication process itself pays off in the end, as this data publication can be presented to new potential funders. On the other hand, research data emerged from a public funded project, could be considered as public good that should be made open for the public.

Given the complexity of contemporary science, researchers have to act against fraud and misconduct. Publication of research data helps to promote research integrity and accountability. By making the data available to one's own peers for re-use, one receives direct feedback on the quality of the research, which is verified in this way. This can have a positive effect on researchers' reputations too.

Overall, the exchange of data with colleagues promotes new collaborations and also new insights. Van Horik, Dillo, and Doorn (2013) give examples on how fast the awareness and the practice of data management can positively change. The authors took Archeology, Oral History and Qualitative Social Science, Virology and Veterinary Medicine as an example, where data transparency and open access to data became the new scientific practice.

When publishing research data, the scientist may prevent unnecessary costs for gathering the same data twice. It allows a more efficient allocation of these resources in different projects and to gather more visibility. Furthermore, data put in a repository helps to prevent data loss.

Making data publicly and openly available facilitates therefore the re-use, verification, replication, meta-analysis and robustness check of the research. It supports more efficient and excellent science and leads to increase the trust and confidence in research processes.

Research Data in Learning Analytics

Similarly, digitization has helped to really bring Learning Analytics (LA) into existence. The use of Learning Management Systems (LMS) and Virtual-Learning-Environments (VLE) increased. Learning processes are increasingly taking place online, especially now during the COVID19 pandemic. As a result, large amount of learning and learners' data is generated every day. This information enables learning and teaching to become more personalized (Ferguson, 2012; Long & Siemens, 2011; Papamitsiou & Economides, 2014). These technical advances led to the development of a new field of research: Learning Analytics.

The range of research data in the field of Learning Analytics varies as much as the definition of the subject area itself. Scientists from computer science, educational research, psychology, as well as from all didactic subjects can identify themselves with this field of work. The community is roughly divided into three areas: Learning Analytics and Knowledge, Educational Data Mining and Academic Analytics. With different methods (such as data mining, qualitative analysis or statistics) research data is collected, which should help to model student behaviour, predict performance or make resource recommendations (Papamitsiou & Economides, 2014).

In semi-structured interviews (Biernacka, 2020a, 2020b, 2020c, 2020d), Learning Analytics scientists from Computer Science from Germany, India, China and

Peru have identified the following data types as their research data: process data, questionnaires, interview data, log data, audio-video data, multimodal data produced by sensors (e.g. ECG, EEG, GSR, vital data), assessment data, annotated text data, sociodemographic data, data from learning platforms (e.g. behaviour data), learning performance, online user behaviour, MOOC data, focus group observations, runtime data and many more. One can therefore clearly see the diversity of the research data, both qualitative and quantitative. A general research data management workflow will be only of little help here – all these types need different handling, in particular when legal aspects are considered. The data sensitivity shows large variation, but in most of the cases the scientist indeed deal with personal, or sometimes even sensitive data[11].

Barriers of Publishing Research Data in Learning Analytics

Despite the many advantages of publishing research data presented in the section before, in many disciplines data publication is still rare (Alsheikh-Ali, Qureshi, Al-Mallah, & Ioannidis, 2011; H. A. Piwowar, 2011; Schofield et al., 2009; Vanpaemel, Vermorgen, Deriemaecker, & Storms, 2015; Vision, 2010). Some studies already identified factors that prevent researchers from the publication of their research data. They include the "*fear for misuse and misinterpretation of data*" (Van den Eynden et al., 2016), "*the desire to publish results before releasing data*" (Schmidt, Gemeinholzer, & Treloar, 2016), "*lack of journal requirements*" (Lucraft, Allin, Baynes, & Sakellaropoulou, 2019) or "*not common in the community*" (Houtkoop et al., 2018). Besides the barriers mentioned, regular factors are connected to ethical concerns, legal constraints, not having the rights to make data accessible or to the anonymization process are identified (Cheah et al., 2015; Meyer, 2018; Schmidt et al., 2016). Already in these studies it becomes clear, that the different disciplines require different handling of their research data.

However, none of these studies have specifically addressed the concerns and needs of the scientists from Learning Analytics. In the HEADT Centre project, the researchers are looking in particular at the handling of research data and their publication in Learning Analytics in four different countries: Germany, India, China and Peru (Biernacka, 2019; Biernacka & Huaroto, 2020; Biernacka & Pinkwart, 2020). In addition to very different cultural perspectives, the different countries also show great differences in legal regulations. The authors consider distinctive issues that may arise considering these circumstances with the focus on the publication of data about learners' behaviour and try to find out why the LA researcher are reluctant to publish their research data.

To understand the concerns about research data publishing in their domain, a semi-structured interview study with scientists in Learning Analytics was used. In total 13 scientists from Germany, Peru, India and China were questioned (compare sampling in *Table 2*). The qualitative research was conducted between July 2019 and January 2020. Both, junior (2 to 4 years of experience) and senior scientists (more than 5 years of experience) were included. Researcher with longer professional experience seemed to be more willing to participate in an interview. Newcomer and scientists in early stages of their careers may have more inhabitations about expressing their opinion. The authors experienced some difficulties in finding researchers in this research field in Peru and India, where the awareness and understanding of Learning Analytics and the related issues in the data-driven society is still missing (Cobo & Aguerrebere, 2018). The terms "analysis of educational data", "data-based feedback" or "data-based actions" seem to be more common.

Table 2. Sampling for the semi-structured interviews in Germany, Peru, India and China (2019-2020)

	Germany	Peru	India	China
No. of junior scientists	2	0	0	1
No. of senior scientists	3	2	1	4
No. of institutions	5	1	1	2
Total no. of interviews	5	2	1	5

The semi-structured interview study gave an insight of how the research data is handled in LA in general. Questions about their work and the research data their working with were asked. In the second part of the interview, the interviewer asked whether the researcher has published his/her data. Ten of the thirteen interviewed scientists answered "no" to this question, of which four are "*uncertain what is allowed*". Another person who indicated this factor, published his/her data only aggregated as an evaluation in a paper. This result already shows one of the biggest challenges. This lies in an unclear legal situation with regard to research data. This problem seems to be not only in Germany (or Europe, where the GDPR [12]applies), but worldwide: both India and China have mentioned this factor too. In the remained case that indicated "*uncertainty what is allowed*" we have no information about whether he/she published the research data.

A junior scientist from Germany concludes:

On the other side, especially because media is big on (unintelligible) about data security and data usage, everyone is very, very insecure: What can I do? (Junior Scientist, Germany (Biernacka, 2020c, p. 3 in os_013))

In total, 27 different barriers to the publication of research data were mentioned by the scientists (see Figure 4). Those barriers and concerns can be clustered around five dimensions (see *Table 3*):

- Authority or practice considerations
- Technical or processing constraints
- Legal concerns
- Loss of control of data
- Resource constraints.

Table 3. The five dimensions of barriers to publication of research data emerged from the semi-structured interviews

Authority or practice considerations	Technical or processing constraints	Legal concerns	Loss of control of data	Resource constraints
No extrinsic motivation or obligation	Anonymisation – conducting the anonymization process	Anonymisation – no complete security	Anonymisation – loss of information	Costs
No sharing culture	Big data	Balancing privacy and openness	Competition	Missing infrastructure
Non-visible value	Complexity of the publication process	Consequences	Fear of misinterpretation	Time and/or work effort
Not established in community	Unclear which infrastructure	"I'm not allowed to publish"	Quality of the data	
	Unfamiliarity with the publication process	Legal regulations	Vulnerability	
		Licenses		
		Personal / sensitive data		
		Uncertainty what is allowed		
		Uncertainty who owns the data		
		Unclear responsibility		

Figure 4. The occurrence of emerged codes for the barriers to the publication of research data in Learning Analytics in Germany, Peru, India and China

Codesystem	LA Germany	LA Peru	LA India	LA China	SUMME
Barriers to and problems with publication of research data					0
patents					0
embargo					0
big data				■	1
unfamiliarity with the publication process				■	1
unfamiliarity with the legal regulations					0
legal regulations			■		1
quality of the data			■		1
loss of control					0
licenses			■	■	2
stealing ideas					0
mistrust					0
missing peer-review					0
fear of misinterpretation		■			1
anlysis is easier to understand than the raw data					0
no extrinsic motivation or obligation		■			1
no sharing-culture			■		1
costs	■				1
not established in community		■		■	2
vulnerability		■			1
uncertainty who owns the data				■	1
uncertainty what is allowed	■		■	■	3
"I'm not allowed to publish"	■			■	2
balancing privacy and openness	■			■	2
consequences	■				1
unclear responsibility	■				1
personal / sensitive data	■				1
non-visible value	■				1
complexity of the publication process	■				1
missing infrastructure		■			1
unclear which infrastructure	■			■	2
anonymisation					0
no complete security	■			■	2
conducting the anonymisation process	■			■	2
loss of information	■			■	2
time and/or work effort	■		■	■	3
competition	■	■			2
Σ SUMME	15	6	6	13	40

The "*uncertainty what is allowed*" is followed by the two codes that have to do with the anonymization process: "*no complete security*" and the "*loss of information*". While the first one underpins the unfamiliarity with the legal regulations and the uncertainty with all that is associates with it, it also shows the concerns about the potential harm that might arise out of the identification of the participants. The interviewees expressed their concerns that the publication of data could compromise the participants' confidentiality as the risk could not always be fully mitigated by the de-identification process of individual data:

What is behind it is of course, that anonymized data will never provide full security. There are enough examples where anonymous data sets has been combined with others and in the end you could filter out individual persons through certain features. (Senior Scientist, Germany (Biernacka, 2020c, p. 2 in os_002))

or

I can not take the risk of explosion [sic exposure]... some, eh.. some data of others. (Senior Scientist, China (Biernacka, 2020b, p. 3 in os_029))

The "*loss of information*" through conducting the anonymization process is relevant in Learning Analytics indeed too. As the discipline lives from analyzing personal and behavior data, it is exactly what is needed for the evaluation or for the training of the e.g. machine learning. If these data are anonymized too early it can have huge influence on the results of the research project:

(...) the question about anonymisation has to be looked at critically. Because... at the beginning of the research you don't really know, what are the important factors. (Junior Scientist, Germany (Biernacka, 2020c, p. 2 in os_013))

On the other hand, publishing anonymized data in a discipline that works on the personalization of learning arises doubts too:

I would at least secure that some kind of information can be gained from the data. If that is not the case, you have to ask yourself why you even work on it. (Senior Scientist, Germany (Biernacka, 2020c, p. 3 in os_024))

Research data in Learning Analytics is based on collecting information about the learner, his/her learning behavior and achievements. Since it's the ground for the personalization of the learning and teaching experience, these data are particularly subject to data protection laws and regulations. According to Pardo and Siemens (2014), a clear definition of *privacy* in LA is elusive and has to be addressed from different angles. Issues like confidentiality, trust or data ownership have to be dealt with (Drachsler & Greller, 2016; Pardo & Siemens, 2014). While in Germany and China the legal concerns form more than 50% of the named factors that prevent publishing of research data (64% and 55% respectively), it's only 33% in India and not a single one in Peru. In the latter case the publication process for research data is "*not established in the community*" yet. At this point one should bear in mind that this field of research in Latin America is still fundamentally new and all processes here are still being redefined (Biernacka & Huaroto, 2020). The researchers express their concerns:

They think that the data that will be shared will be measured or will have other results and will contradict the work that they are doing. (Senior Scientist, Peru (Biernacka, 2020a, pp. 3 in os_018, translated))

The re-analysis of their data can lead to different conclusions or in some cases, even identify mistakes in the raw research data or the original data analysis. Such a situation can possibly cause reputational damage to the researcher or their whole institution.

In India the researchers are more concerned about the *"quality of data"*. The published research data should be of good quality and therefore curated and validated:

I'm expecting to take that to a certain quality, a certain format before I publish. (Senior Scientist, India (Biernacka, 2020d, p. 4 in os_032))

Another big hurdle to overcome, is the "*time and/or work effort*" that has to be undertaken. Making research data accessible costs time and human resources for the preparation and publication of the data. Researchers prefer to invest this time in the research itself rather than in the management of the data:

And, so we think, a lot of work needs to be done before this kind of data can be published. (Senior Scientist, China (Biernacka, 2020b, p. 5 in os_007))

Moreover, funds are rarely made available for this purpose. In low-income countries this barrier is emphasized even more when it comes to costs for storage and archiving.

Five Dimensions of Barriers

In the previous sections the authors outlined on the one hand the benefits of the publication of research data, and on the other hand the factors that prevent scientist from publishing research data according to a semi-structured interview study with scientist in Learning Analytics from Germany, Peru, India and China. The potential advantages do not seem sufficient so far to motivate the researchers, in particular from low-income countries, to make their data publicly available; even though many of the interviewees stated that they had an interest in Open Data and Open Science in general.

In this section, the authors will give a wider explanation of the five dimensions of barriers to the publication of research data.

Authority or Practice Considerations

The main findings of this study show, that publication of research data among Learning Analytics researchers is not a common practice yet. Even though it is considered as desirable, the time and work effort needed to prepare good-quality data is too high. The processes of scientific article publication, which have been imprinted for decades as the highest mark of recognition in other, older disciplines, also leave their mark in this young research domain. Furthermore, the publication of Learning Analytics data requires in most of the cases an anonymization process that leads to loss of the most important information in the dataset.

There are different steps that have to be done to overcome these barriers. It is not easy to change thinking patterns and the scientific publishing world is not making it easier. The system has to be adopted. Increasing the value of publication of the research data or its citation would be of great help. It should not only be the publication of scientific articles that contributes to the reputation of the researcher, but also providing high-quality research data. Mandatory or rewarded data publishing, enforced by institutions, journals or funders would be highly efficient in increasing the motivation for the publication of research data.

Technical or Processing Constraints

Many of the barriers mentioned show clear problems with the technical system or related processes. Digitization brings with it a large flood of data. This data is on the one hand very complex and on the other hand very extensive and therefore requires a lot of storage space. Transferring many terabytes from the local laboratory server to a repository and at the same time making them available in a form that potential re-users can work with this research data is beyond the means of many researchers.

This brings up the question of which system or which repository is suitable for this. Many researchers would not even know where to start looking for a suitable repository, and what "suitable" means in this context.

Furthermore, researchers are often not sufficiently trained to publish research data in a way that complies with scientific publication standards. There are uncertainties in the processes involved, from the correct administration to anonymization and the publication of research data.

Legal Concerns

When publishing research data, many scientists face a number of legal challenges or uncertainties. Whether it is a matter of researchers working together in collaborations and not knowing what they are allowed to do by contract, or whether the question of who owns the data has not yet been clarified. The question of legal liability also often arises: what happens if data is published illegally? Is it the scientist who is accountable, his or her supervisor, or the institution? The consequences of data publication can be difficult to assess and it is difficult to decide which license best protects the interests of the study participants and the scientist while at the same time acting in the spirit of Open Science.

Rarely is the publication of data planned from the outset and therefore not included in the informed consent. This leads to problems at a later stage, as it is often not possible or too costly to obtain a publication permit at a later stage. According to the GDPR, the processing of personal data is only possible if it follows the six principles: lawfulness, fairness and transparency, purpose limitation, data minimization, accuracy, storage limitation and integrity and confidentiality. This means that the participants need to know what will happen with their data, the minimum of data needed is collected and that this data stays confidential. Person-related information shall be eliminated before the data can be published. Some can argue though, that the process of anonymization is not sufficiently secure to guarantee protection of the research subjects as it is not possible to know what other data was already published or leaked about the participants.

Loss of Control of Data

A major problem in the publication of research data is competition and the fear of misuse of the data. Researchers do not want to lose control over their data and want to know who is using it and for what purpose. They are afraid that the data will be used unintentionally (e.g. by one of the well-known data power-houses for commercial purposes). Others consider their data to be of insufficient relevance or quality. The last point is difficult to determine because there is no established peer-review process for research data. The curation of data always has to take place on two levels (technical and content-related) (Callaghan et al., 2012) and thus costs a lot of effort. Furthermore, the publication of research data carries the risk that weaknesses in data collection and analysis may become visible and errors being exposed.

To guarantee a high security of anonymity, it is necessary to eliminate a large amount of information from the data. This does not happen without losing value of data, and then the question arises as to why one wants to do the effort at all.

Resource Constraints

The barriers that arise regarding resources refer mainly to four types of resources: human, time, financial and infrastructural.

The time and human resources required for the preparation of research data are often ignored in project planning, which in turn is a major problem later on. Additional data managers cannot be paid for, but the scientists' time is too valuable at that moment to put it into administration. Researchers prefer to invest time in the research itself rather than in the management of their research data for later publication.

Often the supporting infrastructure is also missing at the institutions. There are no points of contact for support during the various stages of the research process and Data Protection Officers are often left to manage the high number of requests on their own (as shown in Ostendorff and Linke (2019) too). This problem is even more visible in the low-income countries and thus worse possibilities to guarantee additional personnel or technical systems.

RECOMMENDATIONS FOR THE PUBLICATION OF RESEARCH DATA IN LEARNING ANALYTICS

Solutions can be found for all five dimensions of barriers introduced in the section before. In this section the authors will give recommendations for tools and further reading tips for those researchers in Learning Analytics that want to publish his or her research data but faced the barriers mentioned before. During the semi-structured interviews, the participants suggested solutions on how to address these barriers and concerns which will be included here too.

The recommendations consist of two parts: a toolkit and guidelines.

The toolkit (see p. 14) is a collection of suggested and exemplary tools and services, as well as further reading suggestions. The resources are available (mostly) for free online and shall help the Learning Analytics researcher to overcome the barriers to the publication of research data. The proposed further sources for reading can be websites or scientific articles where the researchers can go into the deep of the topic.

The guidelines (see p. 14) can be regarded as an extension of the DELICATE checklist (Drachsler & Greller, 2016) and thus shows step by step what the researcher can and should do before publishing his or her research data.

FUTURE RESEARCH DIRECTIONS

The HEADT Centre research project consists of three phases: qualitative research, quantitative research, and findings implementation. Only the results of the first phase are presented in this chapter.

Table 4. Toolkit

	Tools & Services	Further reading
Authority or practice considerations	http://www.imsglobal.org/learningdesign/index.html - IMS Learning Design	Lee, B. D. (2018). Ten simple rules for documenting scientific software. PLoS Comput Biol, 14(12), e1006561. doi:10.1371/journal.pcbi.1006561
	http://dublincore.org/documents/dces/ - Dublin Core Metadata Element Set	Biernacka, K., Bierwirth, M, Buchholz, P., Dolzycka, D., Helbig, K., Neumann, J., Odebrecht, C., Wiljes, C., & Wuttke, Ulrike. (2020). Train-the-Trainer Concept on Research Data Management (Version 3.0). Zenodo. doi:10.5281/zenodo.4071471
	http://ltsc.ieee.org/wg12/files/LOM_1484_12_1_v1_Final_Draft.pdf - Draft Standard for Learning Object Metadata	Tennant, J. (2020). The [R]evolution of Open Science.
	https://rdmpromotion.rbind.io/ - Research data management Promotion material	
Technical or processing constraints	https://re3data.org - Registry of Research Data Repositories	
	https://pslcdatashop.web.cmu.edu/ - DataShop – a data analysis service for the learning science community	
	https://zenodo.org - Multidisciplinary repository	
Legal concerns	https://choosealicense.com/ - Choose an open source license	https://www.ukdataservice.ac.uk/manage-data/legal-ethical/gdpr-in-research/consent.aspx - Applying GDPR in research
	https://creativecommons.org/share-your-work/ - Creative Commons tools to help share your work	Meyer, M. N. (2018). Practical Tips for Ethical Data Sharing. Association for Psychological Science, 1(1), 131-144.
	https://aircloak.com/top-5-free-data-anonymization-tools/ - Top 5 Free Data Anonymization Tools	Guibault, L., & Wiebe, A. (2013). Safe to be open. Study on the protection of research data and recommendations for access and usage.
		Drachsler, H., & Greller, W. (2016). Privacy and analytics. Paper presented at the Proceedings of the Sixth International Conference on Learning Analytics & Knowledge - LAK '16.
Loss of control of data	https://osf.io/ - Platform to support your research and enable collaboration	Wallis, J. C., Borgman, C. L., & Mayernik, M. (2007). Know Thy Sensor: Trust, Data Quality, and Data Integrity in Scientific Digital Libraries. UCLA Papers. doi:10.1007/978-3-540-74851-9_32
	https://originstamp.com - Create secure timestamps using blockchain technology	
	https://citation.crosscite.org - Citation Formatter	
Resource constraints	https://ukdataservice.ac.uk/media/622368/costingtool.pdf - Data management costing tool	
	https://v2.sherpa.ac.uk/juliet - SHERPA/JULIIET – Research Funders' Open Access Policies	
	https://dmponline.dcc.ac.uk/ - Helps to create, review and share data management plans	

Table 5. Guidelines for publication of research data in Learning Analytics

1. Create a consent form before collecting data	
Try to think of everything, that you want to do with the collected data. Don't forget to mention the evaluation, archiving, and publication. Your participants need to be informed about all the steps you want to undertake. Here you can already put the information about the repository and the licenses you want to give your data. If you need to anonymize data, mention it as well and explain to your participants at which point of your research you want to do that, what happens to the raw data, and how will you provide data protection before you anonymize the research data. Let all your participants sign a consent before the study starts.	• Why do you want to apply Learning Analytics? • What is the added value of your research? • What will happen to the collected data? How will you process the research data? • Do you need to collect personal or even sensitive data? • Why are you allowed to collect the data? • Where will you store your data? • How will you protect your research data? • Will you share your data and with whom? • Will you publish the research data? Where? Under what license? • Where will the data and its documentation be stored after the end of the project? • How long should the data be kept?
2. Document all your steps	
Most of the documentation is simply good research practice, so you are probably doing it anyway, just write it down step by step. Start with it as early as possible and document consistently throughout the project. Try not to leave the documentation at the very end of your research project. Write it down as long as you have it fresh in your mind and try to think about, what information is needed to understand your data. You can write it down in a separate document called README, in a data dictionary or a codebook (or combining all three forms if needed).	• What information would you need to understand the data? • For what purpose was the research data created/collected? • What does the dataset contain? • How was the research data collected? • Who collected the data? • When was the research data collected? • What data cleansing processes were undertaken? • How was the quality of the research data ensured? • In which formats is the data available? • How can the data be accessed?
3. Think about where to publish your data as early as possible	
Data Journals and repositories can follow specific metadata standards, controlled vocabulary or have other requirements to your data (e.g. formats). The most popular discipline-specific repository for LA is probably DataShop. You can decide for a generic repository like Zenodo or an institutional repository too. The choice depends on your needs, but all of those are a good choice. The important thing is that the repository provides a DOI (or another persistent identifier) to your data.	• Where do you want to publish? • Are there specific recommendations or requirements coming from the repository or Data Journal? • Is the repository trustworthy? Does it have a seal? • Does the repository provide a DOI (or another persistent identifier)? • How durable is the service provider? • What terms of use of the data are possible? • What access is there to the data?
4. Define different levels of processing[13] and de-personalize data	
Before you can publish your data, you have to get sure that your data is de-personalized. Delete all person-related information. If this is not possible for you, you should consider publishing the metadata including the documentation instead of the dataset itself. You can define different levels of processing, e.g. 0 Raw data; full data 1 Pseudonomized data (full data with redaction for direct and indirect identifiers) 2 Anonymized data (de-identification via direct or indirect identifiers not possible)	• Is it possible to anonymize your research data? • When do you pseudonomize your data? • Are there technical procedures to guarantee privacy? • Does the data storage or externals fulfill highest international security standards?

continues on following page

Table 5. Continued

5. Choose a license[14]	
There are different licenses you can choose from for your research data depending on the format of the data. Try to choose a free and open license like Creative Commons, Open Data Commons or MIT.	• Do you have software as your research data? • Do you want attribution for your work? • Do you want to allow others to use your work commercially? • Do you want to allow others to change, remix, adapt or build upon your work?
6. Choose the right format	
Choose open formats and try to avoid proprietary formats to support re-use. Not everybody can afford to buy the use licenses. Use a format that is readable by machines and humans. Learning Analytics comes with a wide variety of formats, so it's difficult to make clear recommendation. Compare it with the actual recommendation for long time archiving.	• Is the format you're using proprietary? • Is the software you used widely distributed? • Is the format well established in the community? • Is it a compressed file format? • Would it be better to make the research data available in the source format and additionally in a widely used export format (e.g. PDF/A)?
7. Consider all the related legal aspects[15]	
Get sure that all the legal aspects are clarified before you publish.	• Which legal provisions exist in general? • Are there any patents pending? • Are you allowed to publish the data? • Who owns the data? • Does the research data fall under the Copyright Act? • Are there any agreements on the intellectual property of the research data? • Are there any predetermined requirements of the funding agencies?
8. Define the access levels[16]	
Before you publish your data, you should think about different access levels to control the re-use, e.g you can define different access levels: Open – Data is freely available for re-use Restricted – Data is available for re-use with access restriction Controlled – Data can be shared after approved by the researcher Closed – Data cannot be shared. Data can only be used by the researcher or for archival purpose	• What data can be published openly (Open Data without any restriction)? • What data should have restricted access (data available when a user meets standard criteria)? • Were any agreements made regarding data accessibility? • What data should have controlled access (data available only when e.g. a user is approved by the original researcher)?
9. FAIR Data Principles[17]	
Check your data complies with the FAIR Data Principles. If you cannot assure the privacy protection of your participants consider preparing your metadata for publication. You don't have to make your data open. Maybe conditional access is the better choice: the metadata record is available to the public but access to the research data themselves occurs only after pre-determined conditions are met.	• Is your data described by rich metadata? • Can you put your metadata online in a searchable repository or catalogue? • Does the metadata record specify the persistent identifier? • Can the metadata be accessible, even if the data aren't? • Does the metadata provided follow relevant standards? • Did you use controlled vocabularies, keywords, thesauri or ontologies? • Are qualified references and links provided to other related data?
10. Publish	
You are ready: Take the step, and publish your research data (or metadata if nothing else is possible)!	

In the second step, the hypotheses that emerged from the semi-structured interviews will be revised through a wide-spread online-survey. Thus, by incorporating a quantitative analysis, the authors wish to resolve some of the limitations of the qualitative phase of the study.

In order to better understand the influence factors on the publication of research data in general, two more disciplines should be considered: medicine and climate impact research. These disciplines show a wide variation in the research data types, particularly in terms of the data sensitivity.

In the final phase of research, in addition to the guidelines and recommendations, technical implementations for repositories will be proposed and best practices for researchers will be developed.

CONCLUSION

Learning Analytics present significant opportunities for a change of teaching and learning experiences. It is particularly useful because it incorporates computational analysis techniques to the already established research on evidence and improvement of teaching and learning. It is also based on algorithms and methods that require and produce a lot of data. According to Drachsler and Greller (2016) researchers and institutions dealing with Learning Analytics are seeing privacy as a big concern. The authors emphasize that most of the people are not aware of the legal boundaries. The semi-structured interview study of the HEADT Centre underpins this observation and focuses on the publication of data in LA that would be so important in this area. It can be extrapolated from the research trends in other disciplines, that the scientists in Learning Analytics put their focus on the publication of scientific articles, including the results of their research, rather than publishing the underlying research data.

In 2014 Scheffel, Drachsler, Stoyanov, and Specht (2014) it is already shown that two of the most important topics in Learning Analytics are: the openness and transparency of the used data, and the data privacy . But still, it can be said that the process of publishing research data in Learning Analytics has not yet been fully established. A complete openness of data also seems quite unlikely in this case due to the processing of personal data. Although the participants in the interviews and surveys from related research come from different countries and are therefore subject to different data protection regulations, they agreed that "*uncertainty about what is allowed*" or legal issues in general (data privacy in particular) is the biggest factor preventing them from publishing their research data. Ignoring these fears can lead to a lack of acceptance from the research participants and to the hesitation of publishing research data from the researchers.

In all phases of research data management, the most diverse areas of law must be considered. This fact alone overwhelms many researchers even before they start preparing research data for publication. Rights of use, science law, fundamental rights, international law, patent law, competition law, copyright law, contracts, policies, labor law and above all - concerning almost every phase of the research data life cycle – the data protection law.

Learning Analytics as a subject has a difficult starting position, because research here is based on individual data to enable personalized teaching and learning in order to achieve even better learning results. Basically, beginning with the planning of a research project and through to the collection of the research data, it must be considered whether these data have a personal reference and whether this personal information is important for the research to be conducted. If this is the case, the informed consent of the research participants is essential. The data should be made anonymous as soon as the research purpose allows it. If it is not possible from the beginning, other protective measures must be conducted (e.g. pseudonymization). Anonymization should only be postponed in research projects if those features that can be used to identify a person are really needed to achieve the research purpose or individual research steps. Anonymization can be seen as an enabler for the publication of data and it reduces the fear of privacy breaches too. However, caution must be paid: in many cases of automated anonymization it is at best a pseudonymization. In this case, the data, in combination with other data sources, can lead to the de-anonymization or identification of the persons (Drachsler & Greller, 2016).

The publication of research data is still a tough issue in some areas. This is also true for Learning Analytics, the value of such data publication is not yet apparent to researchers. The frequent barriers associated with the many legal aspects create uncertainty. With this chapter, the authors launch a call to break through these fears and show the benefits of publishing and citing data. Other ways are also pointed out in the very difficult cases where complete opening of research data is not possible. In many cases the data is not validated or not all information can be shared, but perhaps new collaborations or meta-analyses can emerge from FAIR metadata alone.

The road to truly open and FAIR published data is still long and certainly challenging. The basic data protection regulation rightly protects the participants in the research, but at the same time it spreads a large degree of uncertainty among scientists when publishing research data.

REFERENCES

Alexander, S. M., Jones, K., Bennett, N. J., Budden, A., Cox, M., Crosas, M., Game, E. T., Geary, J., Hardy, R. D., Johnson, J. T., Karcher, S., Motzer, N., Pittman, J., Randell, H., Silva, J. A., da Silva, P. P., Strasser, C., Strawhacker, C., & Stuhl, A. (2019). Qualitative data sharing and synthesis for sustainability science. *Nature Sustainability*. Advance online publication. doi:10.103841893-019-0434-8

ALLEA. (2017). *The European Code of Conduct for Research Integrity*. ALLEA - All European Academies.

Alsheikh-Ali, A. A., Qureshi, W., Al-Mallah, M. H., & Ioannidis, J. P. (2011). Public availability of published research data in high-impact journals. *PLoS One*, *6*(9), e24357. doi:10.1371/journal.pone.0024357 PMID:21915316

Biernacka, K. (2019). *Research Integrity and Privacy*. Retrieved from https://headt.eu/Research-Integrity-Technology-and-GDPR

Biernacka, K. (2020a). *Perspectiva de los Investigadores sobre la Publicación de Datos de Investigación: Entrevistas Semiestructuradas de Perú*. edoc-Server, Humboldt-Universität zu Berlin. Berlin, Germany. doi:10.18452/21394

Biernacka, K. (2020b). *Researchers' Perspective on the Publication of Research Data: Semi-structured Interviews from China*. edoc-Server, Humboldt-Universität zu Berlin. Berlin, Germany. doi:10.18452/21330

Biernacka, K. (2020c). *Researchers' Perspective on the Publication of Research Data: Semi-structured Interviews from Germany*. edoc-Server, Humboldt-Universität zu Berlin. Berlin, Germany. doi:10.18452/21644

Biernacka, K. (2020d). *Researchers' Perspective on the Publication of Research Data: Semi-structured Interviews from India*. edoc-Server, Humboldt-Universität zu Berlin. Berlin, Germany. doi:10.18452/21378

Biernacka, K., & Huaroto, L. (2020). *Learning Analytics in Relation to Open Access to Research Data in Peru. An Interdisciplinary Comparison*. Paper presented at the LALA 2020, Cuenca, Ecuador.

Biernacka, K., & Pinkwart, N. (2020). *Barriers and Hurdles to the Publication of Learning Analytics Data*. Paper presented at the 10th International Learning Analytics and Knowledge (LAK), Frankfurt (Oder), Germany.

Callaghan, S., Donegan, S., Pepler, S., Thorley, M., Cunningham, N., Kirsch, P., Ault, L., Bell, P., Bowie, R., Leadbetter, A., Lowry, R., Moncoiffé, G., Harrison, K., Smith-Haddon, B., Weatherby, A., & Wright, D. (2012). Making Data a First Class Scientific Output: Data Citation and Publication by NERC's Environmental Data Centres. *International Journal of Digital Curation, 7*(1), 107–113. doi:10.2218/ijdc.v7i1.218

Catlin-Groves, C. L. (2012). The Citizen Science Landscape: From Volunteers to Citizen Sensors and Beyond. *International Journal of Zoology, 2012*, 1–14. doi:10.1155/2012/349630

Chan, L., Cuplinskasm, D., Eisen, M., Friend, F., Genova, Y., Guédon, J.-C., Hagemann, M., Harnad, S., Johnson, R., Kupryte, R., La Manna, M., Rév, I., Segbert, M., de Souza, S., Suber, P., & Velterop, J. (2002). *Budapest Open Access Initiative*. Retrieved from https://www.budapestopenaccessinitiative.org/read

Cheah, P. Y., Tangseefa, D., Somsaman, A., Chunsuttiwat, T., Nosten, F., Day, N. P., Bull, S., & Parker, M. (2015). Perceived Benefits, Harms, and Views About How to Share Data Responsibly: A Qualitative Study of Experiences With and Attitudes Toward Data Sharing Among Research Staff and Community Representatives in Thailand. *Journal of Empirical Research on Human Research Ethics; JERHRE, 10*(3), 278–289. doi:10.1177/1556264615592388 PMID:26297749

Cobo, C., & Aguerrebere, C. (2018). Building Capacity for Learning Analytics in Latin America. In C. Ping Lim & V. L. Tinio (Eds.), *Learning Analytics for the Global South* (pp. 58–67). Foundation for Information Technology Education and Development.

Colavizza, G., Hrynaszkiewicz, I., Staden, I., Whitaker, K., & McGillivray, B. (2019). *The Citation Advantage of Linking Publications to Research Data*. https://arxiv.org/abs/1907.02565

DCC (Digital Curation Centre). (n.d.). *Overview offunders' data policies*. Retrieved from https://www.dcc.ac.uk/resources/policy-and-legal/overview-funders-data-policies

Deutsche Forschungsgemeinschaft. (2019). Guidelines for Safeguarding Good Research Practice. Code of Conduct. In (pp. 29). doi:10.5281/zenodo.3923602

Drachsler, H., & Greller, W. (2016). Privacy and analytics. *Proceedings of the Sixth International Conference on Learning Analytics & Knowledge - LAK '16*. 10.1145/2883851.2883893

Ebner, M., & Maurer, H. (2008). *Can Microblogs and Weblogs change traditional scientific writing?* Paper presented at the E-Learn: World Conference on E-Learning in Corporate, Government, Healthcare, and Higher Education 2008, Las Vegas, NV.

European Commission. (2014). *Background Document. Public Consultation 'Science 2.0': Science in Transition*. Author.

European Commission. (2016). *H2020 Programme. Guidelines on FAIR Data Management in Horizon 2020*. European Commission.

Fecher, B., & Friesike, S. (2014). Open Science: One Term, Five Schools of Thought. In S. Bartling & S. Friesike (Eds.), *Opening Science. The Evolving Guide on How the Internet is Changing Research, Collaboration and Scholarly Publishing*. Springer Open. doi:10.1007/978-3-319-00026-8_2

Ferguson, R. (2012). Learning analytics: Drivers, developments and challenges. *International Journal of Technology Enhanced Learning*, *4*(5/6), 304. Advance online publication. doi:10.1504/IJTEL.2012.051816

Gentil-Beccot, A., Mele, S., & Brooks, T. C. (2009). *Citing and Reading Behaviours in High-Energy Physics. How a Community Stopped Worrying about Journals and Learned to Love Repositories*. https://arxiv.org/abs/0906.5418

Gezelter, D. (2011). *An informal definition of Open Science*. Retrieved from http://opensscience.org/an-informal-definition-of-openscience

Gleditsch, N. P., Metelits, C., & Strand, H. v. (2003). Symposium on Replication in International Studies Research. *International Studies Perspectives*, *4*(1), 89–97.

HartmannT. (2019). *Rechtsfragen. Institutioneller Rahmen und Handlungsopitonen für universtiäres FDM*. Frankfurt (Oder): Europa-Universität Viadrina Frankfurt (Oder). doi:10.5281/zenodo.2654306

House of Commons Science and Technology Committee. (2011). *Science and Technology Committee – Eighth Report. Peer review in scientific publications*. Retrieved from https://www.publications.parliament.uk/pa/cm201012/cmselect/cmsctech/856/85602.htm

Houtkoop, B. L., Chambers, C., Macleod, M., Bishop, D. V. M., Nichols, T. E., & Wagenmakers, E.-J. (2018). Data Sharing in Psychology: A Survey on Barriers and Preconditions. *APS, 1*(1), 70-85. doi:10.1177/2515245917751886

Ince, D. (2011). The Duke University scandal - what can be done? *Significance*, 3. doi:10.1111/j.1740-9713.2011.00505.x

Irwin, A. (1995). *Citizen Science: A Study of People, Expertise and Development (Environment and Society)*. Routledge.

Jones, L., Grant, R., & Hrynaszkiewicz, I. (2019). Implementing publisher policies that inform, support and encourage authors to share data: two case studies. *Insights the UKSG Journal, 32*, 11. doi:10.1629/uksg.463

Jones, S., & Grootveld, M. (2017). *How FAIR are your data?* (2nd ed.)., doi:10.5281/zenodo.1065990

Kim, J. (2019). Overview of disciplinary data sharing practices and promotion of open data in science. *Science Editing, 6*(1), 3–9. doi:10.6087/kcse.149

Kratz, J., & Strasser, C. (2014). Data publication consensus and controversies. *F1000 Research, 3*, 94. doi:10.12688/f1000research.3979.3 PMID:25075301

Larivière, V., Sugimoto, C. R., Macaluso, B., Milojević, S. a., Cronin, B., & Thelwall, M. (2013). *arXiv e-prints and the journal of record: An analysis of roles and relationships*. https://arxiv.org/abs/1306.3261

Long, P., & Siemens, G. (2011). Penetrating the Fog: Analytics in Learning and Education. *EDUCAUSE Review*.

LucraftM.AllinK.BaynesG.SakellaropoulouR. (2019). Challenges and Opportunities for Data Sharing in China. In (Journal contribution ed.): figshare. doi:10.6084/m9.figshare.7718441.v1

Meyer, M. N. (2018). Practical Tips for Ethical Data Sharing. *Association for Psychological Science, 1*(1), 131–144.

Nielsen, M. (2012). *Reinventing Discovery. The New Era of Networked Science*. Princeton University Press.

Open Knowledge Foundation. (2015). *Open Definition 2.1*. Retrieved from http://opendefinition.org/

Open Knowledge Foundation (Producer). (2019). *Open Data Handbook*. Retrieved from http://opendatahandbook.org

Open Science and Research Intitiative. (2014). *The Open Science and Research Handbook*. Retrieved from https://www.fosteropenscience.eu/content/open-science-and-research-handbook

Ostendorff, P., & Linke, D. (2019). Best-Practices im Umgang mit rechtlichen Fragestellungen zum Forschungsdatenmanagement (FDM). *Bibliotheksdienst, 53*(10-11), 717–723. doi:10.1515/bd-2019-0098

Papamitsiou, Z., & Economides, A. A. (2014). Learning Analytics and Educatinal Data Mining in Practice: A Systematic Literature Review of Empirical Evidence. *Journal of Educational Technology & Society*, *17*(4), 49–64.

Pardo, A., & Siemens, G. (2014). Ethical and privacy principles for learning analytics. *British Journal of Educational Technology*, *45*(3), 438–450. doi:10.1111/bjet.12152

Peng, R. D. (2011). Reproducible Research in Computational Science. *Science*, *334*(6060), 2. doi:10.1126cience.1213847 PMID:22144613

Pienta, A. M., Alter, G., & Lyle, J. (2010). The Enduring Value of Social Science Research: The Use and Reuse of Primary Research Data. In Inter-university Consortium for Political and Social Research. Institute for Social Research, University of Michigan. http://hdl.handle.net/2027.42/78307

Piwowar, H. A. (2011). Who shares? Who doesn't? Factors associated with openly archiving raw research data. *PLoS One*, *6*(7), e18657. doi:10.1371/journal.pone.0018657 PMID:21765886

Piwowar, H. A., & Vision, T. J. (2013). Data reuse and the open data citation advantage. *PeerJ,* (1), 25. doi:10.7717/peerj.175

Pontika, N., Knoth, P., Cancellieri, M., & Pearce, S. (2015). Fostering open science to research using a taxonomy and an eLearning portal. *Proceedings of the 15th International Conference on Knowledge Technologies and Data-driven Business - i-KNOW '15*. 10.1145/2809563.2809571

Priem, J., Taraborelli, D., Groth, P., & Neylon, C. (2010). *Altmetrics: A manifesto*. Retrieved from http://altmetrics.org/manifesto

Rentier, B. (2016). Open science: A revolution in sight? *Interlending & Document Supply*, *44*(4), 155–160. doi:10.1108/ILDS-06-2016-0020

Scheffel, M., Drachsler, H., Stoyanov, S., & Specht, M. (2014). Quality Indicators for Learning Analytics. *International Forum of Educational Technology & Society, 17*(4), 117-132. Retrieved from https://www.jstor.org/stable/10.2307/jeductechsoci.17.4.117

Schmidt, B., Gemeinholzer, B., & Treloar, A. (2016). Open Data in Global Environmental Research: The Belmont Forum's Open Data Survey. *PLoS One*, *11*(1), e0146695. doi:10.1371/journal.pone.0146695 PMID:26771577

Schofield, P. N., Bubela, T., Weaver, T., Portilla, L., Brown, S. D., Hancock, J. M., David, E., Tocchini-Valentini, G., Hrabe de Angelis, M., & Rosenthal, N. (2009). Post-publication sharing of data and tools. *Nature*, *461*(10), 171–173. doi:10.1038/461171a PMID:19741686

TED. (2020). *TED. Our Mission: Spread ideas*. Retrieved from https://www.ted.com/about/our-organization

Van den Eynden V. Knight G. Vlad A. Radler B. Tenopir C. Leon D. Manista F. Whitworth J. Corti L. (2016). Towards Open Research. Practices, experiences, barriers and opportunities: Welcome Trust. doi:10.6084/m9.figshare.4055448

Van Horik, R., Dillo, I., & Doorn, P. (2013). Lies, Damned Lies and Research Data: Can Data Sharing Prevent Data Fraud? *International Journal of Digital Curation*, *8*(1), 229–243. doi:10.2218/ijdc.v8i1.256

Vanpaemel, W., Vermorgen, M., Deriemaecker, L., & Storms, G. (2015). Are We Wasting a Good Crisis? The Availability of Psychological Research Data after the Storm. *Collabra*, *1*(1). Advance online publication. doi:10.1525/collabra.13

Vicente-Saez, R., & Martinez-Fuentes, C. (2018). Open Science now: A systematic literature review for an integrated definition. *Journal of Business Research*, *88*, 428–436. doi:10.1016/j.jbusres.2017.12.043

Vision, T. J. (2010). Open Data and the Social Contract of Scientific Publishing. *Bioscience*, *60*(5), 330–331. doi:10.1525/bio.2010.60.5.2

Wilkinson, M. D., Dumontier, M., Aalbersberg, I. J., Appleton, G., Axton, M., Baak, A., Blomberg, N., Boiten, J.-W., da Silva Santos, L. B., Bourne, P. E., Bouwman, J., Brookes, A. J., Clark, T., Crosas, M., Dillo, I., Dumon, O., Edmunds, S., Evelo, C. T., Finkers, R., ... Mons, B. (2016). The FAIR Guiding Principles for scientific data management and stewardship. *Scientific Data*, *3*(1), 9. doi:10.1038data.2016.18 PMID:26978244

ADDITIONAL READING

Bezjak, S., Clyburne-Sherin, A., Conzett, P., Fernandes, P., Görögh, E., Helbig, K., Kramer, B., Labastida, I., Niemeyer, K., Psomopoulos, F., Ross-Hellauer, T., Schneider, R., Tennant, J., Verbakel, E., Brinken, H., & Heller, L. (2018). *The Open Science Training Handbook* (Version 1.0): Zenodo. doi:10.5281/zenodo.1212495

Corti, L., Van den Eynden, V., Bishop, D. V. M., & Woollard, M. (2014). *Managing and Sharing Research Data: A Guide to Good Practice*. Sage.

European Commission. (2018). *Ethics and Data Protection*. European Commission.

Ferguson, R. (2012). Learning analytics: Drivers, developments and challenges. *International Journal of Technology Enhanced Learning*, *4*(5/6), 304. Advance online publication. doi:10.1504/IJTEL.2012.051816

Jensen, U., Netscher, S., & Weller, K. (2019). *Forschungsdatenmanagement sozialwissenschaftlicher Umfragedaten. Grundlagen und praktische Lösungen für den Umgang mit quantitativen Forschungsdaten.* Verlag Barbara Budrich. doi:10.3224/84742233

Kalkman, S., Mostert, M., Udo-Beauvisage, N., van Delden, J. J., & van Thiel, G. J. (2019). Responsible data sharing in a big data-driven translational research platform: Lessons learned. *BMC Medical Informatics and Decision Making*, *19*(1), 283. doi:10.118612911-019-1001-y PMID:31888593

Majid, S., Foo, S., & Zhang, X. (2018). Research Data Management by Academics and Researchers: Perceptions, Knowledge and Practices. In Maturity and Innovation in Digital Libraries (pp. 166-178).

KEY TERMS AND DEFINITIONS

Altmetrics: An alternative way to record and document the use and impact of science.

Metadata: Structured data that provides basic description of other data.

Metadata Standard: Used for the standard definition of related data in terms of content and structure.

Open Data: Data that can be freely accessed, modified, processed and re-used by everyone for any purpose.

Repository: Infrastructure and the corresponding service that enables digital resources (e.g. data, code or documents) to be permanently, efficiently and sustainably stored.

Research Data: Data that are produced during the research process. It includes all data from the planning of the process to the outcome thereof.

Research Data Management: Includes all activities related to the collection, storage, preservation and publication of research data.

Research Integrity: Research Integrity refers to a set of principles that lead to good scientific practice. These include: reliability, honesty, respect and accountability.

ENDNOTES

1 https://headt.eu/

2 A collaborative project among mathematicians started in 2009 on Timothy Gowers' blog.

3 The Budapest Open Access Initiative was formed during a meeting convened in Budapest by the Open Society Foundations (OSF) on December 1-2, 2001.

4 https://arxiv.org/

5 https://peerj.com/preprints/

6 Kratz and Strasser (2014) distinguish between "published" data and "Published" data. Their definition of "published" data matches the term "shared" data in this chapter. However, when talking about published data in this chapter, this refers to "Published" data in the sense of Kratz and Strasser (2014)(formal publishing).

7 e.g. https://www.re3data.org/

8 https://www.doi.org/

9 https://creativecommons.org/

10 Although a complete opening of the data would be desired, it is not always possible due to personal data. Therefore, in this definition of Open Research Data it is considered that for those data that cannot be de-personalized, limited access or only the publication of metadata may be required.

11 Sensitive data are particular personal data, which require an increased protection: racial and ethnic origin, political opinions, religious or philosophical beliefs, union membership, genetic and biometric data, health data, data on sex life or sexual orientation.

12 General Data Protection Regulation (GDPR) valid from May 2018 in the European Union.

13 Based on Alexander et al. (2019)

14 Questions based on the Creative Commons Chooser https://chooser-beta.creativecommons.org/

15 Compare with Hartmann (2019)

16 Based on Alexander et al. (2019)

17 Compare with S. Jones and Grootveld (2017)

Chapter 3
Reflections on Adaptive Learning Analytics:
Adaptive Learning Analytics

Ahmet Dogukan Sarıyalçınkaya
https://orcid.org/0000-0002-1388-5114
Computer Programming Department, Vezirkopru Vocational School, Ondokuz Mayıs University, Turkey

Hasan Karal
Department of Computer Education and Instructional Technology, Faculty of Education, Trabzon University, Turkey

Fahriye Altinay
Societal Research and Development Center, Faculty of Education, Institute of Graduate Studies, Near East University, Cyprus

Zehra Altinay
Societal Research and Development Center, Faculty of Education, Near East University, Cyprus

ABSTRACT

Learning analytics is developed from the big data approach and plays an important role in the adaptive learning model. Learning analytics is individualized to provide more effective learning experiences and opportunities. Learning analytics can support learning and teaching a structured intervention model developed for those learning to improve their performance. This research chapter explains the two concepts from general to specific also the imperatives and distinctions between the two concepts. This chapter reveals that adaptive learning analytics can be defined as a subset of learning analytics that provides content to provide learners with more effective and adaptive learning opportunities. Learning analytics which is associated with adaptive learning calls upon adaptive learning analytics to create accurate individualized learning.

DOI: 10.4018/978-1-7998-7103-3.ch003

INTRODUCTION

One of the most important transformations spoken in the world today is the change that education and training methods, which have been going on for hundreds of years in parallel with the development of online resources, must live for the Y and Z generations. The system in which the student is passive in the classroom and the teacher is active has become inoperable. The most important thing is the use of information. Information is everywhere now. The transfer of information is not only done through trainers today. The educator should no longer be a wise man but a moderator. Learning analytics become more important in education process.

Accordingly, learning analytics is defined as the understanding of learning and learning environment to improve about learners and their context by collection, measurement, analysis and reporting.(LAK,2011). Learning Analytics is the use of intelligent data, learned information, and analysis models to predict people's learning and get ideas, and explore information and social relationships. It has a multidisciplinary structure, formed by combining fields such as artificial intelligence, machine learning, data mining and statistics. Data, users, purposes and methods are handled in different dimensions and these dimensions are searched for answers to what, who, why and how questions are assessed in learning analytics respectively.

The Purpose of adaptive education learning, is to provide easier and more efficient access to user presentation media systems useful need in learning process in addition to providing many features, by creating special, information-based content support. Varying student level for the best learning and most relevant content is purchased by adaptability of learning analytics that have different messages found different forwarding and different messages in the navigation of the structure area.

Learning analytics "effective learning/ efficient learning hypothesis "is important for realization (Siemens, 2010).Adaptive learning technologies are used for effective learning (Johnson, Adams Becker, Cummins, Estrada, Freeman and Ludgate, 2013; Johnson, AdamsBecker, Cummins, Estrada, Freeman and Hall, 2016). Adaptive learning technologies has two progressive stages. In the first stage, reaction is made according to individual user data. And the teaching material is adapted accordingly. In the second stage, a large user data collected from the sample is used for the design and adaptation of the curriculum.

Adaptive learning creates a fully customized learning path and adapts it to the student's abilities, using the power of analysis by the use of learning analytics.

The relationship between learning analytics and adaptive learning has not been clearly defined yet. The boundaries have not been drawn in an understandable matter. Because the issues related to analytics are still new. It is seen that researches are disrupted. The main reason for this glitch is that is not enough studies for intervention between the adaptive learning and learning analytics. This chapter explains the relationship between adaptive learning and learning analytics hierarchically in this section. This research chapter explains the two concepts from general to specific also the imperatives and distinctions between the two concepts. The holistic multi-case design, one of the case study designs, was used in the study. In holistic multistate patterns, more than one is self-holistic. There is a situation that can be perceived as. Each situation is holistic in itself treated as and then compared to each other. According to the case studies, the models used in adaptive learning environments were tried to be expressed under a common belief. Later, how the learning analytics would be used in adaptive learning was tried to be examined according to these models is expressed.

BACKGROUND

Designing appropriate environments for the individual is the most common basic tips of instructional design. Teaching based on learning theories design becomes more application oriented with design models and the steps to be taken in design can be clearly stated. The common point of different design models with theoretical infrastructures are the learning features. Interaction with learning environment according to constructivist learning theory as a result, the individual creates his own meaning personally; the teacher instead of getting the information it conveys as it is, every individual learns his own way by choosing the method. Constructivist theory has flexible and adaptable principles in basic instructional approaches to field learning from active and self-learning that make it responsible.

Adaptable learning environments identify learning preferences and characteristics of learners and provides learning content and interface suitable for these features; each from the traditional model in which the same type of teacher transfers the content to the student learning to a student with the understanding of a teacher it is personalized. In the 2000s, learning environments have become flexible due to the learner-centered approach, design and development learning features and needs have come to the fore in their processes and personalization has gained importance. Learners has different personality traits, learning styles, learning backgrounds, learning needs, expectations, interests and learning speeds. Therefore, standard learning environments prepared for all learners and their content may be insufficient in learning processes. Learning environments for learners with different characteristics designed, personalized and adapted according to the increase efficiency in the learning process.

Adaptive learning environments for different learning styles and individual needs offers tools for design (Truong, 2015). In this context, adaptive learning environments are unique to individuals. It can be used to design and develop personalized learning environments. Nowadays the return of digital age, technological change and transformation increases knowledge in a difficult way to measure. This situation is a messy of available information causing it to show structure. Educational institutions to increase the available knowledge it also has the function of transforming scattered knowledge into skill. But education designing learning environments according to the group characteristics of the institutions, conversion to skill affects its function negatively. Because individuals have different personality features and learning styles, processing information in different ways and different information preferring to use their resources, learning needs even when using the same environment (Riding and Rayner, 1998). The adaptive learning approach (ALA) has an important place in learning environment based on the characteristics of the individual and suitable for the individual in the solution of the problems.

Adaptive learning systems named with different concepts in the literature (Kim, Lee and Ryu, 2013), intelligent teaching environments (Tuna & Öztürk, 2015) adaptive educational hypermedia systems (Schneider, 2018) and intelligent adaptive learning systems (Hou and Fidopiastis, 2017)indicates an individualized and personalized learning approach. Although systems and models are defined differently, the main purpose of all to provide a learning environment suitable for its characteristics. The system specified in this scope and all of the models are called ALA (Adaptive learning approach). ALA, is the learning that is shaped according to the preferences and needs of learners throughout the teaching process presents the environment (Somyürek, 2009). In addition, ALA enables people to learn in different ways and it was developed in order to eliminate differences in learning by taking into account variability (Mulwa, Lawless, Sharp, Arnedillo-Sanchez and Wade, 2010). The main purpose of each learning approach to provide efficient learning and to overcome the differences of learning with existing methods considering that it is, it can be thought that the ALA has evolved to the present day. ALA based on learning mechanisms that is included Skinner' s (1958) using operant conditioning. However, Skinner's learning mechanisms has adaptations according to the characteristics of the learning object rather than its interests and needs. This regardless of the prior knowledge provided to the learner, motivation and learning characteristics of the learner in the relevant learning mechanism by giving instant feedback and reinforcers of knowledge. Carroll (1963), has designed a model of school learning in which expressing that learning will be provided with appropriate opportunities and time for the learner apart from the appropriate time given to the learner in the model, learning objects providing editing possibilities provides adaptability of the model. Skinner and while Carroll's models provide adaptation through learning materials in general, Keller's (1968) individualized learning approach is based on individual needs advocates adaptation based on differences. Skinner, Carroll and Keller are different from their perspectives, they combine their models that advocate ALA in Bloom (1979) mastery learning model. The basic principle of the mastery learning model is by determining the qualifications of the learner. realization of learning design. Preliminary information that constitutes the learner qualifications. The provision of learning-teaching materials suitable for academic learning ensures complete learning. Bloom's model individual characteristics of the learner has demonstrated that learning objects and services can be adapted accordingly.

Adaptive learning environments, offers personalized learning with a learning experience parallel to new web Technologies by the use of the artificial intelligence algorithms (Kim, Lee & Ryu, 2013). Personalized learning support, the system's personal characteristics of the user determining and adjusting the way the information is presented according to these characteristics characterized in that; hypermedia systems, intelligent teaching systems and learning / content management systems personalized learning options presenting adaptable environments (Yang, Hwang & Yang, 2013). Adaptable to different learner features learning environments such as visited pages and browsing times personality traits, prior knowledge, interest personal learning option by collecting information about the target. Learning with personalization in addition to increasing the quantity of their outputs, individuals have a learning experience and more from the learning environment they can be satisfied.

MAIN FOCUS OF THE CHAPTER[1]

The relationship between learning analytics and adaptive learning has not been clearly defined yet. The boundaries have not been drawn in an understandable matter. Because the issues related to learning analytics and adaptive learning are still new. It is seen that researches are disrupted. The main reason for this glitch is that is not enough studies for intervention between the adaptive learning and learning analytics. This chapter explains the relationship between adaptive learning and learning analytics hierarchically in this section. This chapter shows the main approachs, models and process of adaptive learning and learning analytics to combine adaptive learning analytics in a systematic approach . This research chapter explains the two concepts from general to specific also the imperatives and distinctions between the two concepts. This chapter reveals that adaptive learning analytics can be defined as a subset of learning analytics, that provides content to provide learners with more effective and adaptive learning opportunities.

Issues, Controversies, Problems

Learning Analytics builds a model for a student's activities that other students in the classroom will take with those who have already taken this course, and / or each student will make progress.

In this way, learning analyzes rely on vast amounts of data that most schools and universities collect to find structures that can be used for learning enhancement.

Learning Analytics: What Can It Do?

- Predicting future student performance (based on past learning patterns in various student institutions)
- Providing students with unique feedback tailored to their answers, being able to intervene where they have difficulty
- Personalizing each student's learning process, revealing their strengths and encouraging their development

Adaptive learning is a computer-based education method that organizes and plans the trainings in the most appropriate way, taking into account the different needs of each student. The computer presents the educational material in the most appropriate way to the learning needs of the learner by using learmimg analytics. In order to reach the best practices, it monitors the behavior and experiences of the learner in their previous education and gets to know the learner.

Adaptive learning environments identify learners' learning preferences and characteristics and offers appropriate learning content and interface; traditional, where the same type of teacher passes content on by leaving the model, learning is individualized to a student with the understanding of a teacher (Ocepek, Bosnic,Serbec & Rugejl, 2013). Adaptive learning environments are individualized, providing the user with a more effective learning experience thanks to the artificial intelligence algorithms they use in parallel with new web technologies offers learning opportunities (Kim, Lee & Ryu, 2013; Vandewaetere, Desmet & Clarebout, 2011). Individualized learning support, determining the personal characteristics of the system and the presentation of information is the feature of adjusting according to; hypermedia systems, intelligent teaching systems, and learning / content management systems are adaptable environments that offer individualized learning options.

Mampadi, Chen, Ghinea & Chen (2011) designed a hypermedia learning environment adaptable to learners' cognitive styles. The cognitive styles of learners are based on Pask's linear-holisticserialistic classification. Learners who adopt the approach can be provided with the knowledge that can be obtained from the transfer of learning to learning experience, while the learner can finish one topic and move on to another. Individuals who prefer both approaches after entering their enterprise with the learning environment learning performance and two learning perceptions were examined, and the individuals who preferred each cognitive style indexes are included. It was revealed that there was an increase in their prior knowledge level and their positive perceptions about the environment.

Kim, Lee & Ryu (2013), developed principles for the design of adaptive learning environments by examining their relationships with personality options and preferences in e-learning environments. They are really using e-learning environments according to personality types in the first of two different experiments they performed. They took out their profiles; getting help, wandering time, number of repetitions and time spent on a learning module Maybe they revealed their learning preferences. In the second experiment, the content and interface design of the profile-appropriate learning environment was performed.

Graf, Kinshuk & Ives (2010) realized a design study of a learning management system based on learning styles. The learning objects of the components that should be in the system were developed in accordance with the learning styles. Learning objects should be included in the learning management system for all components (content, quiz, exercises, animations, self-assessment, real-life experience, self-assessment questionnaires etc.) designed. After that, units and course segments were created by combining different learning objects. Footnote Of the system is adaptive annotation and adaptive sorting approaches were used to adapt them to different learning styles. Adaptive annotation, best suited to the user's learning styles. It detects the segments where the learning objects are located and makes suggestions for the user to visit that page during interaction.

Yang, Hwang & Yang (2013), have realized cognitive styles (Vitkin's domain dependent-domainindependent styles) and learning styles (Felder-Silverman learning styles) had a major effect in adaptable learning environment development. With an adaptable experimental environment, the traditional learning students participating in both groups by creating a learning environment performance, cognitive load effect and motivations for learning compared in terms according to the personal characteristics specified in the study. The adaptive environment developed consists of 4 parts:

Learning content development module: Raw of text and images to produce content presentations suitable for individual characteristics by grouping content, adding examples and supporting information to basic information,

Adaptable presentation module: The presentation plan suitable for cognitive styles adjusting. For example, for individuals in the domain dependent style, it is simpler interface and less information presentation at a time are adapted in this module,

Adaptive content module: Learning styles scale embedded in this module determining the user's learning styles (active-reflective; sensory-intuitive; visual-verbal and sequential-holistic) is the section where it was created.

The learning module combines content and interface, making .It is the last part where the presentation is made.

In the 1980s, technological developments enabled the use of computers in the adaptive learning analytics (ALA) . The use of computer-aided adaptive learning environments within the scope, is turning in the ALA. Wenger (1987) in this period, has designed a computer aided adaptive learning environment. It consists of four main components: (i) field knowledge, (ii) user interface, (iii) communication strategies and (iv) student model. Field information from these components is defines the learning content. How the interface learner interacts with the learning environment user, including how to set up and how to organize feedback to the learner. It is the module. Communication strategies decide when and how the content will be presented to the learner and is designed as a smart system. Student model, learner's current academic and it represents motivational state.

Structure of Adaptive Learning Environment

Adaptive learning environments according to the personal characteristics of the users automatically offering learning options, so that the environments that provide learning experience more effective. These environments both personalize the presentation of the learning content and the system adapts its interface and navigation according to user characteristics. Adaptive learning systems traditionally have two types as separate components or 'models'. While different sets of models are presented, most systems include some or all of the following models (sometimes with different names):

Content(Expert) model: Model with information to be taught.
Student(User)model:The model that monitors and learns the student
Teaching model: The model that actually transmits information
Teaching environment: User interface for interacting with the system

1. User Model

Learner preliminary information, demographic features include defining information about learning preferences. For example, depending on the visual or textual preferences of the user, personal features of the user with the system materials can be presented. It can be determined at the first stage of interaction and can remain constant during use, or it can be determined and updated at certain stages in the interaction process. Brusilovsky (2001) targets user characteristics to be adapted to the environment, experiences, interests, preferences and personal characteristics. User interests, especially in information retrieval (Information Retrieval, IR) the search terms that the user is interested in saving and filtering the data and developing search suggestions is an important feature used. Users interests in information search (IR), analysis of the preferences and search behavior of the user cognitive load by preventing loss, filtering unnecessary information and content about individual's learning status in mitigation and e-learning environments can give information users individual and personality types, cognitive characteristics and learning styles consists of factors. Personal factors with various psychological tests determined are more permanent features than interests and preferences., the user of adaptable environments in terms of instructional design stated that the following three features should be addressed in his modeling:

Personality traits that determine the attitude towards learning or environment, auxiliary features that determine the user's area information and processing the information cognitive features that reflect the process.

2. Content Model

Appropriate to the learning objectives and knowledge level of the learner determination of concepts and appropriate learning objects includes creation. Content consisting of related structures and connections belonging to certain disciplines and this about the transfer and evaluation of the content (guides for authors) contains information in creating a content model, stated that approaches can be adopted:

Content-independent approach suitable for the delivery of all types of content; same all kinds of information to meet the needs of all users can pull over the internet. Flexible approach designed for different user characteristics and scalable that can be shaped according to increasing user needs and demands content model. Content, specified features and repetition in adaptive learning environments. It consists of learning objects because it is available. The structures that make up the content can be listed as follows:

Basic knowledge: Definitions, examples, supporting information (visuals, videos etc.), basic content like formulas.

Operational information: Following a certain order, certain steps information that includes relationships and is divided into sub-steps.

Conceptual information: Relationships and relations between other pieces of information relational information.

Studies on adaptive learning environments research, micro level user modeling and different content that can be shared and reused by systems was developing towards the design of its objects.

3. Teaching model:

In this model presentations and demonstrations are prepared in accordance with their goals. In this model, the most suitable course for the user's personal preferences and interests will interact with the presentation. In line with user features as well as the learning object packages offered on the page

Features such as the list of works, discussion platform, calendar are also will be found. The user created during the user's interaction with the system records are transferred to the user model with the help of log analysis. It will allow the profile to be updated dynamically. There is a need for a teaching model that organizes the lessons by looking at and evaluating more advanced student models based on concepts. Having generic concept-based tips are offered, these multi-concept weaknesses can be influenced by the teaching model, or all of the tips-question-specific overlap can be in this case student, instructor and expert models.

Adaptation mechanism: User, content and teaching models consists of algorithms that bring together. The following questions in the adaptation process answer should be followed to answer in order:

- What can we adapt? - user features
- What will we adapt to? - system
- Why do we adapt it? - better learning performance or satisfaction
- Where will we adapt? - which stage or system of adaptation will we perform in the sections?
- When will we adapt?
- How do we adapt it?

Learning by matching user model and content model It is the stage where the activities,

4. Teaching Environment

Learning Management Systems

Learning management systems (LMS) are web-based applications that provide and organize to access educational web 2.0 systems that stores the content and that content within the student's specific rules. These systems use various modules to manage the course process assignments, exams, follow-up of course success. They perform operations such as learner-student-content interactions. Simko, Barla & Bieliková (2010), stated that learning based on Web 2.0 technologies should include the following features in the design of management systems:

- Learning content and metadata can be reused, stored and must be manageable.
  - System should be based on a user model, so different user can be adapted according to their characteristics.
- Active participation of users in the system should be ensured. Collaboration, interaction, content created, edited, shared by users and organization learning management systems from being an educational presentation and makes it a personalized, interactive system.

Adaptive learning states that the management system should have the following features:

Shareability or interoperability (Sharable/ interoperability): Connect the system with different systems and the content can be used in different systems.

Reusability: Learning content is to be able to develop new objects by using metadata of objects.

Learning shareable and reusable learning objects the preparation and transmission of reliable content in its environment, so that the learning environment meets standards and the content is different provides work on platforms.

Using Agents

Agents can be adapted for their autonomy, pre-efficacy, and responsiveness to organize the content by collecting the information related to the user in the systems. In adaptive systems, agents can learn the content. It is used in proper arrangement. System's needs and features. It can be used by creating different types of agents.

Adaptive Learning Analytics

Applying Learning Analytics to Adaptive Learning

With the effect of the learner-centered approach in the 2000s, learning environments became flexible, learning features and needs have come to the fore in the processes and personalization has gained importance in design and development of adaptive learning. Learners have different personality traits, learning styles, learning backgrounds, learning needs, expectations, interests and learning speeds. Therefore, standard learning environments prepared for all learners and their contents may be insufficient in learning processes. Learning environments to learners with different characteristics designed, personalized and adapted according to the increase of effectiveness and efficiency in the learning process. Adaptive learning environments are designed for different learning styles and individual needs provides tools for design (Truong, 2015). In this context, adaptive learning environments can be used in designing and developing personalized learning environments by using learning analytics.

Learners learn about learning processes while using on line learning environments many data are collected in logs. The purpose of adaptive learning analytics is to learn using this data to determine the effectiveness of the process and to reveal how learning takes place (Mah, 2016). The reports provided by the learning analytics are presented to the stakeholders in the process. It enables the detection of defects. So the learners are learning their own while learning about their processes, trainers also know the effectiveness of the learning process they have the opportunity to evaluate. Gašević, Dawson and according to Siemens (2015), can make an estimate of the individual's learning and provide effective feedback states that learning analytics are the two most important consequences. Adaptive learning analytics data in the system within the framework of certain algorithms are solutions. Different processes are passed while reporting the data stored in the logs. Baker and Yacef (2009) used to make sense of learning analytics data processes for estimation, classification, relational mining data to make inference of individuals are the processes of purification and discovery with models whereas learning analytics makes the user learn modeling and experiences, profiling, learning areas / interests modeling of areas, analysis of the course, individualization and adaptation states that their processes are used. Daniel (2015) is also, examined learning analytics in three groups according to the type of data they use and how they interpret in adaptive learning analytics:

Descriptive analytics: The purpose of these analytics, learners, teaching and to collect data about administrative processes. Rather learning introduction to management system, page view, activity completion, course completion rates and performs the analysis by using graded assessments.

Predictive analytics: These analytics are historical data and current tries to identify possible risks and opportunities in the future by examining the trends. With this aspect it gives institutions the chance to make better decisions and take action. Descriptive analytics with the demographic information and activity completion rates can reveal relationships. Instructors are at risk of failing the course or to identify students who show risky behavior at the point of quitting can help.

Preventative analytics (Prescriptive analytics): While evaluating the data, a valid and consistent data based on data also helps the learner make a choice. Both descriptive analytics and prediction by combining the results obtained from analytics, to reach the desired results provides information.

The Approaches of Adaptive Learning by Learning Analytics

Adaptive learning analytics changes concepts, but inconsistent concept definitions or technical approaches and theoretical as a result of the disconnection between their expectations, the basic principles and historical development of realized systems is ignored. While looking at the historical devolopment there are, four main approaches identifiable in creating adaptable learning environments by learning analytics:

Macro-adaptive approach, micro-adaptive approach, aptitude treatment approach and constructivist - collaborative approach.

1. Macro-Adaptive Approach

Macro adaptive teaching is the adaptation of instruction at the macro level. Based on the adaptation of teaching to the differences of individuals in school education many examples have emerged, and many examples today are in classroom teaching continues to be used. The appearance of the macro adaptive approach is seen from the 1960s and 70s, learning objectives of education, detailed levels of knowledge and at the macro level, such as allowing some different alternatives to be selected define adaptation. In this approach, learning alternatives are often called learning objectives that involves general abilities and success according to the student's curriculum selected depending on the level .

One of the macro approachs, first used in the individualization of teaching is the Keller plan. This approach based on Keller's based on the individualized learning model in which teaching should be adapted to the learner's individual speed with different learning for each individual speed and ratio. Evaluation of student performance and appropriate feedback individual characteristics should be taken into account in providing Keller plan by choosing the learning module suitable for the student's needs program for learning in accordance with needs (Flanagan, Shanner, Brudner & Marker, 1975) and Bloom taxonomy is also the first to be used in the adaptation of teaching are some of the approaches. This approach has been developed as an alternative to traditional step-by-step group learning applied in school settings, and is used in educational goals, in the depth of curriculum content, distribution systems, etc. used in many adaptive learning systems that allow changes. The use of macro adaptive systems is practical and two approaches are used to created(Thompson, 2013):

1- Media, content or learning styles are adapted according to the personal preferences of the learners; however, additional content development studies are needed in this process.

2- The current skill or knowledge levels of the learners are determined by pretesting. These systems Save learners' time by measuring the level of knowledge of learners instantly they provide

2. Aptitude–Treatment Approach

In this approach, educational processes and strategies are adapted based on learners-specific characteristics. This approach requires the identification of the most appropriate teaching method and educational strategies that facilitate the learning process of the learners and determining the characteristics or abilities of the learners on the subject. Aptitude-treatment approach is adapted specific strategies of teaching students according to its features. As Cronbach (1957) points out, the top e-learning systems that try to reach a wide range of students for level learning should provide a wide range of suitable environments for these individuals. Aptitude-treatment interaction approach, different teaching styles for different students recommends different types of media. Many studies have been done to explain the relationship between learning and talent in the learning environment, the individual's ability and functioning adaptations made in line with the interaction of the environment, can increase student satisfaction and the efficiency, (Cronbach and Snow, 1977). The most important student characteristics that can be evaluated with the interaction approach; mental skills, cognitive styles, learning styles, prior knowledge level, anxiety, can be summarized as motivation and competence to achieve in aptitude-treatment. The quality and quantity of learning to increase the method that will provide maximum benefit from the learning environment in order to apply teaching to the individual characteristics of the learner and is a talented design approach. It consists of variables such as specified ability factor attitudes, cognitive skills (information processing capacity, perception, attention), pre knowledge, skills, learning styles, cognitive styles, self-efficacy, motivation.

3. Micro Adaptive Approach

Micro-adaptive approach can be defined as the provision of the level of special learning needs of students and the appropriate guidelines for them in micro-learning process. Researchers tried to determine the measurements obtained during the task instead of the pre-task measurements. According to the micro adaptive approach by monitoring their behavior and performance behavior and arrangement of the teaching environment can be determined with users wrong answers, in their answers delays, emotional states, etc. One-on-one learning is mentioned to be the most typical example of micro - adaptive learning

In this type of learning, the teacher has the most appropriate level of knowledge for the student. By student's level of knowledge, motivation and learning ability chooses according to his assessment and materials. Then the teacher follows the student by constantly, and evaluates by monitoring what the next learning action will be? According to the situation of the individual during the learning activity to identify changing specific needs and organize the activity accordingly is a dynamic approach. Intelligent teaching including artificial intelligence techniques systems, web-based teaching environments (Web 2.0 and semantic web technologies) and hypermedia systems are micro approach that makes adaptations in the system by determining the needs and requirements samples. Mathematical model, navigation model, bayesian model and algorithmic model.

In micro - adaptive approach the amount of content that will be basically presented with the approach or the content a limited amount of learning variables such as sequencing can be adapted by micro adaptable approach. In this approach, specific learning needs for students are determined and training instructions are created for these needs where smart teaching systems can be given as an example. Micro adaptive systems are more effective than macro adaptive systems for personalization, and in these systems, the level of learning is constantly updated and adapted according to the actions of the learners at each step (Thompson, 2013). The system performs operations automatically. Thompson (2013) divided micro adaptive learning types into three:

Rule Based Systems: These systems based on programming by how the system will respond to the actions of the learners. The process is organized according to learner responses and actions. These systems can be applied in basic mathematics and basic science.

Preference Based Systems: As learners progress through the process, their special preferences are learned and accordingly content is presented.

Algorithm Based Systems: Determining the most appropriate learning order for each learner algorithms are used, and ranking is changed in parallel with the progress.

4. Contructivist Collabarative Approach

In another approach, the e-learning approach of the constructivist teaching approach systems and how they can be used in the learning process is stated. Constructivist learning theory, emphasizes that the student has a great role in constructing self-knowledge in the target area of his/her studying process (Park and Lee,2004). Rather than providing students with target information, in order to have learning experiences in line with their goals, they analyze the interaction between the sequence learning situation over a certain period of time they have presented a system called INCENSE that adapts itself.

One of the new approaches in adaptive e-learning is the the use of collaborative technologies seen as an indispensable part. Researchers took the collaborative teaching approach in the late nineties.

They started to work on its use in adaptive teaching systems (Modritscher et al., 2004). Use of collaborative technologies can be expanded from individuals to groups with adaptable and different learning experiences can be created in e-learning.

SOLUTIONS AND RECOMMENDATIONS

In an adaptive learning system the type of adaptation performed (content / navigation), adaptation technique used (link generation / description of links / annotations etc), the techniques are applied, characteristics based on its development (with the task relevance / compliance with prior information etc.) and modeling and inference mechanisms (created by hand rules / fuzzy logic / bayes networks) as they differ the usefulness / effectiveness of the environment varies.

With the developments in e-learning technologies considering differences between users and differentiating according to the personal needs of the user; Designing and developing "adaptive environments" has become possible with using learning analytics.

User, content and teaching models consists of algorithms that bring together. The following questions in the adaptation process answer should be followed to answer in order:

- What can we adapt? - user features
- What will we adapt to? - system
- Why do we adapt it? - better learning performance or satisfaction
- Where will we adapt? - which stage or system of adaptation will we perform in the sections?
- When will we adapt?
- How do we adapt it?

Learning by matching user model and content model it is the stage where the activities. According to this process an adaptive learning analytics mechanism can be like this adaptivity that is shown in table 1 below. The mechanisms of "how" technology adapts to students has several variations as it is shown in figure 1.

Figure 1. Adaptive learning mechanism

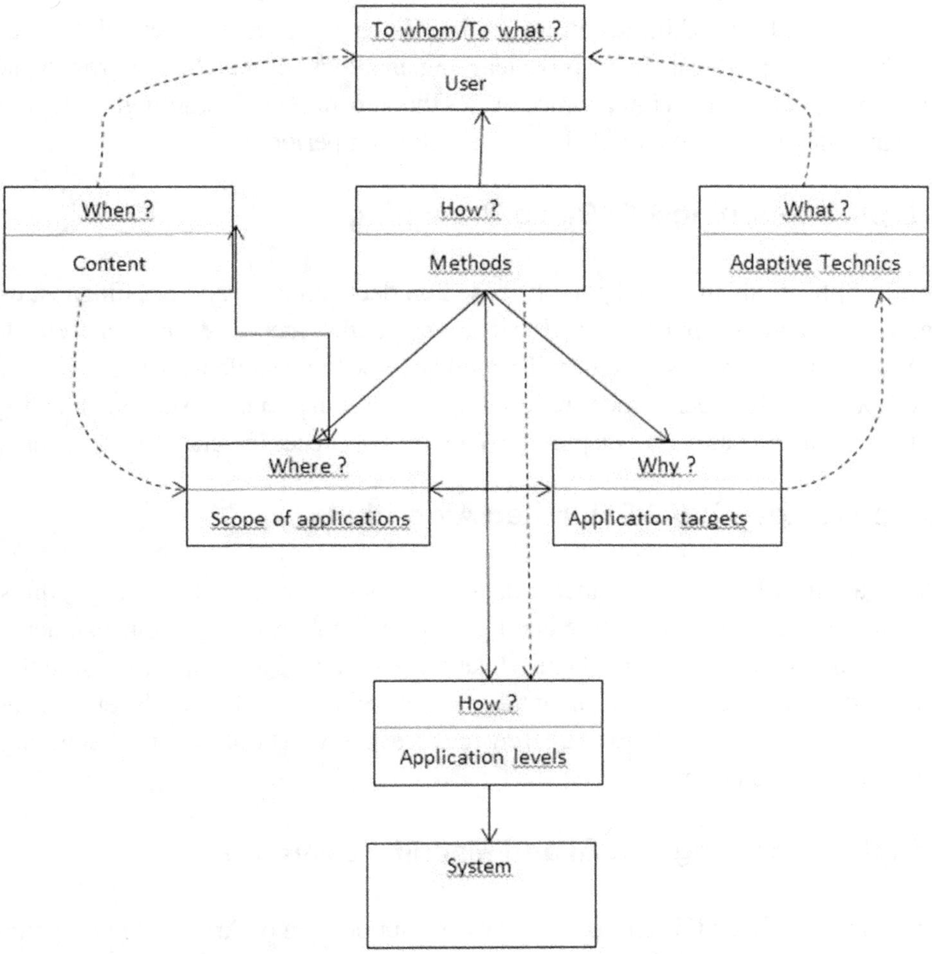

FUTURE RESEARCH DIRECTIONS

Adaptive learning platforms use advanced algorithms that evaluate the student's level, provide the learner with the right difficulty and content at the right level, do not tire the person with excessive information that will not work and ensure that they can make the most of their learning skills. Combining learning analytics to adaptive learning has a multidisciplinary structure, formed by combining fields such as artificial intelligence, machine learning, data mining and statistics. Data, users, purposes and methods are handled in different dimensions and these dimensions are searched for answers to what, who, why and how questions are assessed in learning analytics respectively.

It would make more sense for both researchers and practitioners to divide adaptive learning into periods and versions, such as the development of the web concept (web1.0-web2.0-web 3.0), according to models, approaches, the technology used and the needs of students in adaptive learning analytics. Especially the growth and development of artificial intelligence makes this seperations. Accordingly, adaptive learning analytics can be divided into the following periods:

Adaptive Learning 1.0: Basic Branching

These applications make adaptations based on decision trees and pre-diagnostics. Learning Analytics applications collect data, analyze data, generate reports and enable interventions, regardless of students' preferences (without students being aware of). The types of analysis performed are variable. However, it initially involves evaluating historical student data to create predictive models of successful and at-risk students.

Adaptive Learning 2.0: Limited Algorithms

These applications make limited adaptations based on simplified algorithms. System-generated interventions can range from a simple warning about a student's likelihood of success to asking them to take specific actions to explain their situation with students at risk. Learning analytics can help educators identify the efforts and abilities that students who are struggling to achieve. It will be slow at the beginning, put into success later on.

Adaptive Learning 3.0: AI and Machine Learning

Adaptive Learning 3.0 is characterized by the application of Artificial intelligence techniques to real world situations whether an adaptive system that applies. In other words, its effectiveness, providing efficiency and user satisfaction evaluation to determine if it does not provide is necessary reduction in learning times. Unlike the real classroom environment, a lesson in an e-environment using learning analytics allows each student to answer all questions and interact with all the material of the course. Learning analysis can be customized to student needs, allowing students to view their performance better and faster. Learning analysis can identify common wrong answers and generate tailored feedback to get the details of each specific wrong answer. Learning analysis allows on line peer assessment and self-assessment so educators can track students' past performance and teacher / peer / self-assessment.

CONCLUSION

Accordingly, learning analytics is defined as the understanding of learning and learning environment to improve about learners and their context by collection, measurement, analysis and reporting. Learning analytics is the use of intelligent data, learned information, and analysis models to predict people's learning and get ideas, and explore information and social relationships. It has a multidisciplinary structure, formed by combining fields such as artificial intelligence, machine learning, data mining and statistics. Data, users, purposes and methods are handled in different dimensions and these dimensions are searched for answers to what, who, why and how questions are assessed in learning analytics respectively.

One of the most important points to be considered to benefit from learning analytics is the need to follow a bottom-up approach with a focus on the needs of learners. If a top-down approach is followed, undesirable situations such as educational institutions, companies and governments putting pressure on students, employees and citizens may occur. Adaptive learning can be defined as the self-adaptation of the system according to the learners, instead of presenting the same content to each learner in e-learning systems for this purpose, learning models are created according to different components such as learning styles, prior knowledge levels, motivation levels used to model the learning processes of learners more adaptive learning can be achieved thanks to adaptive learning analytics, which is created by the use of adaptive learning and learning analytics that is called as adaptive learning analytics.

Adaptive learning systems try to determine the characteristics of the students and according to the requests and characters of the students . Each student has a different background, needs, knowledge level and learning style. Making it suitable with the adaptation process that we call adaptive, adapting to the conditions effective learning the system takes into account each student's individuality to ensure . In adaptive processing the main goal is personalization. The adaptive personalization system provides the training content to the users in different ways, according to the needs Adaptive education systems, user goals, inputs and system creating a learning model for the user as a result of interactions, structuring the learning environment and personalizes teaching for the user. To improve the learning performance of learners, Adaptive Learning analytics are a very important force to increase the efficiency of learning.

REFERENCES

Akhras, F. N., & Self, J. A. (2000). System intelligence in constructivist learning. *International Journal of Artificial Intelligence in Education, 11*(4), 344–376.

Baker, R. S., & Yacef, K. (2009). The state of educational data mining in 2009: A review and future visions. *Journal of Educational Data Mining, 1*(1), 3-17.

Bloom, B. S. (1979). *Taxonomy of educational objectives: the classification of educational goals book 1 cognitive domain*. Longman.

Burrows, P. (2016). *Adaptive learning: Can industry's most provocative software make a difference in the classroom?* EdSurge. https://www.edsurge.com/research/special-reports/adaptive-learning/

Carroll, J. B. (1963). A model of school learning. *Teachers College.*

Cronbach, L. J. (1957). The two disciplines of scientific psychology. *The American Psychologist, 12*(11), 671–684. doi:10.1037/h0043943

Daniel, B. (2015). B ig D ata and analytics in higher education: Opportunities and challenges. *British Journal of Educational Technology, 46*(5), 904–920. doi:10.1111/bjet.12230

Flanagan, J. C., Shanner, W. M., Brudner, H. J., & Marker, R. W. (1975). An individualized instructional system: PLAN. *Systems of Individualized Education*, 136-167.

Gašević, D., Dawson, S., & Siemens, G. (2015). Let's not forget: Learning analytics are about learning. *TechTrends, 59*(1), 64–71. doi:10.100711528-014-0822-x

Geller, E. S. (2005). Behavior-based safety and occupational risk management. *Behavior Modification, 29*(3), 539–561. doi:10.1177/0145445504273287 PMID:15784754

Graf, S. (2010). A Flexible Mechanism for Providing Adaptivity Based on Learning Styles in Learning Management Systems. *Adv. Learn. Technol.*, 30-34.

Hou, M., & Fidopiastis, C. (2017). A generic framework of intelligent adaptive learning systems: From learning effectiveness to training transfer. *Theoretical Issues in Ergonomics Science, 18*(2), 167–183. doi:10.1080/1463922X.2016.1166405

Keller, F. S. (1968). Good-bye, teacher.... *Journal of Applied Behavior Analysis, 1*(1), 79–89. doi:10.1901/jaba.1968.1-79 PMID:16795164

Kennedy-Clark, S., & Thompson, K. (2013). Collaborative Process Analysis Coding Scheme (CPACS): Examining the macro-and micro-level of students' discourse in a virtual world. *International Journal of Virtual and Personal Learning Environments*, *4*(2), 19–49. doi:10.4018/jvple.2013040102

Kim, J., Lee, A., & Ryu, H. (2013). Personality and its effects on learning performance: Design guidelines for an adaptive e-learning system based on a user model. *International Journal of Industrial Ergonomics*, *43*(5), 450–461. doi:10.1016/j.ergon.2013.03.001

Mah, D. K. (2016). Learning analytics and digital badges: Potential impact on student retention in higher education. *Technology. Knowledge and Learning*, *21*(3), 285–305. doi:10.100710758-016-9286-8

Mampadi, F., Chen, S. Y., Ghinea, G., & Chen, M. P. (2011). Design of adaptive hypermedia learning systems: A cognitive style approach. *Computers & Education*, *56*(4), 1003–1011. doi:10.1016/j.compedu.2010.11.018

Mödritscher, F., Garcia-Barrios, V. M., & Gütl, C. (2004). The Past, the Present and the Future of adaptive E-Learning. *Proceedings of ICL 2004*.

Mulwa, C., Lawless, S., Sharp, M., Arnedillo-Sanchez, I., & Wade, V. (2010, October). Adaptive educational hypermedia systems in technology enhanced learning: a literature review. In *Proceedings of the 2010 ACM conference on Information technology education* (pp. 73-84). 10.1145/1867651.1867672

Pardo, A., & Dawson, S. (2016). *Learning Analytics: How Can Data Be Used to Improve Learning Practice?* Academic Press.

Riding, R., & Rayner, S. (1998). *Cognitive styles and learning strategies: Understanding style differences in learning and behavior*. Routledge.

Schneider, J., Di Mitri, D., Limbu, B., & Drachsler, H. (2018, September). Multimodal learning hub: A tool for capturing customizable multimodal learning experiences. In *European Conference on Technology Enhanced Learning* (pp. 45-58). Springer. 10.1007/978-3-319-98572-5_4

Siemens, G. (2013). Learning analytics: The emergence of a discipline. *The American Behavioral Scientist*, *57*(10), 1380–1400. doi:10.1177/0002764213498851

Šimko, M., Barla, M., & Bieliková, M. (2010, September). ALEF: A framework for adaptive web-based learning 2.0. In *IFIP International Conference on Key Competencies in the Knowledge Society* (pp. 367-378). Springer. 10.1007/978-3-642-15378-5_36

Skinner, B. F. (1958). Teaching machines. *Science*, *128*(3330), 969–977. doi:10.1126cience.128.3330.969 PMID:13592277

Somyürek, S. (2009). Student modeling: Recognizing the individual needs of users in e-learning environments. *Journal of Human Sciences*, *6*(2), 429–450.

Truong, N. B., Lee, G. M., & Ghamri-Doudane, Y. (2015, May). Software defined networking-based vehicular adhoc network with fog computing. In *2015 IFIP/IEEE International Symposium on Integrated Network Management (IM)* (pp. 1202-1207). IEEE. 10.1109/INM.2015.7140467

Tuna, G., & Öztürk, A. (2015). Zeki ve uyarlanabilir e-öğrenme ortamları. In *International Distance Education Conference* (pp. 2-4). Academic Press.

Tzelepi, M. (2014, July). Personalizing learning analytics to support collaborative learning design and community building. In *2014 IEEE 14th International Conference on Advanced Learning Technologies* (pp. 771-773). IEEE. 10.1109/ICALT.2014.226

Wenger, R. H. (1987). Cognitive science and algebra learning. *Cognitive Science and Mathematics Education*, 217-251.

Yang, T. C., Hwang, G. J., & Yang, S. J. H. (2013). Development of an adaptive learning system with multiple perspectives based on students' learning styles and cognitive styles. *Journal of Educational Technology & Society*, *16*(4), 185–200.

KEY TERMS AND DEFINITIONS

Adaptive Learning: Adaptive learning designs an education according to his / her learning method after evaluating the learner's knowledge. This system also organizes and changes the way the learner develops in the relevant subject.

Adaptive Learning Analytics: Learning analytics which is associated with adaptive learning is called as adaptive learning analytics to accurate individualized learning.

Aptitude Treatment: Aptitude-treatment approach is adapted specific strategies of teaching students according to its features.

Contructivist Collabarative Approach: Adaptive systems that make motivation adaptations differentiate the way of teaching the same subject by adapting it to the motivation status of the student.

Intervention: An adaptation is also sentenced to be intervention when the teacher changes the teaching material.

Learning Analytics: Appropriate technology to facilitate learning and increase performance ethics of creating, using and evaluating processes and resources is the application

Macro-Adaptive: Macro adaptive teaching is the adaptation of instruction at the macro level.

Micro-Adaptive: Micro-adaptive approach can be defined as the provision of the level of special learning needs of students and the appropriate guidelines for them in micro-learning process.

APPENDIX

The Institute of Museum and Library Services has collected some interesting statistics indicating that despite the sharp decline in library usage over the last ten years, libraries have actually seen an *increase* in the number of people who come through their doors annually since the beginning of the current recessionary period in 2008. Was this a contradiction, or some kind of error? Table 1 shows the data in question.

Table 2. Visits to public libraries

Year	Per Capita Visit to Public Library	Year	Per Capita Visit to Public Library
1998	4.2	2003	4.6
1999	4.3	2004	4.6
2000	4.3	2005	4.7
2001	4.4	2006	4.8
2002	4.4	2007	5.0

(Data Source: National Center for Education Statistics, 1998-2007)

Section 2
Organizational Issues

Chapter 4
Ethics in Predictive Learning Analytics:
An Empirical Case Study on Students Perceptions in a Northern Irish University

Paul Joseph-Richard
https://orcid.org/0000-0003-4176-419X
Ulster University, UK

James Uhomoibhi
Ulster University, UK

ABSTRACT

Most universities collect large amounts of students' data to enhance teaching, understand student behaviour, and predict their success. However, such practices raise privacy and ethical issues due to sensitive data harvesting practices. Despite the recognised importance of this topic, few empirical studies address how students perceive the ethical issues related to predictive learning analytics (PLA). To redress this, interview data collected from 42 undergraduate and postgraduate students in a Northern Irish university were thematically analysed. Findings suggest that there are at least three distinct groups of students having varying assumptions about ethics in PLA. They are (1) naïve and trusting, (2) cautious and compromising, and (3) enlightened and demanding, and all of them tend to narrowly focus only on the issue of informed consent. An empirically supported argument for the need for PLA researchers to recognise the within-group variations in student populations and to educate all types of students in issues related to ethics is presented.

DOI: 10.4018/978-1-7998-7103-3.ch004

INTRODUCTION

Higher education institutions use a variety of computation-based technologies to gather and analyse data while students interact in a learning environment, for activities such as completion of online tasks, accessing learning materials, submitting assignments and create postings in discussion forums. As students leave their digital footprints, several issues emerge in relation to the rights and responsibilities stakeholders have in relation to students' data, the ways of obtaining an informed consent from students, and whether students can opt out of institutional data collection practices, to name a few. There is an increasing scholarly and practitioner interest in understanding more about students' awareness, consent, data ownership and control, the obligation to act, the kinds of institutional interventions, and the impacts on student behaviour. This body of literature forms the field of *ethics in learning analytics* and it is steadily growing. Learning Analytics (LA), is often defined as "the measurement, collection, analysis and reporting of data about learners and their contexts, for purposes of understanding and optimising learning and the environments in which it occurs" (Siemens, 2011). LA is used to understand students' learning needs, build better pedagogies, target at-risk students, assess factors affecting student successes, allocate resources and inform institutional strategies on student retention and progression (Rienties et al. 2016). Within this broader field of learning analytics, descriptive learning analytics presents what happened in a learning context, diagnostic learning analytics explains why something has happened, predictive learning analytics (PLA) forecasts what might happen and prescriptive learning analytics instructs how could institutions make something happen (Davis, 2013). Scholars tend to agree that students' engagement in LA in general, and in PLA discourses in particular, has been neglected in literature (West et al. 2020), and therefore, the ethical issues triggered by students' disengagement in PLA is the focus of this chapter. We present an empirical case study that seeks to explore students' perceptions on their personal data is being utilised by the University for the purposes of making predictions about their academic success.

This study contributes to the PLA literature at least three ways: first, we empirically establish that students have a relatively a narrower view of ethics in LA than what is presented in the literature and they focus only on a limited set of issues, related to informed consent. Second, it highlights the importance of including students as key stakeholders in the conversations about ethics in PLA. Third, it emphasises the need to recognise the within-group variations in student populations, and to educate all types of students in issues related to ethics so that students as a collective, develop a more holistic understanding of this complex issue of ethics in PLA.

Background

Within the LA literature, in general, scholars lament that "the topics of privacy and ethics have been widely under-represented in the learning analytics literature" (Davis, 2013; p.2). In a special issue on ethics in learning analytics, the editors (Gasevic, Dawson and Jovanovic, 2016) acknowledge that questions related to this ethics "have been an ongoing concern since the early days of learning analytics" (p. 1). In recent years, however, a growing number of conceptual papers discuss questions related to the ownership and protection of personal data, data sharing and access, ethical use of data, and ethical implications of the use of learning analytics (e.g. Pardo and Siemens, 2014; Drachsler and Greller, 2016; Prinsloo and Slade, 2015; 2017a; 2017b; 2017c; 2018). To guide institutions, and to reassure students and staff, in undertaking ethics-informed LA, a range of frameworks and guidelines for ethics in learning analytics have been produced, so that student privacy is respected and potential harms avoided, at a more general level (Slade and Prinsloo, 2013, Jisc, 2015), national level (Sclater, 2014a; Oliver, 2020) and global level (Slade and Tait, 2019). While recognising the possibility of key legislative, logistic and cultural factors (e.g. the EU's General Data Protection Regulation (2018) and the OECD's Fair Information Practice Principles; also refer to Jaakonmaki et al. 2020 for an overview), which are contributing to ethical issues in specific contexts, these broad sets of principles duly acknowledge their own limitations in what they could realistically do in a given context. However, some critics continue to argue (e.g. Kitto and Knight, 2019) that these guidelines fail to help practitioners in addressing the problems that they face in building LA for institutional adoption. Nevertheless, taken together, these frameworks help researchers and practitioners broaden their understanding of ethics in LA; and they repeatedly highlight a number of core issues that are to be considered when using learning analytics in ethics-informed ways. These issues include the need for transparency, quality, management, validity, ownership and control of data, the impact of surveillance, different understandings of informed consent and privacy, responsibilities of student and institutions, the need for clear institutional policies and the significance of standardised communications (Slade and Prinsloo, 2013; Sclater, 2014; Slade and Tait, 2019). Increasingly, these issues are understood as separate but interconnected problems (Drachsler et al. 2015). For example, Ferguson (2019) usefully group these challenges into six categories: duty to act, informed consent, safeguarding, equality and justice, data ownership and protection, and privacy and integrity of self. Although on the one hand, our understanding of the challenges associated with these issues is growing, scholars (e.g. Rubel and Jones, 2016; Griffiths, 2020) are also concerned with the intrusive and coercive ways in which students' information is accessed and gathered, the use of LA as an enabling technology for management, and the implications of the link between surveillance and trust, and the issues that are linked with student autonomy. In fact, Rubel and Jones (2016) questioned whether or not LA can be justified given the potential distribution of consequences and benefits, and doubt whether LA really advances the aims of higher education.

The growing mistrust in the ways institutions use students' data is in part due to the fact that students' participation in LA related discourses is limited in most institutions. Students' engagement has been relatively thin in the LA empirical literature (Tsai et al. 2020). In the new and emerging area of predictive learning analytics (PLA) examining students' perspectives is even rarer. But there are benefits of engaging students in the application of LA in universities. It has been recognised that through students' engagement in the development and implementation of LA, institutions can achieve a more accurate interpretation of behavioural data, a better understanding of what types of interventions and support might work for a group of students, an enhanced perspective on how to personalise learning pathways and a more reliable way of producing student-centred outcomes (Slade and Tait, 2019). By engaging in LA implementations, they too can be reminded of their own responsibilities for the ethical and safe use of personal information and by giving informed and more meaningful consent. As a consequence, published empirical studies that explore students' perceptions of LA are on the increase (e.g. Ifenthaler, D., and Schumacher, 2016; Roberts, et al. 2016; Schumacher and Ifenthaler, 2018; Slade, Prinsloo and Khalil, 2019; Tsai, Perrotta, and Gašević, 2020; Whitelock and Wainwright et al. 2020). For example, Tsai, Whitelock-Wainwright and Gasevic (2020), in their mixed method study, aimed to identify gaps between what students' desire and what they expect to happen or choose to do in reality when it comes to privacy protection. They highlight that purpose, access, and anonymity are key benchmarks of ethics and privacy integrity; that transparency and communication are key levers for learning analytics adoption; and that information asymmetry can impede the active participation of students in learning analytics. Despite a handful of studies, West et al. (2020), in their recent review of LA practices in European higher education institutions, conclude that an academic, teacher-centric or institutional view of LA is prevalent in theory and practice, reflecting a paternalistic approach to students. Selwyn (2019) cautions that "there is an emerging suspicion (warranted or not) that students are not the primary beneficiaries of the Learning Analytics technologies they are subjected to during their school or university education". Therefore, Prinsloo (2019) encourages questioning "the very existence of Learning Analytics". In fact, institutions have been cautioned that they should not assume that they know what students actually want, what students' concerns are and how the data should be presented to them (West et al. 2020). To redress this gap, this study focuses on students' perspectives on institutional use of their learning data.

More specifically, we focus on the ethical issues in the area of Predictive LA, in which students' data is used to predict which of them are at greater risk of dropping out or failing and to use statistics as the basis for a differentiated treatment of 'at risk' students. Scholes (2016) is concerned with the practice of using 'group risk statistics' to identify at-risk students and argues that PLA fails to recognise students as individuals. His view is that the instructional designs that use individual learner-based statistics might mitigate such ethical issues. Recently, Selwyn (2020), reflecting on the ongoing 'datafication' of contemporary education (Selwyn, 2015), highlights the experiences of non-conforming learners, such as non-traditional/transgender students and unrecognisable forms of learning; he provocatively argues that LA can be experienced as "discriminatory, oppressive and ultimately disadvantaging across whole student populations." The debate is continuing, and the issues related to privacy and ethics that emerge in this context "are tightly interconnected with other aspects such as trust, accountability, and transparency" (Pardo & Siemens, 2014 p. 438). It is in this context that, to contribute to the small number of student-focused empirical studies, we approached 46 of our students and asked them what they think about the university using their data for a range of teaching, learning and institutional purposes. This chapter summarises the findings and highlights their implications for PLA.

METHODOLOGY

Institutional Context

Ulster University, in Northern Ireland (UK), has approximately 27,000 students studying in four locations within the region. It also has 1600 fully online students, from 48 unique countries, studying courses that are offered in blended or fully online modes. As students use online learning systems, their digital footprints are recorded continually in the university systems, along with their data on attendance at formal/online lectures, assignment submissions, academic achievements, and the use of library facilities, among others. Using this data, the university personalises learning contents, and customises student support and feedback, and empowers teachers to make real-time pedagogical decisions related to course structures, learning design and programme provision.

Within the European Union, Ulster University is the first institution to use *Blackboard Predict*, a commercial solution that leverages a predictive model to identify at-risk students. The university has implemented a pilot project on predictive learning analytics in less than a year of its introduction in 2017. Through the application of a predictive model, this initiative allowed professors, instructors, and student advisors to make early interventions when a student triggers an early warning system. The project aimed at enhancing intervention strategies that use just-in-time data and encouraging data-informed decision making. Based on its prior implementation expertise in descriptive analytics, the university had a good understanding of how its Learning Management System was being utilised and how different learning support materials were being used by students. Driven by a clear strategic intent to adopt a more student-focused approach, a project board was established. A wide representation from faculties, and other professional services departments such as Student Support, ICT services, Student Administration, and the Quality Management Unit characterised this board. Before making the system institutionally available, several groups worked on issues related to data cleansing, ethics, governance, implementation policy and staff training. Following a substantial period of data integration and model testing, the PLA dashboards were created. These dashboards, displayed the probability a student will succeed with 50% or more. For example, if the dashboard indicator shows 25% against a student, it underlines the prediction that it is only 25% probability that the student will succeed with a 50% grade or higher. The system also helps us identify those students, through available engagement indicators, who show similarities with students who have previously dropped out or failed to achieve 50% or above. These dashboards were made available only to academic staff and to those who engage in student support activities across the institution, and not for the students. At the time of this study, the institution, paused for an interim evaluation and wanted to know students' views on the utilisation of their data for predictive purposes before embarking on an institutional level rollout. The transitional time offered the researchers an opportunity to understand learners' perceptions on ethics and privacy issues related to LA and PLA. In a larger study, we explored what types of datasets were perceived by students as important and useful in student-facing LA dashboards. A PLA-related question was added in that broader inquiry to explore students' perceptions on using their data to predict student outcomes. One research question guided the inquiry: How do students perceive the fact that their personal data is being utilised by the University for the purposes of making predictions about their academic success? The methodology is explained next section.

Research Process

On obtaining approval from the University Ethics Committee, a multi-qualitative methods design was used in the study. Although one-to-one interviews were preferred as a method for this study to capture students' perceptions on ethical issues related to PLA, the researchers ended up with conducting three paired interviews, and two focus groups, along with sixteen one-to-one semi-structured interviews.

Researchers invited student volunteers to take part in the study through online posters, student representatives and personal emails. Among those who responded, sixteen undergraduate students were purposively sampled using a maximum variation strategy. All of them received an information sheet detailing the study and they signed consent forms prior to the interviews. Interviews took place during lunch breaks, and when students did not have scheduled lectures. After a set of introductory questions, all of them were asked the two main questions: How do you feel about your personal data being used by the university so that it can make predictions about your academic success? What are your thoughts on your data being utilised in learning dashboards? Follow-up questions were used only to elicit more specific, in-depth information, whenever required. After the 16th one-to-one interview, students volunteered themselves to take part in this research, not as individuals, but as pairs. Mindful of the ethical and privacy concerns of undertaking a systematic study, we clarified their intentions behind their interest in doing paired interviews. Students convinced us that they normally do their reading and prepare for assessments in pairs, and they were comfortable in discussing the issues explained in the participant information sheet. Volunteering pairs were purposively selected, and the procedures given in Wilson, Onwuegbuzie and Manning (2016) and Morgan et al (2013) were used when conducting the paired interviews. These interviews were conducted in the same place, having both the volunteers available at the same time, and using the same questions that were used in the individual interviews. The difference was that the researchers spent, relatively, a longer time discussing their learning practices, and their views on ethics and privacy. The focus was to understand how the pair, as social learners, perceive the issues related ethics in PLA. Three paired interviews (n=6) were conducted by the lead researcher and a research assistant recorded the conversations for later analysis. The co-researcher observed the non-verbal cues of the dyad and their interactions, as they engage in the conversation.

Learning from this experience, and also in the interests of accommodating the postgraduate students' in-campus availability, an invitation was extended to postgraduates to take part in the focus groups. 31 postgraduate students from one cohort agreed to take part in two focus group interviews. Using a maximum variation sampling strategy, we purposefully selected two sets of postgraduate volunteers (n=20). They assured the researchers that they were comfortable with each other in sharing ideas about PLA ethics. Similar to the paired interviews, we conducted each session having all the volunteers available at the same time, in the same place, using the same interview questions, which is in line with the guidelines offered by Morgan (1996). Our focus was to understand how a group of learners perceive the issues related to ethics in PLA. A research assistant handled the logistics, took notes, observed the seating arrangements, and monitored the audio-recording process. The lead researcher facilitated both of the events, which took approximately 110 minutes each, and concluded the sessions with a summary. Thus, 22 undergraduate and 20 postgraduate students made up our sample. It contained almost equal representation of male and female students with the following characteristics: they were relatively young (n = 30 were 20– 30 years old; n = 12 were 30–40 years old); had studied two management specialisms (i.e., human resources management and business innovation) within the business school, as undergraduates (n = 22) and postgraduates (n = 20); had direct industry work experience (range 2 -10 years); and are from international (n=48%) and home (n=52%) institutions. A professional firm transcribed all recordings verbatim.

Data Analysis: The data comprised transcripts of the conversations with individuals, with the pairs and with focus group participants, along with handwritten notes from the lead researchers and the research assistants. We analysed these various types of data using Braun and Clarke's (2012) thematic analysis guidelines. Accordingly, we familiarised ourselves with the data, generated initial codes, searched for a patterned response or meaning within the dataset, reviewed potential themes, and finally defined and named the themes before writing up the Findings section. During the analytical process, we noted how a comment was made (intensity and emotion), how often (frequency), and by how many students (extensiveness). We captured the big ideas and selected illustrative quotes. We wrote up our analytical interpretation based on the research questions and highlighted the big themes. To enhance trustworthiness of our study, we used researcher triangulation, team vetting of themes, and reflexive journaling in the process. The research assistants kept records of all the raw data, field notes, transcripts, team meetings, and a reflexive journal of how and when we made analytical decisions. In the next section, the findings of our study are presented, using illustrative quotes and pseudonyms.

Findings

As a result of the thematic analysis, three dominant themes emerged in this study: trust, awareness and caution. Utilising the students' own words, we name them as (1) Naïve and Trusting: 'I don't have a problem with the University using my data!' and (2) Cautious and Compromising: 'Some data can be used without my consent, but it is nice to be transparent!' and (3) Enlightened and Demanding: 'It is my data and I must give consent.'

Category 1: NAIVE and TRUSTING - "I Don't Have Problem With the University Using My Data!'

This theme maps the participants' experiences of trusting the university to use the data for the good of the students. There is little or no tension in the ways that they approach the issue of their personal data being utilised by the university for the purposes of predicting academic success. They believe that their data is already available in many places, and that the university has access to most of it. They trust that their university will use this data in ways that support the students and they do not have any doubt in their capacity to use data for the benefit of all students. Some students in this category tend to dismiss the idea that they do not bother about this very much, and they tend to argue if the staff want to see the data, they should be able to see what is required. These students are ignorant of the possible misuse of data, and there is an excessive naivety, and that was evident in their expressions:

[The university using my data] ... doesn't bother me personally, but I can understand how it would bother other people ...I've confidence in the university.

If it benefits the greater good of students within the university, I'd be more than happy for the university to use my data (Bolden).

I don't have a problem with it; yes, I've never really gave it much thought because I've never cared about this personally... I think the data should be accessible to all staff.. if someone wants to see it, they should be able to see it (Clement).

Students believe in the university staff because the employees are seen as 'professionals' who could be trusted and they should be allowed to do their job by using the students' data, as illustrated in Jeevan's quote below:

With the mental health data and stuff like that... if they are going to nip something in the bud, it is good – if the data flag something up...show red flags that there is a pattern in a students' behaviour who experience mental health issue... if they can nip it in the bud ...it is good....! I look at them as professionals and I would be happy enough leaving my data and letting them do the work .... (Jeevan).

In line with the above sentiments of innocence and trust, two international students said that they would be happy for the university to use their data, and, to some extent, they would even be happy to not be informed of all the different ways the university uses the data:

I'd rather the university be using my data than someone else (Juan)

(Referring to the need for university's openness in informing students how their data is used)... *I'd be confident enough in the university to not let me know that information to a certain extent* (Wang Lei).

In essence, there was a blind belief in the university staff's perceived professionalism and an unquestionable acceptance in anyone being able to use the students' data, and a dismissive 'it doesn't bother me' attitude that characterise the students who belong to this category.

Category 2: CAUTIOUS and COMPROMISING - 'Some Data Can Be Used Without My Consent, But It Is Nice to Be Transparent!'

This theme focuses on the participants' attitude that is cautious and compromising towards data use in the university. Students in this category are, first of all, aware of the various datasets, such as their personal data and learning behaviour data, and the intrinsic variation in the nature of that data. They are able to differentiate the personal and sensitive data from those that are campus-based, and institutional-system-generated behavioural data. They believe that the university could use the learning behaviour data for enhancing their experience of teaching and learning, and for supporting them in achieving their study goals. However, they believe that it is better for universities to be transparent about data use. These students do not see student consent as a necessary condition for the institutional usage of student data. They softly acknowledge that it is 'nice' for universities to be transparent in communicating what happens to the data and for what purposes the students' data have been used.

Non-university digital footprints should not be used without my consent. The other things are already with them anyway. They can use them and inform me (Ancilla).

I think... when you're signing up for it during admission, they should explicitly say, here's what we're using... here's how we're going to use this, and this is what you'll be shown [on a dashboard], and this is what we will see. And I think as long as it's just open and transparent about its usage, I wouldn't mind too much (Gopal).

I think the issue has two sides: I mean on the right hand cushy side, it's very important for students that their university monitors its student behaviours...what they read, when do they attend the lectures and how do they engage with the teachers and so on. But on the other hand, the problematic side.... some students may have mental problems, but they don't want other people [to] know about it; some have health issues, personal problems, domestic issues, questionable social life etc. University should not try to steal them without the students' knowledge. When you try to access, I could be informed in advance... (Sharma).

Referring to the Northern Irish context and her own Black and Minority Ethnic (BAME) community status, Jamila argued that for marketing and brand management purposes, universities could use students' data on national and cultural affiliations. She also pointed out that there are datasets that are more sensitive and personal, and institutions should be cautious in using them:

(Data usage by universities)... is good and bad. Good because, for instance, using data on 'gender' and 'ethnicity' within Northern Ireland context..... is useful to explore what type of successes female students from Black and Minority Ethnic communities have had in the university OR how to actually bring in more international students to this university and so on. University can make use of the data without asking my permission. But, I do think that there is some sensitive data... you really don't want the university to know what you're doing (Jamila).

In summary, an ability to differentiate between a range of datasets, to discern the boundaries of personal and institutional responsibilities, and to recognise the need of students to have some degree of privacy and trust from these institutions, in order for them to develop as autonomous learners and human beings, characterise the students who belong to this category.

Category 3: ENLIGHTENED and DEMANDING - 'It Is My Data and I Must Give Consent'

This theme outlines the ways that participants demonstrated awareness about their rights and responsibilities of handling those people who use the students' data. Obtaining consent from students for using their data is important to them. They demand that students should be informed well in advance of the reasons for collecting and using data. They go beyond the issue of student consent by saying that they want to know how 'at risk' predictions are made, and from what datasets the predictions are based upon. They believe that their lecturers should be able to justify why a student is flagged 'at risk', and be able to explain why such decisions are not biased in any way. Unlike the two previous groups of students, those, who are in this category, go even further in expecting universities to protect students' data and identity, and should allow students to 'opt out' of institutional data collection attempts. The following quotes illustrate their awareness and the consequent demands that knowledge of this situation triggers:

If I see a visualisation on the screen, I would like to know all the pieces of data that contributed to that prediction. Because...it's my data at the end of the day – so – if it's mine, I feel I'm entitled to see it (Audrey).

I believe that there's no reason to hide anything, So I believe, yes, it's good to be open to see what happens to the data and how it is used. They [the university] can always review and see how it's gone after a period. Yes, I think it's certainly important (Geoff).

I think we should be well aware of what your data is being used for (William).

Oliver, a postgraduate student voiced his opinion in the focus group emphatically, and the other nine participants in the group acknowledged it when he compared students' data to a property that 'has been lent to the university':

Your data is personal to you. You own it. You're only lending it to the university. If I were to lend an item I own to someone I know, I want to know how it's being used and I want them to be transparent with me on how it's being used. I think that the university has to 1) say how they're gonna protect it and, 2) how it's gonna be used; because it would be a breach of trust between the individual and the university if it was being used in a way that wasn't previously agreed......... I think, if it was used in a way that wasn't previously agreed then the individual would have a right to withdraw that data away from the university. I should be allowed to opt out of that process, if they cannot handle my data in the way it had been agreed with me (Oliver).

In essence, there is an awareness of several dimensions of the ethical use of student data, such as protecting student data, using the data only in ways that are agreed with students, the possibility of students opting out of the data collection process, institutional transparency in what datasets are collected, how they are used, why and for what purposes, and a noticeable tension, assumed to exist between the owners and users of data, characterise the students who belong to this category.

Taken together, all the three thematic categories collectively point to the rich variation in students' perspectives on the use of student data. The findings suggest that students have a range of beliefs and assumptions about how their data should be used and what a university should do when using their data. The in-group variation in students has important implications for PLA researchers, LA practitioners and institutional decision makers, and we discuss these issues next.

Discussion

The aim of this research was to understand students' perceptions on the institutional use of students' personal data for the purposes of making predictions about their academic success. In this quest, we uncovered a rich variation in students' attitudes to ethics in PLA. We revealed three categories of learners: first, the *naïve and trusting* learners; second, the *cautious and compromising* learners; and third, the *enlightened and demanding* learners. All three categories have resonance with student groups found in the literature. For example, the naïve and trusting students, in category 1, are similar to those who were found to be comfortable with the collection of personal data "in exchange for more effective, personalised support and services" in Slade, Prinsloo, & Khalil's (2019, p. 242) study, and those who were labelled as 'uninformed and uncertain' in Roberts et al.'s (2016) study. This group of students tend to overlook the possibility of the data being (mis)used in ways for example, to invading their privacy, exploiting them commercially by selling their data to third parties or targeted marketing of further educational products (Sclater, 2014), although the students in Category 2 tend to show some level of awareness of these issues. Even the Category 2 'cautious and compromising' students while recognising the potential benefit from the additional support provided through learning analytics, are not concerned about the potential inequities that may arise from learning analytics (e.g., some people receiving personalised support than others) as revealed in Roberts et al (2016). Collectively, their unquestioning trust in the institution's ability to care for their data is striking. The 'enlightened and demanding' students, in category 3, have similar attitudinal orientation to those who were found to question 'where will it stop" in Roberts et al.'s (2016) study. These demanding students point to the need to have some choice regarding the implementation of their of dashboard analytics and to the importance of including students' voice in the development of [predictive] learning analytics, a recommended ethical principle (Roberts, Chang and Gibson, 2016).

While our study confirms students' attitudinal differences found in the literature, it brings to light an important critical dimension that characterises them; namely, we found that their views of ethics are centred only around the issue of 'informed consent' whilst ignoring many of the other ethical aspects, such as data ownership and protection, safeguarding students' rights and interests, equality and justice. Although Category 3 students showed an interest to 'opt out' of their data being collected, they showed little interest in other issues that such a scheme might trigger. For example, those who opted out could miss out the personalised support their institution could offer in increasing their chances of success, and those who opted in could be denied the benefits of learning from institutional level big data insights (Sclater, 2014b). These students were less concerned with the ownership and protection of personal data, data sharing and access, ethical use of data, and ethical implications of the use of learning analytics in education. They tend to value more the university's responsibility to gain students' consent, while caring less about its contextual integrity, i.e., whether information flows are appropriate to specific contexts, and are shared by specific actors, under specific 'terms and conditions' (Nissenbaum, 2010). Across the sample, there is also a lack of clarity in their understanding of 'privacy with respect to whom' and 'privacy about what' (Rubel and Jones, 2016). None of our participants expressed a desire to be active agents in the implementation of PLA, engaging in activities such as committing to a self-regulated learning regime when prompted by LA, creating a personalised learning path for themselves or engaging in peer development interventions. No one has asked for opportunities to update their own data and consent agreements at regular intervals. In contrast to the views of institutional leaders and academic staff, revealed in West, Huijser and Heath (2016), our findings show students' views did not align with established ethical principles, and the language used to express their views are one-dimensional, simplistic and linear. Overall, a narrower, a-contextual, consent-focused, self-focused view of ethics appears to be the source of within-group variation in students. It is because of this tunnel vision that students tend to approach the issue of ethics in PLA with naivety, caution or persistence.

There are several implications of recognising the within-group variation that we identified in this study. For example, when recognising the intrusive nature of data harvesting practices and the depth and breadth of the data that the institutions collect, naïve students (in Category 1) could ignore the data exploitation practices of those who do not have the best interests of their students at heart; cautious students (in Category 2) could game the system so that they leave only the desirable, *digital breadcrumbs* (EDUCAUSE, 2011), and the enlightened and demanding group of students (in Category 3) could end up avoiding such courses or engaging in legal action. It is important to recognise that there exists a heavy imbalance of power with regard to harvesting, analysing and exploiting data in HEIs. The power lies with the institution as a provider, who has a duty of care to ensure transparency and security. Therefore, it is important that they make their terms and conditions accessible and understandable to all groups of students; they have to clarify what data are being collected, for what purpose and with whom they are being shared. They should also provide students with access to information and the data held about them, as well as ensure that they are able to verify and update personal information as and when required. At the same time, institutions should not assume that all of their students belong to a homogenous group of innocent learners who view PLA in a uniform way. Not all of them are always ready to learn and understand the complex rights and responsibilities of data handling and safeguarding. Although institutions have a duty to *optimise learning and the environments in which it occurs* (Long and Siemens, 2011, p. 34), if they are not able to justify their data collection using specific criteria, then it is possible that many student groups could experience PLA as discriminatory, oppressive and disadvantaging, as Selwyn (2020) lamented. Therefore, we argue that when it comes to ethics in PLA, institutions should adopt a differentiated approach to educating each of the subgroups of students, which are identified in this study. Students, according to their attitudinal diversity, should be give specific tools that will help them to understand what they are consenting to, and what is the pedagogic value of the information that is being collected. Bespoke training interventions, based on students' within-group variation, hold promise for developing the students' awareness about ethics in PLA. We join Deborah West and her colleagues in emphasising the point that institutions must not assume that *they know what students want, what their concerns are or how they would like data presented* (West et al. 2020).

The study has at least three limitations. First, this research was conducted with students in one business school in Northern Ireland. Their departmental and geographical context may influence their views on ethics and PLA, when compared with students in other schools, such as health and sports, and when situated in wider national and international contexts. Interdisciplinary, cross-cultural and international research is required to understand the rich differences in student attitudes toward ethics in PLA. Second, when we conducted the original, larger piece of research on learning analytics, we introduced a range of datasets (e.g. library history, prior educational data, personal and social background data, demographic info, fee status, within-course comparison, building usage data, and student engagement data) and then asked them to answer the research question explained in this paper. Using these datasets may have biased student attitudes towards ethics. It would be of interest to explore if student perceptions of ethics in PLA differ if students are not presented with any clues about the datasets that were used. Measuring students' prior understanding of what PLA is may also provide universities with a clearer understanding of what, and why, students view something as ethical and acceptable. Third, our focus was on understanding students' views on ethics in PLA, predicated on the relative absence of the student engagement in learning analytics research. Future research could compare perceptions of other key stakeholders, such as academics, teaching assistants, managers, learning technologists and institutional decision makers, on ethics in PLA.

CONCLUSION

This chapter has examined ethics in predictive learning analytics with a focus on students' perception in a northern Irish university. Our study paints a richer picture of within-group variations among students; it identifies three categories of students, the naïve, the cautious and the enlightened. The findings also highlight the need to develop policies and implementation of practice that involves the raising of ethics awareness amongst the students. Our study repeats previous calls for actively engaging users in the process of decision making relating to PLA data (Roberts et al. 2016; Beattie, Woodley and Souter, 2014; Slade and Prinsloo, 2014; 2013); even more so, in these unprecedented times, where the majority of teaching and learning activities take place online, the purpose and the boundaries regarding the use of LA and PLA need to be well defined and visible to the students. The study goes further in highlighting the need to recognise the within-group variation in students' attitudes towards ethics in PLA, revealed in this chapter. Recognising these variations is important for unpacking complexities of learning analytics adoption and integrating students in PLA-related policy making. It is equally important to equip *all* types of students with data literacy skills, so that they broaden their understanding of ethics, and are sufficiently informed to give or withhold consent to the use of data in PLA; it is even more important that those efforts differentially target those who are naïve, cautious and enlightened so that every one of them enhances their understanding of the use, value, ownership, and control of data. We hope that our study marks a first step in understanding students' views on ethics in PLA and future empirical studies might reveal how these various student groups could be meaningfully educated and empowered to develop broader ethical literacy.

REFERENCES

Atif, A., Richards D., Danny Liu D., & Bilgin A. A. (2020). Perceived benefits and barriers of a prototype early alert system to detect engagement and support 'at-risk' students: The teacher perspective. *Computers & Education, 156,* 1-20.

Beattie, S., Woodley, C., & Souter, K. (2014). Creepy analytics and learner data rights. *Rhetoric and Reality. Critical Perspectives on Educational Technology-Conference Proceedings.*

Braun, V., & Clarke, V. (2012). Thematic analysis. In H. Cooper, P. M. Camic, D. L. Long, A. T. Panter, D. Rindskopf, & K. J. Sher (Eds.), APA handbooks in psychology®. APA handbook of research methods in psychology, Vol. 2. Research designs: Quantitative, qualitative, neuropsychological, and biological (p. 57–71). American Psychological Association. doi:10.1037/13620-004

Drachsler, H., & Greller, W. (2016, April). Privacy and analytics: it's a DELICATE issue a checklist for trusted learning analytics. In *Proceedings of the sixth international conference on learning analytics & knowledge* (pp. 89-98). 10.1145/2883851.2883893

Drachsler, H., Hoel, T., Scheffel, M., Kismihók, G., Berg, A., Ferguson, R., ... Manderveld, J. (2015, March). Ethical and privacy issues in the application of learning analytics. In *Proceedings of the Fifth International Conference on Learning Analytics and Knowledge* (pp. 390-391). 10.1145/2723576.2723642

EDUCAUSE Learning Initiative. (2011). *7 Things you should know about learning analytics*. Washingon, DC: EDUCAUSE Learning Initiative. https://www.educause.edu/eli

Ferguson, R. (2019). Ethical Challenges for Learning Analytics. *Journal of Learning Analytics*, *6*(3), 25–30. doi:10.18608/jla.2019.63.5

Ferguson, R., Hoel, T., Scheffel, M., & Drachsler, H. (2016). Guest editorial: Ethics and privacy in learning analytics. *Journal of Learning Analytics*, *3*(1), 5–15. doi:10.18608/jla.2016.31.2

Gasevic, D., Dawson, S., & Jovanovic, J. (2016). Ethics and privacy as enablers of learning analytics. *Journal of Learning Analytics*, *3*(1), 1–4. doi:10.18608/jla.2016.31.1

Gavison, R. (1980). Privacy and the limits of law. *The Yale Law Journal*, *89*(3), 421–471. doi:10.2307/795891

Griffiths, D. (2020). The Ethical Issues of Learning Analytics in Their Historical Context. In *Radical Solutions and Open Science* (pp. 39–55). Springer. doi:10.1007/978-981-15-4276-3_3

Ifenthaler, D., & Schumacher, C. (2016). Student perceptions of privacy principles for learning analytics. *Educational Technology Research and Development*, *64*(5), 923–938. doi:10.100711423-016-9477-y

Jaakonmäki, R., vom Brocke, J., Dietze, S., Drachsler, H., Fortenbacher, A., Helbig, R., & Yun, H. (2020). Responsible Cooking with Learning Analytics. In *Learning Analytics Cookbook* (pp. 15–30). Springer. doi:10.1007/978-3-030-43377-2_3

JISC. (2015). *Code of practice for learning analytics*. https://www.jisc.ac.uk/guides/code-of-practice-for-learning-analytics#

Jones, K. M. L. (2019). "Just Because You Can Doesn't Mean You Should": Practitioner Perceptions of Learning Analytics Ethics. portal. *Portal (Baltimore, Md.)*, *19*(3), 407–428. doi:10.1353/pla.2019.0025

Marshall, S. (2014). Exploring the ethical implications of MOOCs. *Distance Education, 35*(2), 250-262. doi:10.1080/01587919.2014.917706

Morgan, D. L. (1996). Focus groups. *Annual Review of Sociology*, *22*(1), 129–152. doi:10.1146/annurev.soc.22.1.129

Morgan, D. L., Ataie, J., Carder, P., & Hoffman, K. (2013). Introducing dyadic interviews as a method for collecting qualitative data. *Qualitative Health Research, 23*(9), 1276–1284. doi:10.1177/1049732313501889 PMID:23925406

Olivier, J. (2020). Research Ethics Guidelines for Personalized Learning and Teaching Through Big Data. In *Radical Solutions and Learning Analytics* (pp. 37–55). Springer. doi:10.1007/978-981-15-4526-9_3

Pardo, A., & Siemens, G. (2014). Ethical and privacy principles for learning analytics. *British Journal of Educational Technology, 45*(3), 438–450. doi:10.1111/bjet.12152

Phillips, R., Maor, D., Preston, G., & Cumming-Potvin, W. (2012). Exploring learning analytics as indicators of study behaviour. In *World conference on educational multimedia, hypermedia and telecommunications* (pp. 2861–2867). Denver, CO: EDMEDIA.

Prinsloo, P. (2019). Learning analytics: Mapping a critique and agenda. *Journal of Learning Analytics, 6*(3), 20–24.

Prinsloo, P., & Slade, S. (2015). Student privacy self-management: implications for learning analytics. *Proceedings of the Fifth International Conference on Learning Analytics and Knowledge*, 83–92. 10.1145/2723576.2723585

Prinsloo, P., & Slade, S. (2017a, March). An elephant in the learning analytics room: the obligation to act. In *Proceedings of the seventh international learning analytics & knowledge conference* (pp. 46-55). 10.1145/3027385.3027406

Prinsloo, P., & Slade, S. (2017b). Ethics and Learning Analytics: Charting the (Un) Charted. In Handbook of Learning Analytics. SOLAR.

Prinsloo, P., & Slade, S. (2017c). Big Data, Higher Education and Learning Analytics: Beyond Justice, Towards an Ethics of Care. In B. Kei Daniel (Ed.), *Big Data and Learning Analytics in Higher Education*. Springer. doi:10.1007/978-3-319-06520-5_8

Prinsloo, P., & Slade, S. (2018). Student Consent in Learning Analytics: The Devil in the Details? In J. Lester, C. Klein, H. Rangwala, & A. Johri (Eds.), *Learning analytics in higher education: Current innovations, future potential, and practical applications* (pp. 118–139). Routledge. doi:10.4324/9780203731864-6

Rienties, B., Boroowa, A., Cross, S., Kubiak, C., Mayles, K., & Murphy, S. (2016). Analytics4Action Evaluation Framework: A Review of Evidence-Based Learning Analytics Interventions at the Open University UK. *Journal of Interactive Media in Education, 2016*(1).

Roberts, L., Chang, V., & Gibson, D. (2016). Ethical considerations in adopting a university- and system-wide approach to data and learning analytics. In B. Kei Daniel (Ed.), *Big Data and Learning Analytics in Higher Education* (pp. 89–108). Springer.

Roberts, L. D., Howell, J. A., Seaman, K., & Gibson, D. C. (2016). Student attitudes toward learning analytics in higher education: "The fitbit version of the learning world. *Frontiers in Psychology*, *7*, 1959. doi:10.3389/fpsyg.2016.01959 PMID:28066285

Rubel, A., & Jones, K. M. (2016). Student privacy in learning analytics: An information ethics perspective. *The Information Society*, *32*(2), 143–159. doi:10.1080/01972243.2016.1130502

Scholes, V. (2016). The ethics of using learning analytics to categorize students on risk. *Educational Technology Research and Development*, *64*(5), 939–955. doi:10.100711423-016-9458-1

Schumacher, C., & Ifenthaler, D. (2018). Features students really expect from learning analytics. *Computers in Human Behavior*, *78*, 397–407. doi:10.1016/j.chb.2017.06.030

Sclater, N. (2014a). Code of practice for learning analytics: A literature review of the ethical and legal issues. *JISC*. Available online: https://analytics.jiscinvolve.org/wp/2014/12/04/jisc-releases-report-on-ethical-and-legal-challenges-of-learning-analytics/

Sclater, N. (2014b). Snooping professor or friendly don? The ethics of university learning analytics. *The Conversation*. https://theconversation.com/snooping-professor-or-friendly-don-the-ethics-of-university-learning-analytics-23636

Selwyn, N. (2015). Data entry: Towards the critical study of digital data and education. *Learning, Media and Technology*, *40*(1), 64–82. doi:10.1080/17439884.2014.921628

Selwyn, N. (2019). What's the problem with Learning Analytics? *Journal of Learning Analytics*, *6*(3), 11–19. doi:10.18608/jla.2019.63.3

Selwyn, N. (2020). Re-imagining 'Learning Analytics'… a case for starting again? *The Internet and Higher Education*, *46*, 100745. doi:10.1016/j.iheduc.2020.100745

Siemens, G. (2011). Learning and academic analytics. *Learning and Knowledge Analytics, 5.*

Siemens, G., & Long, P. (2011). Penetrating the fog: Analytics in learning and education. *EDUCAUSE Review*, *46*(5), 30.

Slade, P., & Prinsloo, P. (2014). *Student perspectives on the use of their data: between intrusion, surveillance and care*. Paper presented at 8th EDEN Research Workshop, Oxford, UK.

Slade, S., & Prinsloo, P. (2013). Learning analytics: Ethical issues and dilemmas. *The American Behavioral Scientist*, *57*(10), 1510–1529. doi:10.1177/0002764213479366

Slade, S., Prinsloo, P., & Khalil, M. (2019, March). Learning analytics at the intersections of student trust, disclosure and benefit. In *Proceedings of the 9th International Conference on learning analytics & knowledge* (pp. 235-244). 10.1145/3303772.3303796

Slade, S., & Tait, A. (2019). *Global guidelines: Ethics in learning analytics*. Retrieved September 6, 2020 from https://www.learntechlib.org/p/208251/

Tsai, Y. S., Perrotta, C., & Gašević, D. (2020). Empowering learners with personalised learning approaches? Agency, equity and transparency in the context of learning analytics. *Assessment & Evaluation in Higher Education*, *45*(4), 554–567. doi:10.1080/02602938.2019.1676396

Tsai, Y. S., Rates, D., Moreno-Marcos, P. M., Muñoz-Merino, P. J., Jivet, I., Scheffel, M., Drachsler, H., Delgado Kloos, C., & Gašević, D. (2020). Learning analytics in European higher education–trends and barriers. *Computers & Education*, *155*, 103933. doi:10.1016/j.compedu.2020.103933

Tsai, Y. S., Whitelock-Wainwright, A., & Gašević, D. (2020, March). The privacy paradox and its implications for learning analytics. In *Proceedings of the Tenth International Conference on Learning Analytics & Knowledge* (pp. 230-239). 10.1145/3375462.3375536

Viberg, O., Hatakka, M., Balter, O., & Mavroudi, A. (2018). The current landscape of learning analytics in higher education. *Computers in Human Behavior*, *89*, 98–110. doi:10.1016/j.chb.2018.07.027

West, D., Huijser, H., & Heath, D. (2016). Putting an ethical lens on learning analytics. *Educational Technology Research and Development*, *64*(5), 903–922. doi:10.100711423-016-9464-3

West, D., Luzeckyj, A., Toohey, D., Vanderlelie, J., & Searle, B. (2020). Do academics and university administrators really know better? The ethics of positioning student perspectives in learning analytics. *Australasian Journal of Educational Technology*, *36*(2), 60–70. doi:10.14742/ajet.4653

Whitelock-Wainwright, A., Gašević, D., Tsai, Y. S., Drachsler, H., Scheffel, M., Muñoz-Merino, P. J., Tammets, K., & Delgado Kloos, C. (2020). Assessing the validity of a learning analytics expectation instrument: A multinational study. *Journal of Computer Assisted Learning*, *36*(2), 209–240. doi:10.1111/jcal.12401

Wilson, A. D., Onwuegbuzie, A. J., & Manning, L. P. (2016). Using paired depth interviews to collect qualitative data. *Qualitative Report*, *21*(9), 1549.

ADDITIONAL READING

Archer, E., & Prinsloo, P. (2020). Speaking the unspoken in learning analytics: Troubling the defaults. *Assessment & Evaluation in Higher Education*, *45*(6), 888–900. doi:10.1080/02602938.2019.1694863

Ifenthaler, D., Gibson, D., Prasse, D., Shimada, A., & Yamada, M. (2020). Putting learning back into learning analytics: Actions for policy makers, researchers, and practitioners. *Educational Technology Research and Development*, 1–20.

Ifenthaler, D., Mah, D. K., & Yau, J. Y. K. (Eds.). (2019). *Utilizing learning analytics to support study success*. Springer. doi:10.1007/978-3-319-64792-0

Jaakonmäki, R., vom Brocke, J., Dietze, S., Drachsler, H., Fortenbacher, A., Helbig, R., & Yun, H. (2020). Responsible Cooking with Learning Analytics. In *Learning Analytics Cookbook* (pp. 15–30). Springer. doi:10.1007/978-3-030-43377-2_3

Olivier, J. (2020). Research Ethics Guidelines for Personalized Learning and Teaching Through Big Data. In *Radical Solutions and Learning Analytics* (pp. 37–55). Springer. doi:10.1007/978-981-15-4526-9_3

Selwyn, N. (2020). Re-imagining 'Learning Analytics'… a case for starting again? *The Internet and Higher Education*, *46*, 100745. doi:10.1016/j.iheduc.2020.100745

Tsai, Y. S., Whitelock-Wainwright, A., & Gašević, D. (2020, March). The privacy paradox and its implications for learning analytics. In *Proceedings of the Tenth International Conference on Learning Analytics & Knowledge* (pp. 230-239). 10.1145/3375462.3375536

KEY TERMS AND DEFINITIONS

Contextual Integrity: Nissenbaum (1998) developed the concept of privacy as contextual integrity to propose a normative framework that evaluates the flow of information about individuals. It assumes that our privacy is associated with and regulated by the flow of information based on norms that are context-relative. These norms include context, actors, attributes, and transmission principles and they affect the flow of information from information senders to information receivers to information subjects.

Descriptive Learning Analytics: A branch of learning analytics that aims to present what happens/ed in a learning context.

Diagnostic Learning Analytics: A branch of learning analytics that aims to explore why and how something has happened in a learning context.

Ethics: In general, it refers to a philosophy of morality that involves systematising, defending, and recommending concepts of right and wrong conduct; it is a fluctuating moral code of norms and conventions that exist in society externally to a person. In the context of LA, it refers to the systemisation of correct and incorrect behaviour in virtual spaces according to all stakeholders.

Predictive Learning Analytics: A branch of learning analytics that aims to forecast what might happen in a learning context.

Prescriptive Learning Analytics: A branch of learning analytics that aims to instruct how could institutions make something happen in a learning context.

Privacy: Generally, privacy refers to a living concept made out of continuous personal boundary negotiations with the surrounding ethical environment; it is an intrinsic part of a person's identity and integrity. In the context of LA, privacy is defined as the regulation of how personal digital information is being observed by the self or distributed to other observers.

Chapter 5
Learning Analytics and Education Data Mining in Higher Education

Samira ElAtia
The University of Alberta, Canada

Donald Ipperciel
York University, Canada

ABSTRACT

In this chapter, the authors propose an overview on the use of learning analytics (LA) and educational data mining (EDM) in addressing issues related to its uses and applications in higher education. They aim to provide meaningful and substantial answers to how both LA and EDM can advance higher education from a large scale, big data educational research perspective. They present various tasks and applications that already exist in the field of EDM and LA in higher education. They categorize them based on their purposes, their uses, and their impact on various stakeholders. They conclude the chapter by critically analyzing various forecasts regarding the impact that EDM will have on future educational setting, especially in light of the current situation that shifted education worldwide into some form of eLearning models. They also discuss and raise issues regarding fundamentals consideration on ethics and privacy in using EDM and LA in higher education.

DOI: 10.4018/978-1-7998-7103-3.ch005

INTRODUCTION

In this chapter, we present a general survey or overview of the use of Learning Analytics (LA) and Educational Data Mining (EDM) as they relate to higher education. We aim to provide potential answers to how both LA and EDM can advance higher education institutions from a large-scale, big data educational research perspective. For both cognate disciplines, data generated by and available in universities provide a fertile ground for carrying breakthrough research and analyses in understanding and advancing education. This data covers a wide and diverse range of contexts: finances, human resources, the Registrar's Office, maintenance and facilities, internet use, admission, program development, libraries, research, and teaching and learning. In particular, universities are heavily scrutinized for the training and skills they provide to students. Consequently, over the past few decades, universities have been paying close attention to these issues, using tools available through advances in big data analysis, with employability and graduate skills the focus for many institutional programs. For the teaching, learning and services provided to students, it seems that both EDM and LA can become optimal tools to guide universities in adapting to these changes and addressing specific needs for the future.

EDM emerged as a field of its own using data mining techniques in educational environments. There are a variety of methods and applications in EDM that can be classified into two categories. On the one hand, EDM can be used for applied research objectives such as enhancing learning quality. On the other, it can be used as a tool for pure research objectives, which tend to improve our understanding of the learning process (Bakhshinategh, Zaiane, El Atia & Ipperciel 2018). In a multifaceted environment in which data come from different sources and in different forms, EDM offers a wealth of possibilities for understanding and shaping learning (Cios 2007, ElAtia et al. 2012; Hammad, 2009). These techniques are eclectic in nature and combine qualitative and quantitative research approaches. They also enable researchers to analyze big data that are affected by many unknown variables. Han & Kamber (2006) defined data mining as the "analysis of observational datasets to find unsuspected relationships and to summarize the data in novel ways that are both understandable and useful to the data owners. (p. 5)" Data mining is a multidisciplinary field that involves methods at the intersection of artificial intelligence, machine learning, statistics, and database systems.

LA is data analytics in the context of learning and education. It involves collecting data about learner activities and behaviours, as well as educational environments and contexts, using statistics and data mining techniques to extract relevant patterns that reveal how learning takes place. LA can be used (1) to report measures and patterns related to learning activities or (2) to optimize learning strategies and environments. Educational applications of EDM and LA in higher education are an emerging and growing trend resulting from the vast amounts of data becoming available from the growing number of courses delivered in e-learning and hybrid environments. They are a powerful means to systematically analyze the large amount of data produced by institutions of higher education. More on this below.

In the following sections, we engage with the reader in various discussions that are central to LA and EDM from a social-science perspective. To do so, in the first two sections entitled "Potential and Promises of Big Data in Higher Education" and "KDD, Data Warehousing and EDM," we present various tasks and applications that already exist in the field of EDM and LA in higher education and are seen as promising. For the second part, we focus primarily on presenting an overview of various "Stakeholders and Uses of EDM and LA" to brush a broader picture of EDM and LA in the context of their application." We categorize uses based on their purpose, uses, and impact on various stakeholders. Then, we engage in a discussion of the issues around ethical data uses and privacy in the section entitled "Privacy, Confidentiality and Ethical Consideration," and we conclude by contributing to a nascent discussion "At the Intersection of Two Fields" that bridge LA, data mining and higher education. In this context, we explore the possible barriers hindering a wider adoption of EDM and LA, whether as a consequence of ethical considerations or the difficulty to fulfil their interdisciplinary nature.

POTENTIAL AND PROMISES OF BIG DATA IN HIGHER EDUCATION

For Siemens and Long (2011), "the most dramatic factor shaping the future of higher education is something that we can't actually touch or see: *big data and analytics*" (p. 1). Indeed, analyzing educational data has the potential to improve learning experiences and institutional effectiveness (Huebner, 2013). These large amounts of data hold a wealth of knowledge that could be harvested to improve the educational experience as a whole. EDM and LA emerged as fields aiming to make sense of this data in such a way as to produce useful knowledge that could be taken advantage of to address challenges of educational institutions in the 21st century.

The potential of this rapidly accelerating field is immense for educational institutions in Canada as elsewhere. Among the many possible areas of study, the most exciting are perhaps those that aim more specifically to address student-centered issues. Using EDM, researchers and pedagogues can seek to better understand the determinants of student success (by means of emerging patterns and association rule mining), study students' learning patterns (through sequential pattern analysis), identify the factors that influence different aspects of their learning, such as retention, completion and performance (using machine learning techniques and feature selection), and ultimately improve their learning experience. At the same time, modeling students and analyzing their study patterns will help to evaluate the educational systems and their components at an institutional level, and – in the end – improve the quality of education.

The majority of EDM research has been facilitated by the steady use of online web-based educational platforms known as Learning Management Systems (LMS). The extensive and increasing use of LMSs in higher education has provided a rich environment for the systematic and comprehensive collection of data and observations of behaviors of both teachers and students/learners. An LMS provides a centralized virtual space where several educational services and content are systematically grouped and made available for ready consumption: "personal communication (email and instant messages), group communication (chatting and forums), content posting (syllabus, papers, presentations, lesson summaries), performance evaluation (question and answer repositories, self-assessment tests, assignments, quizzes and exams), and instruction management (message and grade posting, surveys, and online office hours)" (Naveh et al. 2012). In Wang (2014) the LMS is defined as "a centralized web-based information systems where the learning content is managed, and learning activities are organized. LMS represents a more general term for a technology framework that supports all aspects of formal and informal learning processes, including learning management, content management, course management, etc." (Stone et al. in Wang 2014). LMSs are a key enablers and catalysts of EDM and LA as they provide a rich data source that allows the study of learning behaviors. Interestingly, as we write these lines, we are in the midst of the COVID-19 pandemic, which has seen the use of LMS surge. In our home institutions, with mandatory online teaching, the use of LMS hovered around 50% of all courses for the past seven years. Currently, we are at 99-100% use of LMS in higher education classes across Canada. This is as much an opportunity (for EDM and LA) as it is a challenge (in terms of pedagogy and instructional design).

In addition to LMS as data generating platforms, web-based synchronous video conferencing platforms are emerging, this year more than ever, as yet another powerful teaching tool that generates a large amount of data that differ significantly from LMS-generated data, yet holds huge potential to direct learning and provide new insight and research application for EDM and LA (Hasan et al. 2020). The web-based video conferencing platform has been appended to the LMS to provide for an integrated virtual meeting space between teachers and their students. As teachers improve their skills in using this tool, they will presumably modify their pedagogical approach and perhaps even their course learning outcomes to best cohere with this new mode of virtual interaction. A new treasure trove of data is just waiting to be analyzed by educational researchers.

That said, it would be wise to heed the lessons learned from the MOOC (Massive Open Online Course) experience, during which the far-ranging and largest ever educational datasets were collected, yet very little insights about teaching and learning have been gained aside from descriptive observations about learners (e.g. prior learning, where students come from, social class based on the latter, etc.). In a 2014 study on MOOCs, Deboer et al. found that almost all measures logged by the MOOC LMS were correlated, e.g. students who do more assignments watch more videos (or perform more of any other learning activity), those who do more of any activity have higher grades, etc., leading to the trivial conclusion that those who do more learn more. In other words, the clicks and tasks provided little insight into learners' thought processes, motivations and attitudes. To avoid the cul-de-sac of haphazardly gathering large datasets that may yield no meaningful or actionable information, it would make sense to tie the data to established learning theories and perhaps, as Reich (2020) suggests, "to invest in online courses that are designed from the beginning not just for student learning but also for conducting research about learning".

KDD, Data Warehousing and EDM

In a multifaceted environment in which data come from different sources and in different shapes, the concepts of Knowledge Discovery in Data (KDD), data warehousing and data mining offer a wealth of possibilities for learning (ElAtia et al. 2012, Hammad 2009). These techniques are eclectic in nature and combine qualitative as well as quantitative research approaches. They also allow researchers to analyze large amounts of data that are impacted by many unknown variables. The context in which datasets continuously flow in large quantities from disparate sources is inherent to Big Data analytics. The three dimensions that characterize Big Data – volume, velocity, and variety – are a reflection of these large amounts of heterogeneous data constantly streaming from different data sources.

So, how is knowledge produced from such fluctuating heterogeneity? The first step of the KDD hybrid model (Hammad, 2009; Cios et al. 2007) starts by understanding the problem domain. Then, it moves to analyzing the problem data and its multiple dimensions using targeted datasets. In a third step, data collection models and a prototype data warehouse are developed. The data warehouse stores collected data in a ready-for-mining format that can be used for dynamic analytical processing. The final step consists in implementing data mining techniques in case studies using sets of actual education data from an institution of higher education, with a view to assist in decision-making processes and improve organizational effectiveness (Huebner, 2013).

Han and Kamber (2006) define data mining as the "analysis of observational datasets to find unsuspected relationships and to summarize the data in novel ways that are both understandable and useful to the data owners." Likewise, Fayyad, Piatetsky-Shapiro, and Smyth (1996) emphasize the fact that the discovered knowledge that ensues from the data mining procedure must be previously unknown, non-trivial, and genuinely useful to the data owners. Data mining is a multidisciplinary field that involves methods at the intersection of artificial intelligence, machine learning, natural language processing, statistics and database systems. Data mining techniques rely on either supervised or unsupervised learning and are mostly grouped into four categories: clustering, association rules, classification and outlier analysis (Cios et al., 2007). These techniques analyze (usually large-scale) data to discover meaningful patterns such as:

a) natural grouping of data records, i.e. cluster analysis,
b) unusual or unexpected records, i.e. anomaly and outlier detection, or/and
c) dependencies, i.e. association rule mining

Data mining techniques have a very broad range of applications: medical, biological, finance, industrial and corporate. Educational applications of data mining and learning analytics are on an emerging and growing trend due to vast data becoming available from the growing number of courses delivered in e-learning and digital environments. In addition, the MOOC trend, despite their announced demise a few years ago, is accelerating the need for advanced and scalable data mining and analytics techniques for educational data ElAtia & Ipperciel 2015, Zaiane & Yacef 2014, 2015).

EDM applies data mining techniques to explore data originating from educational contexts, and to study educational questions (Romero & Ventura 2010). The unique hierarchical features of educational data (Baker, 2011) provide researchers in educational environment with opportunities to use data mining for investigation. Stemming from and building on the field of data mining in educational settings, LA focuses, as described in the introduction to this chapter, on collecting, measuring, and analyzing data about learners and their learning contexts for the purpose of optimizing these learning contexts. LA bridges between the micro level of data mining and the macro level of educational research (Siemens & Baker, 2012) and aims to understand the learning environment. We were saying earlier that Learning Analytics is data analytics in the context of learning and education; that is, the collection of data about learners' activities and behaviour as well as data about the environment and context in which the learning took place; and the analysis of such data using statistics and data mining techniques with the purpose of extracting relevant patterns from this data to better understand the learning that took place. The objectives of Learning Analytics can either be the reporting of measures and patterns from the data for the understanding of learning activities, or the optimization of the learning activities and strategies or the environments in which the learning occurs. Although EDM and LA often overlap in their methods and techniques, authors often highlight key distinctions between the two: whereas EDM is analytical and focuses on elements and their relationships, LA takes a more holistic view; whereas EDM prioritizes algorithmic discovery, LA is more concerned with human judgment (Liñán & Pérez, 2015).

In recent years, the task of would-be educational data miners has been made much easier by the widespread dissemination of EDM tools, which encompass a host of applications, e.g. data manipulation and feature engineering (for the preparation of data), data labeling, database management, data modeling, algorithmic analysis, data visualization, data processing, text mining and analysis, natural language processing, social network analysis, process mining, etc. (Slater et al., 2017). These tools range from the beginner-friendly (e.g. Excel) to programming heavy (e.g. Spark MLLib).

Stakeholders and Uses of EDM and LA

Both EDM and LA are driven by various stakeholders who seek to understand various educational situations. Their usage can provide valuable information to various stakeholders depending on the needs of each. In this respect, EDM applications and LA can be used to address a range of issues that relate to the following groups of stakeholders in figure #1.

Figure 1. EDM Application Stakeholders

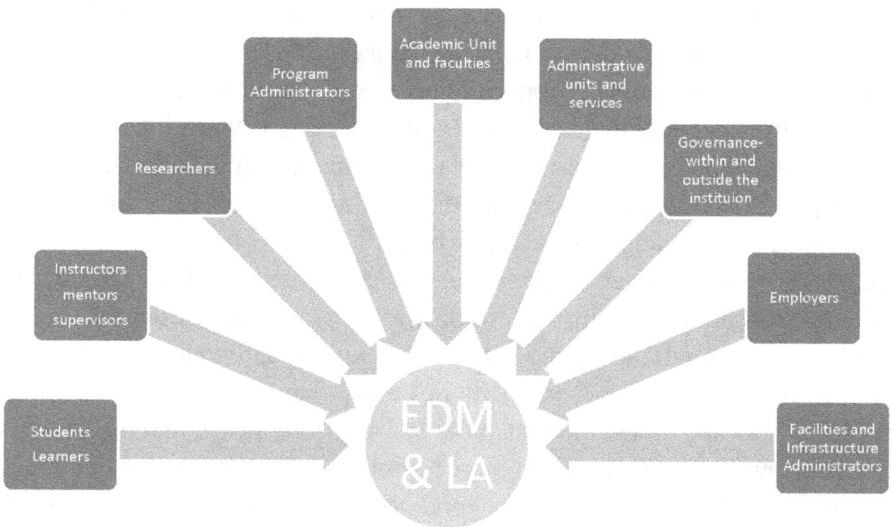

Students, as active participants, are the nucleus of these interdependent relationships. They provide the foundational data for the EDM and LA. Instructors are the other coactive and complementary element of the teaching and learning dyad within the group of stakeholders. By using EDM and LA, and in addition to managing the LMS and supplying data, they seek to understand learner behaviour and interaction with materials, and anticipate news applications within the LMS. They are also attentive to constructive feedback that may redirect their teaching and assessment. For program administrators, applications of EDM and LA can provide evidence related to quality assurance, as well as program and curriculum reviews and revision. For researchers, both in the fields of education and computing sciences, EDM and LA create a new trans- and interdisciplinary tool to conduct research on big data using new methods of data collection and analysis. In our previous work (Behdad et al. 2018), we summarized the various applications of EDM according to stakeholders in a way similar to table 1 below.

Table 1. Stakeholders Uses of EDM Applications (Adapted from Behdad et al 20181)

	Students	Educators	Administrators	Researchers
Predicting performance		X	X	
Predicting characteristics		X	X	
Detecting behaviour (un and desirable)		X	X	
Profiling and Grouping	X	X		
Social Network Analysis		X		X
Providing reports	X	X	X	
Creating and sending alerts		X	X	
Planning and scheduling	X	X	X	
Constructing courseware		X		
Developing Concept Maps		X		X
Generating recommendation	X	X		
Providing feedback	X	X	X	
Evaluation		X	X	
Adaptive systems	X			
Scientific inquiry				X

No matter the stakeholders and their interest and implication, LA and EDM application can be organized into two categories: (a) overall student experience, and (b) overall decision support systems. Back in 2010, Romero & Ventura provided 11 categories for EDM applications, these are:

- Analysis and Visualization of Data
- Providing Feedback for Supporting Instructors
- Recommendations for Students
- Predicting Student's Performance
- Student Modeling
- Detecting Undesirable Student Behaviors
- Grouping Students
- Social Network Analysis
- Developing Concept Maps
- Constructing Courseware
- Planning and Scheduling

Past research has shown that some EDM techniques are best suited to specific pedagogical problems (Aldowah, 2019). For instance, classification has been successfully used to predict – among other things – student performance and dropout, while clustering has been applied to student interaction in a variety of learning situations; association rule has enabled instructors to better structure learning material, while text mining was useful in automatic assessment (as in online discussion forums).

LA and EDM can be powerful tools to address major issues that have been at the center of education, whether for effective teaching and learning, student engagement, retention, promotion of minority groups within certain disciplines or valid and fair assessment. Advances in the field follow two major paths. On the one hand, we have technical advances in the use of AI, algorithms used for LA and EDM, the reporting of results and the visualization used to interpret results (e.g. Wang & Zaiane 2018; Valrstar et al 2020, Lothian et al. 2019; Tan & Wu 2018). On the other hand, the application of these advances can answer research questions related to higher education issues and challenges, ranging from questions of integration of minority and indigenous population (Demmans et al 2017; Demmans & Phirangee 2019), assessment (ElAtia & Ipperciel 2020), student interaction with class materials (Hou et al. 2018), etc. The list is extensive, with multiple scholarly journals around the world dedicated exclusively to LA and EDM. However, as both advances and paths intersect, the important issue of confidentiality and data privacy arises.

As this chapter suggests, it is clear to all that EDM and LA hold immense *potential* in advancing sound pedagogy, student-centered perspectives and curricular improvement, although there is still little substantial scientific evidence of impact and success, mainly because most LA implementations are still in the early phase of adoption (Tsai et al. 2020). In addition, there are major obstacles to the uptake of EDM and LA, the most obvious being the lack of computational and statistical training among most educators, although more and more low- or no-code EDM applications are coming to market and having a mitigating effect. Tsai et al. 2020 identify four challenges that impede LA from developing to its full potential: stakeholder engagement and buy-in, weak pedagogical grounding (which we address below under "At the Intersection of Two Fields"), resource demands and, finally, ethics and privacy. This fourth challenge is the focus of the next section.

Privacy, Confidentiality and Ethical Consideration

Certainly, the issue of privacy as it relates to data mining is more prevalent in situations involving business dealings, targeted advertising, banking, healthcare, social networking, internet searches, genetic material, and the like. In education, this issue has not been much debated, although questions can be raised with regard to its ethicality and legality. The use of technology, of data mining and LA techniques in particular, can be intrusive. According to Holmes (2008), privacy issues historically arose in Canada in the late 1960's when computers were first being used on a large scale by government and large corporations. Even with the best of intentions, as in algorithms attempting to predict future failure or success in students, private information can be improperly gathered. In these cases, as in others, the collection of data is subject to clearly defined rules.

Any attempt to use EDM and LA needs to be anchored and well established within a clearly defined ethics, privacy and confidentiality framework (ElAtia & Ipperciel 2012, 2019). There are dangers of mishandling private and personal data, and we believe that by working in an educational environment, and by collaborating with the institution's Information and Privacy offices, researchers are better poised to safeguard students' and units' privacy and interests. As EDM and LA become more mainstream within our online teaching, especially in the context of the COVID-19 pandemic that gave institutions the much needed push to work online, institutions of higher education will reflect on the tools and protocols that are needed to carry out in-house data mining studies, allowing them to benefit from their own information in ways that align with their mission and vision, without seeking outside help in the matter, a practice that might jeopardize the liberty, integrity, and privacy of both institution and students.

To best avoid the ethical pitfalls tied to mining individual data, one should make sure to respect the basic normative rules of data ethics, i.e. individual control, transparency, accountability and equality (Tranberg et al. 2018). In every study, participants should have control over their data, i.e. which data is collected, how it is used and in which context. The data processes should be transparent to participants, which goes beyond just making the information accessible to users, but also making sure the information is understandable to them. Researchers, teachers and academic administrators should also be accountable in their use of data, making every possible attempt to reduce risk to participants, whether in their own involvement or that of partners and subcontractors. Finally, by adhering to the principle of equality, they remain sensitive to how vulnerable groups fare. This is particular important while using artificial intelligence, where past applications have been discriminatory to protected groups (Prince & Schwarcz, 2020; Todolí-Signes, 2019). In the end, all these principles boil down to the overarching principle of human centeredness. If people remain at the center of all consideration and are thought of as the primary beneficiaries of EDM, the proper ethical conditions should be generally satisfied.

Yet, even when researchers follow all these normative rules and principles with the best of intentions, concerns can be, and are, nonetheless raised. This results from the mere fact that holding vast amounts of private and confidential data is inherently risky. No data custodian intends for their data to be breached, but it happens all the time. This is not an abstract risk. In 2020 alone, major cyberattacks in higher education were conducted against Maastricht University, Niagara University, Simon Fraser University, Illinois Valley Community College, University of Arkansas for Medical Sciences, York University, Ruhr University Bochum, Michigan State University, University of California (San Francisco), Blackbaud (alumni and fundraising), University of Utah, Newcastle University, University Hospital New Jersey, etc. Many of these institutions have had to pay a ransom to hackers (between $220,00 and $1.1M[2]) to avoid private and confidential student data disclosure, and even those who managed to avoid paying ransom incurred hefty recovery costs. Furthermore, the risk of disclosure grows over time, as the volume of data and the technical sophistication for data analysis and cross-reference increase. That is why data collection and storage must constantly be submitted to a cost-benefit analysis, e.g. a balance between the harm to students through data breaches and the benefits of improving the learning experience in a specific project. In the end, there is no easy solution to the ethical conundrums faced by researchers in the field of learning analytics. It is an inherently problematic and thorny aspect of data science (including LA and EDM) to deal with.

And to make things even more complex, the field of education has strong political dimensions that must also be taken into consideration. In this context, issues of "power" are raised (i.e. the exercise of power and the unequal distribution of power between the data scientist and the student), repressive systems that aim to control, the impact on marginalized populations (especially minorities such as queer people, indigenous people, racialized people, etc.), the potential for "administrative violence" of wanting to fit certain people into certain categories, "surveillance capitalism," etc. Debates around these issues in the context of LA are lively and ongoing (Selwyn 2019, 2020; Prinsloo 2019)

To make sure the principles described above are respected and researchers have the proper support in making the cost-benefit analysis, it is common practice to involve institutional ethics review boards in EM and LA projects (Richterich, 2018). These bodies ensure more than legal compliance, which is only a first, albeit necessary, step in approval processes. Beyond legality, it is crucial that researchers, teachers and academic administrators maintain trust and reputational integrity among users (Yoost, 2019). Without such trust, the future of EDM and LA would be rather uncertain.

At the Intersection of Two Fields

Another issue that hampers the advance of LA and EDM relates to its multidisciplinary nature or, more pointedly, to the fact that it seems to be falling between the proverbial two stools. As far back as 2010, *The Chronicles of Higher Education* raised an important issue in an editorial article by Marc Parry. It states that academia is "at a computational crossroads" when it comes to big data and analytics in education. The trans-interdisciplinary nature of EDM and LA squarely sits between two distinct fields of study, i.e. education and computing sciences. Advances in LA and EDM techniques are applied in the context of teaching, assessment, classroom management and curriculum management in education and educational research with an aim to presenting a comprehensive picture and in-depth analyses of specific issues. Yet, for the field of EDM to be truly 'educational' (and for LA to be truly about 'learning'), it would reasonably need to include various stakeholders and researchers in the educational fields proper. However, most of the advances in LA and EDM so far have been carried out with a computing science lens by mainly computing scientists and engineers. Educational researchers have, thus far, played a side role within LA and EDM, with very few exceptions. As a result, advances in LA and EDM often lack the grounding in educational theory. There is arguably a need for new programs that train graduates who can have a foot in both fields, are well versed in both the computational and pedagogical fields and who can truly advance data mining in education.

Being at the juncture of two disciplines, EDM and LA open up knowledge sources in both fields to practitioners, educators, computer scientists, graduate students, and university administrators. EDM and LA can be advanced only if researchers can work with a deep understanding and respect for both the social and computer sciences. This is both a challenge and an opportunity. In our opinion, four issues would need to be addressed to properly implement, use and advance EDM and LA in higher education and in education in general: training, resources, quality assurance, and diversity.

Proper training for practitioners from both fields is essential; on the one hand, learning and teaching methods, learning strategies, and valid assessment methods; on the other hand, learning about the workings of the e-learning environment, coding, data analysis. Instructors, researchers, students and IT personnel all need to be trained to handle both sides of the equation: education and computational techniques. They need to be engaged and aware of strengths and drawbacks in both fields.

Quality assurance in LA and EDM ranges from selecting the proper tools and algorithms to implementing adequate and valid assessment, as well as adopting teaching and delivery methods and shaping learning itself. Quality assurance also addresses issues of reliability and feasibility and validity of EDM results in analyzing educational data. For instance, are the learning outcomes truly reflected in LA/EDM analyses? In the data acquisition model? Quality assurance pertains to the validity and the appropriateness of the instrument itself.

Finally, a major focus of EDM and LA should be diversity. EDM should be viewed as a tool to improve the manifold learning experiences and, ultimately, the richness of higher education in general. It should strive to bring out the unique characteristics of each learning setting and context, each experience, each program and field of study and research. It should certainly not become a pretext for the standardization of practices and course or program content. The temptation is great to have a single all-encompassing mould of learning, which would lead to homogenization and ossification of experiences and knowledge, and consequently to its impoverishment. EDM should certainly seek to appreciate the diversity of learning contents in order to ensure a critical and multifaceted approach to learning in higher education.

CONCLUSION

In the global context, we believe institutions of higher education are well equipped to take on the use of computational resources for educational research that goes beyond current classroom practices, thereby greatly improving the education experience. Using LA and data mining is helpful from a macro-level of assessing students' academic progress for retention and for addressing potential problems (e.g. at-risk students), to a micro-level of ensuring a better learning experience and the involvement of students in taking control and being actively engaged in their own learning. For teaching, EDM and LA are valuable tools for formative feedback on teaching methods and course contents. Kumar & Chadha (2011) presented a survey on case studies that effectively applied educational data mining techniques to improve learners' and teachers' experience.

When data from various units within an institution are made accessible for data mining, new relationships and trends emerge, which are crucial in addressing the major issues of education, such as student retention, assisting at-risk students well in advance of any actual problems, and ensuring that the academic progress is smooth. Data mining techniques on integrated data can enhance general institution decision-making processes, whether in suggesting for example courses that might be more valuable for each class of learners or to assist in admitting students who will most likely do well in their university studies (Romero & Ventura 2010). Furthermore, with the budget crunches that postsecondary institutions have been facing in the current economic climate and the pandemic situation, it would be fruitful to look at the big picture through the wealth of data integrated from all departments and units in an institution. Computational techniques will offer a unique opportunity to show new connections and new insights. LA and EDM at this level aim to find the best way to utilize available resources more effectively, to enhance the educational program and determine the effectiveness of different learning environments such as distance learning.

With data mining, we do not know which ultimate connections will be discovered—it is truly a tool that lets the data speak without any manipulation from outside forces, particularly personal views and researcher biases. Data can reveal patterns that no one could have foreseen. Most importantly, it takes into consideration the uniqueness of elements in the dataset and enables handling data according to the supplied information in a longitudinal manner.

LA, too, holds much potential, although the dearth of implementations is still a major impediment to collecting substantial experimental evidence to its impact on learning. The obstacles against implementation are known and can be addressed at the institutional, stakeholder, pedagogical and resource levels, as well as through an awareness of ethical issues. If EDM and LA projects can be done in an ethical manner that respects basic principles of data ethics and make human centeredness the focus of one's work, and if this emerging field can combine both computational and pedagogical forces, EDM and LA promise to have a tremendous impact on the future educational setting. Indeed, the future will be bright for higher education.

REFERENCES

Aldowah, H., Al-Samarraie, H., & Fauzy, W. M. (2019). Educational data mining and learning analytics for 21st century higher education: A review and synthesis. *Telematics and Informatics, 37*, 13–49.

Baker, R. (2010). Data mining for education. In B. McGaw, P. Peterson, & E. Baker (Eds.), *International encyclopedia of education* (3rd ed., Vol. 7, pp. 112–118). Elsevier. doi:10.1016/B978-0-08-044894-7.01318-X

Baker, R. S., & Yacef, K. (2009). The state of educational data mining in 2009: A review and future visions. *Journal of Educational Data Mining, 1*(1), 3–17.

Bakhshinategh, B., Zaiane, O., ElAtia, S., & Ipperciel, D. (2018). Educational data mining applications and tasks: A Survey of the Last 10 Years. *Journal of Education Information Technology, 23*(1), 537–553. doi:10.100710639-017-9616-z

Cios, K., Pedrycz, W., Swiniarski, R., & Kurgan, L. (2007). *Data mining: A knowledge discovery approach.* Springer.

DeBoer, J., Ho, A. D., Stump, G. S., & Breslow, L. (2014). Changing "Course": Reconceptualizing Educational Variables for Massive Open Online Courses. *Educational Researcher, 43*(2), 74–84. doi:10.3102/0013189X14523038

Demmans Epp, C. (2019). Developing an Adaptive Mobile Tool to Scaffold the Communication and Vocabulary Acquisition of Language Learners. In Y. Zhang & D. Cristol (Eds.), *Handbook of Mobile Teaching and Learning* (2nd ed., pp. 1–26). Springer.

Demmans Epp, C., & Phirangee, K. (2019). Exploring mobile tool integration: Design activities carefully or students may not learn. *Contemporary Educational Psychology, 59*, 101791. doi:10.1016/j.cedpsych.2019.101791

Demmans Epp, C., Phirangee, K., & Hewitt, J. (2017). Talk with Me: Student Behaviours and Pronoun Use as Indicators of Discourse Health across Facilitation Methods. *Journal of Learning Analytics, 4*(3), 47–75. doi:10.18608/jla.2017.43.4

ElAtia, S., & Ipperciel, D. (2011). *Advancing educational research through a Knowledge Discovery in Data (KDD) model.* Paper presented at the American Educational Research Association annual convention, New Orleans, LA.

ElAtia, S., & Ipperciel, D. (2015). At the Intersection of Computer Sciences and Online Education: Fundamental Consideration in MOOCs Education. *Educational Letter, 11*(2), 2–7.

ElAtia,S., Ipperciel, D., Bakhshinategh, B., Zaiane, O.R. & Thibaudeau, P. (2020). Graduate Attribute Assessment Program. *The International Journal of Information and Learning Technology, 38*(3), 25-45.

ElAtia, S., Ipperciel, D., & Hammad, A. (2012). Implications and challenges to using data mining in educational research in the Canadian context. *Canadian Journal of Education, 35*(2), 101–119.

ElAtia, S., Ipperciel, D., & Zaiane, O. R. (2016). *Data Mining and Learning Analytics: Applications in Educational Research*. Wiley & Sons. doi:10.1002/9781118998205

Fayyad, U., Piatetsky-Shapiro, G., & Smyth, P. (1996). From data mining to knowledge discovery in databases. *AI Magazine, 17*(3), 37.

Hammad, A. M. (2009). *An integrated framework for managing labour resources data in industrial construction projects: A Knowledge Discovery in Data (KDD) approach* (Unpublished doctoral dissertation). University of Alberta, Canada.

Han, J., & Kamber, M. (2006). *Data mining: Concepts and techniques*. Morgan Kaufmann.

Hasan, R., Palaniappan, S., Mahmood, S., Abbas, A., Sarker, K. U., & Sattar, M. U. (2020). Predicting Student Performance in Higher Educational Institutions Using Video Learning Analytics and Data Mining Techniques. *Applied Sciences (Basel, Switzerland), 10*(11), 3894. doi:10.3390/app10113894

Hou, Y., Zhou, P., Xu, J., & Wu, D. O. (2018). Course recommendation of MOOC with big data support: A contextual online learning approach. *IEEE INFOCOM 2018 - IEEE Conference on Computer Communications Workshops (INFOCOM WKSHPS)*, 106–111.

Huebner, R. A. (2013). A survey of educational data-mining research. *Journal of Research In Higher Education*. Retrieved on February 20, 2013 from http://www.aabri.com/manuscripts/121328. pdf

Ipperciel, D., & ElAtia, S. (2015). Towards a 21st Century Competency-Based Model of Higher Education: The pragmatics of Accountability. *International Journal of Advances in Education, 1*(1), 5–12.

Kumar, V., & Chadha, A. (2011). An empirical study of the applications of data mining techniques in higher education. *International Journal of Advanced Computer Science and Applications, 2*(3), 80–84.

Liñán, C., & Pérez, J. (2015). Educational Data Mining and Learning Analytics: Differences, similarities, and time evolution. RUSC. *Universities and Knowledge Society Journal, 12*(3), 98–112. doi:10.7238/rusc.v12i3.2515

Lothian, D., Akcayir, G., & Demmans Epp, C. (2019). Accommodating Indigenous People When Using Technology to Learn Their Ancestral Language. In O. (Adewoyin) Olakanmi, O. Ishola, G. McCalla, I. Adaji, & F. J. Gutierrez (Eds.), *International Workshop on Supporting Lifelong Learning co-located with the 20th International Conference on Artificial Intelligence in Education.* Academic Press.

Naveh, G., Tubin, D., & Pliskin, N. (2012). Student satisfaction with learning management systems: A lens of critical success factors. *Technology, Pedagogy and Education, 21*(3), 337–350. doi:10.1080/1475939X.2012.720413

Parry, M. (2010). The Humanities Go Google. *The Chronicles of Higher Education.* http://chronicle.com/article/The-Humanities-Go-Google/65713/

Prince, A. E. R., & Schwarcz, D. (2020, March). Proxy Discrimination in the Age of Artificial Intelligence and Big Data. *Iowa Law Review, 105*(3), 1257.

Prinsloo, P. (2019). Learning analytics: Mapping a critique and agenda. *Journal of Learning Analytics, 6*(3), 20–24.

Reich, J. (2020). *Failure to Disrupt. Why Technology Alone Can't Transform Education.* Harvard University Press. doi:10.4159/9780674249684

Richterich, A. (2018). *The Big Data Agenda : Data Ethics and Critical Data Studies.* University of Westminster Press. doi:10.2307/j.ctv5vddsw

Romero, C., & Ventura, S. (2010). Educational data mining: A review of the state of the art. *Systems, Man, and Cybernetics, Part C: Applications and Reviews, IEEE Transactions on, 40*(6), 601-618.

Selwyn, N. (2019). What's the problem with Learning Analytics? *Journal of Learning Analytics, 6*(3), 11–19. doi:10.18608/jla.2019.63.3

Selwyn, N. (2020). Re-imagining 'Learning Analytics'… a case for starting again? *The Internet and Higher Education, 46,* 1–5. doi:10.1016/j.iheduc.2020.100745

Siemens, G., & Baker, R. (2012). Learning analytics and educational data mining: Towards communication and collaboration. *Proceedings of the 2nd International Conference on Learning Analytics and Knowledge,* 252-254. 10.1145/2330601.2330661

Siemens, G., & Long, P. (2011). Penetrating the fog: Analytics in learning and education. *EDUCAUSE Review, 46*(5), 31–40.

Slater, S., Joksimović, S., Kovanovic, V., Baker, R. S., & Gasevic, D. (2017). Tools for Educational Data Mining: A Review. *Journal of Educational and Behavioral Statistics*, *42*(1), 85–106. doi:10.3102/1076998616666808

Tan, M., & Wu, M. (2018). An Association Rule Model of Course Recommendation in MOOCs: Based on edX Platform. *European Scientific Journal*, *14*(25), 284. doi:10.19044/esj.2018.v14n25p284

Todolí-Signes, A. (2019). Algorithms, artificial intelligence and automated decisions concerning workers and the risks of discrimination: The necessary collective governance of data protection. *Transfer: European Review of Labour and Research*, *25*(4), 465–481. doi:10.1177/1024258919876416

Tranberg, P., Hasselbalch, G., Olsen, B. K., & Byrne, C. S. (2018). *Data Ethics. Principles and Guidelines for Companies, Authorities & Organisations*. DataEthics.eu. The Independent Thinktank.

Tsai, Y. S., Rates, D., Moreno-Marcos, P. M., Muñoz-Merino, P. J., Jivet, I., Scheffel, M., ... Gašević, D. (2020). Learning analytics in European higher education–trends and barriers. *Computers & Education*, *1555*, 1–16.

Valstar, S., Sih, C., Krause-Levy, S., Porter, L., & Griswold, W. G. (2020). A Quantitative Study of Faculty Views on the Goals of an Undergraduate CS Program and Preparing Students for Industry. *Proceedings of the 2020 ACM Conference on International Computing Education Research*, 113–123.

Wang, R., & Zaïane, O. R. (2018). Sequence-Based Approaches to Course Recommender Systems. In S. Hartmann, H. Ma, A. Hameurlain, G. Pernul, & R. R. Wagner (Eds.), Database and Expert Systems Applications (Vol. 11029, pp. 35–50). Springer International Publishing. doi:10.1007/978-3-319-98809-2_3

Wang, V. C. (2014). *Handbook of research on education and technology in a changing society*. IGI Global. doi:10.4018/978-1-4666-6046-5

Yoost, D. (2019). Data Ethics: Beyond Legal Compliance. *The RMA Journal, 101*(8), 16–23.

Zaiane, O. R., & Yacef, K. (2015). MOOCs are not MOOCs Yet: Requirements for a True MOOC or MOOC 2.0. *Educational Letter*, *11*(2), 17–21.

ENDNOTES

1 This is adapted from our previous work on a survey of EDM application in the last 10 years.

2 Maastricht University: $220,000; University of California, San Francisco: $1.4M (hackers invited BBC to the negotiations), University of Utah: $457,000; University Hospital New Jersey: $670,000. For the most dramatic occurrence at University of California, San Francisco.

Chapter 6
The Practice of Gaining Universal Values Based on Learning Analytics Framework:
Universal Values and Learning Analytics

Nedime Karasel Ayda
Faculty of Education, University of Kyrenia, Cyprus

Zehra Altinay
Societal Research and Development Center, Faculty of Education, Near East University, Cyprus

Fahriye Altinay
Societal Research and Development Center, Faculty of Education, Institute of Graduate Studies, Near East University, Cyprus

Gokmen Dagli
University of Kyrenia, Cyprus

Ebba Ossiannilsson
https://orcid.org/0000-0002-8488-5787
International Council for Open and Distance Education (ICDE), Norway & European Distance and e-Learning Network (EDEN), UK & Swedish Association for Distance Education (SADE), Sweden

DOI: 10.4018/978-1-7998-7103-3.ch006

ABSTRACT

This chapter encapsulates the framework of learning analytics. It is aimed to evaluate leisure activities and practices of students in learning outcomes based on the role of learning analytics framework. Qualitative research method was employed, and action research was conducted through activities to the 33 students. Data was analyzed based on content analysis. Metaphoric understanding and analysis of perceptions on activities were evaluated within the framework of learning analytics. It is seen that students felt the value of practice-based activities, and they become satisfied in their leisure times with different activities. In-service training is essential for teachers to develop the practice of leisure education.

INTRODUCTION

Education has changed its nature and transformation become crucial. Re-construction of knowledge becomes important and there is a need to foster an engaged learning and collective learning environments based on sharing, practicing and experiences. Therefore, learning process encapsulates the importance of values, feelings while making learning sustainable and ongoing for the life standandards. Information technology, and the use of technology makes learners connected and enriches the meaningful learning (Altınay Altınay, Dagli, Altınay, 2018). Collaboration and coordination to diffuse transformation in educational activities is important. Therefore, agile management in schools for adapting changes and development is essential. In practicing leisure activities in more efficient way, school management and culture is also needed (Tokel at. al, 2019).

In today's context, learning analytics is important to give directions of learners based on learning environments and management. In this respect, learning analytics is defined as the use of advanced tools in learnin and instruction. It is a level of analyzing for construction educational data mining. The use of online learning environments plays a great role to foster learning analytics. In this respect, it is the measurement, collection, analysis and reporting of data about learners and learners' contexts (Gašević at. al., 2015).

Improving students learning in education is crucial aspects of sustainable quality in the practices. Teachers need to focus on activities and give importance to leisure times to put a balance between cognitive goals with psychomotor and emotional learning goals. To support learning of learners, there is an intensified need to concentrate on universal values to add a value for lifelong learning experiences. In this respect, leisure education is crucial and social learning analytics makes a stance for supporting learning (Shum and Ferguson, 2012). Participatory learning enriches the merits of merging with theory and practice withing the construction of knowledge. Therefore, focusing on the feelings and perceptions of learners while engaging activities create a database on intrinsic motivations and intentions to the learning.

This research was adapted to the learning analytics framework while students have engaged learning activities based on universal values. It is aimed to evaluate leisure activities and practices of students in learning outcomes based on the role of learning analytics framework.

THEORETICAL FRAMEWORK

Universal Values and Value Education

Value is the sensitivity of a person against any individual, situation, event or entity, based on the concept of human (Yaman, 2012). Value; These are common thoughts, goals, basic moral principles or beliefs that are accepted as right and necessary by the majority of its members in order to ensure and sustain a society or group's own existence, unity, functioning and continuity (Özgüven, 1999). Value; that we attach importance to in life and determines the direction of our lives (Doğanay, 2006); showing the desired and desired situations and undesirable situations (Gari, Mylonas and Karagianni, 2005); showing accepted and approved standards of behavior (Yılmaz, 2008); It consists of attitudes, beliefs and thoughts that affect behaviors (Demircioğlu, 2013).

The values adopted in a society can vary between societies. The reason for this is that the values adopted in societies are shaped depending on the cultural structure of the society. For example; hospitality (Turkey), courage (Japan), gizlikik (USA) and so on. value is values that vary by country. These variable structures of values are one of their most fundamental properties. However, there are values that are accepted as common by the countries of the world. These values are accepted as "Universal Values" by researchers. According to Taşçı and Koç (2007), there are positive features that can be used by every person without geographical limitation and these features do not differ from society to society. For example; There are also universal values such as love, respect, diligence and tolerance that are accepted as common for countries.

Most of the studies on universal values and education (Yıldırım and Turan, 2015; Candan and Ergen, 2014; Yalar and Yelken, 2011; Memiş and Gedik, 2010), concepts such as "righteousness, justice, family, love, respect, tolerance, peace, honesty, cleanliness" have been analyzed and accepted as universal values. However, concepts such as "equality, respect for differences, diversity and acceptance, and consideration of the well-being of others", which have an important place in our lives and that we constantly encounter in our lives, have been ignored in studies (Karasel, Altınay, Altınay and Dağlı, 2018).

In addition to keeping up with the developing and changing world, every society has an effort to convey social culture and these sensitivities to future generations. At this point, value education to be given to individuals gains importance. It is seen in the literature researches that there are many definitions about value education. If we look at some of these definitions; Values Education Study (VES) value education; while explaining values as skills and activities to be used in the step of acquiring knowledge of values, understanding values and applying values (2003); Dilmaç (1999) sees value education as a versatile combination of education and ethics. Kaplan (2014) sees value education as a tool to create the desired behavioral change in societies and to increase the right behavior. Demircioğlu and Demircioğlu (2014) as a process of transferring and adopting value education, acceptable behaviors in the society we live in; Ekşi (2003) defines it as appeasing individuals who are academically successful and respect the basic values adopted by the society.

We can say that value education studies with a history dating back to ancient times started from the schools established in the Chinese and Sumerians period. When the writings written by the Sumerians were examined; values such as justice, truthfulness, forgiveness and freedom are given importance (Kramer, 2002); In Chinese schools, it can be said that the education of values is emphasized in the teachings of Buddha and Confucius (Küken, 2003).

Value education studies started to take place in education as concepts of "moral and value education", especially with the opening of systematic schools in the late 19th and early 20th centuries (VES, 2003). While the researches on character education in the USA in the 1920s continued in a popular manner in the early years, this popularity declined in the 1930s and did not show a great improvement until the 1960s. However, in the second half of the 1960s, with the effects of the World War, the education of national goals gains importance again (Kirschenbaum, 2000). While names such as How, Harmin and Krischenbaum came to the fore with their works in the period that developed after the World War II, the concept of character education leaves its place to the concept of "value education" (Arthur, 2005).

Learning Analytics

Learning analytics is the collection, measurement, analysis and reporting of data on learners and their situations in order to understand and optimize learning and learning environments (Siemens and Gasevic 2012). Learning analytics are more specific than academic analytics. In learning analytics; While focusing on the learning process, including the analysis of the relationship between learner, content, institution and trainer; academic analytics mostly focus on institutional level analysis (Long and Siemens, 2011).

The purpose of learning analytics is to allow teachers and schools to adapt educational opportunities according to the needs and skill levels of each student (Freeman, Becker, Cummins, Davis, and Hall Giesinger, 2017). In the researches; It has been observed that the use of analytics in education has increased in recent years for four main reasons. These; significant increase in the amount of data can be counted as advanced data formats, advances in computational calculations, and the sophistication of existing tools for Analytics (Baker and Siemens, 2014).

The applications of learning analytics also differ according to different purposes. The most common goal estimation studies focusing on the development of managerial decision making (Barngrover, 2017). Structure discovery studies, on the other hand, focus on finding the structure in data without a prior idea of what needs to be found (Baker and Siemens, 2014). Similarly, it is possible to talk about many different learning analytics applications such as relationship mining, usage tracking, content analysis, semantic analysis, suggestion engine.

The methods and techniques used for different learning analytics applications are also changing. Structure discovery algorithms try to find the structure in the data without a prior idea of what needs to be found (Baker and Siemens, 2014). In the predictive model, there is a certain variable that is tried to be modeled. Clustering analysis, on the other hand, is a classification method used to categorize data into groups, and the purpose of the method is to classify ungrouped data according to their similarities and provide summary information to the researcher. In Factor Analysis, the purpose is to find variables that are naturally grouped together and to separate the variable set into a series of implicit factors that cannot be directly observed in contrast to data points (Baker and Siemens, 2014). Factor analysis is also used to develop predictive models in learning environments. Social Network Analysis (SNA) refers to the analysis of metadata to determine the types of students' participation in educational environments (Avella, Kebritchi, and G. Nunn, 2016). Social Network Analysis aims to examine the relationships between individuals instead of individual characteristics or these characteristics, and to create models from patterns emerging from these relationships (Baker and Siemens, 2014). Domain Structure Discovery; It consists of finding the structure of knowledge in an educational field, such as how a certain content is mapped from student to student according to certain components of knowledge or skills (Baker and Siemens, 2014). In Association Rule Mining, the goal is to explore the relationships between variables in a data set containing a large number of variables. A simple association rule expresses the relationship of one item to another, that is, a simple linear relationship (Daniel, 2015). In this method, conditional statements (if / then / else) are used to reveal the relationship between information in the database. The purpose of its associated rules is to find regular patterns that occur in a data set over a period of time (Poonsirivong, 2018).

METHOD

Model of the Research

This research is modeled with qualitative research method. Qualitative research method is a method preferred especially in the field of social sciences, aiming to examine human behavior and the causes of these behaviors deeply (Güler, at. al.,2013). According to the "action research" Stringer (2008), which is used in the research and now known as "action research" or "teacher research"; the process of conducting systematic experiments and applying solutions to find solutions to the problems encountered in one's life; According to the definition of Kemims, McTaggart and Nixon (2014), it is a spiral cycle such as planning, implementation, reflection, re-planning, trying the new, detecting new reflections after the problem is detected.

Sample of the Study

In this research, which was carried out using the Action Research method, a class and students to determine the implementation plan were determined in accordance with the action research. Since the researcher was also a classroom teacher, he preferred to carry out the practices in his class for 15 weeks. Accordingly, the student group of the research consists of 33 students studying in the 3rd grade, which is the researcher's own class.

In the study, the student group purpose sampling approach was selected in accordance with the "easily accessible case sampling". Easily accessible status sampling generally refers to a working environment where the researcher's transportation is comfortable and where he / she will not have any problems while getting permission (Yıldırım and Şimşek, 2018). Easily accessible or "convenient sampling" is based on the items that are completely available, fast and easy to access (Patton, 2005).

Data Collection Tool and Data Collection

In order to provide students with some values within the scope of value education, metaphor study was carried out in the classroom where the applications were made, in the 3rd week of the application process, in order to reveal the views of the students about the applications. The concept of metaphor; is the explanation of a concept, phenomenon or event by comparing it to another concept, phenomenon or event (Oxford et al., 1998). Metaphors; expressing a person in a way he perceives a concept or phenomenon, i.e. using analogies (Aydın, 2010).

The second activity for collecting data was to get opinions from students. The interviews were held in class environment, groups of three with similar characteristics were held and the focus group interview technique was used. Focus group interviews; It is a qualitative data collection technique that prioritizes the subjectivity of individuals and is used in action researches recently (Yılmaz and Oğuz, 2011).

Application Steps of the Research

The framework of the research relies on learning analytics. Measurement, collection, analysis and reporting of data about learners and their contexts have done based on learning analytics. In the applications performed, different activities were carried out, and each activity is directed towards a universal value previously determined by the researchers. The applications / activities and the values aimed to be taught are as follows:

Intended Values and Course Objectives

- Developing self-confidence
- Discovering individual differences
- Respecting people's differences
- Using body language
- Creating environmental awareness
- To gain respect for the environment
- Empathy with the carcass he watches
- Creating environmental awareness
- Processing of healthy nutrition
- Awareness raising around people
- To gain problem solving skills
- Gaining love of Atatürk
- Making the given project subject in harmony with the group
- Improving experimental skills
- Curiosity to discover
- Improving creativity
- To gain awareness of waste materials evaluation
- Improving language skills
- Raising awareness of individuals with disabilities
- Act without disrupting group integrity

- Empathizing with people who do not have the ability to speak
- Describing the given animal images using body language
- Improving reasoning skills
- Improving creativity
- To gain the ability to use mathematics in daily life
- Paying attention to what they see and what they see around

Data Analysis

Semi-structured interview forums, metaphors and student drawings used to obtain qualitative data in the research were analyzed by content analysis technique. Content analysis is a systematic analysis of written and oral material, and it is coded and quantitated by spelling (Balcı, 2004). According to Miles and Huberman (1994), the content analysis technique used in the research is done in four stages. These stages are: Data coding, finding and creating themes, organizing data according to codes and themes. Identification and interpretation of the findings.

FINDINGS AND COMMENT

What are the metaphorical symbols expressed by elementary school 3rd grade students for activities aimed at adding value within the scope of learning analytics?

Table 1. Metaphor concepts of students for activities

METAPHOR	f	%
Entertainment	7	21,2
Playing games	6	18,2
Be free	4	12,2
Recress	3	9,1
Learning with fun	2	6,1
Having a good time	2	6,1
Exciting events	2	6,1
Making a project	2	6,1
Have a good time	2	6,1
Once said *	3	9,1
TOTAL	**33**	**100**
*(Lesson, taking responsibility, doing sports)		

The answer from the students is given in table 1. Expressing metaphors about the applications, 33 elementary school students used 13 different metaphors about the applications made for the purpose of value education. While the most used metaphors are “Entertainment” (21.2%) and “Playing” (18.2%), respectively, in alphabetical order; “Lessons, taking responsibility and playing sports” have been the metaphors that are said only once. Examples of the metaphors expressed by students can be given as follows:

“It is similar to entertainment because; Time is very fast and fun in the lessons we do these activities.”(S-12)

“It is like playing games because; in these events we play silent cinema and do ball events.” (S -5)

“It is similar to the lesson because; we do mathematics, life studies lesson.”(S -20)

“It is like doing sports because; we walk and play ball.”(S -13)

“It is like taking responsibility because; we do experiments and we need to bring materials for them. If we do not bring the materials, we cannot experiment.”(S -32)

What feelings did the students feel during the construction of the activities?

Table 2 shows the feelings of children, who are students in the classroom, where the practices are carried out for a period of time. As can be seen in the table, in the classroom of 33 students, students expressed a total of 52 emotions. When the expressed emotions are gathered under two main themes, a very large number of positive emotional expressions (N = 47) come from the students; some (N = 5) negative statements were received.

Table 2. Emotions experienced by students in free time activities

MAIN THEME	THEME	N
Positive emotions	*Fun (N=23)* *Happily (N=14)* *Enjoyable (N=5)* *Funny (N=2)* *Relaxing (N=2)* *Beautiful (N=1)*	47
Negative emotions	*Boring (N=3)* *Compelling (N=2)*	5
	TOTAL	**52**

It is seen in the table that the most frequently said applications from the student emotional expressions are "fun" (N = 23), and the most frequently expressed emotional expressions are the "boring" applications (N = 3). The positive and negative expressions of students about the subject can be exemplified as follows:

"Applications are very fun and enjoyable activities." (S-13)

"These activities, which are made different from other classes in our class, make me happy." (S-5)

"The activities we do outside are enjoyable." (S-15)

"I think applications are very boring. I prefer physical education lesson." (S-7)

"Events are challenging." (S-20)

CONCLUSION AND RECOMMENDATIONS

In the application research conducted to gain universal values to students with the method of learning analytics, it is aimed to ensure that universal values, which are accepted all over the world, are gained to students through activities and practices to be carried out in free time. Depending on this purpose, action research has been carried out with the logic of learning analytics and education has been given gradually. The following results and suggestions have emerged in the training given (Papamitsiou and Economides, 2014).

Within the scope of activities aimed at bringing value to primary school students, it was observed that the students expressed metaphors about more practices and that 33 primary school students used 13 different metaphors about the applications made for the purpose of value education. While the most used metaphors are "Fun" and "Playing", respectively, in alphabetical order; "Lessons, taking responsibility and playing sports" have been the metaphors that are said only once. In the light of these data, we can say that, as part of activities aimed at bringing value to the students, they can gain values in the most entertainment and playing games with their friends especially in the internalization and behavior of the students. Therefore, it can be suggested that teachers give more fun and play to gain value in students.

When the emotions experienced by students during the making of free time activities are evaluated, it is seen that the expressed emotions are gathered under two main themes. While these students received a large number of positive emotional expressions; a small number of negative statements came. It is understood from the student emotional expressions that the most frequently said applications are "fun" and entertainment should be emphasized more widely in values education (Shum and Ferguson, 2012). However, a small number of student groups, on the other hand, seem to complain that the most frequently expressed emotion is negative because the applications are "boring". In the light of these evaluations, it can be suggested from the findings that the Ministry of Education should provide in-service training to the teachers by internalizing the social learning theories within the scope of learning analytics in order to make the activities carried out within the scope of providing values to the teachers.

Using this research and learning analytics method; What kind of work can be done on value education was evaluated. With learning analytics, answers to the questions of how to improve students' learning skills and how to achieve learning were sought and methods for how to gain values to students were determined.

REFERENCES

Altınay, F., Altınay, M., Dagli, G., & Altınay, Z. (2018). Being leader in global citizenship at the information technology age. *Quality & Quantity, 52*(1), 31-42. doi:10.100711135-017-0585-5

Arthur, M. B., Khapova, S. N., & Wilderom, C. P. M. (2005). Career success in a boundaryless career world. *Journal of Organizational Behavior: The International Journal of Industrial. Occupational and Organizational Psychology and Behavior, 26*(2), 177–202. doi:10.1002/job.290

Avella, J. T., Kebritchi, M., Nunn, S. G., & Kanai, T. (2016). Learning analytics methods, benefits, and challenges in higher education: A systematic literature review. *Online Learning, 20*(2), 13–29.

Balcı, A. (2005). *Sosyal bilimlerde araştırma*. PegemA Yayıncılık.

Berland, M., Baker, R. S., & Blikstein, P. (2014). Educational data mining and learning analytics: Applications to constructionist research. *Technology. Knowledge and Learning, 19*(1-2), 205–220. doi:10.100710758-014-9223-7

Demircioğlu, E. & Demircioğlu, İ. H. (2013). Türk Dünyası bilgeleri ve değer eğitimi. *Türk Dünyası Bilgeler Zirvesi: Gönül Sultanları Buluşması*, 26-28.

Dilmaç, B. (1999). *İlköğretim öğrencilerine insani değerler eğitimi verilmesi ve ahlaki olgunluk ölçeği ile eğitimin sınanması* (Unpublished Master's Thesis). Marmara University, İstanbul.

Doğanay, A. (2009). *Değerler eğitimi, hayat bilgisi ve sosyal bilgiler öğretimi yapılandırmacı bir yaklaşım* (C. Öztürk, Ed.). Pegem-A Yayıncılık.

Ekşi, H. (2003). Temel insani değerlerin kazandırılmasında bir yaklaşım: Karakter eğitimi programları. *Değerler Eğitimi Dergisi, 1*(1), 79–96.

Gari, A., Mylonas, K., & Karagianni, D. (2005). Political and religious group membership, value priorities and educational values. *Journal of Beliefs & Values, 26*(3), 301–310. doi:10.1080/13617670500371917

Gašević, D., Dawson, S., & Siemens, G. (2015). Let's not forget: Learning analytics are about learning. *TechTrends, 59*(1), 64–71. doi:10.100711528-014-0822-x

Güler, A., Halıcıoğlu, M. B. & Taşğın, S. (2013). Sosyal bilimlerde nitel araştırma yöntemleri. Ankara: Seçkin Yayıncılık.

Harguess, J., Barngrover, C., & Rahimi, A. (2017, May). An analysis of optical flow on real and simulated data with degradations. In *Geospatial Informatics, Fusion, and Motion Video Analytics VII* (Vol. 10199, p. 1019905). International Society for Optics and Photonics. doi:10.1117/12.2265850

Karasel, N., Altınay, F., Dagli, G., & Altınay, Z. (2018). An investigation of universal values and disability awareness in course books. *Quality & Quantity, 52*(2), 1235–1243. doi:10.100711135-018-0693-x

Kemmis, S., McTaggart, R. & Nixon, R. (2014). Introducing critical participatory action research. In The action research planner (pp. 1-31). Springer.

Kirschenbaum, H. (2000). From values clarification to character education: A personal journey. *The Journal of Humanistic Counseling, Education and Development, 39*(1), 4–20. doi:10.1002/j.2164-490X.2000.tb00088.x

Kramer, N. S. (2002). Tarih Sümer'de başlar (Yazılı Tarihteki Otuzdokuz İlk). İstanbul: Kabalcı Yay.

Küken, G. (2003). *Ilkçağda eğitim felsefesi.* Alfa Yayınları.

Memiş, A., & Gedik, E. G. (2010). *Sınıf öğretmenlerinin değer yönelimleri.* http://dergipark.gov.tr/download/article-file/302478

Miles, H. B., & Huberman, A. M. (1994). *Qualitative data analysis: An expanded sourcebook.* Sage.

Oxford, R. L., Tomlinson, S., Barcelos, A., Harrington, C., Lavine, R. Z., Saleh, A., & Longhini, A. (1998). Clashing metaphors about classroom teachers: Toward a systematic typology for the language teaching field. *System*, *26*(1), 3–50. doi:10.1016/S0346-251X(97)00071-7

Özgüven, İ.E. (1994). Psikolojik Testler. Ankara: Psikolojik Danısma, Rehberlik Egitim Merkezi (PEDREM).

Papamitsiou, Z., & Economides, A. (2014). Learning analytics and educational data mining in practice: A systematic literature review of empirical evidence. *Journal of Educational Technology & Society*, *17*(4), 49–64.

Patton, M. Q. (2014). *Nitel araştırma ve değerlendirme yöntemleri*. Pegem Akademi.

Poonsirivong, K., & Jittawiriaynukoon, C. (2018, March). Big data analytics using association rules in eLearning. In *2018 IEEE 3rd International Conference on Big Data Analysis (ICBDA)* (pp. 14-18). IEEE. 10.1109/ICBDA.2018.8367643

Shum, S. B., & Ferguson, R. (2012). Learning and Knowledge Analytics. *Journal of Educational Technology & Society*, *15*(3), 3–26.

Siemens, G., & Gasevic, D. (2012). Guest editorial-learning and knowledge analytics. *Journal of Educational Technology & Society*, *15*(3), 1–2.

Siemens, G., & Long, P. (2011). Penetrating the fog: Analytics in learning and education. *EDUCAUSE Review*, *46*(5), 30.

Stringer, E. T. (2004). *Action research in education*. Pearson/ Merrill/ Prentice Hall.

Taşçı, D. & Koç, U. (2007). Örgütsel vatandaşlık davranışı-örgütsel öğrenme değerleri ilişkisi: Akademisyenler üzerinde görgül bir araştırma. *Anadolu Üniversitesi Eğitim Fakültesi Dergisi*, *7*(2), 373–382.

Tokel, A., Dagli, G., Altinay, Z., & Altinay, F. (2019). The role of learning management in agile management for consensus culture. *The International Journal of Information and Learning Technology*, *36*(4), 364–372. doi:10.1108/IJILT-02-2019-0017

Valus Education Study Final Report (VES). (2003). *Australian Government, Department of Education, Science and Training*. http://www.curriculum.edu.au/verve/resources/VES_Final_Report14Nov.pdf

Yalar, T., & Yelken, T. Y. (2011). Değerler eğitiminin iyileştirilmesi ile ilgili öğretmen görüşlerinin belirlenmesi ve bir program modülü örneğinin geliştirilmesi. *Elektronik Sosyal Bilimler Dergisi*, *38*(38).

Yaman, E. (2012). *Değerler eğitimi*. Akçağ Yayınları.

Yıldırım, A., & Simsek, H. (2018). *Sosyal bilimlerde nitel araştırma yöntemleri*. Seçkin Yayıncılık.

Yıldırım, N., & Turan, S. (2015). Opinions of primary school classroom teachers about distribution process of values in social science course curriculum [Sınıf öğretmenlerinin hayat bilgisi dersi öğretim programındaki değerlerin kazandırılma sürecine yönelik görüşleri]. *Eğitimde Kuram ve Uygulama*, *11*(2), 420–437.

Yılmaz, K., & Oğuz, E. (2011). Nitel bir görüşme yöntemi: Odak grup görüşmesi. *Kuramsal Eğitimbilim Dergisi*, *4*(1), 95–107.

Section 3
Application Cases

Chapter 7
Learning Analytics in the Monitoring of Learning Processes:
3D Educational Collaborative Virtual Environments

Rosa Reis
GILT, ISEP, Instituto Politécnico do Porto, Portugal

Bertil P. Marques
GILT, ISEP, Instituto Politécnico do Porto, Portugal

ABSTRACT

During the last few years, learning analytics (LA) has gained the interest of researchers in the field of education. Generally, LA is related with the development of methods that use educational data sets to support the learning process. Therefore, there is a need understanding how learners, educators, and institutions can best support this process. Thus, a framework is presented that tries to extend the collaborative three-dimensional virtual environments for educational by integrating a LA tool. The aim is to help the teacher to monitor and evaluate the students' learning process in these types of environments. It is the intention include a (1) comprehensive analysis of the currently available LA tools for educational, (2) design of a user-centered framework based the requirements gathered from the analysis, and (3) thorough evaluation of framework to allow identify possible behavior patterns of students within the environment, related to your preferences for materials and expertise.

DOI: 10.4018/978-1-7998-7103-3.ch007

INTRODUCTION

In recent years, there has been a great technological evolution that has allowed a change in the way of working in various areas of society, namely in education. At this level, different technologies have been applied to create new ways of teaching, communicating, and representing knowledge, benefiting from the advantages that these technological resources offer.

Teaching goes beyond the classroom, leading teachers to think about new learning strategies. Among the existing solutions, there are the three-dimensional virtual environments, which can be used as a support for carrying out collaborative activities between students. However, although these environments have peculiar characteristics, such as a sense of immersion, a sense of presence, communication and interactivity, which assist teachers and students in carrying out the proposed educational activities, they do not have components that allow monitoring and recording all actions carried out by students throughout their learning process. In order to minimize this gap, we propose a framework that integrates a learning analytics tool with a collaborative, three-dimensional virtual educational environment developed under a platform for the development of virtual worlds. The objective of this framework is to assist the teacher in assessing the performance of each student, helping him to visualize the entire learning process, through the quantitative and qualitative analysis of the collected data, from the students' interactions in the three-dimensional collaborative virtual environment.

From a technological point of view, framework will use the Opensource platform, called OpenSim, which allows the development of immersive and private three-dimensional environments and allows connection to MySQL database. All actions performed by students will be recorded in database, using a scripting language, called OSSL (OpenSimulator Scripting Language).

Based on these premises, the first part of the chapter will introduce the reader the concepts related to three-dimensional collaborative virtual environments, and the technological infrastructure used for the development of the collaborative three-dimensional virtual environment (OpenSim), will be characterized. In the second part, a brief description of the Learning Analytics concept and how it can bring advantages in the improvement and performance of students will be made. In the third part there will be a short explanation about each of the most popular learning analytics tools. Subsequently, it will be explained how the framework will be developed, presenting its architecture and the way of extracting data from the database. Finally, the last part will comprise the evaluation of the framework throughout its development, where a set of quality criteria will be applied.

Three-Dimensional Collaborative Virtual Environments

Three-dimensional Collaborative Virtual Environments (3DCVEs) are simulated persistent virtual spaces based on the interaction by computer, inhabited by several users, who are represented by iconic images called avatars, who can communicate with each other's and the world in a synchronized way" (Reis *et al.*, 2012) .

Looking at the definition we identify some key elements:

Shared space: the world allows many users to participate at once. All the users have the feeling of being in the same place, room, land. The shared space is a common location where interactions occur. The place can be real or fictional, but it should exhibit the same characteristics for all participants.

Immersion and Interactivity: allow users to interact with the environment, to change, develop, build, and submit content. The user must feel immersed in the environment and fully engaged with the activities being under- taken. This is normally achieved through representation of the user and environment in world.

Persistence: the world's existence continues regardless of whether individual users are logged in or not. The persistence of the world leads us to the immediacy feedback and synchronous use of the actions that take place in the world.

Immediacy: An immediate virtual world allows real-time interaction between the user and the world.

Socialization: interaction with others, working as teams to create communities.

These key elements contribute to represent different categories of information in a virtual environment by means of three-dimensional objects that enable the development of a real life-like world. They are dynamic spaces, that are constantly changing, that is that is, what a user sees when they are connected to the environment at a given time, it may not be the same as what him saw on the last connection.

These environments are rich in interaction for students because the students can have different ways of experimenting and learning. They stimulate exchange of information and active participation, supporting different learning styles and giving opportunities for free or guided exploration (Calonge, 2007), personalizing the experience of each user, adapting to their previous knowledge (Chittaro & Ranon,2007). Also, they enable more dynamic learning, based on research and the constant search for knowledge (Bertagnolli *et al.*, 2007).

If we want to apply these types of environments to the educational context and that the learning is collaborative, then we must take into account the communication, the coordination and the cooperation because group work will allow interdependence between activities. It forcing the students learn to collaborate/cooperate with each other´s to understand the environment and solve problems (Johnson et *al*., 1999), (Roussos *et al*., 1999).

Development Platforms for Three-Dimensional Collaborative Virtual Environments

New technologies have been developed to support the construction of collaborative three-dimensional virtual environments, in a simpler and more effective way. Of these technologies, there are several platforms for building environments that provide support for 3D modeling, with the ability to pre-program the behavior of 3D objects. On these platforms, objects are described using a scripting language or using a programming language supported by the platform itself. These behaviors tend to be pre-defined actions that are initiated by the user himself using the mouse, keyboard, or input devices.

From the vast set of tools available in the market, we selected the OpenSimulator (OpenSim). The OpenSim is a freely available, open-source software system that allows to integrate different technologies, allowing the presentation of e-learning materials and e-content, narratives based on social interactions, sharing documents and files, holding meetings and events, and providing spaces for sharing research results and meetings with national and international colleagues (Bettencourt & Abade, 2008). The OpenSim is a platform where the creation of users' static content is simple while interactive objects must be programmed. Installation and maintenance require system administration skills. This platform can be run in standalone mode, a property that allows us to easily manage content electronically and make backups of the 3D world. It allows the creation of content in real time, using its own tools that allow the sharing of text, images and video. The environments created on this platform are similar to real life, which can work in standalone mode (individual) or in grid mode (multiuser).

One of the great advantages of OpenSim is the possibility of developing collaborative work. In this type of environment, it is possible for two or more people to work synchronously or asynchronously, from physically different locations, on the same resources. These resources can be shared and used by others, which are organized in a resource repository.

In OpenSim, each user, represented by an avatar, can store the objects he builds or collects, and they are accessible by himself, in his inventory. This allows that at any time, the avatar can replace and use the objects in his inventory.

At the level of execution, this platform uses configuration files to define the parameters necessary for its startup and operation. The central file is OpenSim.ini, located in the / bin directory, which contains most of the restrictions for system configuration. This file is supported by other region configuration files (based on XML), network services and various cache configuration files.

The OpenSimulator provides an API to interact with external applications. This is how the framework components interact with it.

DESIGN SPECIFICATION OF 3DVE

Collaborative three-dimensional virtual environments are open environments that lead participants, represented by avatars, to browse through different scenarios at random. This leads to some shortcomings, especially in terms of navigation and interaction, leading to disorientation and discouragement of users. These aspects must have to be taken into attention when we design a 3DVE, because a system of collaborative learning through three-dimensional environments, allows students to solve problems and share knowledge with other students and teachers in real time. Thus, it is possible to build more dynamic learning experiences, but this makes design much more complex. We believe that it is necessary to define a set of guidelines for their design in order to improve their usefulness, reducing construction time and increase the performance of environments in terms of usability and functionality e also, increase student learning performance.

As one of the main objective is to increase the students' learning performance, through the monitoring and evaluation of educational tasks performed at 3DVE, an aspect that is not provided by these environments, believe that LA can solve this gap. Teacher cannot be everywhere all the time to monitor the interactions performed by users. Considering these problems, a set of guidelines is presented that can help the teacher to verify what activities were performed in this environment and assist the development team in designing of this type environments. These guidelines were based on identifying the problems assigned to development and are submitted to help the designer to avoid the usability problems and improve the performance of students, i.e., it's may serve as a guideline for teachers in implementing a course to engage their students through at 3DVE. The figure 1shows the basic guidelines of 3DVE development.

Identify the scope, target audience, learning outcomes and the results required to the target audience - In the construction of 3D collaborative virtual environments, it is necessary to be aware who is target audience, the purpose of learning, the results required to the students, the contents, in order to allow us to take maximum advantage of using 3DVE for educational purposes.

Figure 1. The basic guidelines of 3DVE development

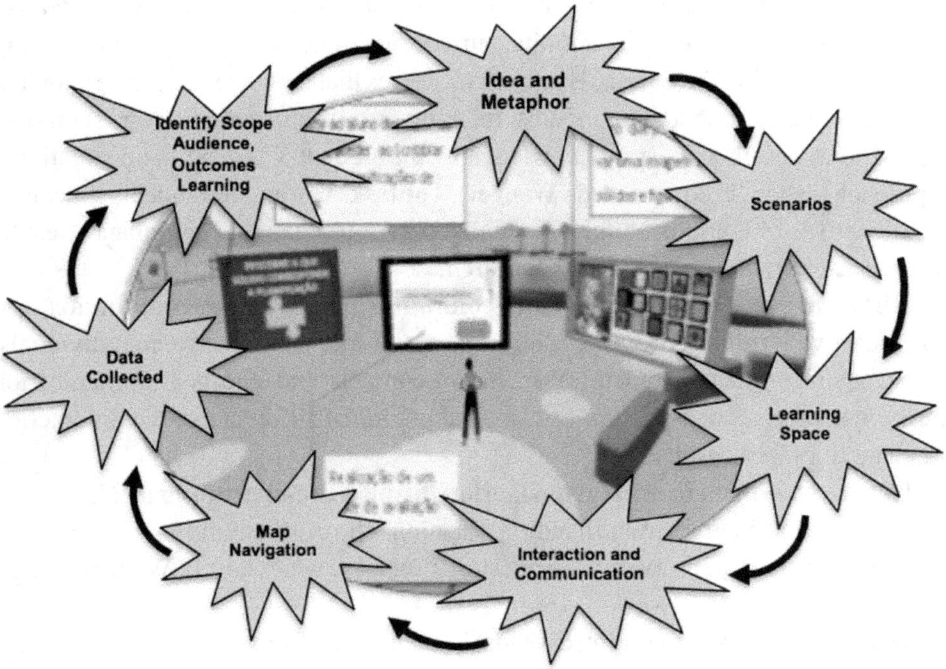

Identify the idea, define a metaphor that allows creating a teaching situation - The metaphor is the bridge between the real and the virtual worlds. The world's structure and organization make it easy to build navigation and increase the interaction quality.

If the 3D collaborative virtual environment model is not representative of the real, the user does not build a consistent mental model with the reality. Moreover, the representation of the real can capture attention and influence the student involvement, because the realism is one of the characteristics of 3D collaborative virtual environment.

Define scenarios with their objects (fixed and dynamic) and content - The scenarios should be created considering the different learning styles students and the different ways of acquiring knowledge. For objects, it is important to define their behavior, which can be interactive, autonomous, connected to other objects as well as without behavior. For objects without behavior (known as fixed), it is necessary to define their positions in the scenario. The contents should be defined and structured according to how we want the users should be involved in learning process. These can be static, allowing users to explore, observe, and do not interact. It allows users touch objects, start a task, select to customize, or modify a specific content.

Define the learning space – to determine the learning strategies and types of tasks that are appropriate to the environment purposes. An education 3D collaborative virtual environment should be examined in a pedagogical perspective of the learning activities, including the type and learning strategies that it is necessary to be adopted. We can include associative models (task-oriented approaches), constructivism (approaches based on existing knowledge by the student-Vygotsky) and situational (approaches socially constructed - Wenger). The tasks that enable students to achieve the objectives of learning should be idealized in order that the performance results are consistent with the knowledge acquired.

Different types of interaction and communication between individuals - 3D collaborative virtual environments allow a greater interaction between individuals, namely among students, student(s)/teacher(s), contents, and objects. Communication can be synchronous or asynchronous. A combination of different forms of interaction can lead to richest results.

Create a map that facilitates navigation through the environment - Navigation is the foundation for a useful and handy application. The world should have information that helps the user to answer basic questions such as, where am I? Where can I go from here?

Define which data to analyze – This data can come from interactions of avatars with other avatars, or with the 3D objects of the at 3DVE, or of the 3DVE itself (for example, frequency of use, performing tasks, movement patterns, preferred locations) (Cruz-Benito, *et al.*, 2014) (Cruz-Benito, *et al*, 2015) The data obtained by 3DVE itself allows a deeper analysis of the time spend of exercises and also visualizing timeline patterns of date trails created during the experiments. This will allow data analysis on students who use the environment to identify patterns of behavior, assess the learning process, improve the overall learning experience and give the opportunity to use this information to reflect on the students' learning activity (Einhardt, L., *et al,* 2016) (Gros, 2016).

LEARNING ANALYTICS

Learning Analytics (LA) as emerging field has many definitions. If one takes a closer analyze at these definitions, we can verify that all emphasize data collection that allows extracting information for instructors to take actions that can improve the teaching-learning process. These data can come from centralized educational systems, distributed learning environments, open data sets, personal learning environments, adaptive systems/ITS, web-based courses, social media, student information systems, and mobile devices (Lukarov *et al.*, 2014)

LA is an iterative process that is carried out in a series of steps, which aims is to make effective LA. According to Dyckhoff *et a*l. (Dyckhoff *et al.*, 2012), the LA process begins with data collection, followed by a data extraction process. This extraction can be presented as a widget integrated into the learning environment, and from the graphical analysis of the data, teachers must be able to interpret and assess whether the objectives have been achieved.

An LA approach which depicted a life cycle (see figure 2) was introduced by Doug Clow (Clow, 2012), with a focus on allowing the 'learner' can perform activities in a traditional learning setting such as a classroom or in virtual environments. This approach starts with the learners. The next step is the generation and capture of data about learners, for instance, clickstream data generated by learners; postings to a forum; assessment results and so on. The third phase consists the processing of this data using metrics or analytics, which provide some insight into the learning process. Finally, the last phase is called by intervention. The intervention uses the metrics to drive the instructor in building some alternatives to the learning process that have some effect on learners. However, learning analytics does not necessarily include all fours steps. A project that created reports about learners, but without any mechanism can feed this back into an improved learning experience, but not a very effective one (Clow, 2012).

Figure 2. Process of learning analytics (clow, 2012)

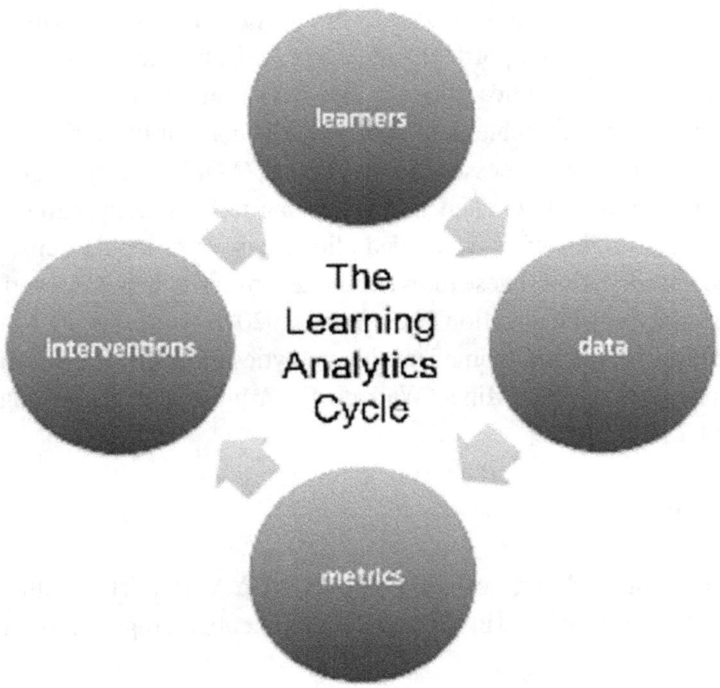

Through learning analytics, the teacher can understand students' progress over a course or discipline and to effectively evaluate students' actions, providing immediate feedback and adjust content and activities in a personalized way. This is possible, because LA uses large datasets to provide real-time information about efficiency of features of learning environments. The recent LA approaches apply several analytics methods developed in domain of data science, artificial intelligence, and business intelligence. Also, the techniques developed in these domains make it possible to identify trends and patterns, and then benchmark individuals or groups against these trends. As examples of these techniques we emphasize the prediction analysis (analysis of current and historical facts to predict trends and behavioral patterns for application to any type of unknown, whether in past, present or future (Padgett, 2014); Social Network Analysis (in which the connection between students and teachers is analyzed, depending on their frequency, quality or importance) (Buckingham & Ferguson, 2012); Natural Language Processing (NLP) because the lexical, syntactic and semantic analysis of a text can show a student's level of interest and depth in a given subject and others.

LA can help to identify at-risk learners, transform pedagogical approaches, and help students gain insight into their own learning.

LEARNING ANALYTICS TOOLS

In the last years, the area of information technology that has had growing importance with respect to decision support and predictive analysis in the current world is data mining. Research and studies indicate that data mining plays a significant role in helping companies evaluate data and, as such, make informed decisions about different aspects of their processes and operations, (Madhuri, 2013). This awakened the academic community to a new and promising field of study, called of learning analytics. Many studies were developed allowing several tools to emerge that are been applied in education. These tools conducted to clarify benefices and challenges of learning analytics in education (Reis *et al.*, 2020).

This section will present some learning analytics tools that are been application in education, namely RapidMiner, Waikato Environment for Knowledge Analysis (Weka) and Tableau.

RapidMiner

The software RapidMiner, formerly known as YALE (Yet Another Learning Environment), was developed in 2001 by Ralf Klinkenberg, Ingo Mierswa and Simon

Fischer in the Artificial Intelligence Unit of the Technical University of Dortmund (Rapidminder, s.d.a).

The Rapid Miner tool (Deutsch, 2010) is a tool that provides several data mining and other functionalities (ETL, reporting, etc.). This tool compatible with Windows, UNIX and Linux. The data source systems available in Rapid Miner range from excel files, through text files, to the most popular DBMS (e.g., Microsoft SQL Server, Oracle, MySQL, Sybase, etc.).

This tool has some characteristic features, of which we highlight (Rapidminder, s.d.b): Data Mining Tools; Statistical analysis; Machine learning; Data extraction; Connected data management.

This software uses a client/server model with the server offered on-site or in public or private cloud infrastructures (Reis *et al.*, 2020).

Weka

The Weka software package (Waikato Environment for Knowledge Analysis) started to be written in 1993, using Java, at the University of Waikato, New Zealand and was later acquired by a company in late 2006. Weka is licensed under General Public License therefore it is possible to study and change the respective source code (Weka, s.d.).

The Weka is one of the most popular data mining tools. Although well known, it is typically used only for teaching purposes (in data mining courses) or in small experiments. However, the tool provides a very powerful and flexible Java API that allows its integration with any type of Java system. Weka has consolidated itself as the most used data mining tool in the academic environment. It is applied not only in scientific research, but also for didactics (Silva, 2015).

The Weka offers some features like (Silva, 2015) (Holmes & Donkin, 1994):

- Prediction: Weka provides algorithms that allow the computer to learn, that is, through existing patterns in the data at the time of the analysis, the computer can predict possible future events;
- Classification and regression: the tool implement classification and regression algorithms, these, like the forecasting algorithms, aim to predict future occurrences of data through current standards;
- Clustering: by applying clustering algorithms, users are able to identify data that share similar trends and patterns.

Tableau

Tableau Software is an American interactive data visualization software company founded in January 2003 by Christian Chabot, Pat Hanrahan and Chris Stolte, in Mountain View, California. The company is currently headquartered in Seattle, Washington, United States focused on business intelligence.[3] . On August 1, 2019, Salesforce acquired Tableau. The Tableau Tool is a powerful data visualization tool used in business intelligence and data analysis (Tableau, s.d.) (Reis *et al.*, 2020).

Tableau products query relational databases, online analytical processing cubes, cloud databases, and spreadsheets to generate graph-type data visualizations. The products can also extract, store, and retrieve data from an in-memory data engine.

The visualization provided by Tableau has completely enhanced the ability to gain more knowledge about the data we are working on and can be used to provide more accurate predictions. Tableau also has functionality for building rich and interactive dashboards, capable of displaying dynamic real-time visualizations to end users. However, Tableau's functionality is limited to this; it does not support predictive analytics or relational data mining.

Comparative Analysis

Making now a comparative analysis between that 3 software's, it will help us to choose which tool to use and how it is to be used in our project. All the tools presented were studied. These were subject to comparison and critical analysis, in the end one of them will be chosen for a practical applicability problem. The chosen tool was then used to create a practical proof of concept, aiming to show the quality of the solution produced by this type of tool (Silva, 2015).

The criteria chosen to carry out this analysis are presented in the table 1 and were based on the following assumptions *(Reis et al., 2020)*:

1. **Usability** - This feature determines the usability of each tool. This describes which user interface is comparatively easier to use.
2. **Speed** - is an important distinguishing factor among different data mining tools. It helps to understand how system configuration impacts the working of a particular data mining tool.
3. **Visualization** - Visualization is the most important feature of a data mining tool.
4. Algorithms supported - This feature classifies data mining tools based on the algorithm implementation supported by them and the descriptor selection choice available.

5. **Data Set Size** - Smaller or larger data set support is another comparable feature among different data mining tools.
6. **Databases** - This item is very important because some platforms of virtual world's development only allow you to connect to some databases. So, the LA tools should allow connection to different database, such as Oracle, Microsoft SQL Server, MySQL and access to Excel, Access as well as numerous other data formats. In our case, OpenSim use MySQL.

Table 1. Comparative Features (Reis et al., 2020)

	RapidMiner	**Weka**	**Tableau**
Usability	• Easy to use	• Easiest to use	• Simple to use
Speed	• Requires more memory to operate	• Works faster on any machine.	• Works fast on any machine
Visualization	• More options but less than Tableau	• Less options	• Many visualization options
Algorithms supported	• Classification and Clustering	• Classification and Clustering	• Not used to implement algorithms
Data Set Size	• Supports large and small data set	• Supports only small data sets	• Supports any data se
Databases	• Oracle, Microsoft SQL Server, MySQL. ..	• Oracle, Microsoft SQL Server, MySQL. ..	• Oracle, Microsoft SQL Server, MySQL. ..

Based on this study we decide to choose the Weka tool, because:

- Its graphical user interfaces allow the platform to be used more simply and easily.
- It is compatible with almost all modern platforms,
- Not require the ability to manipulate SQL statements and files as the RapidMiner tool.
- Provides access to SQL databases through Java Database Connectivity and can process the results obtained by querying the database.
- Support a comprehensive collection of data preprocessing and modeling techniques.

RELATED WORKS

Learning in the virtual world or e-learning has become increasingly popular around the world as information and Internet technologies advance. Young people today grow up in a digital world surrounded by smartphones, computers, the Internet, and video games. "Digital Native" is a term that describes this group of people who are born in a. digital environment: so, they are well acquainted with the computerization technologies that have been evolving (Selywn, 2009). They live in a world full of multimedia. The unique immersive environment existing in virtual worlds allows users to have a learning experience that meets their own needs and provides them with greater learning autonomy (Field, 2007).). It has been reported that virtual environments such as computer games can motivate students to engage in learning activities and have achieved promising results (Li, *et al.*, 2013) (Asgari & Kaufman, 2004) as well as the use of virtual reality in work such as that of Tseng *et al.(* 2020)

Research shows that such innovative educational averages and motivated users to have better collaboration and communication, which creates an effective motivation for learning environment and support for students (Bronack *et al.*, 2008). Itis common that three-dimensional virtual do worlds such as Second Life can model the real world even more realistic than the text-based or two-dimensional environments, and this greater degree of realism can lead to a better involvement of students in learning activities (Tashiro & Dunlap, 2007).

The flexibility of virtual world platforms also brings the possibility of more interactive distance learning. The virtual platform on the Internet has overcome barriers of distance, time, and location. It has been suggested that a virtual social space with essential interaction to improve education (Berge & Colins, 1995) (Reisoğlu, *et al.,* 2017). From experiences and other researchers (Jones,2019) (Kim,2019) (Vicente-Saez & Martinez-Fuentes, 2018),the use of the virtual world as a distance learning platform brings satisfactory and promising results to the courses (Ritzema & Harris,2008). (Recent studies/investigations confirm that recent the theme associated with the most diverse areas of education remains a current and interesting topic, without even reaching a saturation point.

In the table below we will indicate some of these works found and that intersect with this work, indicating its references, and each article by itself still has references to outros other works, of very recent data and whose development /methodology crosses in some points of this work.

Writing a section on this part would practically consider writing a magazine article or a book chapter by the wealth of information that was found in snowball effect (See Table 1).

Table 2. Similar works on the same related field

Article Title	Reference
Collaborative Immersive Virtual Environments for Education in Geography	(Šašinka,2019)
A Learning Analytics Theoretical Framework for STEM Education Virtual Reality Applications	(Christopoulos,2020)
Artificial Intelligence and Emerging Technologies in Schools	(Southgate, 2018)
Games, Simulations, Immersive Environments and Emerging Technologies	(George, 2019)
A Critical look at Educational Technology from a Distance Education Perspective	(Anderson, 2020)

In all the papers read and analyzed, one of the common points was to verify that the most of the students found that the learning experience in the virtual world is intriguing and fascinating enough to trigger a motivation and a more in-depth study of the topic involved..

According to constructivist theory, the student must interact with meaning activities with learning experiences in order to generate knowledge based on his own experience already lived (Field, 2007).). The virtual world simulates the real-world environment in which the learner can learn in an environment close to reality.

The realism of the virtual world can further enhance the learning experience. In addition, students can gain a better understanding of the conceptual context by performing specific tasks in the virtual world, or by interacting with virtual objects (Bricken & Byrne,1994) and virtual environment from a first-person perspective.

Second Life is a flexible and user-friendly platform with high usability for educational purposes. However, some of these schools provided only exhibits for their research and virtual classrooms in Second Life for experimentation, so the authors have many references in the article covering nearly two decades of research, as this topic was begun to be investigated by the late 1990's and interest and usefulness has grown, remaining useful to the scientific community to this day. . Very few of these schools have used Second Life for information system learning in an experiential learning approach. In addition, few of these studies have evaluated the efficacy of using Second Life in education. The work of Lucia *et al.* (2009) is one of the few examples. They evaluated the aspects of presence, awareness, communication, comfort and perceived sociability of the 3D virtual world environment. However, they did not evaluate the learning outcomes of the program. Another example is the work of Ritzema & Harris (2008) where users were asked to create an object in Second Life. Both tasks involve experiential learning.

FRAMEWORK PROPOSED

The proposed framework aims to improve content and courses quality helping in discovering which resources work and which don't, identify the appropriate type of content to improve learning, the correct monitoring of students in the application of educational strategies in online environments. We believe that is possible to increase student performance if we use three-dimensional virtual educational environments, together with a learning analytics tool. Our main idea is to implement mechanisms that make it easier to connect the LA tool, regardless of the platform used to create 3DECVEs.

From the LA tool chosen we intend that the teacher can analyze the student's activities and predict their performance and progress in the identified learning outcomes. The metrics used to analyze the performance of the activities are the ones that the tool supports.

Methodology

Linking the LA concept with the three-dimensional virtual environments, which have been used for collaborative teaching, there has been interest in analyzing the usage data and from here the LA frameworks have made perfect sense. Many studies have been conducted giving interesting perspectives of the various types of uses as presented by Gavilanes-Sagnay et al. (2019). These studies subdivide learning into personalized, adaptive and educational, allowing to diversify the type of LA according to the objectives of the work concerned. Thus, other purposes may arise to work the background of 3CVE to extract the data, process it and subsequently provide the information already interpreted and presented as the user wants to see/use it. This framework aims to help design teams and the educational community improve the management of their pedagogical resources when defined under platforms for the development of three-dimensional virtual environments and improve the application of strategies in order to improve student performance, trying to reduce school failure.

Based on these ideas our framework will be development through an iterative process, composed by four phases as shown in figure 3).

Phase 1 - Development of a three-dimensional virtual environment under a platform of virtual worlds- The teacher and the development team will in a first phase define what educational content to address, type of media to use (video, text, slides, etc.), definition of activities (exercises, quizzes, tests), type of interaction between students and/or teachers.

Figure 3. Development cycle

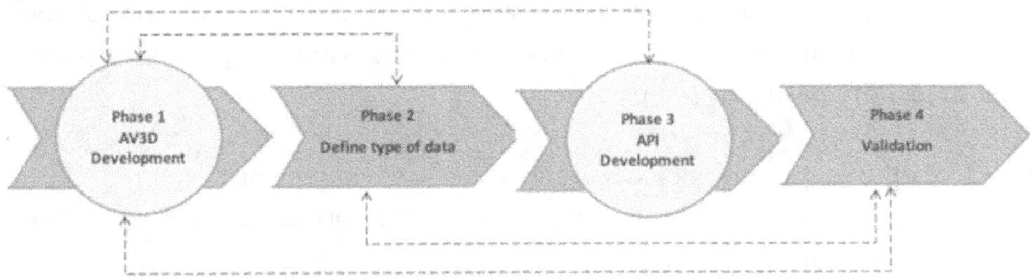

Phase 2 - Define type of data to be collected for student performance analysis. – The teacher must identify the types of data to be collected. These data can be, the contents with greater access, access time in the resolution of activities, number of messages sent to the teacher, messages between students (represented by his avatar), number of questions asked in the discussion forum, final notes, so on.

This information will be automatically stored in a database compatible with the platform used for the development of the three-dimensional virtual environment.

The Data collected by 3D educational virtual environments should only be used for educational purposes. They must have the consent of the students or tutor if the students are minors. The teacher should inform which data to be collected and why.

As a first stage, when developing the virtual environment, the development team should consider the confidentiality of the information collected. This is easily achieved because the different databases on the market already have the resources to provide the security of the information of their products. These features help organizations comply with data protection and privacy standards. These resources supporting data encryption and data masking, mechanisms that are important to protect data outside the database's access control perimeter. Later, the teacher is going to analyze the collected data, and for privacy reasons, there should be no means of identifying the student, the data must be send anonymously to the Learning Analytics tool. We believe that Hoel and Chen's (2018) principles for data protection for LA can be applied:

1. Privacy and data protection in LA are achieved by negotiating data sharing with each student.
2. Openness and transparency are essential and should be an integral part of institutional policies. How the educational institution will use data and act upon the insights of analysis should be clarified in close dialogue with the students.
3. Big data will impact all society. Therefore, in negotiating privacy and data protection measures with students, institutions and researchers should use this opportunity to strengthen their personal data literacies.

Phase 3 - Development of an API that allows you to connect the LA tool to the database for data extraction. These data will be analyzed later, using the LA tool.

Phase 4 – Validation – Components and processes are empirically verified, in order to identify problems such as:

- Does the framework include all the necessary components?
- to what extent API allows you to extract the data correctly to making decisions about the learning process.

After solving these problems, students and teachers will be recruited to participate in this phase, with the aim of improve the learning process. The students will access to 3DVE and the teachers to LA tool. the teachers will analyze the extracted data. From the extracted data, the teacher can perform the analysis of the data and the measurement of the outcomes presented. The teacher will make decisions on how to improve/adapt the contents, exercises, and forms of interaction according to the different learning profiles of their students, i.e., adapt the 3DVE to the profiles of the students. It thus plays an important role within the conceptual structure, as it must be able to gather the necessary qualitative data and incorporate these findings into the decision-making process of adapting learning to the type of student profiles.

Overview of Architecture

The proposed architecture (see Figure 4) is composed of three main components; the first component corresponds to the 3DVE in which the student develops his learning activities, either in groups or individually; and, the second component is the LA tool that will be connected to the platform where environment was developed. It is from this LA tool that the teacher will rigorously analyze the student's performance in the environment, based on the data that was collected by the three-dimensional educational collaborative virtual environment.

Framework Components

3D Educational Collaborative Virtual Environment

The environment as previously discussed will be developed on the platform of collaborative three-dimensional virtual environments, the OpenSim.

Given that the applications developed on these platforms are open spaces and that easily lead to disorientation, distraction and dispersion of students, the environment space will be divided into three main areas: the information space, the activity space and the discussion space. The information space presents all the didactic content to be addressed. Some content can be accessed through Moodle. The activity space has as main objective to present a set of activities that allow students to consolidate the concepts learned. Some of the activities may use collaboration tools found on the Web, such as Scribblar. In the whole area of activities, students can find some problems to be performed. The activities are directed to be carried out in groups. Finally, the discussion space aims to allow teachers to clarify some concepts to students and/or propose something related to the subject being addressed. Thus, students are led to reflect, debate and draw conclusions, that is, to collaborate with each other.

Figure 4. System Architecture

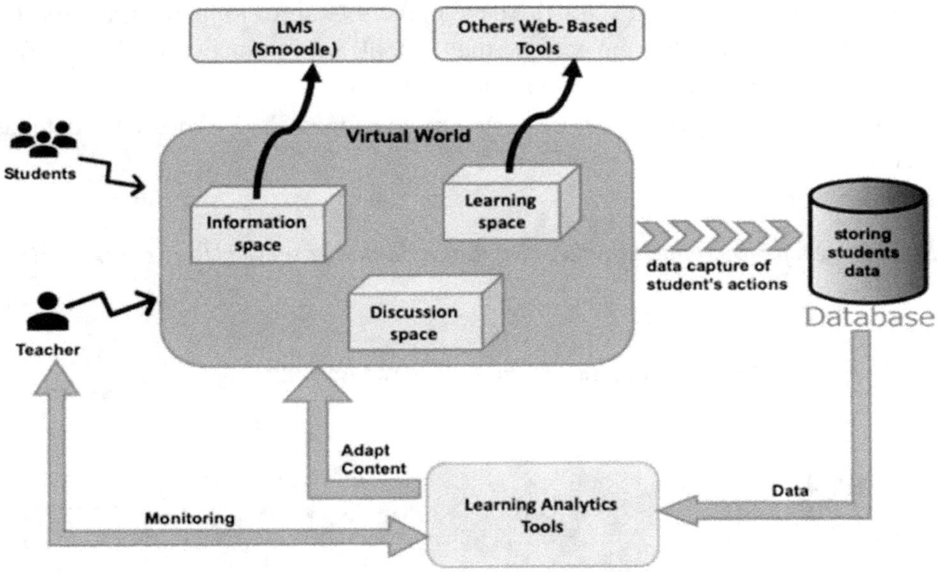

All actions developed in the environment will be stored in a database compatible with the OpenSim platform. For this to be achieved, a set of objects will be developed which, in real time, will store the data. Thus, it will be necessary when defining the environment to define what information should be collected, for example, the period during which the students stayed in a certain place; what actions were performed on the objects; places they visited, so on; and, to design the database schema that allows to store the collected data. To make this possible, it is necessary to create sensors type objects within the environment, such as presence sensors, interaction sensors and geographic sensors. The presence sensors - allows you to control the presence of students in the environment, the interaction sensors - allow capturing student interactions (avatars) in the environment and the geographic sensors - allows to determine which the area(s) more visited by students.

These type of sensors objects, can be programed using the programming language called OSSL. Thus we can capture the data specified previously, which will be sent to the files that performed the treatment and its storage in the database. The learning analytics tool chosen by us will be connect to MySQL database using JDBC Connection object.

Analysis Tool

This analysis tool will be a learning analytics tool that will access the database to extract the data so that the teacher can analyze the students' learning flows.

In order to extract pertinent information about the students' interactions in the environment, it is necessary for the development team to implement an app that allows the database to be connected to the LA tool. So, we can extract the data from the database for the teacher to be able to analyze it.

In Figure 5 you can see the necessary steps to connect the LA tool to the database server.

Figure 5. Steps to connect the LA tool to the database server (Reis et al., 2020)

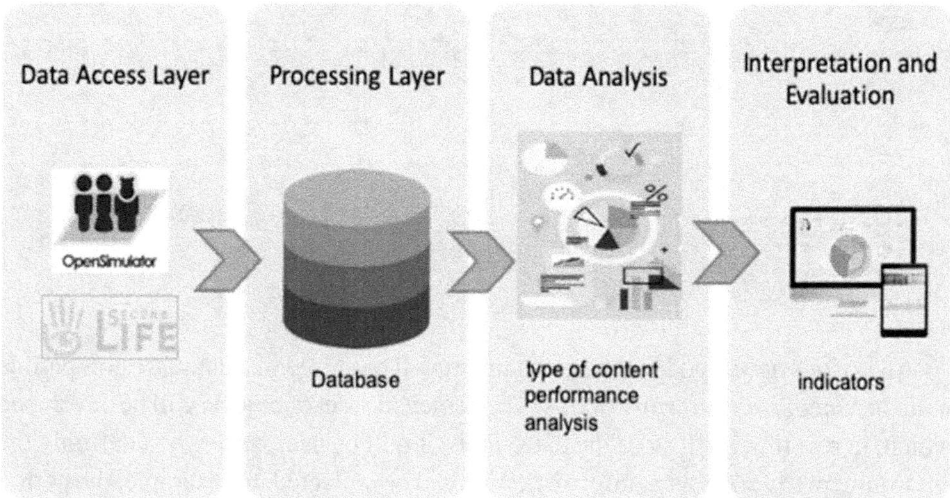

The data access layer should be responsible for allowing access to the existing database. Technologies like Rest API, Open Database Connectivity (ODBC) must be used; The processing layer - will be responsible for processing, in parallel, the large volume of data extracted from the data access layer; Data analysis layer is the process of obtaining actionable insights from the collected data. Data to be extracted are stored and processed pseudonymized to protect the users (students) and prevent data misuse. We do not want to examine records of individual students. Rather, we intend to analyze data of subgroups with specific characteristics for drawing conclusions on learning processes. Finally, the last step will allow the teacher to interpret and evaluate students' behavior patterns and to predict and detect risk of failure, such as new forms of interventions to facilitate student progress and learning. This is possible through La tools, in this case through the Weka Tool.

The proposed architecture can be used as a possible solution the proposed architecture can be used as a possible solution to bring analyzes and suggestions to improve the teaching-learning process in AVA's environments, providing for predicting and detecting risk of failures, as well as forms of interventions to facilitate the progress and learning of students. This because we believe that we will be contributing to the unification and formation of a new paradigm of education.

Framework Evaluation

During the evaluation phase of framework design process, we decided to focus on two main issues. First, the evaluation was focused on design of scenarios created for the 3DCVE, using for this purpose a quality model called the Qualitative Evaluation Framework (QEF) developed by Escudeiro (Escudeiro, 2007). This model evaluates the educational software quality and gives us degree of freedom to choose the criteria, which can be ´using in any domain and ´valence. It is based on the standard of reference ISO 9126 (is an international standard for the evaluation of software) and measures the quality relatively to a hypothetical ideal system, whose quality is assumed to be 100%.

In this assessment, was emphasized three aspects: technical/functional, educational/didactic and usability. These aspects were intrinsically dependent, because a collaborative educational virtual environment must allow an improvement in the teaching/learning process, which is not possible to carry out using traditional methods. It must provide a high degree of interactivity, encouraging the teamwork, according to the needs and preferences giving the user the feeling of presence which promotes the learning process (Reis *et al.*, 2013).

Second, the evaluation was consisted of verifying whether the integration of the learning analytic tool allows verifying that all data are extracted from the database correctly.

As part of the aims a pilot project will be carried out. This pilot project will allow to identify possible behavior patterns of students within the environment, related to their preference for materials and expertise. The following research questions will be answer:

R1: How the learning analytics can be improving the learning of students in 3D Educational Collaborative Virtual Environment?

R2: Given that learning analytics is about using data to help improve learning, what data that students are like more in accessing and exploring?

As shown in figure 6, this pilot project will start with a specific target audience exploring the collaborative virtual environment allowing that the data of students' different learning activities will be collected. The data extraction will be transferred into a separate database. In a second phase (after students have explored the environment) teachers will analyze the data collected through the graphical visualizations of learning analytics tool. Teachers are supposed to be able to more quickly interpret the visualized information, reflect on the impact of their teaching method on the learning behavior and performance of their students, and draw first conclusions about the effectiveness of their teaching, i.e., consider if their goals have been reached (Dyckhoff *et al.*, 2012).

Figure 6. Pilot project process

	RapidMiner	**Weka**	**Tableau**
Usability	• Easy to use	• Easiest to use	• Simple to use
Speed	• Requires more memory to operate	• Works faster on any machine.	• Works fast on any machine
Visualization	• More options but less than Tableau	• Less options	• Many visualization options
Algorithms supported	• Classification and Clustering	• Classification and Clustering	• Not used to implement algorithms
Data Set Size	• Supports large and small data set	• Supports only small data sets	• Supports any data se
Databases	• Oracle, Microsoft SQL Server, MySQL. ..	• Oracle, Microsoft SQL Server, MySQL. ..	• Oracle, Microsoft SQL Server, MySQL. ..

FUTURE RESEARCH DIRECTIONS

The immediate future work for this study consists of developing a detailed textual documentation to explain the results obtained during the pilot study. These results will allow to answer the research questions described in the previous section and will help to improve some teaching strategies form learning improvement and the application of adequate interventions. Tomorrow's instructors must think about increasing the intrinsic motivation of students by improving didactic approaches and the instructional design of their courses (Khalil, 2018). The evidences collected from pilot project can allow conclude that LA integrated with the educational virtual environments improve student engagements in teaching process. Through the analytics interpretation, the teachers can realize what is working and what is not in their classes. Subsequently they can make adjustments that requires intervention their teaching style with respect to learning.

Another interesting research is the practical issues of ethical constraints and privacy. Studies have shown that issues of privacy (data protection) are essential to implementation of systems that using learning analytics tools. Thus, these issues must be considered in applications development and a policy development in learning analytics practices must be required. This require an investigation which hopefully will be done in the next step.

CONCLUSION

In this paper, we presented the theoretical background, design, implementation, and evaluation details that are at the base of the framework development. Throughout the description of the theoretical background, some work related to the areas in question was analyzed. Some guidelines for the development of frameworks that allow to connect LA tools in 3DVE were identified. These guidelines highlight the type of data to be considered for analysis of students' performance, namely all activities of the learning process and alert to data protection and privacy issues.

One of the important aspects in 3DVE is an interaction between students because they are continuous and as the space is opened a high number of activities are not supported by the teacher, leading to many of the students to the disinterest of their learning process. To avoid this situation, if we incorporate a learning analytics tool into the environment, we were able to analyze the students' performance in order to improve the educational content and the type of activities according to the student's profile. The framework presented in this paper describes the main components needed to get connect the LA tool that automatically extract the learning flow undertaken by students in 3DVE.

The authors intend that teachers to monitor and analyze their teaching activities. The main objective of framework is improved student's performance because with the framework, teachers are enabled to explore, reflect and evaluate teaching interventions based on their interests. We believe that the teachers can take actions to solve problems with the low performance of students if they use the learning analytics in the tridimensional virtual environments. We are aware of the importance of LA, in which the data sets generated from the learning processes within virtual environments are used for educational improvement, can lead to greater dynamization and optimization of this process.

Currently, this framework is being built to support teachers in their ongoing reflection, evaluation and improvement of their instructional design and in a near future, we plan to demonstrate the utility of LA in learning process, showing also the possibilities and new metrics that could be gathered.

REFERENCES

Anderson, T., & Rivera-Vargas, P. (2020). A Critical look at Educational Technology from a Distance Education Perspective. *Digital Education Review, 37*, 208-229. HTTPS://DOI.ORG/10.1344/DER.2020.37.208-229

Asgari, M., & Kaufman, D. (2004). Relationships among computer games, fantasy, and learning. *Proceedings, Educating Imaginative Minds: 2nd Annual Conference on Imagination and Education.*

Berge, Z., & Collins, M. (1995). Computer-mediated communication and the online classroom in distance learning. *Computer-Mediated Communication Magazine, 2*(4), 6–13.

Bertagnolli, S., Wagner, M., Amorim, J., & Sanches, L. (2007). Bibliotecas Digitais Integradas a Ambientes Virtuais de Aprendizagem. *RENOTE, 5*(2). Advance online publication. doi:10.22456/1679-1916.14247

Bettencourt, T., & Abade, A. (2008). Mundos Virtuais de Aprendizagem e de Ensino - uma caracterização inicial. *IE Comunicaciones: Revista Iberoamericana de Informática Educativa, 4574*(7), 3-16.

Bricken, M., & Byrne, C. M. (1994). Summer students in virtual reality: a pilot study on educational applications of virtual reality technology. In A. Wexelblat (Ed.), *Virtual Reality: Applications and Explorations* (pp. 199–218). Academic Press.

Bronack, S., Sanders, R., Cheney, A., Riedl, R., Tashner, J., & Matzen, N. (2008). Presence pedagogy: Teaching and learning in a 3D virtual immersive world. *International Journal on Teaching and Learning in Higher Education, 20*(1), 59–69.

Buckingham, S., & Ferguson, R. (2012). Social Learning Analytics. *Journal of Educational Technology & Society, 15*, 3–26.

Calonge, C. (2007). Using Second Life for immersive learning (Podcast). *Educase 2007 Seminars on Academic Computing Conference*. Retrieved April 15, 2020 from http://connect.educause.edu/blog/gbayne/podcastusingsecondlifefor/44967

Chittaro, L., & Ranon, R. (2007). Web3D technologies in learning, education and training: Motivations, issues, opportunities. *Computers & Education*, *49*(1), 3–18. doi:10.1016/j.compedu.2005.06.002

Christopoulos, A., Pellas, N., & Laakso, M.-J. (2020). A Learning Analytics Theoretical Framework for STEM Education Virtual Reality Applications. *Education in Science*, *10*(11), 317. doi:10.3390/educsci10110317

Clow, D. (2012). The learning analytics cycle: Closing the loop effectively. *ACM International Conference Proceeding Series*. 10.1145/2330601.2330636

Cruz-Benito, J., Therón, R., García-Peñalvo, F., & Lucas, E. (2015). Discovering usage behaviors and engagement in an Educational Virtual World. *Computers in Human Behavior*, *47*(1), 18–25. doi:10.1016/j.chb.2014.11.028

Cruz-Benito, J., Therón, R., García-Peñalvo, F., Maderuelo, C., Pérez-Blanco, J., Zazo, H., & ... . (2014) Monitoring and feedback of learning processes in virtual worlds through analytics architectures: a real case. *9th Iberian Conference on Information Systems and Technologies (CISTI)*, 1–6. 10.1109/CISTI.2014.6877097

De Lucia, A., Francese, R., Passero, I., & Tortora, G. (2009). Development and evaluation of a virtual campus on Second Life: The case of Second DMI. *Computers & Education*, *52*(1), 220–233. doi:10.1016/j.compedu.2008.08.001

Deutsch, G. (2010). *RapidMiner from Rapid-I at CeBIT 2010*. Data Mining Blog.

Dyckhoff, A., Zielke, D., Bültmann, M., Chatti, M., & Schroeder, U. (2012). Design and Implementation of a Learning Analytics Toolkit for Teachers. *Journal of Educational Technology & Society*, 15.

Einhardt, L., Tavares, T., & Cechinel, C. (2016). Moodle analytics dashboard: a learning analytics tool to visualize users interactions in moodle. *Proceedings - 2016 11th Latin American Conference on Learning Objects and Technology*, 1–6. 10.1109/LACLO.2016.7751805

Escudeiro, P. (2007). X-TEC Model and QEF Model: A Case Study. In T. Bastiaens & S. Carliner (Eds.), *Proceedings of E-Learn 2007--World Conference on E-Learning in Corporate, Government, Healthcare, and Higher Education* (pp. 258-265). Quebec City, Canada: Association for the Advancement of Computing in Education (AACE).

Field, J. (2007). Looking outwards, not inwards. *ELT Journal, 61*(1), 30–38. doi:10.1093/elt/ccl042

Gavilanes-Sagnay, F., Loza-Aguirre, E., Riofrío-Luzcando, D., & Segura-Morales, M. (2019) Improving the Use of Virtual Worlds in Education Through Learning Analytics: A State of Art. In *Proceedings of the Future Technologies Conference (FTC) 2018. FTC 2018. Advances in Intelligent Systems and Computing* (vol. 880). Springer. 10.1007/978-3-030-02686-8_83

George, S. (2019). Games, Simulations, Immersive Environments, and Emerging Technologies. In A. Tatnall (Ed.), *Encyclopedia of Education and Information Technologies*. Springer. doi:10.1007/978-3-319-60013-0_36-1

Gros, B. (2016). The design of smart educational environments. *Smart Learn. Environ., 3*(15), 1–11.

Hoel, T., & Chen, W. (2018). Privacy and data protection in learning analytics should be motivated by an educational maxim-towards a proposal. *Research and Practice in Technology Enhanced Learning, 13*(1), 20. doi:10.118641039-018-0086-8 PMID:30595748

Holmes, G., & Donkin, A. (1994). Weka: A Machine Learning Workbench. *Proc Second Australia and New Zealand Conference on Intelligent Information Systems.*

Johnson, M. J., Schwab, R. L., & Foa, L. (1999). Technology as a change agent for the teaching process. *Theory into Practice, 38*(1), 24–30. doi:10.1080/00405849909543827

Jones, L., Grant, R., & Hrynaszkiewicz, I. (2019). Implementing publisher policies that inform, support and encourage authors to share data: two case studies. *Insights the UKSG Journal, 32*, 11. doi:10.1629/uksg.463

Khalil, M. (2018). *Learning Analytics in Massive Open Online Courses. Ph.D These.* Graz University of Technology.

Kim, J. (2019). Overview of disciplinary data sharing practices and promotion of open data in science. *Science Editing, 6*(1), 3–9. doi:10.6087/kcse.149

Li, T. M. H., Chau, M., Wong, P. W. C., Lai, E. S. Y., & Yip, P. S. F. (2013). Evaluation of a web-based social network electronic game in enhancing mental health literacy for young people. *Journal of Medical Internet Research, 15*(5), e80. doi:10.2196/jmir.2316 PMID:23676714

Lukarov, V., Chatti, M. A., Ths, H. F., Kia, S., Muslim, A., Greven, C., & Schroeder, U. (2014). Data models in learning analytics. CEUR Workshops, 1227, 88-95.

Madhuri, J. V. (March 2013). Significance of data warehousing and data mining in business applications. *International Journal of Soft Computing and Engineering, 3*(1).

Padgett, S. (2014). *Profiling The Fraudster: Removing the Mask to Prevent and Detect Fraud.* . doi:10.1002/9781118929773

RapidMinder. (n.d.a). *Information about.* https://pt.wikipedia.org/wiki/RapidMiner

RapidMinder. (n.d.b). *More Information about.* https://www.capterra.com.br/software/148220/rapidminer

Reis, R. & Escudeiro, P. & Escudeiro, N. (2012). Comparing Social Virtual Worlds for Educational Purposes. *Education, 1,* 21-26. doi:10.5923/j.edu.20110101.04

Reis, R. & Fonseca, B. & Escudeiro, P. (2013). *A Structured Approach to Evaluate Collaborative Educational Virtual Environments.* . doi:10.2991/iccnce.2013.54

Reis, R., Marques, B. P., & Sampaio, I. (2020) Learning Analytics Framework for Improving Performance to Students through Educational Virtual Worlds. *International Journal of Education and Information Technologies, 14*, 8-13. Doi:10.46300/9109.2020.14.2

Reisoğlu, İ., Topu, F., Yilmaz, R., Karakus Yılmaz, T., & Goktas, Y. (2017). 3D virtual learning environments in education: a meta-review. *Asia Pacific Education Review, 18.* doi:10.100712564-016-9467-0

Ritzema, T., & Harris, B. (2008). The use of Second Life for distance education. *Journal of Computing Sciences in Colleges, 23*(6).

Roussos, M., Johnson, A., Moher, T., Leigh, J., Vasilakis, C., & Barnes, C. (1999). Learning and Building Together in an Immersive Virtual World. Presence, 8(3), 247-263. doi:10.1162/105474699566215

Šašinka, Č., Stachoň, Z., Sedlák, M., Chmelík, J., Herman, L., Kubíček, P., Šašinková, A., Doležal, M., Tejkl, H., Urbánek, T., Svatoňová, H., Ugwitz, P., & Juřík, V. (2019). Collaborative Immersive Virtual Environments for Education in Geography. *Int. ISPRS. J. Geo-Inf., 8*, 3.

Schunk, D. H. (1991). *Learning Theories: An Educational Perspective.* Merrill.

Selywn, N. (2009). The digital native- myth and reality. *Aslib Proceedings, 61*(4), 364–379. doi:10.1108/00012530910973776

Silva, T. (2015). *Ferramentas Gratuitas para Desenvolvimento de Soluções de Business Intelligence. Master Tese Degree.* Escola Superior de Tecnologia e Gestão de Viseu. Instituto Politécnico de Viseu.

Southgate, E., Blackmore, K., Pieschl, S., Grimes, S., McGuire, J., & Smithers, K. (2018). *Artificial intelligence and emerging technologies (virtual, augmented and mixed reality) in schools: A research report*. University of Newcastle, Australia.

Tableau. (n.d.). *Information about*. https://en.wikipedia.org/wiki/Tableau_Software

Tashiro, J.S., & Dunlap, D., (2007). The impact of realism on learning engagement in educational games. *Proceedings of Future Play 2007*.

Tseng, W., Liou, H., & Chu, H. (2020). Vocabulary learning in virtual environments: Learner autonomy and collaboration. *System, 88*. doi:10.1016/j.system.2019.102190

Vicente-Saez, R., & Martinez-Fuentes, C. (2018). Open Science now: A systematic literature review for an integrated definition. *Journal of Business Research, 88*, 428–436. doi:10.1016/j.jbusres.2017.12.043

Weka. (n.d.). *Information about*. https://pt.wikipedia.org/wiki/Weka

ADDITIONAL READING

Araka, E., Maina, E., Gitonga, R., & Oboko, R. (2020). *Research trends in measurement and intervention tools for self-regulated learning for e-learning environments - systematic review (2008–2018)* (Vol. 15). Research and Practice in Technology Enhanced Learning.

Bahritidinov, B., de Lis, J. S., Sánchez, E., & Lama, M. (2010). Supporting Adaptive Learning with a Student Model Repository and Shared Adaptive Variables. In X. Luo, M. Spaniol, L. Wang, Q. Li, W. Nejdl, & W. Zhang (Eds.), Lecture Notes in Computer Science: Vol. 6483. *Advances in Web-Based Learning – ICWL 2010*. Springer., doi:10.1007/978-3-642-17407-0_1

Burgos, D. (2012) "How to use IMS-LD to support eLearning in an effective way (invited talk)," in *2012 International Symposium on Computers in Education (SIIE 2012)*, Andorra la Vella, 2012 pp.1-1.

Correia, A., Fonseca, B., Paredes, H., Martins, P., & Morgado, L. (2016). Computer-Simulated 3D Virtual Environments in Collaborative Learning and Training: Meta-Review, Refinement, and Roadmap. In Y. Sivan (Ed.), *Handbook on 3D3C Platforms. Progress in IS*. Springer., doi:10.1007/978-3-319-22041-3_15

Fernández-Gallego, B., Lama, M., Vidal, J. C., & Mucientes, M. (2013). Learning Analytics Framework for Educational Virtual Worlds, *Procedia Computer Science*, Volume 25, pp. 443-447, ISSN 1877-0509, doi:10.1016/j.procs.2013.11.056

Fernández-Gallego, B., Lama, M., Vidal, J. C., Sánchez, E., & Bugarín, A. (2010). OPENET4VE: A platform for the execution of IMS LD units of learning in virtual environments. In: *Jemni M, Kinshuk, Sampson D, Spector JM, editors*. Proceedings of the 10th IEEE International Conference on Advanced Learning Technologies, ICALT 2010, Los Alamitos, California: IEEE Computer Society; pp. 472-474. 10.1109/ICALT.2010.137

KEY TERMS AND DEFINITIONS

Collaborative Learning: The interaction between students that allow to engage in group the students to enhance learning through working together. They work together to solve problems or learn new concepts.

Evaluation: Systematic process of collecting, analysing, and interpreting information. In this chapter the evaluation is related with evaluation of framework whose purpose the measure the final quality of environment based on some quality criteria.

Framework Design: The basic structure that allow organizing the overall all design flow into a set of steps.

Learning Analytics: An evidence-based approach that from data generated by students as they learn, to allow are measured and analysis for purposes of understanding and optimising learning and the environments in which it occurs.

OpenSim: Open-source multi-platform where we can create complex 3D environments and includes facilities for creating custom avatars, chatting with others in the environment, building 3D content in world.

Privacy: Related to with students because the aim is to analyse the information extracted in their learning process.

User-Centered Design: Iterative design process in which designers focus on the users and their needs in each phase of the design process.

Virtual Environments: Open environments that lead the participants to browse through different scenarios at random.

Weka: Learning analytics tools which contains some visualization tools and machine learning algorithms for data mining tasks.

Chapter 8
Learning Analytics as a Tool for Planning, Evaluating, and Improving a SMOOC for Teacher Professional Development:
Higher Education Experience in a Brazil

Cristine Martins Gomes de Gusmão
Federal University of Pernambuco, Brazil

Josiane Lemos Machiavelli
https://orcid.org/0000-0001-6469-621X
Federal University of Pernambuco, Brazil

Patricia Smith Cavalcante
Federal University of Pernambuco, Brazil

ABSTRACT

This chapter describes how a public university has met the challenge of changing inside the educational culture and preparing its teachers to manage online teaching-learning processes using learning analytics to contribute to the design, evaluation, and improvement of SMOOC. From the results obtained with a survey answered by the teachers, a twenty-hour class SMOOC was developed that focuses on instrumental aspects of digital technological resources in the teaching and learning contexts, as well as in the pedagogical issues, which concern the appropriate use of digital technologies. The findings of this research demonstrate that the SMOOC has been

DOI: 10.4018/978-1-7998-7103-3.ch008

able to meet the teacher training needs, which are changing the way they work since remote education has been the viable alternative to guarantee the functioning of the university in the coronavirus pandemic period. However, it is believed that the knowledge that teachers are acquiring will contribute to changes in professional practice even post-pandemic.

INTRODUCTION

Professional development is an effort of continuous evolution, ensuring inclusive, equitable, and quality education and promoting lifelong learning opportunities for all, which is a goal of the United Nations 2030 Agenda for Sustainable Development that guides educational actions worldwide.

The digital medium becomes an essential vehicle to guarantee teaching and learning opportunities for all, but, in Brazil, this is a problem because, in addition to the difficulty with physical and technological infrastructure, a lot of teachers are still not sufficiently trained to use *information and communications technologies (ICT)* in teaching and learning activities. This aspect was evident in the coronavirus pandemic period when the population needed to adopt physical distancing to prevent the spread of the disease. In this scenario, emergency remote teaching was an alternative for maintaining, at least in part, the functions of the schools and universities, but the lack of preparation of many teachers to deal with digital technological resources made the process difficult.

How did the Federal University of Pernambuco (UFPE), a Brazilian Public University, respond to that? A *Small Open Online Course (SMOOC)* to facilitate the digital inclusion of professors and technical support personnel was designed, and an opportunity to exchange experiences and collaborative construction of knowledge was created. This chapter will describe how UFPE, which has been mostly based on offline teaching and learning, has met the challenge of changing the inside educational culture, preparing their team to manage online teaching and learning processes, and learning how analytics has contributed to SMOOC planning, evaluation, and improvement.

BACKGROUND

In order to understand the course design presented in this chapter, the authors consider it important to clarify aspects that involve the challenges of teacher training in Brazil and what massive open online courses are, as well as the context of this initiative.

Teacher Professional Development in Brazil: Barriers and Possible Solutions

One of the great deficiencies of teachers working in higher education is that, in many cases, they are not sufficiently prepared for the teaching profession. Although most of them have master's or doctorate degrees and relevant professional experience, unpreparedness to deal with teaching and learning processes still predominates (Almeida, 2012). Much of what teachers know about teaching and learning processes are the result of their life history, especially the history of school and university life, as well as what they learn in practice and from interactions with other teachers (Tardif, 2000).

When considering the insertion of ICT in teaching practice, the problems become even more serious, because this theme is not sufficiently explored in the training processes, initial or continued, making many teachers resistant to the use of ICT in their daily profession. In addition to this issue, when specifically analyzing continuing teacher education initiatives, many other problems are highlighted, such as:

- Frequently, they are still done traditionally, through lectures, seminars, or short courses that do not usually meet the real needs of teachers. Also, they have little practical applicability (Abrucio, 2016; Ramos & Filgueiras, 2014);
- For costs reasons, they often end up not including all teachers or, in some cases, are offered to other professionals in the education departments, who become multipliers for teachers in the education network (Davis, 2012);
- It is common for training activities to be given by people without adequate preparation in the training content or with little knowledge about the institutional context and the public they are forming (Davis, 2012; Ramos & Filgueiras, 2014);
- Considering that many training courses are still carried out in face to face design (Universities UK, 2013), it is difficult to reconcile the absence of the teachers in the classroom with the need to participate in training processes, not to mention that the costs of these training courses are usually high (Davis, 2012).

To minimize these problems, some strategies that can be used are (Davis, 2012; Hollands, 2014; Todos Pela Educação, 2014):

- Work on the professional development of teachers in the perspective of lifelong learning, so that they have the opportunity to stay up to date throughout their professional trajectory;

- Understand the profiles and needs of teachers and considered this information in the design of training processes;
- Integrate theory and practice in the formative processes, so teachers can more easily identify possibilities to insert the content in their professional practice;
- Encourage the exchange of experiences between teachers;
- Include ICT in training processes, as a way they can foment teachers to rethink their pedagogical practices;
- Involve managers, pedagogical coordinators, and technical support personnel from educational institutions in the training processes, especially those that occur mediated by digital technologies, so that they better understand the potential of ICT in the teaching and learning processes.

Therefore, the authors concluded that online teaching training can contribute to minimizing the problems reported, because, in addition to enabling large-scale provision, it is capable of providing multiple and more flexible teaching and learning structures, which are difficult to achieve through face to face teaching (Gatti, 2016; Ramos & Filgueiras, 2014). However, a lot of online teaching training models also deserve to be rethought because, frequently, they have only reproduced what is done in face-to-face teaching, without taking advantage of the potential that digital technologies offer from a methodological and pedagogical point of view.

Massive Open Online Courses: Main Definitions

Originally, *massive open online courses (MOOCs)* were online courses, designed to serve numerous participants, which can be accessed by anyone, anywhere, as long as there is an Internet connection, without qualification restrictions. Such courses arose with the proposal to offer complete teaching and learning experiences, online and free (United Nations Educational, Scientific and Cultural Organization, 2016; Yousef et al., 2014; Yuan & Powell, 2013), to assist people who would be excluded from training processes carried out in traditional ways, because of lack of time, geographical distance, costs, or prerequisites (Mazzardo et al., 2017).

The models of MOOCs have evolved rapidly. A series of formats, derived from the first experiences, have emerged, but the literature categorizes MOOCs in two main formats:

- **Connectivist MOOCs (cMOOCs):** Based on a connectivist pedagogical model, which understands that knowledge is formed in a network and learning is the result of interactions that take place in networks, the addition, and removal of connections. In this format, it is the course participants who define their own learning objectives, present their points of view, create and share content and knowledge in a collaborative way (Andrade & Silveira, 2016; Siemens, 2013; Yousef et al., 2014);

- **Extension MOOCs (xMOOCs):** Follow instructional models, based on behaviorist, cognitive, or constructivist theories. They view the teacher as an expert and the students as consumers of the knowledge generated by the teachers. In this course model, the learning objectives, as well as the content, activities, and resources used are previously defined by the teachers responsible for the content (Andrade & Silveira, 2016; Siemens, 2013; Yousef et al., 2014).

From these, other MOOC models have been proposed, such as *small private open online courses*, the main characteristic of which is the offer to a relatively small number of participants. Some studies mention between 100 and 150 students (Mazzardo et al., 2017).

UFPE: A Brief Presentation

Brazil is the largest country in Latin America. According to the Brazilian Institute of Geography and Statistics-IBGE (2020), the Brazilian population exceeds 211.000.000 people, divided into five major regions, which present numerous diversities, social and economic contrasts. Pernambuco is a state located in the northeast region that still has a great lack of assistance to education and health. The higher education institutions, in this context, are fundamental for regional advancement.

The Federal University of Pernambuco is one of the 20 higher education institutions in the region. Pernambuco has four federal higher education institutions. According to QS World University Rankings (2020), which accesses the training of students, research, teachers, and employability, the UFPE is the 14th in Brazil, the only one in the northern and northeastern regions that appears in this ranking of the first 14 positions. The institution has 107 undergraduate courses, with more than 30.000 students, 90 master's degrees, 52 doctoral degrees, and 56 specialization courses, which together have more than 12.000 students and cover different areas of knowledge. Regarding the staff, there are more than 2.500 teachers and 3.800 administrative technicians; most of them are not used to working remotely (Universidade Federal de Pernambuco, 2020).

With the advent of the COVID-19 pandemic, much has been done and rethought. Faced with diversity of funding, higher education, and, in particular, research has advanced in digital transformation. To meet this new context, the training of teachers and technical support personnel is essential, not only for the daily practice of activities, however, it is also important, the vision of the open education movement.

In March 2020, the Federal University of Pernambuco suspended all its prospective activities. Undergraduate courses in distance learning also had their activities suspended, with only short courses and specialization courses remaining in operation. During the period of suspension of academic activities, the university defined and developed a training process for its group of civil servants—professors, researchers, and technicians.

In August 2020, 30% of academic activities have returned, with postgraduate courses. The great effort comes this August with the resumption of graduations. The training of the UFPE team to conduct remote classes was essential for this return. Now the effort is to ensure that a base of almost 40.000 students has access to a new format of the learning process and also the knowledge to better develop necessary skills. This scenario confirms the concern and the necessary alignment with the objectives of sustainable development, which highlights the importance of quality education throughout life for all.

PATHS TAKEN FOR COURSE DESIGN

Given the need to prepare the UFPE team to carry out activities that involve remote activities during the coronavirus pandemic, a SMOOC was proposed. To guide training planning, an initial survey was applied to the UFPE team to learn about their experience with the use of technological resources in professional practice, especially the G Suite, a set of Google services implemented at the university to support administrative activities and teachers.

Data from the 914 survey participants demonstrated that 48,5% of them did not feel comfortable using technologies in their professional practice and that 72,6% never had specific training for this. It was also observed that even among people who say that use technological resources in their professional practice, the emphasis was on communication tools (such as instant messaging and e-mail) and text editors, presentations, and spreadsheets. When asked about the use of G Suite, only 25% of them had used Google Classroom, and 47% of them had used Google Meet, resources considered important to support online education.

This preliminary data showed that the use of digital technologies at the Federal University of Pernambuco was distant from real potential to improve and expand teaching and learning opportunities, as well as to develop critical thinking and new skills in their students. That revealed the urgency of promoting a turning point in this situation.

A group of university researchers, students, and some personnel that worked with distance learning were asked by the UFPE central administration to develop and offer a course to UFPE professionals. Our initial data suggested that the course should focus both on instrumental aspects of digital technologic resources in the teaching and learning processes (i.e., what they are and how to use them), as well as pedagogical issues that concern the appropriate use of the digital technologies in different teaching and learning contexts. To define SMOOC, the "Guidance on flexible learning during campus closures: ensuring course quality of higher education in COVID-19 outbreak" (Huang, Liu, Guo, et al., 2020) and the guide for "Curriculum on media literacy and information for teachers" (Wilson, 2013), both published by UNESCO, were used as references.

There was little time to plan and develop the program because of the coronavirus pandemic. Thus, a 20-hour SMOOC was designed to be offered to all UFPE professors and technical support personnel interested, subdivided into seven groups, from May to September 2020. The course was implemented in Google Classroom. Although it is not a platform for offering massive courses, it is the resource that the UFPE team has available for its activities, so we understand that the fact that training takes place in this space would be an opportunity to learn to use the resource through the exploration of the course itself. The SMOOC, planned to be finished for two weeks, has six didactic units, which explores the differences between online and face-to-face teaching, the pedagogical use of the main resources of G Suite, and the organization of one online course based on Google Classroom by each professor.

From the design point of view, the course considers the concept of flexible learning, understood as a teaching and learning process centered on the needs of course participants, which offers varied study options to meet different student profiles,[1] such as the flexibility of times and places (even if virtual) where the participants usually study at home. A variety of resources and pedagogical approaches were used, which can be synchronous and asynchronous, individual and collective (Huang, Liu, Guo, et al., 2020; Huang, Liu, Tlili, et al., 2020). Course participants are encouraged to share their doubts in the comment area available in the virtual classroom, which works similarly to the discussion forums. This favors interaction and exchange of knowledge between the students themselves and between them and the facilitators who mediate the training. The course completion certificate is available to those who participate in the final activity, which involves structuring a classroom in Google Classroom.

Regarding the didactic materials, it used open educational resources (OER), which reduced the time needed to prepare the course and, at the same time, favored the availability of a variety of didactic materials in different formats, attending different styles of learning. At least two online meetings were held with course participants. Previously scheduled, they are not expository classes. These are moments planned to deepen the discussion on the subjects covered in the course and to clarify doubts that arise during the training.

HOW DID LEARNING ANALYTICS HELP US FOR THE COURSE PLANNING, EVALUATION, AND IMPROVEMENT?

According to the Society for Learning Analytics Research—SoLAR (2020), *learning analytics (LA)* is "the measurement, collection, analysis, and reporting of data about learners and their contexts, for purposes of understanding and optimizing learning and the environments in which it occurs (para. 1)." This can happen in several ways, such as (para. 2):

supporting student development of lifelong learning skills and strategies; provision of personalized and timely feedback to students regarding their learning; supporting the development of important skills such as collaboration, critical thinking, communication, and creativity; develop student awareness by supporting self-reflection; support quality learning and teaching by providing empirical evidence on the success of pedagogical innovations.

Whereas this is the first time that UFPE has offered SMOOC-based training for its team, in this research, LA was used with the purpose of analysis of student needs, behavior in the virtual learning environment, and satisfaction with the course. In other words, we analyzed data collected from student "life cycles" in the course, from admission to certification. We conducted a qualitative data analysis from surveys, observation of comments on activities, meetings, and the common discussion board. This was done weekly and at the end of each class. This is to say that LA was used both from a theoretical perspective, that is, analyzing data to increase the understanding of learning processes, and from a practical perspective, that is, using data to act and intervene in the learning of individuals, helping them to improve their experience and achieve learning goals (Khalil, 2017).

How has LA helped us with the planning, evaluation, and improvement of the educational offer described here? Table 1 presents some decisions that were taken from LA. With adaptations from papers published by Chatti et al. (2012) and Moissa et al. (2014), we present the definitions considered in the "Intervention provided" column shown in the table:

1. **Pedagogical:** These data helped us in the planning and production of the first version of the course;
2. **Monitoring:** These data helped us to follow the path taken by students in the virtual learning environment and supported decision-making in relation to improvements in the way we communicate with students, in the design of the course, in the provision of new materials or in the improvement of didactic materials already made available;

3. **Intervention:** The analysis of this kind of data suggested rapid interventions that could be taken in order to minimize dropout, improve students' performance in the course, and increase graduation rates;
4. **Guidance:** These are data that revealed the need to provide additional guidance to students.

Table 1. How LA helped us plan, evaluate, and improve the course

Data	Project moment when the data was useful	Intervention provided	Taken decisions
Low number of participants who used or knew Google Classroom before training	Planning	Pedagogical	Google Classroom course designs were developed to learn the Google Classroom content at the same time participants were learning the course content. The course was an experience of being a teacher and a learner at the same time.
Low UFPE team proficiency in using other resources available in the G Suite	Planning	Pedagogical	Start with an instrumental perspective of ICT resources and progressively move towards a pedagogical perspective with case discussions and activities in which participants were invited to use the main apps available on G Suite.
Excessive number of people who did not receive training in the use of digital technologies in teaching and learning processes	Planning	Pedagogical	Course design to attend instrumental and pedagogical aspects of digital technologies for teaching practice.
Students who did not access the course in the first week of the offer	Evaluation and improvement	Monitoring, Intervention	Adjustments were made in the way of communicating at the beginning of the course, including personal e-mails and UFPE institutional electronic platform of internal communications to ensure that information was reaching all participants.
Number of comments questioning how to start studies or students saying they are lost in the virtual learning environment	Evaluation and improvement	Intervention, Guidance, Pedagogical	This course was designed to support self-directed study. However, some participants were not used to it. We created discussions with participants about teaching methods that are less teacher-centered, which encourage students to take the lead in defining their learning paths based on their real needs. We also encourage participants to read the tutorials that guided the use of the platform, as many who said they were lost had not even seen the tutorials.

continues on following page

Table 1. Continued

Data	Project moment when the data was useful	Intervention provided	Taken decisions
Number of new conversation topics posted on the common online board regarding subjects that were explained in the course materials	Evaluation and improvement	Intervention, Guidance, Pedagogical	For many participants, it seemed easier to ask than to seek information that was already available in the course. So, we reinforced the logic of self-directed study and encouraged them to read and learn the teaching materials available before asking. Two other decisions were made regarding an FAQ addressing the most frequent doubts and a limit on the number of new conversation topics on the common discussion board. So, we focused on the main doubts, placed them inside the common online board, and concentrated doubts in a single space. By doing this, participants were driven to focus on the answers already produced.
Number of students reporting difficulty using the "Google Meet" because it is not like a regular lecture	Evaluation and improvement	Intervention, Guidance, Pedagogical	We explained in more detail the purpose of the virtual meetings and how to use the tool.
Number of people reporting that they do not know what open educational resources are when we report that the course was produced from OER	Evaluation and improvement	Intervention, Guidance, Pedagogical	We include materials in the course that clarified what OER are, because, in addition to helping participants better to understand how the course was structured, they could also use these resources in their teaching practice, improving and streamlining their activities.
Low access to materials that guided the use of tools such as Google forms and Jamboard, among others, and low adherence to offline tasks that encouraged the use of these tools	Evaluation and improvement	Intervention, Pedagogical	We started using them in real time with them during virtual meetings; that is, we did exercises using these tools so that participants could put the hands-on, thus facilitating the understanding of how they can use them in teaching practice.
Number of questions generated in thematic meetings that could not be answered due to lack of time	Evaluation and improvement	Guidance, Pedagogical	Participation in meetings was much higher than we imagined, leaving some doubts unanswered. So, during meetings, we answered the most questions we could, and after the meeting, we posted the remaining answers to the common discussion board.
Number of participants, especially teachers, reporting difficulty in planning their remote classes with regard to the definition of workload and quantity of teaching materials	Evaluation and improvement	Guidance, Pedagogical	Although this question was not foreseen as the content of this course, we make new teaching materials available dealing with this topic and also explore it during meetings.
Number of graduates after two weeks of course	Evaluation and improvement	Intervention, Pedagogical	We revised the schedule and extended the course by one week, which greatly increased the number of graduates. For future offers, training hours will also need to be revised.

RESULTS

UFPE has just over 2.500 teachers and 3.800 administrative technicians. Everyone was invited to participate in the training presented here. There were 1.563 enrolled, 983 accessed the course at least once, and of these, 87,2% completed the final activity, a requirement to receive the certificate of course completion. The activity requested the sending of a print screen proving the structuring of a classroom or other workspace in Google Classroom. Student dropout in MOOCs is a major concern. The literature have shown significant dropout rates, normally around 90% (Atiaja & Proenza, 2016; Bezerra & Silva, 2017; Dillenbourg et al., 2014), but in this research we had good results, less than 15%.

The analysis of the platform and didactic materials accessed by participants, attendance at online meetings carried out during the course, and the other activities and course evaluation survey, answered by 790 students, demonstrated that UFPE SMOOC succeeded. It met the expectations of the participants and designers. Some data to support this information are presented below:

- 97,9% of respondents considered that the content presented in the training was important or very important for professional practice;
- 93% agreed, totally or partially, that they learned to interact quickly with the didactic resources of the course;
- 91,4% agreed, totally or partially, that the design of the course facilitates learning;
- 93,2% of the participants considered that navigation in the virtual learning environment worked well and occurred free of technical problems;
- 99,1% wished to participate in other training about the use of digital resources in the teaching and learning processes;
- 99% would recommend the course to interested colleagues.

When analyzing how the participants used the virtual learning environment and the feedback left in the survey in which they participated at the end of the course, some comments draw attention, such as: the course recognition to improve participants practice and assist in the transposition of their routine, from a very focused on face to face teaching to online teaching; the indication that the course contributed to participants confidence to use digital technologies in their daily bases work; and the interest for the continuity of the training processes based on MOOCs.

Criticisms were received, related to having little familiarity with the G Suite, a lack of study of the materials available during training weeks, or attempts to fit the course into the characteristics of traditional classroom teaching. Therefore, they are not problems related to the technological resources used, curricula, or the performance of the academic support team.

One of the suggestions for improvement concerns the time and duration of the course. Some participants consider that 20 hours and two weeks were insufficient for adequate development of the suggested studies and activities. Estimating the time in online courses is not an easy task, as it is influenced by several factors, such as the complexity of the content presented in the course, the profile of course participants, and the number of learning objects available. Considering the little familiarity with virtual learning environments and G Suite resources, it is likely that participants felt they needed more time to complete their studies than the one initially planned.

Another important aspect was the need for linear and hierarchical learning methods, which are very present in the Brazilian teaching and learning processes. The freedom to develop studies at one's own pace, with the possibility of accessing didactic materials according to individual interests, learning needs, and time availability, as well as the self-learning method that systematically required online presence and production of activities, led some participants confused or insecure. These findings were not seen as course design problems but as aspects to be better explored with the participants in the subsequent classes. Even so, adjustments are being made to the next course groups of participants, as an evaluation design-based cycle seeking for course excellence.

SOLUTIONS AND RECOMMENDATIONS

Although the results have shown that the UFPE course is well-received and seems to be effective, at the same time, they revealed other problems that need to be addressed:

1. Lack of intimacy with the use of online platforms and participation in MOOC-based course models;
2. Oral orientation culture instead of autonomous tutorial study culture;
3. Bending online learning to fit regular face-to-face classroom teaching strategies;
4. Lack of free time to attend an immersive course;
5. Course participants' linear and hierarchical mindset to study.

Concerning the UFPE team's lack of online platforms intimacy, UFPE managers made two different decisions. They opened the possibilities for teachers' and personnel's free choice to adopt different platforms and social networks of their preferences and proficiencies while preparing other Google Classroom and Moodle courses. By doing that, UFPE seeks to expand the repertoire of teaching platforms, ensuring a certain level of teaching comfort and a smooth learning process.

Brazilian oral communication culture is very strong and impacts teaching and learning strategies. Direct questions and answers are a student's first choice rather than seeking information from written materials, such as articles or tutorials. It was observed the same behavior with our course participants. As a solution, the UFPE course created direct relationships between the activities and the written material, so that there is no way to carry out the activities without reading.

As a predominantly on-site educational institution, with little online didactic experience, teachers' first online classrooms were based on their previous lessons, mirroring face-to-face classes in online media. To help teachers to migrate to a real online model, presentation, and analysis sessions of several examples of online classrooms have been added.

To address the participants' lack of time to attend the course properly, UFPE has extended it from two to four weeks of course time. With that, the learning activities of the last groups were developed in enough time.

Finally, we have a mindset issue. Part of the teacher's work is to organize and structure the contents in the best possible way to enhance learning. Therefore, it is expected that teachers have more linear and hierarchical thinking of classes. As a way of introducing new ideas, examples of classrooms based on themes, learning methods, weeks per month, among others, were inserted in the course. Thus, teachers could observe different forms of curriculum content organization.

This experience strongly suggests that constant course adjustments have to be made according to group data and individual participants as well. One of the strengths of the UFPE course is the importance for each person and their difficulties and interests. Our results demonstrate that humanization and empathy in education, even in MOOCs, make a difference in student satisfaction and in course completion rates.

FUTURE RESEARCH DIRECTIONS

The digital transformation encourages professionals due to the diversity of tools and approaches that favor the acquisition of knowledge; however, some challenges are also imposed. To meet the dynamics and demands of the market, a greater number of people are submitted to training and courses in the most diverse modalities to add value to the professional skills and institutions to which they are linked. Working on real-world problems often requires the combination of different types of specialized and context-dependent knowledge, as well as different forms of knowledge. A set of actions was essential to guarantee the training of UFPE professionals. The development of the approach to meet the educational needs, in a time of emergency activities, like the coronavirus pandemic, brought reflections, which can give rise to research:

1. Define a team of multidisciplinary professionals to support educational activities: the importance of knowledge in virtual environments, flexible and innovative pedagogical practices, experiences in virtual rooms with many students, short courses, but intensive in content. Challenges in structuring the technological platform to be used but also in the pedagogical knowledge necessary to meet the requirement of distance education;
2. Promote digital inclusion: meeting the daily expectations of the academic community;
3. Explore the activities of educational practice in the workplace: the need to understand that the daily practice of actions requires different forms of knowledge to deal with a specific situation, differential provided by the periodic monitoring strategies of professionals in training;
4. Encourage the development and use of open educational resources and participation in courses based on MOOCs: The digital medium becomes a fundamental vehicle to guarantee teaching and learning opportunities for all, but in Brazil, it is still a problem. In addition to the difficulty of physical and technological infrastructure, teachers still need the training to use technology, as well as the application of active methodologies in their face-to-face classroom or digital activities. In this scenario, the movement open educational practices have become an element of great interest to maintain, at least in part, the functioning of schools and universities and improve the quality of education;
5. Expand the use of learning analytics: investing more in research that involves learning analytics, which gives us the possibility to better understand the behavior and the real learning needs of students and intervene from there, is a good strategy to improve the quality of the design of these courses, increase student satisfaction and reduce dropout rates. So, we intend to make this type of analysis more frequent in our courses and publish the results achieved.

CONCLUSION

The literature shows that learning analytics has been widely used to study factors of retention, behavior, participation, and performance in online courses, but to a lesser extent, it has been investigated to support the design of MOOCs, as well as their improvement, work that researchers sought to do in this chapter, with the proposal to improve the learning experience of the course participants.

Drachsler and Kalz (2016) point out that

MOOCs are courses and not just published resources. A course differs from open educational resources in the sense that there is an underlying teaching concept in a digital environment based on a coherent topic divided into subtopics and implemented based on a pedagogical theory or an instructional design approach (p. 3).

However, it seems that sometimes we realize that just making a series of contents available in the virtual learning environment and letting students do what we want with them is enough. Our work seeks to demonstrate that this may not be the best way. The excellent results achieved in this research, that is, the satisfaction of the students and completion rates, are the result of intense work, made possible by what the LA presents us.

A careful analysis of the responses by the course participants in the questionnaire made available before we started the course development, which knows their level of proficiency in the use of digital technologies and the G Suite tools, we are qualified to model the first version of the course in a way that sought to meet the real needs of our target audience, with speed, quality, low cost and with the possibility of reaching hundreds of participants, contrary to what is observed in many traditional teacher training processes. Besides that, the attention and observation of what was going on in the virtual learning environment during the course offer made possible immediate interventions, which made it even more assertive.

Being assertive, meeting people's real learning needs, should be the premises of any educational process. We know that learning success does not depend exclusively on the content, the teachers, or the people who design the courses or disciplines, students are key players in this process, and LA helps us to better understand how the learning experience of students has been and to improve our work continuously.

ACKNOWLEDGMENT

The authors would like to thank the team that contributed to the idealization of this SMOOC, the UFPE team who have participated assiduously in this professional development initiative and sought to rethink their professional practice to improve your performance in an atypical moment like the coronavirus pandemic, as well as the UFPE managers, for the opportunity to conduct initiative of such importance to the Brazilian education.

REFERENCES

Abrucio, F. L. (2016). *Formação de professores no Brasil: Diagnóstico, agenda de políticas e estratégias para a mudança*. Editora Moderna. https://www.todospelaeducacao.org.br/arquivos/biblioteca/formacao_de_professores_no_brasil_diagnostico_agenda_de_politicas_e_estrategias_para_a_mudanca_todos_pela_educacao.pdf

Almeida, M. I. D. (2012). *Formação do professor do ensino superior: Desafios e políticas institucionais*. Cortez.

Andrade, M. V. M., & Silveira, I. F. (2016). Panorama da aplicação de Massive Open Online Course (MOOC) no ensino superior: Desafios e possibilidades. *Revista EAD em Foco, 6*(3), 2177–8310. https://eademfoco.cecierj.edu.br/index.php/Revista/article/view/392

Atiaja, L. N. A., & Proenza, R. S. G. (2016). MOOCS: Origin, characterization, principal problems and challenges in higher education. *Journal of e-Learning and Knowledge Society, 12*(1), 65–76. https://pdfs.semanticscholar.org/df33/d3707dfbc14dac4c2827109af8f825377036.pdf

Bezerra, L. N. M., & da Silva, M. T. (2017). A review of literature on the reasons that cause the high dropout rates in the MOOCS. *Revista Espacios, 38*(5), 11-24. http://www.revistaespacios.com/a17v38n05/a17v38n05p11.pdf

Brazilian Institute of Geography and Statistics. (2020). *Projeção da população do Brasil e das unidades da federação*. https://www.ibge.gov.br/apps/populacao/projecao

Chatti, M. A., Dyckhoff, A. L., Schroeder, U., & Thus, H. (2012). A reference model for leaning analytics. *International Journal of Technology Enhanced Learning, 4*(5–6), 318–331. doi:10.1504/IJTEL.2012.051815

Davis, C. L. F. (2012). *Formação continuada de professores: Uma análise das modalidades e práticas em estados e municípios brasileiros*. Fundação Carlos Chagas. http://publicacoes.fcc.org.br/ojs/index.php/textosfcc/article/view/2452

Dillenbourg, P., Fox, A., Kirchner, C., Mitchel, J., & Wirsing, M. (2014). Massive open online courses: Current state and perspectives. *Proceedings of Dagstuhl Perspectives Workshop*. http://citeseerx.ist.psu.edu/viewdoc/download?doi=10.1.1.657.4811&rep=rep1&type=pdf

Drachsler, H., & Kalz, M. (2016). The MOOC and learning analytics innovation cycle (MOLAC): A reflective summary of ongoing research and its challenges. *Journal of Computer Assisted Learning, 32*(3), 281–290. doi:10.1111/jcal.12135

Gatti, B. A. (2016). Formação de professores: Condições e problemas atuais. *Revista Internacional de Formação de Professores, 1*(2), 161–171. https://periodicos.itp.ifsp.edu.br/index.php/RIFP/article/view/347

Hollands, F. M. (2014). Why do institutions offer MOOCs? *Online Learning, 18*(3), 1–20. https://eric.ed.gov/?id=EJ1043160

Huang, R. H., Liu, D. J., Guo, J., Yang, J. F., Zhao, J. H., Wei, X. F., Knyazeva, S., Li, M., Zhuang, R. X., Looi, C. K., & Chang, T. W. (2020). *Guidance on flexible learning during campus closures: Ensuring course quality of higher education in COVID-19 outbreak.* Smart Learning Institute of Beijing Normal University. https://iite.unesco.org/wp-content/uploads/2020/05/Guidance-on-Flexible-Learning-during-Campus-Closures-in-COVID-19-outbreak-SLIBNU-V1.2_0508.pdf

Huang, R. H., Liu, D. J., Tlili, A., Yang, J. F., & Wang, H. H. (2020). *Handbook on facilitating flexible learning during educational disruption: The Chinese experience in maintaining undisrupted learning in COVID-19 outbreak.* Smart Learning Institute of Beijing Normal University. https://iite.unesco.org/wp-content/uploads/2020/03/Handbook-on-Facilitating-Flexible-Learning-in-COVID-19-Outbreak-SLIBNU_V2.0_20200324.pdf

Khalil, M. (2017). *Learning analytics in massive open online courses* [Doctoral thesis]. Universidad Carlos III de Madrid.

Mazzardo, M. D., Nobre, A. M. D. J. F., & Mallmann, E. M. (2017). Small open online course e recursos educacionais abertos na formação continuada de professores do ensino médio no Brasil. *Indagatio Didactica, 9*(2), 175–194. https://repositorioaberto.uab.pt/bitstream/10400.2/6901/1/Small Open Online Course e Recursos Educacionais Abertos.pdf

Moissa, B., Gasparini, I., & Kemczinski, A. (2014). Learning analytics: um mapeamento sistemático. *Proceedings of XIX Conferência Internacional sobre Informática na Educação.* http://www.tise.cl/volumen10/TISE2014/tise2014_submission_262.pdf

QS World University Rankings. (2020). *QS World University Rankings 2021*. https://www.topuniversities.com/university-rankings/world-university-rankings/2021

Ramos, M. N., & Filgueiras, T. (2014). *Formação continuada de professores no Brasil: Acelerando o desenvolvimento dos nossos educadores.* Instituto Ayrton Senna. https://www.observatoriodopne.org.br/_uploads/_posts/46.pdf?1140547125

Siemens, G. (2013). Massive open online courses: innovation in education? In R. Mcgreal, W. Kinuthia, & S. Marshall (Org.), *Open educational resources: Innovation, research and practice* (pp. 5–15). Athabasca University. https://oerknowledgecloud.org/sites/oerknowledgecloud.org/files/pub_PS_OER-IRP_web.pdf#page=31

Society for Learning Analytics Research. (2020). *What is Learning Analytics*? https://www.solaresearch.org/about/what-is-learning-analytics

Tardif, M. (2000). Saberes profissionais dos professores e conhecimentos universitários: Elementos para uma epistemologia da prática profissional dos professores e suas conseqüências em relação à formação para o magistério. *Revista Brasileira de Educação, 13*, 5–24. http://anped.tempsite.ws/novo_portal/rbe/rbedigital/RBDE13/RBDE13_05_MAURICE_TARDIF.pdf

Todos Pela Educação. (2014). *Inovações tecnológicas na educação: Contribuições para gestores públicos*. Inspirare Instituto. https://porvir.org/wp-content/uploads/2014/08/Inova%C3%A7%C3%B5es-Tecnol%C3%B3gicas-na-Educa%C3%A7%C3%A3o_Constribui%C3%A7%C3%B5es-para-gestores-p%C3%BAblicos-1.pdf

United Nations Educational, Scientific and Cultural Organization. (2016). *Making sense of MOOCs: A guide for policy-makers in developing cauntries*. United Nations Educational, Scientific and Cultural Organization (UNESCO). https://unesdoc.unesco.org/ark:/48223/pf0000245122

Universidade Federal de Pernambuco. (2020). *UFPE em números*. https://www.ufpe.br/institucional/ufpe-em-numeros

Universities, U. K. (2013). *Massive open online courses: Higher education's digital moment?* https://www.universitiesuk.ac.uk/policy-and-analysis/reports/Documents/2013/massive-open-online-courses.pdf

Wilson, C. (2013). *Alfabetização midiática e informacional: Currículo para formação de professores*. UNESCO, UFTM. https://unesdoc.unesco.org/ark:/48223/pf0000220418

Yousef, A. M. F., Chatti, M. A., Schroeder, U., Wosnitza, M., & Jakobs, H. (2014). MOOCs: A review of the state-of-the-art. *Proceedings of 6th International Conference on Computer Supported Education*, 9–20. https://www.researchgate.net/publication/275823066_MOOCs_a_review_of_the_state-of-the-a

Yuan, L., & Powell, S. (2013). *MOOCS and Open Education: Implications For Higher Education*. Centre for Educational Technology, Interoperability and Standards (CETIS). https://publications.cetis.org.uk/wp-content/uploads/2013/03/MOOCs-and-Open-Education.pdf

ADDITIONAL READING

Shum, S. B. (2012). *Learning Analytics*. https://iite.unesco.org/pics/publications/en/files/3214711.pdf

Spyropoulou, N., Pierrakeas, C., & Kameas, A. (2014). Creating MOOC guidelines based on best practices. *Proceedings of 6th International Conference on Education and New Learning Technologies*. https://www.researchgate.net/publication/281555098_Creating_MOOC_Guidelines_based_on_best_practices

United Nations Educational, Scientific and Cultural Organization. (2018). *Unesco ICT competency framework for teachers*. https://unesdoc.unesco.org/ark:/48223/pf0000265721

United Nations Educational, Scientific and Cultural Organization. (2019). *Open Educational Resources (OER)*. https://en.unesco.org/themes/building-knowledge-societies/oer

KEY TERMS AND DEFINITIONS

Common Online Board: It is a feature, similar to a discussion forum, which in Google Classroom is called Class Stream, through which people can interact asynchronously, posting, commenting, or responding to comments and questions.

Digital Inclusion: It refers to the activities necessary to ensure that people have access to and use Information and Communication Technologies (ICTs).

Dropout Rates: Number of students who do not complete a training activity, such as a course.

Information and Communications Technologies (ICT): Communication technologies, such as the Internet, wireless networks, cell phones, computers, software, middleware, videoconferencing, social networks, and other media services used to access, retrieve, store, send, and manipulate information in digital format.

Lifelong Learning: Involves all the learning activities that people experience during their lives and that do not occur only in the formal teaching-learning spaces, aimed at improving knowledge, skills, and competencies, whether from a personal, civic, social, or professional point of view.

Open Educational Resources (OER): The term refers to free teaching, learning or research resources offered to users, whether in the public domain or with an open copyright license, which allows the use, reuse, modification, sharing, remixing, always referring to the authors who produce the resources.

Remote Classes: Classes offered online.

Self-Directed Study: A form of learning in which students identify their needs and learning objectives, as well as define the strategies and resources they will use for learning, and evaluate their performance on their own.

Small Open Online Course (SMOOC): Massive, open, online courses (MOOCs) offered to a small number of participants, usually around 100-150.

Virtual Learning Environments: Teaching and learning system that generally uses the Internet and special software for students and teachers to participate in classes and courses.

ENDNOTE

1 It is important to keep in mind that the course presented here was offered to all interested UFPE professors and technical support personnel. So, from now on, when we refer to students or participants in training, we are talking about UFPE professors and technical support personnel.

Chapter 9
Social Learning Analytics:
Learning How We Learn on YouTube

Mustafa Şahin Bülbül
Kafkas University, Turkey

ABSTRACT

Despite the idea that learning is individual, the YouTube channel has been examined to explain how learning is controlled in social networks. What kind of mechanism does the YouTube channel, which deeply influences the education world, work with and what does this structure tell the educators? What do data such as the number of views and comments on YouTube mean? Also, what kind of a model can be established between the video proposition system and our individual and social learning? This study has been prepared to shed light on the questions mentioned.

INTRODUCTION

We communicate in daily life to learn. Modern humans use written communication channels in addition to verbal communication. Reading is a bridge between the past and the future, it brings far distances closer and the author's perception of the world transfers to the reader. Although it is also possible to teach and learn foreign languages with sound and pictures, reading is not as effective on language learning skills as videos. For this reason, videos are indispensable resources for pronunciation teaching and multi-language education (Watkins & Wilkins, 2011).

Internet sites that provide information by reading are classic websites and are called as web 1.0. Internet sites (such as YouTube ©) that contain larger files (Abhari & Soraya, 2010) and change according to the website visitor's choices are known as new web or web 2.0 (Gill, Arlitt & Mahanti, 2007). People's interactions with

DOI: 10.4018/978-1-7998-7103-3.ch009

each other and with information occur not only through one social media, but also through multiple interrelated social media; social network (Lange, 2007).

People acquire most of the vital knowledge they acquire from their social environment, and the education of the social environment is carried out by the media, which has long been called newspapers, radio and television; YouTube © is new media (Snickars & Vonderau, 2009). It is a social effect that can cause not only social culture but also individual accumulation and culture to affect society (Chau, 2010). For this reason, one of the indicators of the learning of the society and the individual is social media analysis (Haridakis & Hanson, 2009).

Today, it is possible to extract / produce data using artificial intelligence without purchasing a direct data set from YouTube © (Abu-El-Haija, Kothari, Lee, Natsev, Toderici, Varadarajan & Vijayanarasimhan, 2016). For this reason, there are different explanations about different studies and operation of the system (Adhikari, Jain, Chen & Zhang, 2012; Hoßfeld, Seufert, Hirth, Zinner, Tran-Gia & Schatz, 2011). This study includes the current literature and some applied reviews.

The way of learning and teaching has changed after the inclusion of YouTube © in our education life; It is possible to watch educational videos by pausing, slowing down and reading the subtitle. Also; In addition to teachers, new trainers called phenomena contributed to our education life with many videos (Clifton & Mann, 2011). Because of the large number of videos, teachers should also teach students to be critical and choose educational videos (Jones & Cuthrell, 2011). Misinformation especially in the field of health has the potential to create irreversible effects (Keelan, Pavri-Garcia, Tomlinson & Wilson, 2007; Jaffar, 2012; Madathil, Rivera-Rodriguez, Greenstein & Gramopadhye, 2015). Students are required to take responsibility for their learning using YouTube ©. Students' critical approach to videos and their own research on YouTube's © video suggestion system can help them take on learning responsibilities.

As a result of the influence of the individual on the society and the society on the individual, both the thoughts of the individual and some of the thoughts that are valid in the general society may change. The issue of which video should be watched by teachers who want to change the thoughts of both the student and the class on the subject to be discussed is important. The aim of this study is to diversify learning analytics through a system such as Youtube (c) that uses big data, by showing that the presented and tested model can contribute to the video selection criteria and video preparation stages of the educators. Showing that such open systems, which are directed by the society and the individual while guiding the society and the individual, work in a manner similar to the laws of nature, is what makes this study unique and important.

The process of collecting, measuring, analyzing and reporting information about learners and their contexts in order to make learning environments more qualified can be called learning analytics (LAK, 2011). Therefore, learning analytics is a new, emerging field where advanced analysis tools are used for learning and teaching purposes and is related to many other fields such as education and work (Del Blanco, Serrano, Freire, Martínez-Ortiz & Fernández-Manjón, 2013). In this section, what kind of information and comments we can reach by examining the individual and social video watching of learners. Understanding the relationship between the number of general audiences and individual preferences and directions through a model will pave the way for further research.

MAIN FOCUS OF THE CHAPTER

Personal and Social Learning Analytics

YouTube © is the most popular video search and viewing site in the world, founded in 2005, constantly developing. Which videos are featured in searches and which videos are recommended for viewing depends on a specific algorithm. While some of the propositions reflect the choice of society, some focus on individual preferences as much as possible (Davidson, Liebald, Liu, Nandy & Van Vleet, 2010). Before a video recommendation, both the user's preferences and the preferences of other users are compared and the characteristics of the video are also evaluated. Many factors such as the noise contained in the video, the presence of a cover image and the duration of the video are used in the evaluation of the videos (Covington, Adams & Sargin, 2016).

The content of the videos is decided by the video creators, but this choice is not only the result of their own decisions. Video watchers influence and direct the video creators by watching, commenting and liking (Khan, 2017). The video creator also impresses the watcher with his/her videos and a mutual interaction takes place (Figure 1). Therefore, both the published videos are a product of interaction and the videos suggested to the watcher are the result of previous individual and social interactions (Susarla, Oh & Tan, 2012).

Figure 1. Interaction between video creator and watcher

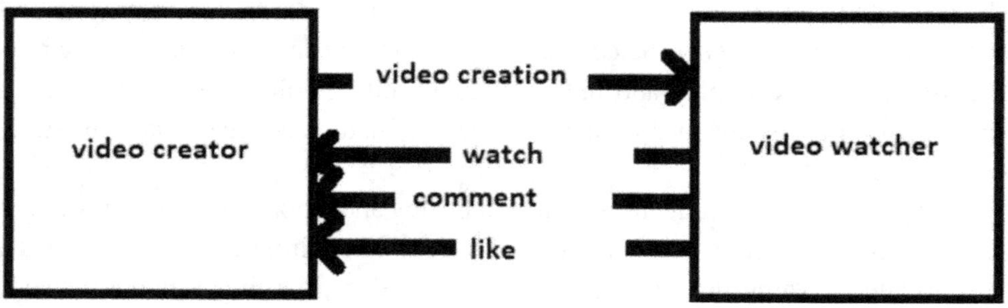

Over 10 categories when uploading videos (Film and Animation, Cars and Vehicles, Music, Pets and Wild Animals, Sports, Travel and Events, Gaming, People and Blogs, Comedy, Entertainment, News and Politics, Practical Knowledge and Style, Education, Science and Technology). The video creator is expected to match one of these categories to /her/his video. When this is the case, videos are produced in line with the expectations of the society from the videos. In other words, those who produce videos in line with the expectations of the society become more popular. In short, music and entertainment channels are watched more than science channels and the watcher is drawn towards these channels (Cheng, Dale & Liu, 2008; Shifman, 2012).

Sometimes, video creators create content that will flame watchers and discuss opposing views by writing with each other, and each discussion increases the viewing rate (Moor, Heuvelman & Verleur, 2010). Although YouTube © has the feature of closing comments, video creators do not use this feature frequently.

It is a strategy that is thought to be effective in the 2016 USA elections, both by giving the watcher the opportunity to comment and by enabling them to discuss with other viewers, collecting data and processing this data, both developing policies and trying to convince users by suggesting videos (Tufekci, 2018). For this reason, the videos that the society and the individual prefer to watch with their curiosity are data on learning analytics for researchers.

Self-Learning and Distance Learning Analytics

Self-learning and distance education studies, which are widely used in developed countries, have started to be seen in all countries with the pandemic process (Bao, 2020). There are different learning opportunities that broadcast over the Internet. They may prefer to learn through text-heavy sites (Wiki, etc.) or through sites that provide visual and audio narration (YouTube ©, etc.). In order for the sought video to be useful, video creators need to produce a lot of quality videos. Few and unqualified videos will push the video watcher to other searches. For example; The concepts of Brain, Language, Science, Philosophy and Physics create different search graphics both in Google © search engine and YouTube © search engine (Figure 2).

If there are factors such as the curriculum, periodic ups and downs are seen in the technical terms in the program, as in the A graph in Figure 2. The video watching method, which is an easy way to obtain information for people, directs the watchers and this affects the number of views and suggestions (Figure 2, B). When the video suggestion system of YouTube © is examined, it is known that not only popular videos are recommended, but also videos waiting to be discovered (Zhou, Khemmarat & Gao, 2010).

Figure 2. Search graphs with Google Trends ©

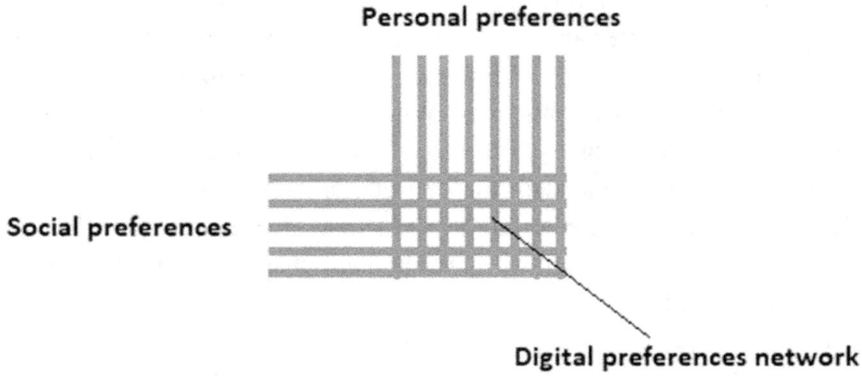

What implications does the YouTube © video suggestion system offer us for users and educators, progressing with our individual interests but also influencing the preferences of all viewers? This structure, which progresses with the choices of human beings, resembles to which systems the human is included and produced by himself?

Game is the most important action that affects children's learning. This action can sometimes be influenced by watching the player. For example; A child who watches a game video is more successful when playing a game than a child who has never watched a game video. This success shows that even viewing for entertainment purposes is associated with learning. In game videos, viewers can gain experience by seeing success or failure (Akour, Alsghaier, & Aldiabat, 2020). It informs us that it is a mechanism not only for educational videos but also for videos for other purposes, that those who want to gain experience gather in some game videos and recommend them to the audience as the number of views increases. Game videos recorded and watched by remote users are very important for individual learning by watching. Therefore, this importance may be related to social behaviors and laws related to gathering in nature. This possibility forms the basis of the model in the section. An example of testing both the model and the model will be presented in the following lines.

General Relativity and Social Learning Model

Social learning model is a learning theory that combines behavioral and cognitive learning models and describes the processes of learning to perceive and develop behaviors needed in social environments (Bandura, 1969; Bandura, 1986). The social dimension of learning increases the importance of the social learning model to explain behaviors such as watching trending videos, which are a social activity, and watching videos according to recommendations. The similarity of the YouTube © algorithm examined in this study to the General Relativity Theory (GRT) can explain the majority's desire to watch videos.

The explanatory model proposed in this study was inspired by Einstein's GRT. This theory explains the cause of gravity based on the principles of geometry by combining the geometric properties of four-dimensional space-time with the generalized form of special relativity (Carrol, 2004; Gron & Hervik, 2007). According to this theory, space and time are flat and taut like a sheet. The space-time plane bends in proportion to the size of the mass when mass is placed on it (Arnowitt, Deser & Misner, 1962). Similarly, personal and social monitoring preferences form the digital preference network (Figure 3). Video channels on this network create some bends, and videos suggested to the viewer vary according to these bends.

Figure 3. Components of digital preferences network

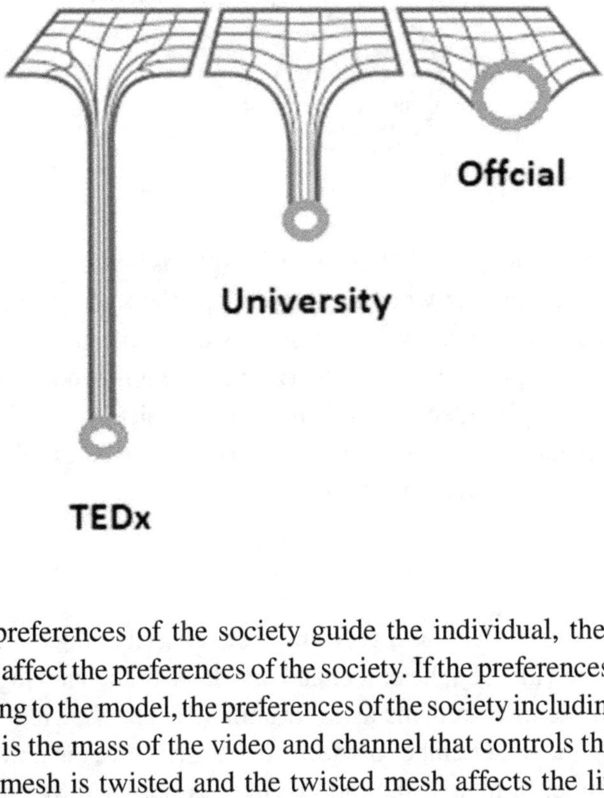

While the preferences of the society guide the individual, the choices of the individual also affect the preferences of the society. If the preferences of the personal change according to the model, the preferences of the society including the individual also change. It is the mass of the video and channel that controls this change. With this mass, the mesh is twisted and the twisted mesh affects the linear movement of preferences. This effect results in not being presented the same suggestions to every user.

Individual channels and large corporate channels are not as effective on the network. For example; As TEDx © bends space-time like a black hole bends, a university channel can show the effect of a neutron star (Figure 4).

Figure 4. The channels warp the digital preferences network

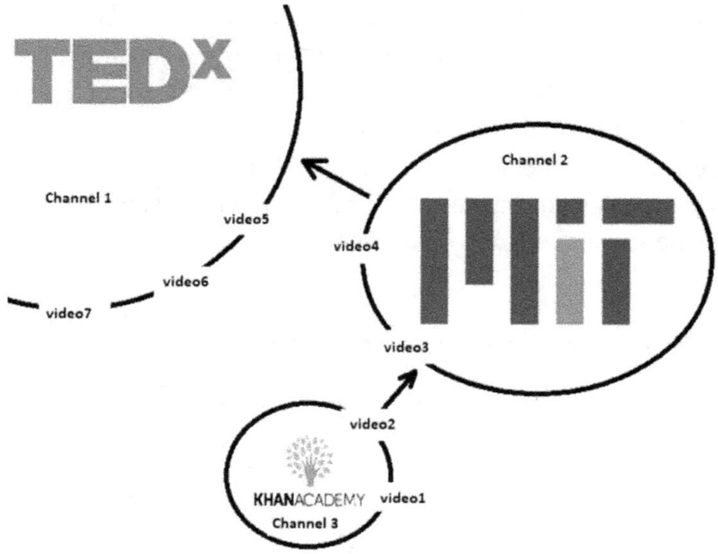

Like the general theory of relativity, which explains how two masses attract each other, this model can predict which of the proposed videos will be after watching a video. Even if it is official, a video channel is as qualified as the channel of the university and cannot produce more videos, so the recommended video will be the video of the university's video channel after a few choices.

The mass of a channel depends on the number of subscribers of that video channel and the mass of its videos as in formula (1).

$$\Omega = \tau\,(\Sigma\,\Phi) \quad (1)$$

(Ω: Channelmass, Φ: Videomass, τ: Number of subscribers)

The mass of the video, on the other hand, is related to the viewing rate, the liking rate and the number of comments as in formula (2). The viewing rate is obtained by proportioning the total number of views to the time from the upload of the video to the analysis time. Similarly, the ratio of likes is obtained by proportioning the number of likes to the number of dislikes.

$$\Phi = \alpha(\beta + \gamma) \quad (2)$$

(Φ: Videomass, α: View rate, β: Liking rate, γ: Number of comments)

Testing the Model

Numerous attempts have been made to test the model presented, but only one is presented in this section. In the shared review, it started with the keyword "physics" and seven videos were watched with the suggested videos. The masses of a total of seven videos and channels were also calculated (Table 1).

Table 1. Videomass and Channelmass values of tested videos

Video Code	*Videomass (Φ)*	*Channelmass (Ω)*
Video1	67897345	>100M
Video2	43546578	
Video3	76443234	>10G
Video4	49304934	
Video5	126756908	>100G
Video6	111327468	
Video7	98032395	

The YouTube © video suggestion system has suggested videos from low-value video to large-value video. Similarly, the masses of the channels on which these videos are broadcast have increased as the videos progressed. The increase in mass is shown in Figure 5 in a way to be represented by the size of the circle where the logo of the relevant channel is located.

Khanacademy © is an education channel. There is a presenter and images related to the subject presented on the screen. It has content that goes parallel with normal/formal education. In this sense, it is an institutional (official) YouTube © channel that has an important role in eliminating inequality in schools (Thompson, 2011). On the other hand, due to the number of students like Massachusetts Institute of Technology (MIT) and the accumulation of many years, there is a larger area of attraction. We see that the recommended 3rd and 4th videos in the application are suggested from the 2nd channel. The last three videos are provided by the TEDx © channel (Figure 5). Even though the playlist is not selected, suggestions coming from the same channel one after the other indicates that there are many videos with similar content on that video channel and the mass of these videos is larger/bigger.

Figure 5. An example map of a recommendation video proposition series

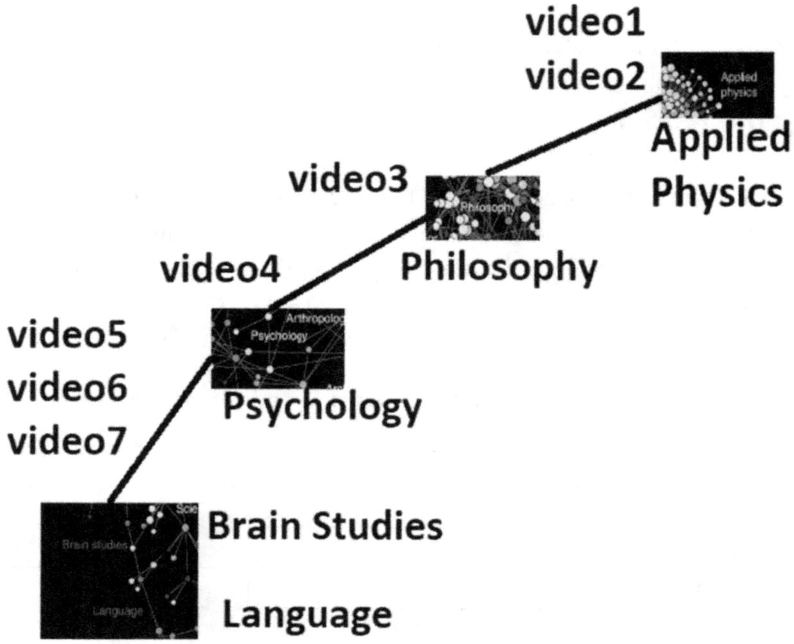

TEDx © videos are videos taken when an expert in his/her field gives a brief presentation in front of the community. The presence of an audience here, the presentation of an institutionally selected expert with visuals, and the short duration of the presentations will increase the number of views of the video and the number of subscribers of the channel (Romanelli, Cain & McNamara, 2014). So, no matter which of the scientific topics you choose, if you follow the recommendations, you may find yourself watching TEDx © videos after a while. In this sense, TEDx © videos can be examined in many areas from training of teachers (DaVia Rubenstein, 2012) to creating a data set in the field of education (Taibi, Chawla, Dietze, Marenzi & Fetahu, 2015).

TEDx's © impact on science is very strong. Generally, academics talk. Academics also speak on university channels but cannot create the impact of TEDx © (Caliendo & Compagnone, 2014). TEDx © is making science popular; Scientific talks are in demand compared to unread articles and books. TEDx © has categories belonging to various fields of science and life. These categories have transitions with each other. Some categories are close to each other, while some are far away. Similarly, in scientific disciplines, there are closeness or distances to each other. There are also studies to map science by analyzing publishing journals (Bollen, Van de Sompel,

Hagberg, Bettencourt, Chute, Rodriguez & Balakireva, 2009; Boyack & Klavans, 2014). When the content of the videos of the suggestions for testing the model and the shared application are examined; Applied physics, philosophy, psychology, brain studies and language study areas come across (Figure 6).

Figure 6. An example case analysis: links of disciplines in line with recommended videos

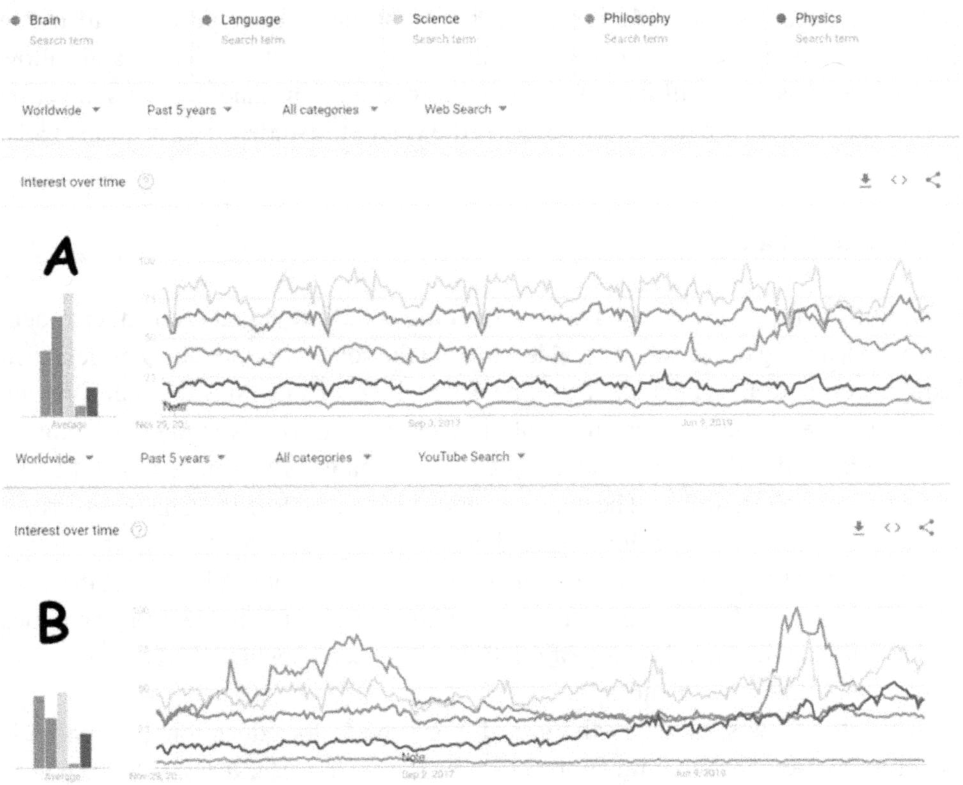

The orientation towards the concept reached from the initial concept is shaped by the interaction of both personal interests and social preferences, similar to the structure mentioned earlier in the model. The inter-sciences relationship created by the society is also available on YouTube ©, and videos on a stream sequence from the field where the concept of starting towards the field of interest by watching continuously are suggested on this subject. Since the researcher is not interested in the fields of chemistry or medicine, the video suggestions are moving towards the areas of interest to the areas of interest to the society and which have a great impact.

If the review continues and the videos in the relevant field are finished, the referral to the next high-interest areas will begin.

This shared application will therefore yield different results over another user. Differences between results also inform us about the preferences of both the individual and the society, namely learning tendencies. In this section, educators / readers who realize how videos with known number of views, comments and likes create a field of attraction for other viewers will be able to examine the video suggestion systems more carefully and design their lesson processing flows in a way that offers more natural transitions. Moreover, teachers who have the opportunity to log in from the account the student is using will log in from the target video and follow the suggestions, and will have an individual roadmap for handling the subject by following the reverse path when it comes to the videos the student watches constantly.

CONCLUSION

According to the social learning theory, learning of the individual is not independent from the learning of the society and learning in the society. This study was designed using open data provided by YouTube ©, a video display site that can provide individual and distance learning analytics. According to this study, YouTube © data, suggested videos, some features of video channels can be evaluated as an indicator of social learning. The large values of Videomass (Φ) and Channelmass(Ω) are largely effective in guiding the audience, just as the large mass in the theory of general relativity creates a curve in space-time and creates a large gravitational effect. The explanation, which is presented as an example of social learning analytics and similar to the general theory of relativity, has been shown to fit the situation in a map that relates the sciences.

This study has shown that the use of YouTube © for educational purposes is beyond the use of video with flipped classes (Cargile & Harkness, 2015; Zengin, 2017) first, putting the face-to-face lesson later or for experimental studies (Snelson, 2011). When the suggestions of YouTube © are examined, we see a network that both the user and the community have created jointly. This network has changed and taken its current form and continues to shape over time.

The YouTube © video suggestion system, which is shaped by the interaction of video creators and viewers, social and individual preferences, regular and irregular keywords entered into the search engine, and the digital recommendation network that bends according to the mass of videos and channels formed at the end of the process, is an indicator of social learning and examinations with the methods mentioned on it. It is possible to do. By deepening these studies, it is possible to map the relationship between sciences and concepts in the mind of the YouTube © user, or to create educational video series based on related concepts.

To think that the laws of nature affect all non-human beings, but to think that they do not affect people and society means not understanding the laws of nature. While Einstein's theory explains how masses attract each other, it actually provides an explanation for structures that add up / cluster. Research on clusters is the subject of social research, and it is extremely important to make researches through channels dealing with concepts and concepts as stated in this section, in order to predict new structures and concepts to be formed.

Preferences are meaningful together with their reasons. The example shared in this section reveals the implications for the society formed by people's individual preferences. Similarly, if the number of equivalent channels increases, it becomes important which channel users choose and why. Easier to understand, entertaining, enjoyable and life's narratives may be among the reasons to be preferred. It can be revealed by interviews with these users.

The biggest risk of this model proposal, which will enable us to understand the social structure, is that the system is manipulated by fake and artificial intelligence-based systems. In such a case, the problematic data will make the comments problematic. The new media teaches users this network of relationships while forcing people and human societies to reconsider the numbers and forms of interactions. The similarities and differences between individual learning and society's learning can only be tested with the proposed model.

The digital algorithm created by searches is the main reason why it creates a gravitational field around the searched. The bosses of the new media keep this attraction area active to increase the viewing algorithms. The video search site, which offers the most preferred videos by the society, also cares about the preferences of the individual. Assuming that the individual's calls are meaningful, he establishes relationships between calls, determines the person's need and style, and recommends a video to the person. The transition from one video to another actually tells us the orientation and preferences of both the society and the individual.

Over time, a video search system, which starts to suggest videos suitable for their own searches to the user after analyzing the videos that are searched and watched by different users, but which are made from the same device, aims to be watched more. For this reason, the proposed model requires an algorithm that is meaningful in accordance with the structure of human and nature, focused on preferences and therefore needs. It is no coincidence that the map showing the relationship between the search frequency of the sciences and the publications in the sciences, and the video follow-ups coincide. As researchers who are not the designers of the video search system, we will be able to indirectly understand the individual and society better through this network of relationships we have discovered, and we will see that what we share in virtual environments has become the footprints of the people we have been trying to understand for years.

REFERENCES

Abhari, A., & Soraya, M. (2010). Workload generation for YouTube. *Multimedia Tools and Applications*, *46*(1), 91–118. doi:10.100711042-009-0309-5

Abu-El-Haija, S., Kothari, N., Lee, J., Natsev, P., Toderici, G., Varadarajan, B., & Vijayanarasimhan, S. (2016). *YouTube-8m: A large-scale video classification benchmark*. arXiv preprint arXiv:1609.08675.

Adhikari, V. K., Jain, S., Chen, Y., & Zhang, Z. L. (2012). Vivisecting YouTube: An active measurement study. In 2012 Proceedings IEEE INFOCOM (pp. 2521-2525). IEEE.

Akour, M., Alsghaier, H., & Aldiabat, S. (2020). Game-based learning approach to improve self-learning motivated students. *International Journal of Technology Enhanced Learning*, *12*(2), 146–160. doi:10.1504/IJTEL.2020.106283

Arnowitt, R., Deser, S., & Misner, C. W. (1962). The dynamics of general relativity. In L. Witten (Ed.), *Gravitation: An Introduction to Current Research. Wiley.*

Bandura, A. (1969). Social-learning theory of identificatory processes. Handbook of socialization theory and research, 213, 262.

Bandura, A. (1986). *Social Foundations of Thought and Action*. Prentice-Hall.

Bao, W. (2020). COVID-19 and online teaching in higher education: A case study of Peking University. *Human Behavior and Emerging Technologies*, *2*(2), 113–115. doi:10.1002/hbe2.191 PMID:32510042

Bollen, J., Van de Sompel, H., Hagberg, A., Bettencourt, L., Chute, R., Rodriguez, M. A., & Balakireva, L. (2009). Clickstream data yields high-resolution maps of science. *PLoS One*, *4*(3), e4803. doi:10.1371/journal.pone.0004803 PMID:19277205

Boyack, K. W., & Klavans, R. (2014). Including cited non-source items in a large-scale map of science: What difference does it make? *Journal of Informetrics*, *8*(3), 569–580. doi:10.1016/j.joi.2014.04.001

Caliendo, G., & Compagnone, A. (2014). Expressing epistemic stance in University lectures and TED talks: A contrastive corpu-based analysis. *Lingue e Linguaggi*, *11*, 105–122.

Cargile, L. A., & Harkness, S. S. (2015). Flip or Flop: Are Math Teachers Using Khan Academy as Envisionedby Sal Khan? *TechTrends*, *59*(6), 21–28. doi:10.100711528-015-0900-8

Carroll, S. M. (2004). An introduction to general relativity: spacetime and geometry. Addison Wesley.

Chau, C. (2010). YouTube as a participatory culture. *New Directions for Youth Development*, *2010*(128), 65–74. doi:10.1002/yd.376 PMID:21240954

Cheng, X., Dale, C., & Liu, J. (2008). Statistics and social network of YouTube videos. In *2008 16th Interntional Workshop on Quality of Service* (pp. 229-238). IEEE. 10.1109/IWQOS.2008.32

Clifton, A., & Mann, C. (2011). Can YouTube enhance student nurse learning? *Nurse Education Today*, *31*(4), 311–313. doi:10.1016/j.nedt.2010.10.004 PMID:21036430

Covington, P., Adams, J., & Sargin, E. (2016). Deep neural networks for YouTube recommendations. In *Proceedings of the 10th ACM conference on recommender systems* (pp. 191-198). 10.1145/2959100.2959190

DaVia Rubenstein, L. (2012). Using TED talks to inspire thoughtful practice. *Teacher Educator*, *47*(4), 261–267. doi:10.1080/08878730.2012.713303

Davidson, J., Liebald, B., & Liu, J. Nandy & Van Vleet, (2010). The YouTube video recommendation system. In *Proceedings of the fourth ACM conference on Recommender systems* (pp. 293-296). 10.1145/1864708.1864770

Del Blanco, Á., Serrano, Á., Freire, M., Martínez-Ortiz, I., & Fernández-Manjón, B. (2013). E-Learning standards and learning analytics. Can data collection be improved by using standard data models? In *Global Engineering Education Conference (EDUCON)*, 2013 *IEEE* (pp. 1255-1261). IEEE. 10.1109/EduCon.2013.6530268

Gill, P., Arlitt, M., Li, Z., & Mahanti, A. (2007). YouTube traffic characterization: a view from the edge. In *Proceedings of the 7th ACM SIGCOMM conference on Internet measurement* (pp. 15-28). 10.1145/1298306.1298310

Gron, O., & Hervik, S. (2007). *Einstein's General Theory of Relativity*. Springer. doi:10.1007/978-0-387-69200-5

Haridakis, P., & Hanson, G. (2009). Social interaction and co-viewing with YouTube: Blending mass communication reception and social connection. *Journal of Broadcasting & Electronic Media*, *53*(2), 317–335. doi:10.1080/08838150902908270

Hoßfeld, T., Seufert, M., Hirth, M., Zinner, T., Tran-Gia, P., & Schatz, R. (2011). Quantification of YouTube QoE via crowdsourcing. In *2011 IEEE International Symposium on Multimedia* (pp. 494-499). IEEE. 10.1109/ISM.2011.87

Jaffar, A. A. (2012). YouTube: An emerging tool in anatomy education. *Anatomical Sciences Education*, *5*(3), 158–164. doi:10.1002/ase.1268 PMID:22383096

Jones, T., & Cuthrell, K. (2011). YouTube: Educational potentials and pitfalls. *Computers in the Schools*, *28*(1), 75–85. doi:10.1080/07380569.2011.553149

Keelan, J., Pavri-Garcia, V., Tomlinson, G., & Wilson, K. (2007). YouTube as a source of information on immunization: a content analysis. *JAMA, 298*(21), 2482-2484.

Khan, M. L. (2017). Social media engagement: What motivates user participation and consumption on YouTube? *Computers in Human Behavior*, *66*, 236–247. doi:10.1016/j.chb.2016.09.024

LAK. (2011). *1st International Conference on Learning Analytics and Knowledge*. Banff, Alberta: LAK.

Lange, P. G. (2007). Publicly private and privately public: Social networking on YouTube. *Journal of Computer-Mediated Communication*, *13*(1), 361–380. doi:10.1111/j.1083-6101.2007.00400.x

Madathil, K. C., Rivera-Rodriguez, A. J., Greenstein, J. S., & Gramopadhye, A. K. (2015). Healthcare information on YouTube: A systematic review. *Health Informatics Journal*, *21*(3), 173–194. doi:10.1177/1460458213512220 PMID:24670899

Moor, P. J., Heuvelman, A., & Verleur, R. (2010). Flaming on YouTube. *Computers in Human Behavior*, *26*(6), 1536–1546. doi:10.1016/j.chb.2010.05.023

Romanelli, F., Cain, J., & McNamara, P. J. (2014). Should TED talks be teaching us something? *American Journal of Pharmaceutical Education*, *78*(6), 113. doi:10.5688/ajpe786113 PMID:25147385

Shifman, L. (2012). An anatomy of a YouTube meme. *New Media & Society*, *14*(2), 187–203. doi:10.1177/1461444811412160

Snelson, C. (2011). YouTube across the disciplines: A review of the literature. *Journal of Online Learning and Teaching*.

Snickars, P., & Vonderau, P. (2009). *The YouTube reader*. Kungliga biblioteket.

Susarla, A., Oh, J. H., & Tan, Y. (2012). Social networks and the diffusion of user-generated content: Evidence from YouTube. *Information Systems Research*, *23*(1), 23–41. doi:10.1287/isre.1100.0339

Taibi, D., Chawla, S., Dietze, S., Marenzi, I., & Fetahu, B. (2015). Exploring TED talks as linked data for education. *British Journal of Educational Technology*, *46*(5), 1092–1096. doi:10.1111/bjet.12283

Thompson, C. (2011). How Khan Academy is changing the rules of education. *Wired Magazine*, *126*, 1–5.

Tufekci, Z. (2018). YouTube, the great radicalizer. *The New York Times, 10*.

Watkins, J., & Wilkins, M. (2011). Using YouTube in the EFL classroom. *Language Education in Asia*, *2*(1), 113–119. doi:10.5746/LEiA/11/V2/I1/A09/Watkins_Wilkins

Zengin, Y. (2017). Investigating the use of the Khan Academy and mathematics software with a flipped classroom approach in mathematics teaching. *Journal of Educational Technology & Society*, *20*(2), 89–100.

Zhou, R., Khemmarat, S., & Gao, L. (2010). The impact of YouTube recommendation system on video views. In *Proceedings of the 10th ACM SIGCOMM conference on Internet measurement* (pp. 404-410). 10.1145/1879141.1879193

ADDITIONAL READING

Babo, R. B., Azevedo, A. I., & Suhonen, J. (2015, July). Students' perceptions about assessment using an e-learning platform. In *2015 IEEE 15th International Conference on Advanced Learning Technologies* (pp. 244-246). IEEE.

Kitto, K., Cross, S., Waters, Z., & Lupton, M. (2015, March). Learning analytics beyond the LMS: the connected learning analytics toolkit. In *Proceedings of the fifth international conference on learning analytics and knowledge* (pp. 11-15). 10.1145/2723576.2723627

Lau, K. V., Farooque, P., Leydon, G., Schwartz, M. L., Sadler, R. M., & Moeller, J. J. (2018). Using learning analytics to evaluate a video-based lecture series. *Medical Teacher*, *40*(1), 91–98. doi:10.1080/0142159X.2017.1395001 PMID:29113565

Shoufan, A. (2019). Estimating the cognitive value of YouTube's educational videos: A learning analytics approach. *Computers in Human Behavior*, *92*, 450–458. doi:10.1016/j.chb.2018.03.036

Topps, D., Helmer, J., & Ellaway, R. (2013). YouTube as a platform for publishing clinical skills training videos. *Academic Medicine*, *88*(2), 192–197. doi:10.1097/ACM.0b013e31827c5352 PMID:23269305

Uhomoibhi, J., Azevedo, A. I. R. L., Azevedo, J. M. M. L., & Ossiannilsson, E. (2019). Learning analytics in theory and practice: Guest editorial. *The International Journal of Information and Learning Technology*.

KEY TERMS AND DEFINITIONS

Personal Learning Analytics: Indicators of making sense of the footprints of the individual in the learning process. Based on the individual's freedom of choice, the data obtained from the process are associated with the individual and used in the recognition of the individual. Considering the reasons for the individual's preferences, the society she or he lives in and the individual's savings cannot be seen as insignificant. Therefore, individual learning analytics should be examined together with social learning analytics.

Social Learning Analytics: They are indicators of making sense of the footprints of the society and the individuals who make up the society. In this study, a study was conducted on YouTube © videos, the leading website of distance learning. Using viewing and other open data, it has been tried to be interpreted in a way similar to the General Relativity Theory.

Social Learning Theory: It is the theory that explains how learning takes place through society. This explanation, which is based on the difference between environments where people can interact and environments where self-learning activities can be performed, forms the basis of the need for social learning analytics.

Theory of General Relativity: The theory that explains why planets and stars attract each other in space. According to this theory, large mass bends space-time larger than other small celestial bodies, and this large pit is the cause of the strong gravity.

Section 4
Some Technological Issues

Chapter 10
Big Data Analysis:
Basic Review on Techniques

Arpit Kumar Sharma
Manipal University Jaipur, India

Arvind Dhaka
Manipal University Jaipur, India

Amita Nandal
Manipal University Jaipur, India

Kumar Swastik
Arya Institute of Engineering Technology and Management, Jaipur, India

Sunita Kumari
Arya Institute of Engineering Technology and Management, Jaipur, India

ABSTRACT

The meaning of the term "big data" can be inferred by its name itself (i.e., the collection of large structured or unstructured data sets). In addition to their huge quantity, these data sets are so complex that they cannot be analyzed in any way using the conventional data handling software and hardware tools. If processed judiciously, big data can prove to be a huge advantage for the industries using it. Due to its usefulness, studies are being conducted to create methods to handle the big data. Knowledge extraction from big data is very important. Other than this, there is no purpose for accumulating such volumes of data. Cloud computing is a powerful tool which provides a platform for the storage and computation of massive amounts of data.

DOI: 10.4018/978-1-7998-7103-3.ch010

1. INTRODUCTION

"Data explosion" refers to the sudden and rapid growth of data. Sometimes it is also referred as "data tsunami" (IBM, 2014). There have been many milestones in the history indicating this phenomenon. Each time some new technique for storing information was invented and a period of data explosion followed (Big Data, 2015; Storage Engine, 1951). Data explosion can be dated back to the period when paper and the printing press were invented, and it still occurs with the advancements introduced in the digital media (IBM, 2015). The latest example is the growth in amount of user generated content (UGC) (Backupify, 2015). UGC includes all the images, posts, and videos etc. which are posted online by the users of any social media platform. Keeping aside the fact that it is not easy to handle the big data; its proper analysis can be profitable to the fields concerned with it, for e.g. business, transport, medical services etc (Bhardwaj, 2015). This is because meaningful information can be extracted from big data (through data mining) which has proved to be helpful for making future decisions. Using big data, organizations can know the customers' reactions to the goods and services provided by them, and they can also evaluate how the name of company is faring within the market (Grolinger, 2014; Park, 2015). In this way, big data creates an environment where each and every type of data is available, only the need is to properly analyze it to extract useful information from it and use it in a way for the welfare of the society. Big data is not useful as a whole, only a small part of it can be useful at a time for a specific purpose. The current need of the situation is to recognize the right data and extract it in the most feasible way possible without disturbing the privacy and safety of the data even if it is in large amounts. The structure of the paper starts from the definition of big data, how it is recognized, analysed and transformed, then moves on to the different frameworks and platforms that are used for the analysis, and at last how the machine learning algorithms are integrated in big data analytics.

2. Literature Review

Authors Sanehlata Yadav and Asha Sohal have presented in their research that hadoop is the most widely used framework that is used for processing a large amount of data (Yadav & Sohal, 2017). Syed Umar concluded that search is the most important factor you need to have for the mining, if you are well aware of what is to be searched then it will be lot simpler (Kumar et al., 2014). Kevin Taylor sakyi suggested that big data analytics can help to find the solution of modern analytic problems in the traditional methods which contain structured set that are periodically queried (Taylor, 2016). Nana Kwame Gyamfi, in his paper regarding big data analytics, suggested various efficient techniques like sampling, data condensation, divide and conquer etc. to make the process of handling manageable so as to improve the performance of operators (Gyamfi, 2017). Gyamfi illustrated Knowledge Discovery Database (KDD) as a four-step process involving data clustering, integration, selection, transformation, data pattern, and interpretation/ evaluation to derive relevant information from a database. He also described clustering algorithms, classification algorithms, and frequent pattern mining algorithms (Gyamfi, 2017). D. P. Acharya and Kauser Ahmed P. have classified the challenges faced in big data analysis in four categories, namely data storage and analysis, knowledge discovery and computational complexities, scalability and visualization, and information security (Acharya & Ahmed P, 2016). They have also described some big data processing tools like Hadoop, MapReduce, Mahout, Spark, Jaspersoft etc. Hadoop works by dividing the data into parts and the results are combined after the different parts are analysed by different servers, while Apache Mahout works by presenting different graphs using Python and Scala languages. On the other hand, Apache Spark works by implementing existing machine learning models on big datasets. Khalid adam in his research work "Big data and learning analytics: a big potential to improve E-learning" mentioned that the learning management system generates enormous and several form of data by students activity on using the online content (Adam, 2018).Anthony G. Picciano in his research presented that data driven decision is already started helping institute to take identify and evaluation strategy (Anthony, 2012).Amal Albalowi and Ahmad A Alhamed in their work mentioned that integrated learning analytics is providing solution in making decision concerning individual students (Amal & Ahmad, 2017). Katrina Sin and Loganathan Muthu in their research work pointed that as the data in getting involved in every aspect, the application of Big data techniques became more and more necessary in learning environment (Sin & Muthu, 2015).

3. Big Data Analysis

This section briefly explains about big data, how it is recognized, what is redundancy in big data, the 4V's of big data, how it gets stored, how analysis of the big data is done, what are the frameworks and platforms used in the analysis and how machine learning and its different algorithms are involved in the big data analysis.

3.1 Which Data Can be Considered as BIG DATA?

In 1965, Gordon E. Moore- cofounder of Intel gave a statement that the number of transistors that can be packed into a given unit space will become twice in about every two years. It implied that the storage capacity and speed of computing devices will increase at exponential rate. This observation became true, so later it came to be known as Moore's law (S & Reddy, 2013; Reddi & Indira, 2013; Bifet, 2013).

Since the computing power increases at such a rate, data considered as big in the present may not remain big in the future. So, there is no fixed rule to categorize any data as big data or not. Due to this reason, some characteristics of big data have been identified, which are as follows:

1. The Data Capturing Devices- It can be said that if the data capturing devices are found everywhere or are most likely to become easily available for everyone in near future, then the data stored in these devices will eventually become big data. Such type of devices includes mobile phones, cameras etc.
2. Super Linear Scaling of Data Production Rate- It means that with each addition in the number of data producers, data production also increases at a much greater rate. So with increase in the number of users, the data they are generating will eventually become big data.

3.2 Data Reduction

Big data analysis makes use of data reduction techniques, for the obvious reason that it will be easy to analyze the reduced content which is relevant to the decision to be made. If the required data is known beforehand, then the reduction technique used is a search. Using search, we can retrieve the information we want from a given pool of data, that's why it is the most efficient one. If the user is unsure as to what data will be best suitable, then the reduction technique known as filtering is used. Filter involves the step by step removal of irrelevant data. For example, when a person wants to order any product via Amazon or Flipkart, first we enter the type or name of that product (Hu, 2014). Hundreds or even thousands of similar products are displayed for the buyer to browse through. To narrow down this list, various filters are applied like brand name, range of price etc. This process of filtering helps in reducing the initial long list into a smaller one, using which it becomes easier to select the best option (Xu et al., 2012).

3.3 Redundancy in BIG DATA

Big data is so large in terms of volume that there is a huge possibility of data redundancy. Redundant data refers to the data which is of no use, or has become insignificant with time. The presence of such type of data will only add to the volume of big data, without contributing much in its usefulness (Ruimin, 2016; Domenico et al., 2018). Some common reasons for data redundancy have been identified, which are as follows:

1. Data Duplication- This is the most common reason of data redundancy. Whether knowingly or not, people copy their data for various reasons like backup, or to open the same file in another system. It results in generation of multiple copies of the same thing, and it is clear that making copies of any file will not produce any new information.
2. Serial Correlation (also known as autocorrelation)- It refers to the similarity between observations taken at two small instants of time. Video data shows this type of redundancy. The frames of a video can be seen as a flipbook. Like in a flipbook, the consecutive pages show only a little difference, the same happens with the images seen in frames of a video. This is the reason why videos are stored in compressed form.
3. Cross Correlation- In present time, no two events can be considered as totally independent. Each event is the cause or effect of the other. This is applied in big data also. However small this relationship is, it would mean that there is at least some redundancy present.

3.4 V'S of Big Data

According to IBM scientists, there are four dimensions of big data as shows in figure 01:

i. Volume- Each new technology introduced for the generation and storage of data contributes very much to the volume of big data.
ii. Velocity- It refers to the rate at which data is gathered, and flows from one system/device to another.
iii. Variety- The data constituting big data is collected from a variety of sources (like tweets, posts, likes video uploads on social media, web pages etc.) and is stored on different types of formats (like images, videos, files etc.).
iv. Veracity- It refers to the presence of noise, or inaccuracy in big data (Puyun & Miao, 2016; Liou et al., 2015; Li et al., 2017).

3.5 Big Data Analytics Transformation

Conventional methods to analyze data make use of RDBMS (Relational Database Management System). This method is not much useful for decision-making as much as big data can be; therefore new analysis methods are required for this purpose (Li, 2018). Data as a Service (DaaS) is a distribution model in which data files are provided to customers over a network. Similar to DaaS, Kyounghyun Park and his colleagues, in their research of Big Data Software Research Department in South Africa, introduced the idea of setting up Big Data as a service (BDaaS). This platform provides a cloud-based environment to manage big data. Some examples of BDaaS providers are- IBM's Analytics for Twitter service (data analysis for Twitter), Acxiom (sells marketing data) etc (McHugh, et al., 2017). Big data can be handled by incorporating MapReduce and HDFS (Hadoop Distributed File System). MapReduce is a programming paradigm used to process large data sets. This model works by using key, value pairs. In this model, two functions called the Map-function and Reduce-function are used. The map function takes a document as input and for each word, creates key, value pair. The reduce function lists down all the pairs associated with a single key. So, it can be used to count the occurrences of different words in a document.

Figure 1. 4 V's of Big Data (IBM, 2014)

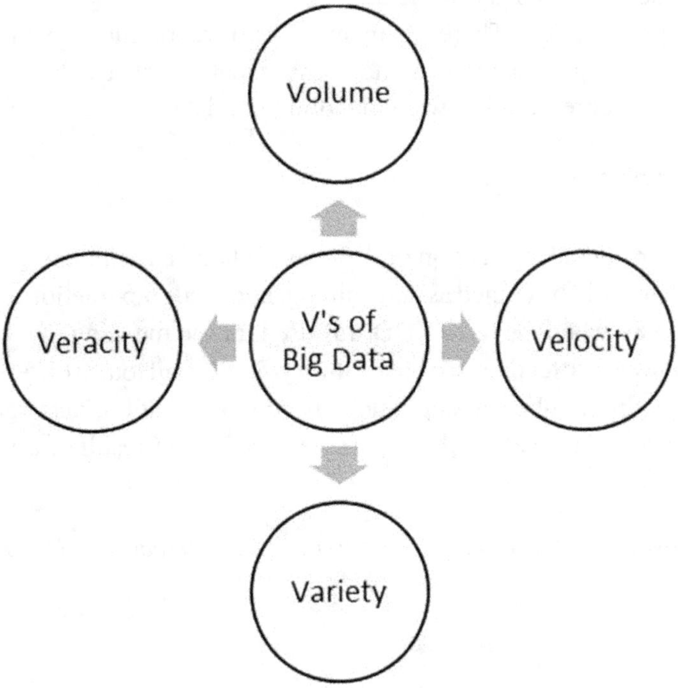

3.6 Data Storage

The first warning sign for the need of more data storage techniques was given in the year 1944 by a Wesleyan University's librarian named Fremont Rider (Chen et al., 2016). He reported that "American University libraries were doubling in size every sixteen years." Therefore, it was necessary to develop new efficient ways to store data. The evolution of data storage saw the rise of punch cards, magnetic tapes, hard drives, floppy disks, compact disks, flash drives, and the latest being cloud (Chen et al., 2016). The capacities of all these storage devices have been increasing with the years passing by. The various inconsistencies in big data are as follows:

1. Management of data life-cycle: The rate of data gathering is increasing day by day. So, the retrieval of useful information is also becoming difficult. As a result, it is necessary to develop a mechanism to handle the data which is not useful for the present time, or is totally useless.
2. Data privacy and security: Big data includes the users' personal information also. Due to this, the privacy of users is a big concern here. Unauthorized access and the use of anyone's personal information without permission is a violation of his/her rights. There must be universal set of guidelines to ensure the privacy and security of the users.
3. Data representation: There are many ways of representing data, like videos, audio recordings, images, texts etc. Consequently, there can be issues for using the correct representation while handling big data.

3.7 Data Analysis

If history is considered, extraction of data from a large amount has been termed in many ways that could be coined as data mining, knowledge extraction, etc. It was the first time in 1989 when the term KDD was used for the meaning that knowledge is the result that we get after data driven discovery. KDD is all total a different approach in which there are number of steps such as, data preparation, data selection, data mining, etc. and at last ends with proper interpretation of result of mining.

Figure 2. Flow of data in KDD process to mine the correct data (IBM, 2015)

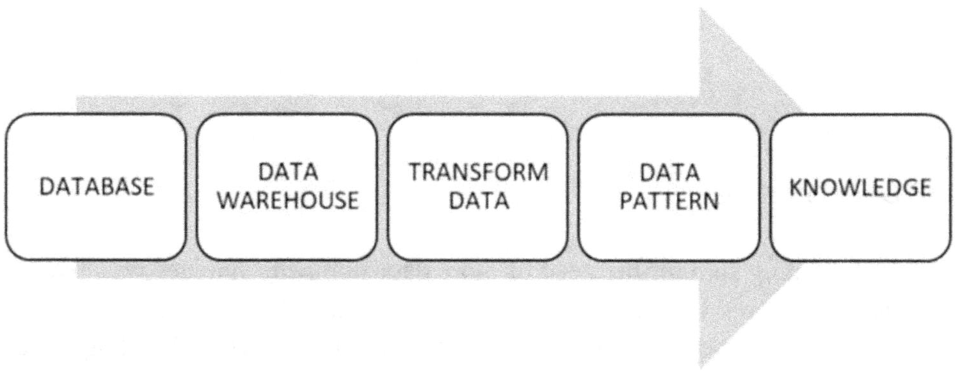

Big Data Analysis

Big Data analysis is the process of storing, analysing and maintaining a huge amount of data sets. In this direction IBM has achieved the biggest achievement by covering large aspects of big data such as analytics for twitter service (data analysis for twitter) and Acxiom (which sells marketing data). IBM has covered the V's of big data analysis viz. variety, volume and velocity. KDD is related to data mining process. In fact, data mining is a process of making or extracting useful things out of waste product shows in figure 02. To enhance data mining speed many technological ways like computing, etc. are added in the process which made it more convenient.

3.8 Limitations of Data Analysis

The different data analysis models have certain limitations which can be described as follows:

- Most of the methods are not able to handle large sets and complex data collections.
- They cannot be dynamically changed according to the data that is entered.
- Usually a method assumes that all the data will be of same set or category or of same type but that's not true always.

3.9 Big Data Analysis Framework and Platforms

In today's world the data is generated from every other appliance. Everything we do even a single step could lead to generate a data and this data will be of huge volume, different characteristics, different way of origin, and many other properties (Bhargava et al., 2017). Thus, to analysis this data we need to look at it from different approaches such as:

- From volume perspective huge amount of data is a problem because a very large amount of data may be a problem for traditional as well new upcoming models.
- From velocity perspective online streaming and other facilities provide data at very speedy rate thus within small time a huge amount of data is presented.
- Data originates from different sources so it can be in a variety of formats like text, video, speech etc. Therefore, another problem for the big data analyst is to convert all the data to a particular format so that the data processing becomes less tedious.

Handling a large amount of data is not possible for any system all at a once, so there is requirement of pre-processing in needed for the input data to system. Some of the traditional methods include compressing the data, etc. These methods are improved into new ways but the data is always needed to be pre-processed before getting into a system. There are various solutions on different basis to handle big data:

1. For processing: Hadoop, NVidia CUDA or Twitter Storm.
2. For storage: Titan, HDFS
3. Analytics: MLPACK, Mahout

As we all know that many technologies have been used along with big data to make its analysis simple and much convenient. The combination or uses of below technologies will be beneficial in that direction.

Hadoop: It is a java-oriented framework to analyse big data, to manage it properly and to create a useful output from the given input framework. This uses multiple path ways to handle the input data and give the required analysed output from given data set in required time (Bhargava et al., 2017).

MapReduce: In this method initially the data is divided into small chunks called as maps and analysed. Then, it is sent to reduce phase by the reducers (Sharma & Sharma, 2017). After analysing the data the frame workers analyse the result of all the framework that is being done and send it to final output.

3.10 Big Data Analysis Algorithms

Mining algorithm: If huge amount of data gets accumulated it is necessary to get the right information out of that heap of data, this algorithm helps in getting good and accurate results.

Clustering algorithm: In this algorithm data can be extracted easily but the problem is that the data should be entered in such a way that they are of same types or categories. Thus, it is difficult to divide into groups while entering of data and forming crystals of same types. Few Researcher divide Clustering Algorithm in various ways:

- Partitioning based clustering algorithms: In parceling based calculations, the huge informational indexes are separated into various allotments, where each segment speaks to a group. Model Algorithm is KNN, and so on (Shoban, 2017).
- Hierarchical based clustering algorithms: hierarchical based algorithms or progressive based calculations enormous information are coordinated in a various leveled way dependent on the mechanism of vicinity. The underlying or root group continuously separates into a few bunches (Shoban, 2017).

- Density based clustering algorithms: density based algorithms clusters or thickness based calculations bunches are shaped dependent on the information objects districts of thickness, network and limit. DENCLUE is one such calculation dependent on thickness based grouping (Shoban, 2017).
- Grid based clustering algorithms: framework base calculations space of information objects are partitioned into number of networks for quick handling. OptiGrid calculation is one such calculation dependent on ideal network apportioning (Shoban, 2017).
- Model based clustering algorithms: model based bunching calculations grouping is principally performed by likelihood appropriation (Shoban, 2017).

Classification algorithm: This algorithm provides different aspects in which things goes on in parallel process. The main aim is to divide the whole dataset into different categories and imply different teams to work on them individually (Bhardwaj, 2015). According to one of researcher Classification divides:

- Decision tree induction classification algorithms: In decision tree induction algorithms or in choice tree acceptance calculations, tree structure has been generally used to speak to grouping models (Shoban, 2017).
- Evolutionary based classification algorithms: Evolutionary algorithms and Transformative calculations use area free method to investigate enormous spaces finding reliably great improvement arrangements (Shoban, 2017).

3.11 Machine Learning or Big Data Mining

Machine learning codes are used to search values by combining traditional methods and can be used to search a particular result efficiently. But the major issue with machine learning method is that it works on a bulk basis as takes all input at once which cannot be possible in case of large amount of data. To solve this issue, we can create a parallel approach then apply machine-learning methods. Figure 3 depicts a parallel model for processing through machine learning. Therefore, to make use of machine learning we must have to do either of two things either make machine learning concept work on parallel platforms or make changes in machine learning concept to make them suitable for being able to do parallel task. Figure 3 is the analysis by the author and author clearly represent the Parallel model for processing through machine learning because all the steps should use in work and challenges both. The pre-processing steps involved in building up a model in parallel mode was analysed and the steps to obtain the final result (model) was computed, all the parallel nodes start with mining the data from a data source through data mining algorithms, and using the data to build logistic models and then combining all the logistic models to present the final model.

Figure 3. Parallel model for processing through machine learning

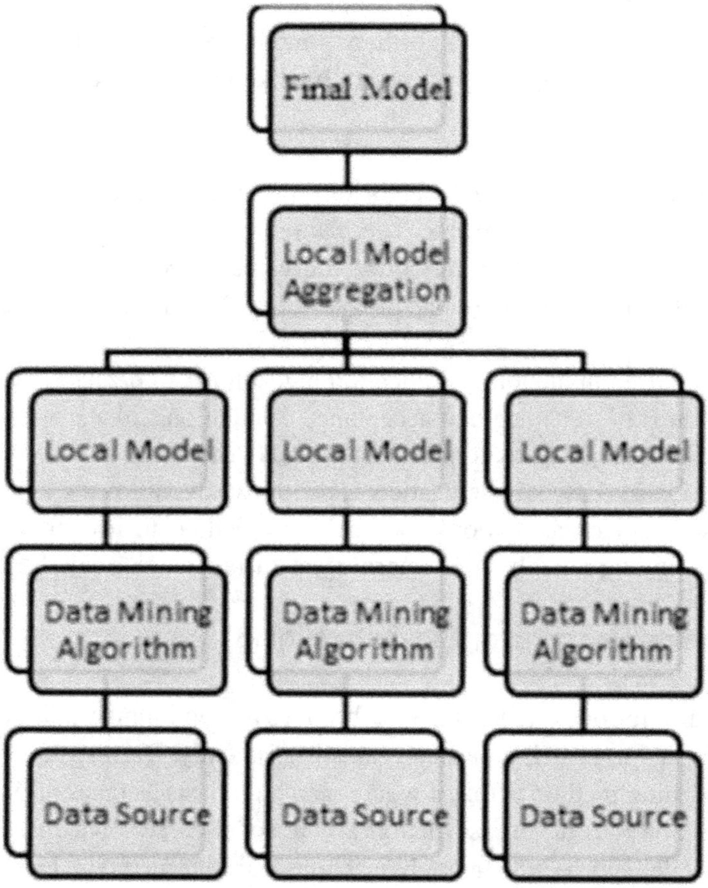

4. Machine Learning Algorithms in Big Data Analytics

Due to its voluminous quantity, handling big data manually will be a tedious task, and analyzing it manually will result in lots of errors. In recent years, data processing and machine learning have been trending due to the excessive production of data. Big data is gaining boom and so is machine learning to provide support in each and every task which requires big data. Machine learning is actually a sub part of data science. It is a process in which data is fed into machines to obtain valuable insights from it. Machine learning models are trained on existing datasets, and their performance improves over time as they learn patterns from the data. A machine learning model performs three basic tasks (Divya et al., 2018):

- First it is given a data set which it learns from
- Then it makes its own set of rules upon that.
- With the help of the set of rules, it predicts the required output for next datasets.

Normally the data is unstructured, may contain irrelevant information, or some data points can be missing too. To get good results, the data needs to be preprocessed and cleaned before being fed to a machine learning model. After preprocessing, a model is developed according to the problem. The dataset is divided into three parts: training data, validation data, and test data. The model is fitted on training data. The validation dataset is used to evaluate the model and also used for tuning the hyperparameters (factors whose values affect the performance of model). Finally, the test data is fed to the model to check how it will perform in the real world. The figure 04 given below mentions the key pathway the machine learning helps the data analytic part in the big data analytics:

4.1 Types of Machine Learning

On the basis of their purpose, machine learning algorithms can be broadly classified into three types (Divya et al., 2018):

4.1.1 Supervised Learning

In supervised learning, the model is trained using a set of inputs along with their corresponding output. Using this data, the model establishes a relationship between the known inputs and outputs in the form of a function, and uses it to predict the output on a new set of inputs (Divya et al., 2018).

Some supervised learning algorithms are (Divya et al., 2018):

- Naive Bayes
- Linear Regression
- Logistic Regression
- Support Vector Machines (SVM)
- Neural Networks

Figure 4. Pathway of machine learning (Divya et al., 2018)

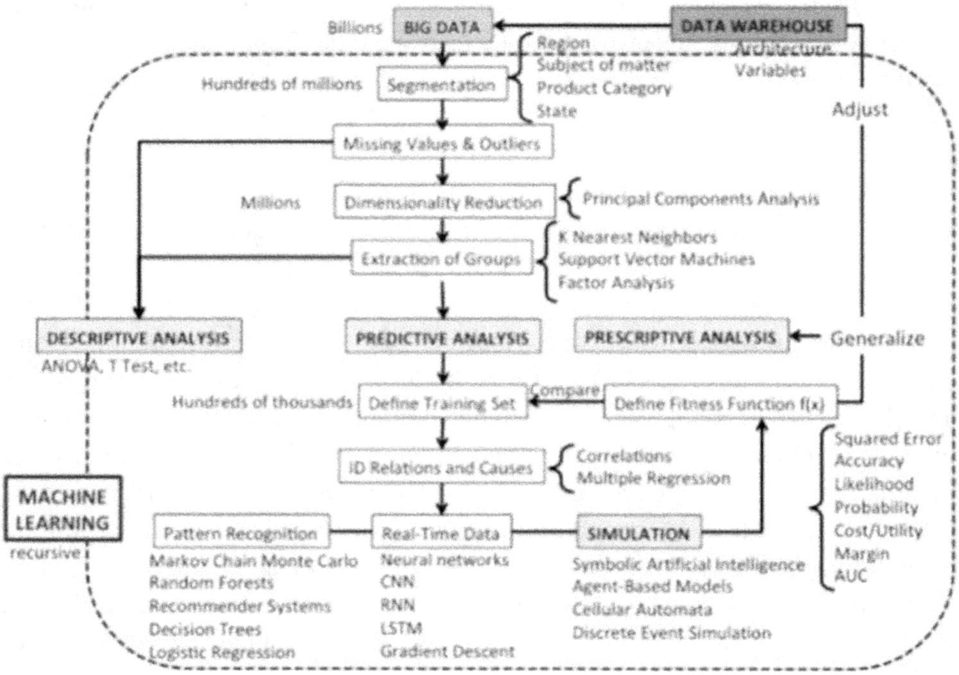

4.1.2 Unsupervised Learning

This type of algorithm is used when it is not known what variable needs to be predicted. The model identifies patterns in the data on its own and these are used to gain insights to the data. It is used for exploratory data analysis, for example, to analyze the current trends in business, to provide recommendations to users by observing what he/ she browses on the internet, etc.

Some unsupervised learning algorithms are (Divya et al., 2018):

- Hidden Markov Models
- K-Means Clustering

4.1.3 Reinforcement Learning

It can be said that reinforcement learning is inclined towards artificial intelligence. This type of algorithm learns continuously from the input and determines what should be its ideal behavior in order to improvise its performance, so as to maximize the reward and minimize the punishment. The most common example of reinforcement learning algorithm can be found in video games. Challenges are given to the player. If the player loses points, it is a reward for the computer and if the player gains points, it is a punishment. Artificial intelligence is used to navigate the game to provide viable challenges.

Some reinforcement learning algorithms are (Divya et al., 2018):

- Q-Learning
- Deep Q Network (DQN)
- State-Action-Reward-State-Action (SARSA)
- Proximal Policy Optimization

4.2 Common Machine Learning Algorithms

4.2.1 Linear Regression

It is the simplest algorithm for solving a regression problem. Regression is a problem in which we want to predict a variable which can take any continuous value. In this algorithm, a relationship between the independent variables (inputs, features or predictors, say x) and dependent variable (target, say y) is described in the form of an equation of the form:

$$y = \beta_0 + \beta_1 x.$$

Comparing above equation with the standard equation of a line, $y=mx+c$, we can say that β_0 is the intercept (also known as bias) and β_1 is the coefficient or slope (also known as weight).there is only one independent variable x, then this type of regression is called simple linear regression.

Figure 5. Example of a simple linear regression plot

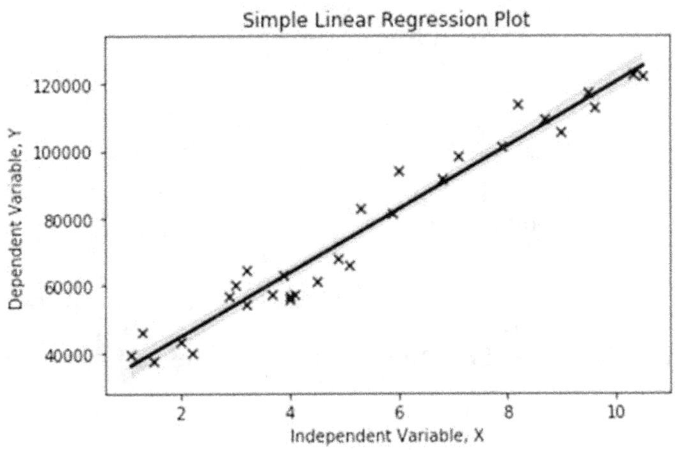

Above figure 05 is a linear regression plot between an independent variable X and a dependent variable Y. The cross marks on the plot represent the actual data points. The dark straight line is the best fitted line obtained by performing linear regression on the given data points.

If there are two or more independent variables, then it is called multiple linear regression. The equation of such a regression line is given by:

$$y = \beta_0 + \beta_1 x_1 + \beta_2 x_2 + \beta_3 x_3 + \beta_4 x_4 + \ldots \text{ and so on}$$

where $x_1, x_2, x_3 \ldots$ are the independent variables and $\beta_1, \beta_2, \beta_0, \ldots$ are their respective individual weights. In multiple linear regression, a plane is found out which best fits the n-dimensional data (Aurelien, 2017).

4.2.2 Decision Tree

Decision trees can perform both classification and regression tasks. While linear and logistic regression techniques are suitable for fairly simple datasets, decision trees can also perform well on complex datasets. A decision tree can either be classification tree or regression tree based on the nature of target variable.

In a decision tree model, the topmost node is called root and on every node, a decision is made on the basis of which it further splits into branches. These are also called internal nodes. Terminal nodes which do not split further are the leaf nodes. Output is obtained at theses leaf nodes as figure 06 as example (Muller & Sarah, 2016).

Figure 6. Basic structure of a decision tree

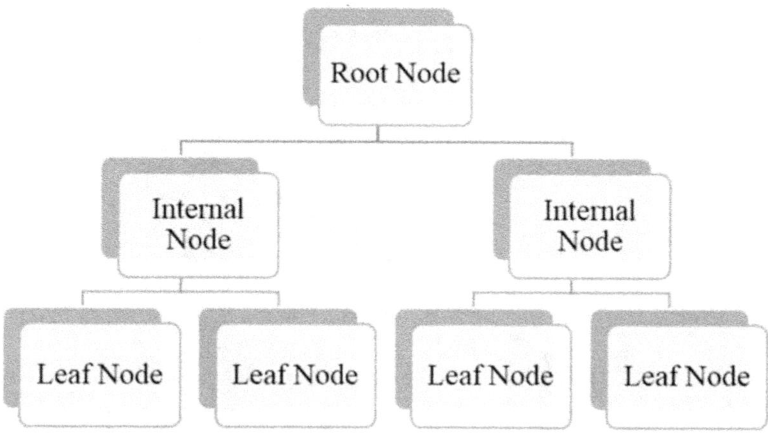

The most suitable root node is that independent variable which has a very strong relation with the outcome. A decision tree learns through a series of if-else type questions as shown in following figure (Muller & Sarah, 2016):

Figure 7. A decision tree to distinguish between four animals

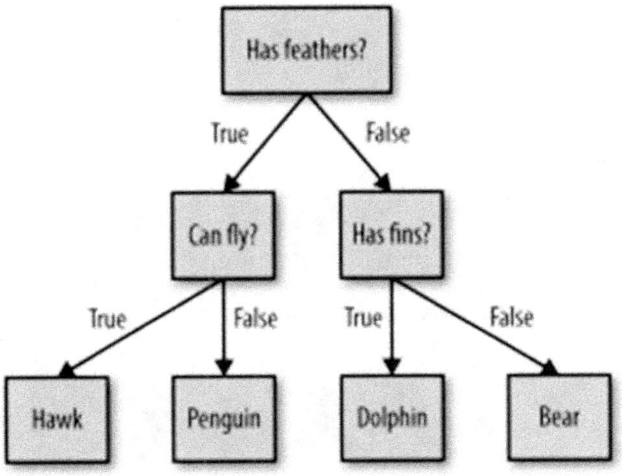

As an example denotes figure 07 in mode of Decision Tree between four animals via author analysis. For real life datasets, decision trees are much more complex due to the large number of independent variables. Without setting a limit on the number of splits, the decision tree obtained is very deep as it makes decisions on every independent variable. To overcome this problem, the tree size is limited to a feasible depth. In this decision tree the use case is taken to distinguish between four animals (viz. hawk, penguin, dolphin, bear), on the basis of their characteristics. The first level of classification is whether the animal have feather or not, this divides them into two groups, first have feather and second does not, now the second level of classification for the animal that have feather, if its able to fly, then it is hawk, and if not it is penguin, and for the animals which does not have feathers if it has fins then it is a dolphin otherwise it is a bear. This was analyzed from the characteristics and then the decision tree was made to classify them accordingly.

4.2.3 Logistic Regression

This algorithm is used for classification problems. It is named 'logistic regression' because its working is somewhat similar to that of linear regression. While in linear regression, we calculate continuous values of target variable, in logistic regression sigmoid function is used in addition to map that real number into a range of (0, 1) to find out in which class the target variable falls in. The formula of sigmoid function is:

$$f(x) = \frac{1}{1+e^{-x}}$$

(a) Linear Regression
(b) Logistic Regression

Figure 8. Linear Regression vs. Logistic Regression

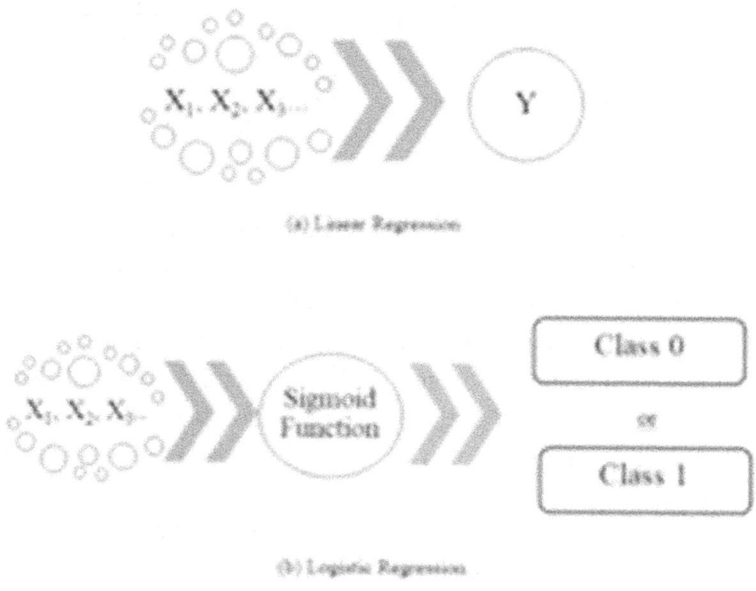

Logistic regression is not only suitable for binary classification, but it can also be used for multiclass classification. In figure 08 shows the comparison between Linear regression and Logistic Regression.

4.2.4 Support Vector Machines (SVM)

These models are very useful for performing linear, as well as nonlinear classification and regression. SVM classifiers aim to find out the widest possible street (margin) between the different classes of data points. The points nearest to the margin lines are called support vectors, and they help in determining the width of the separation. If the classes are to be strictly separated from one another, it is called hard margin classification. Presence of any outliers in this case has a significant effect on the margin. To avoid this problem, the separation can also be determined while maintaining a balance between its width and margin violations. It is called soft margin classification (Muller & Sarah, 2016). This is illustrated in the following figure 09:

Figure 9. Hard Margin and Soft Margin in SVM

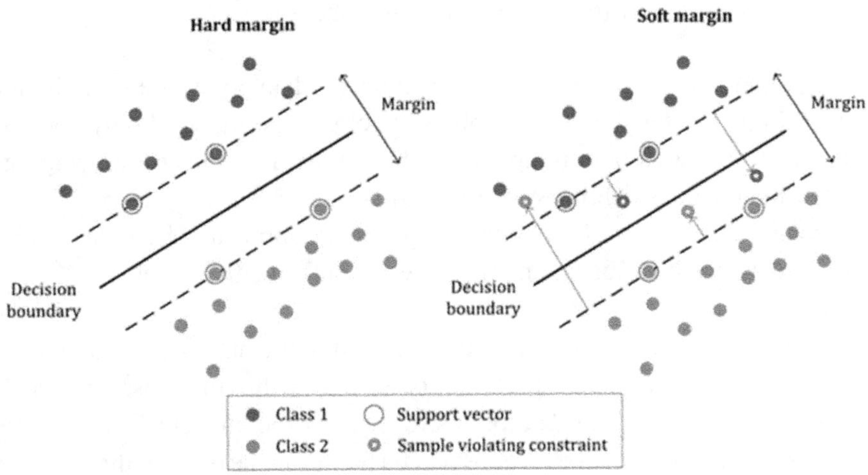

For regression problems, the SVM repressor's try to locate the maximum number of data points possible on the separation boundary area while reducing the margin violations.

4.2.5 K Nearest Neighbors

It follows the assumption that similar data points are always close to each other when plotted on a graph. In this algorithm, the distances between the point of interest (whose value is unknown) and all the other points are calculated. A value for 'K' is chosen. If it is a regression problem, then the output is the mean of all the K closest points. On the other hand, if it is a classification problem, then the label that occurs most in the K closest values is taken to be the output class. The model is trained for multiple values of K and the best one is taken as the final K value (Muller & Sarah, 2016).

4.2.6 Clustering

As the name suggests, this technique involves grouping of data points which are similar in terms of features. Clustering is a type of unsupervised learning. Some types of clustering algorithms are:

Density based clustering - This class of clustering methods forms groups of data points on the basis of their density. A cluster is seen as a collection of data points in space, and higher density points are differentiated from lower density regions. DBSCAN (Density Based Spatial Clustering of Applications with Noise) is the most commonly used density based clustering algorithm (Aurelien, 2017).

Hierarchical clustering - These methods visualize the hierarchy in clusters in a tree-like diagram. It is further divided into two categories:

- Agglomerative clustering - In this method, all data points are initially treated as a single cluster. Then it combines the closest points until only one cluster is left. It follows a bottom up approach, and previous clusters are aggregated to form new ones (Muller & Sarah, 2016).
- Divisive clustering - It follows a top down approach. The data points are treated as one big cluster, and then divided into smaller groups.

Partitioning clustering - These methods partition the data points into k clusters on the basis of an observation. Different types of partitioning clustering methods use different observations in data points to identify the clusters. For example, K means clustering method makes groups of data points on the basis of their individual distances from the centroid. K-medoids algorithm and CLARA (Clustering Large Applications) algorithm are also commonly used partitioning clustering methods.

Grid based clustering - In this approach, the data space is divided into cells to form a grid like structure. All the clustering operations are then performed on this structure.

5. Machine Learning Tools

In the situation of big data, researchers, operators, managers have a large amount of data acquired from the data set. To make the analysis easy, various tools are used so that it takes lesser time to implement. The tools which are used are:

5.1 Map Reduce Frameworks

The core idea working beneath is to divide the data into crunches and each crunch is then analysed by different servers and the collective result of every server forms the actual result. This approach is also utilized as working of the Hadoop framework. On the other hand, apache spark uses the power of interactive graphs and plots by Python and Scala.

The presence of Hadoop over a long tenure attracted a majority of business over the new arrivals viz. spark and Mahout which uses the machine learning approach. Map Reduce frameworks tool also available online[1].

Map Reduce frameworks tool available online -

5.2 Apache Spark

Improving the efficiency in memory management and communication via pipelines, apache spark is a general purpose analytic framework, facilitates the user via APIs in different programming languages such as Scala, R, Python etc.

It acts as a medium to implement existing machine learning algorithms on large datasets and this feature of Spark helps to test out different models on one platform. Apache Sparl tool available online[2].

5.3 Apache Mahout

As shows in figure 10 and it is an open source project from Apache along with java libraries to scale machine learning algorithms. The calculation in Mahout is done in such a way that it includes machine learning terms such as affiliation run examination, bunching, arrangements, and suggestions. In spite of the fact that Mahout is built on the top of Apache Hadoop environment, it is compatible with any framework that supports Map Reduce system (Divya et al., 2018). As Apache Mahout tool available online[3].

6. DISCUSSION

The data and information are two similar terms, the characteristic that distinguishes these two concepts from one another is that data is simply a collection of facts-either related or not. Whereas, information is what we infer after processing the data. Information derived from analysis of data helps in decision making, not the data itself. Since big data contains a significant amount of redundant data in it, the information that can be extracted from it is comparatively very small in size. Data duplication, serial correlation, and cross-correlation are the causes of data redundancy. During data explosion sudden and rapid growth of data occurs. It gives scope to a number of data reduction techniques. This paper also presented the type of data that can be considered as big data. Later on, data redundancy is considered, which deals with topics such as data duplication, serial correlation, cross-correlation, etc. In this paper the different aspects of big data are taken into consideration. We present that how the analytics of big data have been transformed from RDBMS to HADOOP like methods. Table 1 presents a brief discussion about such methods that exist in literature. The needs for those transformation and different phases of transformation are also presented. There is also a consideration to store large amount of data. This paper also describes the inconsistencies that are present inside the data analysis in case of big data analytics. The data analysis process goes from input to output or from user to storage place. Big data analytics frameworks are also discussed in brief. The attention to machine learning in big data is given and its usefulness in the research of big data analytics is presented. As the definition of learning analytics defines, learning analytics is a field of collecting, measuring and analysing the data about the learner and their context, to understand and optimize their learning environment, thus big data is directly related to the key functioning of learning analytics by providing the base to collect and analyse the data and outcomes. Big data is highly related to learning analytics as it shifts the attention from a group of learner to particular learner; it personalized the feed of individual, helping to improve the learning rates. As the big data introduced, we can now find out trends in learning pattern and improve our strategies for better efficiency, thus big data relates to learning analytics to improve efficiency and strategy making. As we are living in the era where everything is data driven, every aspect of our life is being affected by data driven technology, education and learning analytics are finding their scope through these technologies as well, students are hugely contributing to these massive amount of data in the industry and also getting benefited by them as online resource and platform to learn. This transition of education system and teaching manner is praised and criticized at the same time. Praised to let the learners explore everything inside their area of interest at such a easy, helping them to be updated with the research areas of the times, on the other hand criticized for making the student divert themselves from their curriculum studies.

Figure 10. Framework of Apache Mahout

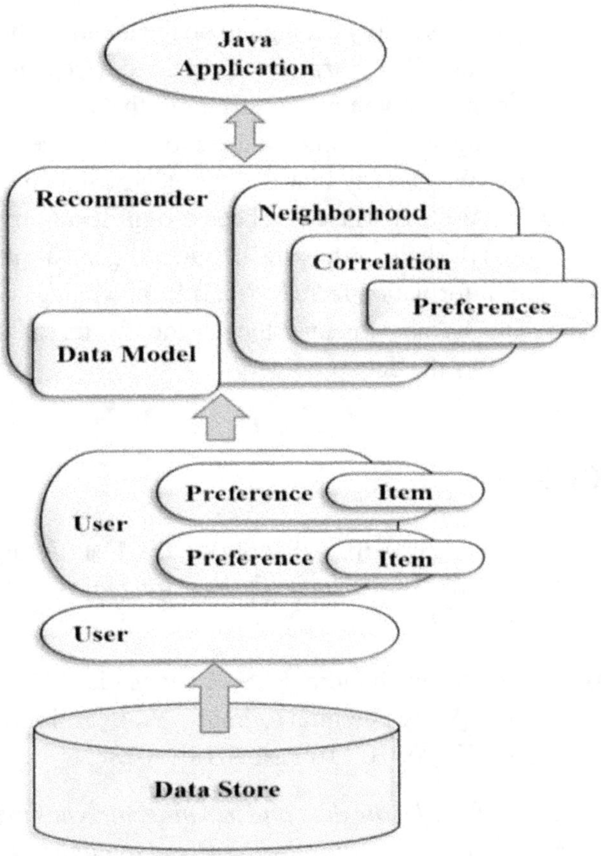

Table 1. Discussion of Literature

Authors	Methodology/Process	Techniques
S. Vikram Phaneendra & E. Madhusudhan Reddy	• capable enough to handle a lot of data • all the 5V's of the big data definition	• Hadoop method
Kiran Kumara Reddi & Dnsvl Indira	• data is a combination of structured, semi-structured, and unstructured data of both homogenous and heterogeneous type	• better model for understanding analysing such a big amount of data
Wei Fan & Albert Bifet	• mining is a process of extracting data from a large set • data of data which of high volume, velocity and variety	• ideas and challenges to be dealt with while incorporating big data analysis

CONCLUSION

The usefulness of big data is totally dependent on the identification of relevant data in it. Any data is only junk if it is irrelevant. Many devices and technologies are available to capture such large volumes of data, but the amount of relevant data in it is very small. Searching and filtering are done to convert the larger data sets into smaller, relevant ones. We can say that the absence of search and filter methods will render all this data useless. There has been a significant growth in the field of big data analytics. With the help of these techniques, organizations dealing with big data are able to derive information from it. Apart from it being such a great help for organizations, big data has many inconsistencies too, the major one being the issue of privacy and security of the data providers.

REFERENCES

Acharjya, D., & Kauser, A. (2016). A Survey on Big Data Analytics: Challenges, Open Research Issues and Tools. *International Journal of Advanced Computer Science and Applications*, 7.

Adam, K., Bakar, N. A. A., Fakhreldin, M. A. I., & Majid, M. A. (2018). Big Data and Learning Analytics: A Big Potential to Improve e-Learning. *Advanced Science Letters*, *6*(10), 7838–7843. doi:10.1166/asl.2018.13028

Amal, A., & Ahmad, A. (2017). *Big data and learning analytics in higher education: Demystifying variety, acquisition, storage, NLP and analytics*. Academic Press.

Anthony, G. (2012). The Evolution of Big Data and Learning Analytics in American Higher Education. *Journal of Asynchronous Learning Networks*, *16*, 9–20.

Backupify. (2015). *Bit & Bytes: A History of Data Storage*. Author.

Batistic, S., & Laken, P. (2019). History, Evolution and Future of Big Data and Analytics: A Bibliometric Analysis of Its Relationship to Performance in Organizations. *British Journal of Management*, *30*(2), 229–251. doi:10.1111/1467-8551.12340

Bhardwaj, V. (2015). Big Data Analysis: Issues and Challenges. *Big Data Analysis: Issues and Challenges*, *1*, 1–3.

Bhargava, N., Sharma, A., Kumar, A., & Rathoe, P. (2017). An adaptive method for edge preserving denoising. *2017 2nd International Conference on Communication and Electronics Systems (ICCES),* 600-604.

Bifet, A. (2013). Mining Big Data in Real Time. *Informatica (Vilnius)*, *37*, 15–20.

Big Data - A Visual History. (2015). *Big Data and the History of Information Storage*. Author.

Chen, J., Jiang, Q., Wang, Y., & Tang, J. (2016). Study of data analysis model based on big data technology. *2016 IEEE International Conference on Big Data Analysis (ICBDA)*, 1-6. 10.1109/ICBDA.2016.7509810

Divya, K., Bhargavi, P., & Singaraju, J. (2018). Machine Learning Algorithms in Big data Analytics. *International Journal on Computer Science and Engineering*, *6*, 63–70.

Géron, A. (2017). Training Models in Hands-on Machine Learning with Scikit-Learn & TensorFlow. O'Reilly Media.

Géron, A. (2017). *Support Vector Machines in Hands-on Machine Learning with Scikit-Learn & TensorFlow. O'Reilly Media.*

Grolinger, K. (2014). Challenges for MapReduce in Big Data. *2014 IEEE 10th World Congress on Services, 1*, 182-183.

Gyamfi, N. (2017). *Big Data Analytics: Survey Paper*. Academic Press.

Hu, H. (2014). Toward Scalable Systems for Big Data Analytics: A Technology Tutorial. *Toward Scalable Systems for Big Data Analytics: A Technology Tutorial, 1*, 658-659, 665.

Hu, R. (2016). Key Technology for Big Visual Data Analysis in Security Space and Its Applications. *International Conference on Advanced Cloud and Big Data (CBD)*, 333-333. 10.1109/CBD.2016.065

IBM100 - The IBM Punched Card. (2015). *The IBM Punched Card*. Author.

IBM Big Data & Analytics Hub. (2014). *The Four V's of Big Data*. Author.

Kumar, D., & Duvvuri, B., Kamesh, K., & Umar, S. (2014). *A Study on Big Data and its Importance*. Academic Press.

Li, B., Ming, X., & Li, G. (2017). Big data analytics platform for flight safety monitoring. *2017 IEEE 2nd International Conference on Big Data Analysis (ICBDA)*, 350-353.

Li, X., Jiang, W., Jiang, Y., & Zou, Q. (2012). Hadoop Applications in Bioinformatics. *Open Cirrus Summit*, *7*, 48–52.

Liao, C., Lei, Y., Liou, K., Lin, J., & Yeh, H. (2015). Using Big Data for Profiling Heavy Users in Top Video Apps. *2015 IEEE International Congress on Big Data*, 381-385. 10.1109/BigDataCongress.2015.63

McHugh, J., Cuddihy, P., Williams, J., Aggour, K., Kumar, V., & Mulwad, V. (2017). Integrated access to big data polystores through a knowledge-driven framework. *2017 IEEE International Conference on Big Data (Big Data),* 1494-1503.

Müller, A., & Guido, S. (2016). *Supervised Learning in Introduction to Machine Learning with Python. O'Reilly Media.*

Müller, A., & Guido, S. (2016). *Unsupervised Learning and Preprocessing in Introduction to Machine Learning with Python. O'Reilly Media.*

Park, K., Nguyen, M. C., & Won, H. (2015). Web-based Collaborative Big Data Analytics on Big Data as a Service Platform. *Web-based Collaborative Big Data Analytics on Big Data as a Service Platform, 1*, 564–566. doi:10.1109/ICACT.2015.7224859

Phaneendra, S., & Reddy, E. (2013). Big Datasolutions for RDBMS problems- A survey. *IEEE/IFIP Network Operations & Management Symposium, 2*.

Puyun, B., & Miao, L. (2016). Research on analysis system of city price based on big data. *2016 IEEE International Conference on Big Data Analysis (ICBDA)*, 1-4. 10.1109/ICBDA.2016.7509819

Redavid, D., Corizzo, R., & Malerba, D. (2018). An OWL Ontology for Supporting Semantic Services in Big Data Platforms. *2018 IEEE International Congress on Big Data (BigData Congress),* 228-231.

Reddi, K., & Indira, D. (2013). Different Technique to Transfer Big Data: Survey. *IEEE Transactions*, *3*, 708–711.

Sharma, S., & Sharma, A. (2017). An adaptive approach for Decomposition of Space Variant Blur and It's Restoration using Blind Deconvolution. *International Journal for Research & Development in Technology*, *7*, 492–496.

Sin, K., & Muthu, L. (2015). Application of Big Data in Education Data Mining and Learning Analytics – A Literature Review. *ICTACT Journal on Soft Computing,* 1035-1049.

Sriramoju, S. (2017). Review on Big Data and Mining Algorithm. *International Journal for Research in Applied Science and Engineering Technology*, *5*(XI), 1238–1243. doi:10.22214/ijraset.2017.11181

Taylor, S. (2016). Big Data: Understanding. *Big Data*.

The Storage Engine. (2015). *1951: Tape unit developed for data storage*. Author.

Yadav, S., & Sohal, A. (2017). *Review Paper on Big Data Analytics in Cloud Computing*. Academic Press.

KEY TERMS AND DEFINITIONS

Big Data: It is the collection of such a huge amount of data (both structured and unstructured) with much complexity that traditional data management tool cannot store or process it efficiently.

Data Redundancy: It is the condition in which same piece of data is stored in two different places in the data base.

Hadoop: Hadoop is an open source distributed processing framework that manages data processing and storage for big data applications in scalable clusters of computer servers.

KDD: Knowledge discovery in database (KDD) is a process to find knowledge or insights from the data.

MapReduce: MapReduce is a programming model and an associated implementation for processing and generating big data sets with a parallel, distributed algorithm on a cluster.

ENDNOTES

1 Map Reduce Frameworks tool https://hadoop.apache.org/docs/r1.2.1/mapred_tutorial.html

2 Apache Spark tool available online - https://spark.apache.org/

3 Apache Mahout tool available online - http://mahout.apache.org/

Chapter 11
Educational Data Mining Techniques and Applications

M. Govindarajan
Annamalai University, India

ABSTRACT

Educational data mining (EDM) creates high impact in the field of academic domain. EDM is concerned with developing new methods to discover knowledge from educational and academic database and can be used for decision making in educational and academic systems. EDM is useful in many different areas including identifying at risk students, identifying priority learning needs for different groups of students, increasing graduation rates, effectively assessing institutional performance, maximizing campus resources, and optimizing subject curriculum renewal. This chapter discusses educational data mining, its applications, and techniques that have to be adopted in order to successfully employ educational data mining and learning analytics for improving teaching and learning. The techniques and applications discussed in this chapter will provide a clear-cut idea to the educational data mining researchers to carry out their work in this field.

INTRODUCTION

Educational Data Mining (EDM) describes a research field concerned with the application of data mining, machine learning and statistics to information generated from educational settings (e.g., universities and intelligent tutoring systems). EDM refers to techniques and tools designed for automatically extracting meaning from large repositories of data generated by people's learning activities in educational settings. At a high level, the field seeks to develop and improve methods for exploring this

DOI: 10.4018/978-1-7998-7103-3.ch011

data, which often has multiple levels of meaningful hierarchy, in order to discover new insights about how people learn in the context of such settings. In doing so, EDM has contributed to theories of learning investigated by researchers in educational psychology and the learning sciences. The field is closely tied to that of learning analytics, and the two have been compared and contrasted. Quite often, this data is extensive, fine-grained, and precise (B.Namratha et al., 2016). This chapter discusses about educational data mining, its techniques and applications that have to be adopted in order to successfully employ educational data mining and learning analytics for improving teaching and learning. The techniques and applications discussed in this chapter will provide a clear cut idea to the educational data mining researchers to carry out their work in this field.

The rest of the chapter is organized as follows: The background section describes the related work. A brief description of what is educational data mining, their techniques and applications and some tools of educational data mining is presented in section of main focus of the chapter and future research directions focuses on future work. Finally concludes the chapter.

BACKGROUND

Brijesh Kumar Baradwaj et al., (2011) designed to justify the capabilities of data mining techniques in context of higher education by offering a data mining model for higher education system in the university. Manoj Bala et al., (2012) addresses the applications of data mining in educational institution to extract useful information from the huge data sets and providing analytical tool to view and use this information for decision making processes by taking real life examples. Rajni Jindal et al., (2013) focuses on components, research trends (1998 to 2012) of EDM highlighting its related Tools, Techniques and educational Outcomes. It also highlights the Challenges EDM. Alejandro Peña-Ayala (2014) pursues a twofold goal, the first is to preserve and enhance the chronicles of recent educational data mining (EDM) advances development; the second is to organize, analyze, and discuss the content of the review based on the outcomes produced by a data mining (DM) approach. Hardeep Kaur (2015) focuses on the applications of data mining in the field of education. A.S. Arunachalam et al., (2016) focuses on educational data mining (EDM) and it discusses on various techniques involved in making EDM for students' knowledge improvement. In this article, the authors also discuss about different types of EDM tools and techniques. Among the different tools and techniques, best categories are suggested for real world usage. Ashish Dutt et al., (2017) provides over three decades long (1983 - 2016) systematic literature review on clustering algorithm and its applicability and usability in the context of EDM. Future insights are outlined based on the literature reviewed, and avenues for further research are identified. VandnaDahiya (2018) presents a survey on various components of educational data mining along with its objectives. HananAldowaha et al., (2019) covered the most relevant studies related to four main dimensions: computer-supported learning analytics (CSLA), computer-supported predictive analytics (CSPA), computer-supported behavioral analytics (CSBA), and computer-supported visualization analytics (CSVA) from 2000 till 2017. SnježanaKrižanic (2020) describes the application of data mining techniques on educational data of a higher education institution in Croatia. Data used for the analysis are event logs downloaded from an e-learning environment of a real e-course. Data mining techniques applied for the research are cluster analysis and decision tree.

MAIN FOCUS OF THE ARTICLE

The purpose of this chapter is to provide a brief description of what is educational data mining, their techniques and applications and present some tools of educational data mining.

Educational Data Mining

Data mining introduces a new technique known as educational mining (EM). In educational mining, data mining concepts are applied to data that is related to field of education. It is the process of remodelling the data assembled by education systems. Educational mining means analysing hidden data that came from educational settings by using new methods for better understanding of students and context they learnt.

Educational mining support distinct tools and algorithms for analyze the data patterns. In EM, data is acquired during learning process and then analysis work can be done with the techniques from statistics, machine learning and other data mining concepts. To extract the hidden knowledge from data came from educational system, the various data mining techniques like classification, clustering and rule mining have been discussed for generating better decisions in educational system.

The academic's responsible and educators worked upon the educational system to strengthen the performance of students. Educational systems include traditional classrooms and some innovative learning methods like e-learning system, intelligent and adaptive web based educational system. The data set can be extracted from students as students are directly connected with educational system. Now the data is given as input to data mining methods and in result it produces guidance to students and to extract new knowledge to the educators by using various data mining techniques like clustering, classification, pattern matching etc (Sharma et. al.,2018).

Objectives of Educational Data Mining

The objectives of educational data mining can be classified into two categories- the educational objectives and the administrative objectives ((Vandna Dahiya, 2018). A new category that is recently becoming very popular is the commercial or the market objectives. The detailed look at the objectives of the educational data mining is as follows:

Educational Objectives

They are also known as the academic objectives and are of great importance when it comes to conception and designing of educational content. They help in doing time-to-time development and improvement required in the study material. Another critical educational use is to bring improvement in academic performance of the learners. So, talking on formal terms the educations objectives can be divided into the following sub-categories:

1. Individual/ Person-oriented- these objectives have a direct contribution to teaching and learning. The person-oriented objectives of educational data mining that exist around us are
   - Student learning
   - Risk
   - Modeling
   - Behavior
   - Cognitive learning
   - Predicting right enrollment decision
   - Performance analysis

There are many more generic and specific factors, both in the conventional and digital environment for faculty modeling, which helps in job performance analysis and satisfaction analysis.

2. Department/Institution-oriented- this is specifically related to certain department or organization with respect to-time, structure, and demand. EDM helps institutes and various educational departments in
   - Redesigning new courses according to industry requirements,
   - Understand real-time field problems
   - Effective research analysis
   - Enhance learning experience and process.

Administrative or Management Objectives

Educational data mining can be applied to optimization of the school, college or any other learning institute. It can be of great use when it comes to the maintenance of educational infrastructure, which is a chief administrative oriented objective and involves the direct participation of higher authorities and senior management.

Commercial Objectives

Commercial objectives are particularly important in case of private education, such as the creation of a niche and capturing the market in terms of enrollments. In higher education system the university and private institution improve their quality by focusing on quality of teaching process, placement details and achieving the certification from various certified agencies and also develop their own infrastructure. The information regarding the private institution and university should be stored in database in such a way that the student can easily visualize these information and on that basis choosing of institution is done followed by various analysis and data mining experiment in educational data base. The data can be effectively used in marketing for student enrollment and capturing the scholars for private institutions and the establishment of a network for innovative research and practices. Other objectives are to

- Automated the decision process of management by analyzing heterogeneous educational data from traditional as well as intelligent tools.
- Experiment with the latest intelligent tools and application of effective techniques used in EDM and
- Understand various real-time challenges faced in EDM.

Educational Data Mining Techniques

Educational data mining methods come from different literature sources including data mining, machine learning, psychometrics, and other areas of computational modelling, statistics, and information visualization. Work in EDM can be divided into two main categories: 1) web mining and 2) statistics and visualization. The category of statistics and visualization has received a prominent place in theoretical discussions and research in EDM (Baker et al., 2009, Romero et al., 2010, Tanimoto, 2007). Another point of view, proposed by Baker et al., (2010), classifies the work in EDM as follows.

1. Prediction.
    a. Classification.
    b. Regression.
    c. Density estimation.
2. Clustering.
3. Relationship mining.
    a. Association rule mining.
    b. Correlation mining.
    c. Sequential pattern mining.
    d. Causal DM.
4. Distillation of data for human judgment.
5. Discovery with models.

The first three categories are largely acknowledged to be universal across types of data mining (albeit in some cases with different names). The fourth and fifth categories achieve particular prominence within educational data mining.

1. Prediction

Prediction aims to predict unknown variables based on history data for the same variable. However, the input variables (predictor variables) can be classified or continue as variables. The effectiveness of the prediction model depends on the type of input variables. The prediction model is required to have limited labelled data for the output variable. The labelled data offers some prior knowledge regarding the variables that we need to predict. However, it is important to consider the effects of quality of the training data in order to achieve the prediction model.

There are three general types of predictions:

- Classification uses prior knowledge to build a learning model and then uses that model as a binary or categorical variable for the new data. Many models have been developed and used as classifiers such as logistic regression and support vector machines (SVM).
- Regression is a model used to predict variables. Different from classification, regression models predict not only variables. Different methods of regression, such as linear regression and neural networks, have been used widely in the area of EDM to predict which students should be classified as at-risk.
- Density estimation is based on a variety of kernel functions including Gaussian functions.

Prediction methodology in EDM is used in different ways. Most commonly, it studies features used for prediction and uses those features in the underlying construct, which predicts student educational outcomes (Romero, 2008). While different approaches try to predict the expected output value based on hidden variables in the data, the obtained output is not clearly defined in the labels data.

For example, if a researcher aims to identify the students most likely to drop out of school, with the large number of schools and students involved, it is difficult to achieve using traditional research methods such as questionnaires. The EDM method, with its limited amount of sample data, can help achieve that aim. It must start by defining at-risk students and follow with defining the variables that affect the students such as their parents' educational backgrounds. The relation between variables and dropping out of school can be used to build a prediction model, which can then predict at-risk students.

Making these predictions early can help organizations avoid problems or reduce the effects of specific issues. Different methods have been developed to evaluate the quality of a predictor including accuracy of linear correlation (Bradley, 1997). However, accuracy is not recommended for evaluating the classification method because it is dependent on the base rates of different classes. In some cases, it is easy to get high accuracy by classifying all data based on the large group of classes sample data. It is also important to calculate the number of missed classifications from the data to measure the sensitivity of the classifier using recall (Liu, 2007).A combined method, such as an F-measure, considers both true and false classification results, which are based on precision and recall, to give an overall evaluation of the classifier.

2. Clustering

Clustering is a method used to separate data into different groups based on certain common features. Different from the classification method, in clustering, the data labels are unknown. The clustering method gives the user a broad view of what is happening in that dataset. Clustering is sometimes known as an unsupervised classification because class labels are unknown (Fayyad et al., 1996).

In clustering, data points are found that naturally group together to split the dataset into different groups. The number of groups can be predefined in the clustering method. Generally, the clustering method is used when the most common group in the dataset is unknown. It is also used to reduce the size of the study area. For example, different schools can be grouped together based on similarities and differences between them (Beal et al., 2006 and Amershi et al., 2006).

3. Relationship Mining

Relationship mining aims to find relationships between different variables in data sets with a large number of variables. This entails finding out which variables are most strongly associated with a specific variable of particular interest.

Relationship mining also measures the strength of the relationships between different variables. Relationships found through relationship mining must satisfy two criteria: statistical significance and interestingness. Large amounts of data contain many variables and hence have many associated rules. Therefore, the measure of interestingness determines the most important rules supported by data for specific interests.

Different interestingness measures have been developed over the years by researchers including support and confidence. However, some research has concluded that lift and cosine are the most relevant used in educational data mining (Merceron et al., 2008). Many types of relationship mining can be used such as association rule mining, sequential pattern mining, and frequent pattern mining. Association rule mining is the most common EDM method. The relationship found in association rule mining is if → then rules. For example, if {Student GPA is less than two, and the student has a job}⇒{ the student is going to drop out of school}. The main goal of relationship mining is to determine whether or not one event causes another event by studying the coverage of the two events in the data set, such as TETRAD (Wallace et al., 1996), or by studying how an event is triggered.

4. Distillation of Data for Human Judgement

Distillation of data for human judgment aims to make data understandable. Presenting the data in different ways helps the human brain discover new knowledge. Different kinds of data require specific methods to visualize it. However, the visualization methods used in educational data mining are different from those used in different data sets (Hershkovitz et al., 2008 and Maisonneuve et al., 2006) in that they consider the structure of the education data and the hidden meaning within it.

Distillation of data for human judgment is applied in educational data for two purposes: classification and/or identification. Data distillation for classification can be a preparation process for building a prediction model (Baker et al., 2008); identification aims to display data such that it is easily identifiable via well known patterns that cannot be formalized (Corbett et al., 1994). As mentioned previously, there is a wide variety of methods used in educational data mining. These methods have been divided into five categories: clustering, prediction, relationship mining, discovery with models, and distillation of data for human judgement.

5. Discovery With Models

In discovery, models are generally based on clustering, prediction, or knowledge engineering using human reasoning rather than automated methods. The developed model is then used as part of other comprehensive models such as relationship mining.

Most of the above mentioned items are considered Data Mining (DM) categories. However, the distillation of data for human judgment is not universally regarded as DM. Historically, relationship mining approaches of various types have been the most noticeable category in EDM research. Discovery with models is perhaps the most unusual category in Bakers EDM taxonomy, from a classical DM perspective.

It has been used widely to model a phenomenon through any process that can be validated in some way. That model is then used as a component in another model such as relationship mining or prediction. This category (discovery with models) has become one of the lesser-known methods in the research area of educational data mining. It seeks to determine which learning material subcategories provide students with the most benefits (Beck et al., 2008), how specific students behavior affects students learning in different ways (Cocea et al., 2009), and how tutorial design affects students learning (Jeong et al., 2008). Historically, relationship mining methods have been the most used in educational data mining research in the last few years.

Other EDM methodologies, which have not been used widely, include the following:

- Outlier detections discover data points that significantly differ from the rest of the data (Hodge et al., 2004). In EDM, they can detect students with learning problems and irregular learning processes by using the learners response time data for e-learning data (Chan, 2007). Moreover, they can also detect a typical behavior via clusters of students in a virtual campus. Outlier detection can also detect irregularities and deviations in the learners or educators actions with others (Muehlenbrock, 2005).
- Text mining can work with semi-structured or unstructured datasets such as text documents, HTML files, emails. It has been used in the area of EDM to analyze data in the discussion board with evaluation between peers in an ILMS (Ueno, 2004 and Dringus et al., 2005). It has also been proposed for use in text mining to construct textbooks automatically via web content mining (Chen et al., 2004). Use of text mining for the clustering of documents based on similarity and topic has been proposed (Tane et al., 2004 and Tang et al., 2000).
- Social Network Analysis (SNA) is a field of study that attempts to understand and measure relationships between entities in networked information. Data

mining approaches can be used with network information to study online interactions (Scott, 2011). In EDM, the approaches can be used for mining group activities (Reyes et al., 2005).

Educational Data Mining Applications

There are many application areas of data mining like customer analytics, Agriculture, banking, Security Applications, Educational data mining, Mass surveillance, Privacy preserving etc. The main concerned area is about data mining applications in educational systems. Educational Data Mining (EDM) is an emerging discipline, concerned with developing methods for exploring the unique types of data that come from educational settings, and using those methods to better understand students and the settings which they learn in. A key area of EDM is mining student's performance. Another key area is mining enrollment data. Key uses of EDM include predicting student performance and studying learning in order to recommend improvements to current educational practice. EDM can be considered one of the learning sciences, as well as an area of data mining (B.Namratha et al., 2016). A list of the primary applications of EDM is provided by Cristobal Romero and Sebastian Ventura (2010). In their taxonomy, the areas of EDM application are:

- Analysis and visualization of data
- Providing feedback for supporting instructors
- Recommendations for students
- Predicting student performance
- Student modeling
- Detecting undesirable student behaviors
- Grouping students
- Social network analysis
- Developing concept maps
- Constructing courseware
- Planning and scheduling

The main applications of EDM are described as follows:

Analysis and Visualization of Data

It is used to highlight useful information and support decision making. In the educational environment, for example, it can help educators and course administrators to analyze the students' course activities and usage information to get a general view of a student's learning. Statistics and visualization information are the two main techniques that have been most widely used for this task. Statistics is a mathematical science concerning the collection, analysis, interpretation or explanation, and presentation of data. It is relatively easy to get basic descriptive statistics from statistical software, such as SPSS. Statistical analysis of educational data (logs files/ databases) can tell us things such as where students enter and exit, the most popular pages students browse, number of downloads of e-learning resources, number of different pages browsed and total time for browsing different pages. It also provides knowledge about usage summaries and reports on weekly and monthly user trends, amount of material students might go through and the order in which students study topics, patterns of studying activity, timing and sequencing of events, and the content analysis of students notes and summaries. Statistical analysis is also very useful to obtain reports assessing how many minutes student worked, number of problems were solved and his correct percentage along with our prediction about his score and performance level.

Visualization uses graphic techniques to help people to understand and analyze data. There are several studies oriented toward visualizing different educational data such as patterns of annual, seasonal, daily and hourly user behavior on online forums. Some of such investigations are statistical graphs to analyze assignments complement, questions admitted, exam score, student tracking data to analyze student's attendance, results on assignments and quizzes, weekly information regarding students and group's activities.

Predicting Student Performance

In this case, the unknown value of a variable that describes the student is estimated. In education, the values normally predicted are student's performance, their knowledge, score, or marks. This value can be numerical/continuous (regression task) or categorical/discrete (classification task). Regression analysis is used to find relation between a dependent variable and one or more independent variables. Classification is used to group individual items based upon quantitative characteristics inherent in the items or on training set of previously labelled items. Prediction of a student's performance is the most popular applications of DM in education. Different techniques and models are applied like neural networks, Bayesian networks, rule based systems, regression, and correlation analysis to analyze educational data. This analysis helps us to predict student's performance i.e. to predict about his success in a course and to predict about his final grade based on features extracted from logged data. Different types of rule-based systems have been applied to predict student's performance (mark prediction) in an e-learning environment (using fuzzy-association rules). Several regression techniques are used to predict student's marks like linear regression for predicting student's academic performance, stepwise linear regression for predicting time to be spent on a learning page, multiple linear regression for identifying variables that could predict success in colleges courses and for predicting exam results in distance education courses.

Grouping Students

In this case groups of students are created according to their customized features, personal characteristics. These clusters/groups of students can be used by the instructor/developer to build a personalized learning system which can promote effective group learning. The DM techniques used in this task are classification and clustering. Different clustering algorithms that are used to group students are hierarchical agglomerative clustering, K-means and model-based clustering. A clustering algorithm is based on large generalized sequences which help to find groups of students with similar learning characteristics like hierarchical clustering algorithm which are used in intelligent e-learning systems to group students according to their individual learning style preferences.

Enrollment Management

This term is frequently used in higher education to describe well-planned strategies and tactics to shape the enrolment of an institution and meet established goals. Enrollment management is an organizational concept and a systematic set of activities designed to enable educational institutions to exert more influence over their student enrollments. Such practices often include marketing, admission policies, retention programs, and financial aid awarding. Strategies and tactics are informed by collection, analysis, and use of data to project successful outcomes.

Activities that produce measurable improvements in yields are continued and/or expanded, but while those activities that do not are discontinued or restructured. Competitive efforts to recruit students are a common emphasis of enrollment managers. The numbers of universities and colleges instituting offices of "enrollment management" have increased in recent years. These offices serve to provide direction and coordination of efforts of multiple offices such as admissions, financial aid, registration and other student services. Often these offices are part of an enrollment management division. Some of the typical aims of enrollment management include

- Improving yields at inquiry, application, and enrollment stages.
- Increasing net revenue, usually by improving the proportion of entering students capable of paying most or all of unsubsidized tuition.
- Increasing demographic diversity
- Improving retention rates

- Increasing applicant pools

Tools of Educational Data Mining

The tools listed in the following section offer a wide range of algorithms and modeling frameworks that can be used to model and predict processes and relationships in educational data (Vandna Dahiya, 2018).

- **WEKA[1] (Waikato Environment for Knowledge Analysis):** The Weka workbench consists of several tools, algorithms and graphics methods that lead to the analysis and predictions. Mostofthealgorithms are inbuilt inthistool.
- **KEEL[2] (Knowledge Extraction Based on Evolutionary Learning):** KEEL as an application is a set of machine learning software that is designed for providing a resolution to numerous data mining problems. It has a collection of software techniques that are involved in data manipulation and analysis before and after the process as well. It applies soft-computing methods in extracting information about learning and knowledge.
- **R (Revolution)[3]:** This is a statistical computing software/ language that are widely used by data miners to perform statistics for learning development solutions. R is an extremely versatile tool that is not only scientifically designed but is also easy to use. So, applyingstatsandformulas in R are convenient.
- **KNIME (Konstanz Information Miner)[4]:** This platform is a widely used open source for data analytics, reporting, and integration. Traditionally used for pharmaceutical research, this business analysis tool is now widely used for Educational Data Mining.
- **ORANGE[5]:** Orange is component-based visual programming software for data mining that is suitable for explorative data analysis, visualization and predictions. It operates perfectly for various exploration techniques and also aids in scoring and filtering data as a part of the post-processing operation.

FUTURE RESEARCH DIRECTIONS

This chapter will be beneficial to the researchers who are willing to get insight knowledge in educational data mining for the selection of educational data mining techniques with their algorithm according to their research area. Future work should describe the growing forms of analytics that are presented in different domains (academic, business, other) and the fundamental role that machine learning and artificial intelligence must face in these processes. It is also expected to continue characterizing in a more granular way in which part of the educational process these techniques of text mining and analytics should impact in the educational field, and know if concepts such as learning analytics and other concepts of these will focus on the teaching process, student process knowledge discovery or educational management (A. Villanueva et al., 2018).

CONCLUSION

Educational Data Mining (EDM) is an emerging field to explore the data from various educational contexts. It provides inherent knowledge about imparting the education, which is used to enhance the quality of teaching and learning (Vandna Dahiya, 2018). EDM can be used in many different areas including identifying at-risk students, identifying priorities for the learning needs of different groups of students, increasing graduation rates, effectively assessing institutional performance, maximizing campus resources, and optimizing subject curriculum renewal (Abdulmohsen Algarni, 2016). This chapter discusses about educational data mining, its applications and techniques to be used in educational data mining. The application of data mining methods in the educational sector is an interesting phenomenon. Data mining techniques in educational organizations help us to learn student performance, student behavior, designing course curriculum and to motivate students on various parameters.

REFERENCES

Aldowah, H., Al-Samarraie, H., & Fauzy, W. M. (2019). Educational data mining and learning analytics for 21st century higher education: A review and synthesis. *Telematics and Informatics*, *37*, 13–49. doi:10.1016/j.tele.2019.01.007

Amershi S., & Conati, C. (2006). Automatic recognition of learner groups in exploratory learning environments. *Intelligent Tutoring Systems*, 463–472.

Arunachalam, A. S., & Velmurugan, T. (2016). A Survey on Educational Data Mining Techniques. *International Journal of Data Mining Techniques and Applications*, *05*(02), 167–171. doi:10.20894/IJDMTA.102.005.002.014

Baker, R. S. D., & Corbett, A. T., & Aleven, V. (2008). More accurate student modeling through contextual estimation of slip and guess probabilities in bayesian knowledge tracing. *Intelligent Tutoring Systems*, 406–415.

Bala, & Ojha. (2012). Study of Applications of Data Mining Techniques in Education. *International Journal of Research in Science and Technology*, *1*(4), 1–10.

Baradwaj, B. K., & Pal, S. (2011). Mining Educational Data to Analyze Students' Performance. *International Journal of Advanced Computer Science and Applications*, *2*(6), 63–69.

Beal, C. R., Qu, L., & Lee, H. (1999). Classifying learner engagement through integration of multiple data sources. *Proceedings of the National Conference on Artificial Intelligence, 21,* 151-156.

Beck J. E. & Mostow, J. (2008). How who should practice: Using learning decomposition to evaluate the efficacy of different types of practice for different types of students. *Intelligent tutoring systems*, 353–362.

Bradley, A. P. (1997). The use of the area under the roc curve in the evaluation of machine learning algorithms. *Pattern Recognition, 30*(7), 1145–1159. doi:10.1016/S0031-3203(96)00142-2

Chan, C. C. (2007). A framework for assessing usage of web-based e-learning systems. *Innovative Computing, Information and Control, 2007.ICICIC '07.Second International Conference on*, 147–147.

Chen, J., Li, Q., Wang, L., & Jia, W. (2004). Automatically generating an e-textbook on the web. *Advances in Web-Based Learning–ICWL 2004*, 35–42.

Cocea, M., Hershkovitz, A., & Baker, R. S. (2009). The impact of off-task and gaming behaviors on learning: immediate or aggregate? *Proceedings of the 2009 conference on Artificial Intelligence in Education: Building Learning Systems that Care: From Knowledge Representation to Affective Modelling*, 507–514.

Corbett, A. T., & Anderson, J. R. (1994). Knowledge tracing: Modeling the acquisition of procedural knowledge. *User Modeling and User-Adapted Interaction*, *4*(4), 253–278. doi:10.1007/BF01099821

Dahiya. (2018). A Survey on Educational Data Mining. *IMPACT: International Journal of Research in Humanities. Arts and Literature*, *6*(5), 23–30.

Dringus, L. P., & Ellis, T. (2005). Using data mining as a strategy for assessing asynchronous discussion forums. *Computers & Education*, *45*(1), 141–160. doi:10.1016/j.compedu.2004.05.003

Dutt, A., Ismail, M. A., & Herawan, T. (2017). A Systematic Review on Educational Data Mining. *IEEE Access: Practical Innovations, Open Solutions*, *5*, 15991–16005. doi:10.1109/ACCESS.2017.2654247

Fayyad, U., Piatetsky-Shapiro, G., & Smyth, P. (1996). The kdd process for extracting useful knowledge from volumes of data. *Communications of the ACM*, *39*(11), 27–34. doi:10.1145/240455.240464

Hershkovitz A., & Nachmias, R. (2008). Developing a log-based motivation measuring tool. *EDM*, 226–233.

Hodge, V. J., & Austin, J. (2004). A survey of outlier detection methodologies. *Artificial Intelligence Review*, *22*(2), 85–126. doi:10.1023/B:AIRE.0000045502.10941.a9

Jeong H., & Biswas, G. (2008). Mining student behavior models in learning by teaching environments. *EDM*, 127–136.

Jindal, R., & Borah, M. D. (2013). A Survey on Educational Data Mining and Research Trends. *International Journal of Database Management Systems*, *5*(3), 53–73. doi:10.5121/ijdms.2013.5304

Kaur, H. (2015). A Review of Applications of Data Mining in the Field of Education. *International Journal of Advanced Research in Computer and Communication Engineering*, *4*(4), 409–412.

Kay, J., Maisonneuve, N., Yacef, K., & Reimann, P. (2006). The big five and visualisations of team work activity. *Intelligent tutoring systems*, 197–206.

Križanic. (2020). Educational data mining using cluster analysis and decision tree technique: A case study. *International Journal of Engineering Business Management*, *12*, 1–9.

Liu, B. (2007). *Web data mining: exploring hyperlinks, contents, and usage data.* Science & Business Media.

Merceron, A., & Yacef, K. (2008). Interestingness measures for associations rules in educational data. *EDM*, *8*, 57–66.

Muehlenbrock, M. (2005). Automatic action analysis in an interactive learning environment. *Proceedings of the 12th International Conference on Artificial Intelligence in Education*, 73–80.

Peña-Ayala, A. (2014). Educational data mining: A survey and a data mining-based analysis of recent works. *Expert Systems with Applications*, *41*(4), 1432–1462. doi:10.1016/j.eswa.2013.08.042

Reyes, P., & Tchounikine, P. (2005). Mining learning groups' activities in forum-type tools. *Proceedings of the 2005 conference on Computer support for collaborative learning: learning 2005: the next 10 years!* 509–513.

Romero, C., Ventura, S., Espejo, P. G., & Herv´as, C. (2008). Data mining algorithms to classify students. *EDM*, 8–17.

Romero, C., Ventura, S., Pechenizkiy, M., & Baker, R. S. (2010). *Handbook of educational data mining*. CRC Press. doi:10.1201/b10274

Scott, J. (2011). Social network analysis: Developments, advances, and prospects. *SOCNET, 1*(1), 21–26. doi:10.100713278-010-0012-6

Tane, J., Schmitz, C., & Stumme, G. (2004). Semantic resource management for the web: an e- learning application. *Proceedings of the 13th international World Wide Web conference on Alternate Track Papers & Posters*, 1–10.

Tang, C., Lau, R. W., Li, Q., Yin, H., Li, T., & Kilis, D. (2000). Personalized courseware construction based on web data mining. *Web Information Systems Engineering, 2000. Proceedings of the First International Conference on, 2,* 204–211.

Tanimoto, S. L. (2007). Improving the prospects for educational data mining. *Track on Educational Data Mining, at the Workshop on Data Mining for User Modeling, at the 11th International Conference on User Modeling*, 1–6.

Ueno, M. (2004). Data mining and text mining technologies for collaborative learning in an ILMS "ssamurai". *Advanced Learning Technologies, 2004. Proceedings. IEEE International Conference on*, 1052–1053.

Wallace, C., Korb, K. B., & Dai, H. (1996). Causal discovery via mml. *ICML, 96,* 516–524.

ADDITIONAL READING

Algarni, A. (2016). Data Mining in Education. *International Journal of Advanced Computer Science and Applications, 7*(6), 456–461. doi:10.14569/IJACSA.2016.070659

Baker, R. S., & Yacef, K. (2009). The state of educational data mining in 2009: A review and future visions. *JEDM-Journal of Educational Data Mining, 1*(1), 3–17.

Dahiya, V. (2018). A Survey on Educational Data Mining. *IMPACT: International Journal of Research in Humanities. Arts and Literature, 6*(5), 23–30.

Romero, C., & Ventura, S. (2010). Educational Data Mining: A Review of the State of the Art. *IEEE Transactions on Systems, Man and Cybernetics. Part C, Applications and Reviews, 40*(6), 601–618. doi:10.1109/TSMCC.2010.2053532

Villanueva, A., Moreno, L. G., & Salinas, M. J. (2018). Data mining techniques applied in educational environments: Literature review. *Digital Education Review*, *33*, 235–266.

KEY TERMS AND DEFINITIONS

Commercial Objectives: Commercial objectives are particularly important in case of private education, such as the creation of a niche and capturing the market in terms of enrollments.

Educational Data Mining: It refers to techniques and tools designed for automatically extracting meaning from large repositories of data generated by peoples learning activities in educational settings.

Educational Data Mining Methods: It come from different literature sources including data mining, machine learning, psychometrics, and other areas of computational modelling, statistics, and information visualization.

Educational Objectives: It also known as the academic objectives and are of great importance when it comes to conception and designing of educational content.

Enrollment Management: This term is frequently used in higher education to describe well-planned strategies and tactics to shape the enrolment of an institution and meet established goals.

Management Objectives: It can be of great use when it comes to the maintenance of educational infrastructure, which is a chief administrative oriented objective and involves the direct participation of higher authorities and senior management.

WEKA: Weka work bench consists of several tools, algorithms and graphics methods that lead to the analysis and predictions.

ENDNOTES

1. https://www.cs.waikato.ac.nz/ml/weka/
2. http://www.keel.es/
3. https://blog.revolutionanalytics.com/2016/01/microsoft-r-open.html
4. https://www.knime.com/
5. https://orange.biolab.si/

Compilation of References

Abhari, A., & Soraya, M. (2010). Workload generation for YouTube. *Multimedia Tools and Applications*, *46*(1), 91–118. doi:10.100711042-009-0309-5

Abhinav, K., Subramanian, V., Dubey, A., Bhat, P., & Venkat, A. D. (2018). LeCoRe: a framework for modeling learner's preference. In *Proceedings of the Eleventh International Conference on Educational Data Mining (EDM' 18).* International Educational Data Mining Society.

Abou-Khalil, V., Flanagan, B., & Ogata, H. (2018). Learning false friends across contexts. In *Proceedings of the Eighth International Conference on Learning Analytics & Knowledge (LAK' 18).* Society for Learning Analytics Research.

Abrucio, F. L. (2016). *Formação de professores no Brasil: Diagnóstico, agenda de políticas e estratégias para a mudança*. Editora Moderna. https://www.todospelaeducacao.org.br/arquivos/biblioteca/formacao_de_professores_no_brasil_diagnostico_agenda_de_politicas_e_estrategias_para_a_mudanca_todos_pela_educacao.pdf

Abu-El-Haija, S., Kothari, N., Lee, J., Natsev, P., Toderici, G., Varadarajan, B., & Vijayanarasimhan, S. (2016). *YouTube-8m: A large-scale video classification benchmark.* arXiv preprint arXiv:1609.08675.

AbuSneineh, W., & Zairi, M. (2010). An evaluation framework for E-learning effectiveness in the Arab World. International Encyclopedia of Education, 521–535. doi:10.1016/B978-0-08-044894-7.01708-5

Acharjya, D., & Kauser, A. (2016). A Survey on Big Data Analytics: Challenges, Open Research Issues and Tools. *International Journal of Advanced Computer Science and Applications*, 7.

Adam, K., Bakar, N. A. A., Fakhreldin, M. A. I., & Majid, M. A. (2018). Big Data and Learning Analytics: A Big Potential to Improve e-Learning. *Advanced Science Letters*, *6*(10), 7838–7843. doi:10.1166/asl.2018.13028

Adhikari, V. K., Jain, S., Chen, Y., & Zhang, Z. L. (2012). Vivisecting YouTube: An active measurement study. In 2012 Proceedings IEEE INFOCOM (pp. 2521-2525). IEEE.

Ai, F., Chen, Y., Guo, Y., Zhao, Y., Wang, Z., & Fu, G. (2019). Concept-aware deep knowledge tracing and exercise recommendation in an online learning system. In *Proceedings of the Twelfth International Conference on Educational Data Mining (EDM' 19)*. International Educational Data Mining Society.

Akhras, F. N., & Self, J. A. (2000). System intelligence in constructivist learning. *International Journal of Artificial Intelligence in Education, 11*(4), 344–376.

Akour, M., Alsghaier, H., & Aldiabat, S. (2020). Game-based learning approach to improve self-learning motivated students. *International Journal of Technology Enhanced Learning, 12*(2), 146–160. doi:10.1504/IJTEL.2020.106283

Aldowah, H., Al-Samarraie, H., & Fauzy, W. M. (2019). Educational data mining and learning analytics for 21st century higher education: A review and synthesis. *Telematics and Informatics, 37*, 13–49.

Aldowah, H., Al-Samarraie, H., & Fauzy, W. M. (2019). Educational data mining and learning analytics for 21st century higher education: A review and synthesis. *Telematics and Informatics, 37*, 13–49. doi:10.1016/j.tele.2019.01.007

Alexander, R. (2008). *Essays on pedagogy*. Routledge.

Alexander, S. M., Jones, K., Bennett, N. J., Budden, A., Cox, M., Crosas, M., Game, E. T., Geary, J., Hardy, R. D., Johnson, J. T., Karcher, S., Motzer, N., Pittman, J., Randell, H., Silva, J. A., da Silva, P. P., Strasser, C., Strawhacker, C., & Stuhl, A. (2019). Qualitative data sharing and synthesis for sustainability science. *Nature Sustainability*. Advance online publication. doi:10.103841893-019-0434-8

ALLEA. (2017). *The European Code of Conduct for Research Integrity*. ALLEA - All European Academies.

Almeida, M. I. D. (2012). *Formação do professor do ensino superior: Desafios e políticas institucionais*. Cortez.

Alsheikh-Ali, A. A., Qureshi, W., Al-Mallah, M. H., & Ioannidis, J. P. (2011). Public availability of published research data in high-impact journals. *PLoS One, 6*(9), e24357. doi:10.1371/journal.pone.0024357 PMID:21915316

Altınay, F., Altınay, M., Dagli, G., & Altınay, Z. (2018). Being leader in global citizenship at the information technology age. *Quality & Quantity, 52*(1), 31-42. doi:10.100711135-017-0585-5

Amal, A., & Ahmad, A. (2017). *Big data and learning analytics in higher education: Demystifying variety, acquisition, storage, NLP and analytics*. Academic Press.

Amershi S., & Conati, C. (2006). Automatic recognition of learner groups in exploratory learning environments. *Intelligent Tutoring Systems*, 463–472.

Anderson, T., & Rivera-Vargas, P. (2020). A Critical look at Educational Technology from a Distance Education Perspective. *Digital Education Review, 37*, 208-229. HTTPS://DOI.ORG/10.1344/DER.2020.37.208-229

Andrade, M. V. M., & Silveira, I. F. (2016). Panorama da aplicação de Massive Open Online Course (MOOC) no ensino superior: Desafios e possibilidades. *Revista EAD em Foco, 6*(3), 2177–8310. https://eademfoco.cecierj.edu.br/index.php/Revista/article/view/392

Angeli, C., & Valanides, N. (2009). Epistemological and methodological issues for the conceptualization, development, and assessment of ICT–TPCK: Advances in technological pedagogical content knowledge (TPCK). *Computers & Education, 52*(1), 154–168. doi:10.1016/j.compedu.2008.07.006

Anthony, G. (2012). The Evolution of Big Data and Learning Analytics in American Higher Education. *Journal of Asynchronous Learning Networks, 16*, 9–20.

Arnowitt, R., Deser, S., & Misner, C. W. (1962). The dynamics of general relativity. In L. Witten (Ed.), *Gravitation: An Introduction to Current Research. Wiley.*

Arthur, M. B., Khapova, S. N., & Wilderom, C. P. M. (2005). Career success in a boundaryless career world. *Journal of Organizational Behavior: The International Journal of Industrial. Occupational and Organizational Psychology and Behavior, 26*(2), 177–202. doi:10.1002/job.290

Arunachalam, A. S., & Velmurugan, T. (2016). A Survey on Educational Data Mining Techniques. *International Journal of Data Mining Techniques and Applications, 05*(02), 167–171. doi:10.20894/IJDMTA.102.005.002.014

Asgari, M., & Kaufman, D. (2004). Relationships among computer games, fantasy, and learning. *Proceedings, Educating Imaginative Minds: 2nd Annual Conference on Imagination and Education.*

Atiaja, L. N. A., & Proenza, R. S. G. (2016). MOOCS: Origin, characterization, principal problems and challenges in higher education. *Journal of e-Learning and Knowledge Society, 12*(1), 65–76. https://pdfs.semanticscholar.org/df33/d3707dfbc14dac4c2827109af8f825377036.pdf

Atif, A., Richards D., Danny Liu D., & Bilgin A. A. (2020). Perceived benefits and barriers of a prototype early alert system to detect engagement and support 'at-risk' students: The teacher perspective. *Computers & Education, 156,* 1-20.

Avella, J. T., Kebritchi, M., Nunn, S. G., & Kanai, T. (2016). Learning analytics methods, benefits, and challenges in higher education: A systematic literature review. *Online Learning, 20*(2), 13–29.

Azcona, D., Hsiao, I.-H., & Smeaton, A. (2018). PredictCS: personalizing programming learning by leveraging learning analytics. In *Proceedings of the Eighth International Conference on Learning Analytics & Knowledge (LAK' 18).* Society for Learning Analytics Research.

Backenköhler, M., Scherzinger, F., Singla, A., & Wolf, V. (2018). Data-driven approach towards a personalized curriculum. In *Proceedings of the Eleventh International Conference on Educational Data Mining (EDM' 18).* International Educational Data Mining Society.

Backupify. (2015). *Bit & Bytes: A History of Data Storage*. Author.

Baker, R. S. D., & Corbett, A. T., & Aleven, V. (2008). More accurate student modeling through contextual estimation of slip and guess probabilities in bayesian knowledge tracing. *Intelligent Tutoring Systems*, 406–415.

Baker, R. S., & Yacef, K. (2009). The state of educational data mining in 2009: A review and future visions. *Journal of Educational Data Mining, 1*(1), 3-17.

Baker, R. (2010). Data mining for education. In B. McGaw, P. Peterson, & E. Baker (Eds.), *International encyclopedia of education* (3rd ed., Vol. 7, pp. 112–118). Elsevier. doi:10.1016/B978-0-08-044894-7.01318-X

Baker, R. S., & Yacef, K. (2009). The state of educational data mining in 2009: A review and future visions. *Journal of Educational Data Mining, 1*(1), 3–17.

Bakharia, A., Corrin, L., De Barba, P., Kennedy, G., Gašević, D., Mulder, R., . . . Lockyer, L. (2016, April). A conceptual framework linking learning design with learning analytics. In *Proceedings of the Sixth International Conference on Learning Analytics & Knowledge (LAK' 16)*. Society for Learning Analytics Research.

Bakhshinategh, B., Zaiane, O., ElAtia, S., & Ipperciel, D. (2018). Educational data mining applications and tasks: A Survey of the Last 10 Years. *Journal of Education Information Technology, 23*(1), 537–553. doi:10.100710639-017-9616-z

Bala, & Ojha. (2012). Study of Applications of Data Mining Techniques in Education. *International Journal of Research in Science and Technology, 1*(4), 1–10.

Balcı, A. (2005). *Sosyal bilimlerde araştırma*. PegemA Yayıncılık.

Bandura, A. (1969). Social-learning theory of identificatory processes. Handbook of socialization theory and research, 213, 262.

Bandura, A. (1986). *Social Foundations of Thought and Action*. Prentice-Hall.

Bao, W. (2020). COVID-19 and online teaching in higher education: A case study of Peking University. *Human Behavior and Emerging Technologies*, *2*(2), 113–115. doi:10.1002/hbe2.191 PMID:32510042

Baradwaj, B. K., & Pal, S. (2011). Mining Educational Data to Analyze Students' Performance. *International Journal of Advanced Computer Science and Applications*, *2*(6), 63–69.

Batistic, S., & Laken, P. (2019). History, Evolution and Future of Big Data and Analytics: A Bibliometric Analysis of Its Relationship to Performance in Organizations. *British Journal of Management, 30*(2), 229–251. doi:10.1111/1467-8551.12340

Beal, C. R., Qu, L., & Lee, H. (1999). Classifying learner engagement through integration of multiple data sources. *Proceedings of the National Conference on Artificial Intelligence, 21,* 151-156.

Beattie, S., Woodley, C., & Souter, K. (2014). Creepy analytics and learner data rights. *Rhetoric and Reality. Critical Perspectives on Educational Technology-Conference Proceedings.*

Beck J. E. & Mostow, J. (2008). How who should practice: Using learning decomposition to evaluate the efficacy of different types of practice for different types of students. *Intelligent tutoring systems*, 353–362.

Berge, Z., & Collins, M. (1995). Computer-mediated communication and the online classroom in distance learning. *Computer-Mediated Communication Magazine*, *2*(4), 6–13.

Berland, M., Baker, R. S., & Blikstein, P. (2014). Educational data mining and learning analytics: Applications to constructionist research. *Technology. Knowledge and Learning*, *19*(1-2), 205–220. doi:10.100710758-014-9223-7

Bertagnolli, S., Wagner, M., Amorim, J., & Sanches, L. (2007). Bibliotecas Digitais Integradas a Ambientes Virtuais de Aprendizagem. *RENOTE*, *5*(2). Advance online publication. doi:10.22456/1679-1916.14247

Bettencourt, T., & Abade, A. (2008). Mundos Virtuais de Aprendizagem e de Ensino - uma caracterização inicial. *IE Comunicaciones: Revista Iberoamericana de Informática Educativa*, *4574*(7), 3-16.

Bezerra, L. N. M., & da Silva, M. T. (2017). A review of literature on the reasons that cause the high dropout rates in the MOOCS. *Revista Espacios, 38*(5), 11-24. http://www.revistaespacios.com/a17v38n05/a17v38n05p11.pdf

Bhardwaj, V. (2015). Big Data Analysis: Issues and Challenges. *Big Data Analysis: Issues and Challenges*, *1*, 1–3.

Bhargava, N., Sharma, A., Kumar, A., & Rathoe, P. (2017). An adaptive method for edge preserving denoising. *2017 2nd International Conference on Communication and Electronics Systems (ICCES),* 600-604.

Biernacka, K. (2019). *Research Integrity and Privacy*. Retrieved from https://headt.eu/Research-Integrity-Technology-and-GDPR

Biernacka, K. (2020a). *Perspectiva de los Investigadores sobre la Publicación de Datos de Investigación: Entrevistas Semiestructuradas de Perú.* edoc-Server, Humboldt-Universität zu Berlin. Berlin, Germany. doi:10.18452/21394

Biernacka, K. (2020b). *Researchers' Perspective on the Publication of Research Data: Semi-structured Interviews from China.* edoc-Server, Humboldt-Universität zu Berlin. Berlin, Germany. doi:10.18452/21330

Biernacka, K. (2020c). *Researchers' Perspective on the Publication of Research Data: Semi-structured Interviews from Germany.* edoc-Server, Humboldt-Universität zu Berlin. Berlin, Germany. doi:10.18452/21644

Biernacka, K. (2020d). *Researchers' Perspective on the Publication of Research Data: Semi-structured Interviews from India*. edoc-Server, Humboldt-Universität zu Berlin. Berlin, Germany. doi:10.18452/21378

Biernacka, K., & Huaroto, L. (2020). *Learning Analytics in Relation to Open Access to Research Data in Peru. An Interdisciplinary Comparison.* Paper presented at the LALA 2020, Cuenca, Ecuador.

Biernacka, K., & Pinkwart, N. (2020). *Barriers and Hurdles to the Publication of Learning Analytics Data.* Paper presented at the 10th International Learning Analytics and Knowledge (LAK), Frankfurt (Oder), Germany.

Bifet, A. (2013). Mining Big Data in Real Time. *Informatica (Vilnius)*, *37*, 15–20.

Big Data - A Visual History. (2015). *Big Data and the History of Information Storage*. Author.

Bloom, B. S. (1979). *Taxonomy of educational objectives: the classification of educational goals book 1 cognitive domain*. Longman.

Bollen, J., Van de Sompel, H., Hagberg, A., Bettencourt, L., Chute, R., Rodriguez, M. A., & Balakireva, L. (2009). Clickstream data yields high-resolution maps of science. *PLoS One*, *4*(3), e4803. doi:10.1371/journal.pone.0004803 PMID:19277205

Boyack, K. W., & Klavans, R. (2014). Including cited non-source items in a large-scale map of science: What difference does it make? *Journal of Informetrics*, *8*(3), 569–580. doi:10.1016/j.joi.2014.04.001

Bradley, A. P. (1997). The use of the area under the roc curve in the evaluation of machine learning algorithms. *Pattern Recognition*, *30*(7), 1145–1159. doi:10.1016/S0031-3203(96)00142-2

Braun, V., & Clarke, V. (2012). Thematic analysis. In H. Cooper, P. M. Camic, D. L. Long, A. T. Panter, D. Rindskopf, & K. J. Sher (Eds.), APA handbooks in psychology®. APA handbook of research methods in psychology, Vol. 2. Research designs: Quantitative, qualitative, neuropsychological, and biological (p. 57–71). American Psychological Association. doi:10.1037/13620-004

Brazilian Institute of Geography and Statistics. (2020). *Projeção da população do Brasil e das unidades da federação*. https://www.ibge.gov.br/apps/populacao/projecao

Bricken, M., & Byrne, C. M. (1994). Summer students in virtual reality: a pilot study on educational applications of virtual reality technology. In A. Wexelblat (Ed.), *Virtual Reality: Applications and Explorations* (pp. 199–218). Academic Press.

Broisin, J., & Hérouard, C. (2019). Design and evaluation of a semantic indicator for automatically supporting programming learning. In *Proceedings of the Twelfth International Conference on Educational Data Mining (EDM' 19)*. International Educational Data Mining Society.

Bronack, S., Sanders, R., Cheney, A., Riedl, R., Tashner, J., & Matzen, N. (2008). Presence pedagogy: Teaching and learning in a 3D virtual immersive world. *International Journal on Teaching and Learning in Higher Education*, *20*(1), 59–69.

Bucic, T., Vigentini, L., & King, M. E. (2018). Juggling system and data streams to personalize feedback: the case of a large first year course. In *Proceedings of the Eighth International Conference on Learning Analytics & Knowledge (LAK' 18)*. Society for Learning Analytics Research.

Buckingham, S., & Ferguson, R. (2012). Social Learning Analytics. *Journal of Educational Technology & Society, 15*, 3–26.

Burrows, P. (2016). *Adaptive learning: Can industry's most provocative software make a difference in the classroom?* EdSurge. https://www.edsurge.com/research/special-reports/adaptive-learning/

Caliendo, G., & Compagnone, A. (2014). Expressing epistemic stance in University lectures and TED talks: A contrastive corpu-based analysis. *Lingue e Linguaggi, 11*, 105–122.

Callaghan, S., Donegan, S., Pepler, S., Thorley, M., Cunningham, N., Kirsch, P., Ault, L., Bell, P., Bowie, R., Leadbetter, A., Lowry, R., Moncoiffé, G., Harrison, K., Smith-Haddon, B., Weatherby, A., & Wright, D. (2012). Making Data a First Class Scientific Output: Data Citation and Publication by NERC's Environmental Data Centres. *International Journal of Digital Curation, 7*(1), 107–113. doi:10.2218/ijdc.v7i1.218

Calonge, C. (2007). Using Second Life for immersive learning (Podcast). *Educase 2007 Seminars on Academic Computing Conference*. Retrieved April 15, 2020 from http://connect.educause.edu/blog/gbayne/podcastusingsecondlifefor/44967

Cargile, L. A., & Harkness, S. S. (2015). Flip or Flop: Are Math Teachers Using Khan Academy as Envisionedby Sal Khan? *TechTrends, 59*(6), 21–28. doi:10.100711528-015-0900-8

Carroll, J. B. (1963). A model of school learning. *Teachers College.*

Carroll, S. M. (2004). An introduction to general relativity: spacetime and geometry. Addison Wesley.

Catlin-Groves, C. L. (2012). The Citizen Science Landscape: From Volunteers to Citizen Sensors and Beyond. *International Journal of Zoology, 2012*, 1–14. doi:10.1155/2012/349630

Chan, C. C. (2007). A framework for assessing usage of web-based e-learning systems. *Innovative Computing, Information and Control, 2007.ICICIC '07.Second International Conference on*, 147–147.

Chan, L., Cuplinskasm, D., Eisen, M., Friend, F., Genova, Y., Guédon, J.-C., Hagemann, M., Harnad, S., Johnson, R., Kupryte, R., La Manna, M., Rév, I., Segbert, M., de Souza, S., Suber, P., & Velterop, J. (2002). *Budapest Open Access Initiative*. Retrieved from https://www.budapestopenaccessinitiative.org/read

Chatti, M. A., Dyckhoff, A. L., Schroeder, U., & Thus, H. (2012). A reference model for leaning analytics. *International Journal of Technology Enhanced Learning, 4*(5–6), 318–331. doi:10.1504/IJTEL.2012.051815

Chau, C. (2010). YouTube as a participatory culture. *New Directions for Youth Development, 2010*(128), 65–74. doi:10.1002/yd.376 PMID:21240954

Cheah, P. Y., Tangseefa, D., Somsaman, A., Chunsuttiwat, T., Nosten, F., Day, N. P., Bull, S., & Parker, M. (2015). Perceived Benefits, Harms, and Views About How to Share Data Responsibly: A Qualitative Study of Experiences With and Attitudes Toward Data Sharing Among Research Staff and Community Representatives in Thailand. *Journal of Empirical Research on Human Research Ethics; JERHRE, 10*(3), 278–289. doi:10.1177/1556264615592388 PMID:26297749

Chen, J., Li, Q., Wang, L., & Jia, W. (2004). Automatically generating an e-textbook on the web. *Advances in Web-Based Learning–ICWL 2004*, 35–42.

Cheng, X., Dale, C., & Liu, J. (2008). Statistics and social network of YouTube videos. In *2008 16th Interntional Workshop on Quality of Service* (pp. 229-238). IEEE. 10.1109/IWQOS.2008.32

Chen, J., Jiang, Q., Wang, Y., & Tang, J. (2016). Study of data analysis model based on big data technology. *2016 IEEE International Conference on Big Data Analysis (ICBDA)*, 1-6. 10.1109/ICBDA.2016.7509810

Chen, L., Gjekmarkaj, E., & Dubrawski, A. (2019). Parent as a Companion for Solving Challenging Math Problems: Insights from Multi-modal Observational Data. In *Proceedings of the Twelfth International Conference on Educational Data Mining (EDM' 19)*. International Educational Data Mining Society.

Chittaro, L., & Ranon, R. (2007). Web3D technologies in learning, education and training: Motivations, issues, opportunities. *Computers & Education, 49*(1), 3–18. doi:10.1016/j.compedu.2005.06.002

Christopoulos, A., Pellas, N., & Laakso, M.-J. (2020). A Learning Analytics Theoretical Framework for STEM Education Virtual Reality Applications. *Education in Science, 10*(11), 317. doi:10.3390/educsci10110317

Ciavarelli, A. (2003). *Assessing the Quality of Online Instruction: Integrating Instructional Quality and Web Usability Assessments*. https://files.eric.ed.gov/fulltext/ED480084.pdf

Cios, K., Pedrycz, W., Swiniarski, R., & Kurgan, L. (2007). *Data mining: A knowledge discovery approach*. Springer.

Clifton, A., & Mann, C. (2011). Can YouTube enhance student nurse learning? *Nurse Education Today, 31*(4), 311–313. doi:10.1016/j.nedt.2010.10.004 PMID:21036430

Clow, D. (2012). The learning analytics cycle: Closing the loop effectively. *ACM International Conference Proceeding Series*. 10.1145/2330601.2330636

Cobo, C., & Aguerrebere, C. (2018). Building Capacity for Learning Analytics in Latin America. In C. Ping Lim & V. L. Tinio (Eds.), *Learning Analytics for the Global South* (pp. 58–67). Foundation for Information Technology Education and Development.

Cocea, M., Hershkovitz, A., & Baker, R. S. (2009). The impact of off-task and gaming behaviors on learning: immediate or aggregate? *Proceedings of the 2009 conference on Artificial Intelligence in Education: Building Learning Systems that Care: From Knowledge Representation to Affective Modelling*, 507–514.

Colavizza, G., Hrynaszkiewicz, I., Staden, I., Whitaker, K., & McGillivray, B. (2019). *The Citation Advantage of Linking Publications to Research Data.* https://arxiv.org/abs/1907.02565

Corbett, A. T., & Anderson, J. R. (1994). Knowledge tracing: Modeling the acquisition of procedural knowledge. *User Modeling and User-Adapted Interaction, 4*(4), 253–278. doi:10.1007/BF01099821

Covington, P., Adams, J., & Sargin, E. (2016). Deep neural networks for YouTube recommendations. In *Proceedings of the 10th ACM conference on recommender systems* (pp. 191-198). 10.1145/2959100.2959190

Cronbach, L. J. (1957). The two disciplines of scientific psychology. *The American Psychologist, 12*(11), 671–684. doi:10.1037/h0043943

Cruz-Benito, J., Therón, R., García-Peñalvo, F., & Lucas, E. (2015). Discovering usage behaviors and engagement in an Educational Virtual World. *Computers in Human Behavior, 47*(1), 18–25. doi:10.1016/j.chb.2014.11.028

Cruz-Benito, J., Therón, R., García-Peñalvo, F., Maderuelo, C., Pérez-Blanco, J., Zazo, H., & ... . (2014) Monitoring and feedback of learning processes in virtual worlds through analytics architectures: a real case. *9th Iberian Conference on Information Systems and Technologies (CISTI),* 1–6. 10.1109/CISTI.2014.6877097

Dahiya. (2018). A Survey on Educational Data Mining. *IMPACT: International Journal of Research in Humanities. Arts and Literature, 6*(5), 23–30.

Daniel, B. (2015). B ig D ata and analytics in higher education: Opportunities and challenges. *British Journal of Educational Technology, 46*(5), 904–920. doi:10.1111/bjet.12230

Dasgupta, C., Magana, A. J., & Vieira, C. (2019). Investigating the affordances of a CAD enabled learning environment for promoting integrated STEM learning. *Computers & Education, 129*, 122–142. doi:10.1016/j.compedu.2018.10.014

DaVia Rubenstein, L. (2012). Using TED talks to inspire thoughtful practice. *Teacher Educator, 47*(4), 261–267. doi:10.1080/08878730.2012.713303

Davidson, J., Liebald, B., & Liu, J. Nandy & Van Vleet, (2010). The YouTube video recommendation system. In *Proceedings of the fourth ACM conference on Recommender systems* (pp. 293-296). 10.1145/1864708.1864770

Davis, C. L. F. (2012). *Formação continuada de professores: Uma análise das modalidades e práticas em estados e municípios brasileiros.* Fundação Carlos Chagas. http://publicacoes.fcc.org.br/ojs/index.php/textosfcc/article/view/2452

Davis, G. M., Wang, C., & Yuan, C. (2019). N-gram graphs for topic extraction in educational forums. In *Proceedings of the Twelfth International Conference on Educational Data Mining (EDM' 19).* International Educational Data Mining Society.

DCC (Digital Curation Centre). (n.d.). *Overview of funders' data policies.* Retrieved from https://www.dcc.ac.uk/resources/policy-and-legal/overview-funders-data-policies

De Lucia, A., Francese, R., Passero, I., & Tortora, G. (2009). Development and evaluation of a virtual campus on Second Life: The case of Second DMI. *Computers & Education*, *52*(1), 220–233. doi:10.1016/j.compedu.2008.08.001

DeBoer, J., Ho, A. D., Stump, G. S., & Breslow, L. (2014). Changing "Course": Reconceptualizing Educational Variables for Massive Open Online Courses. *Educational Researcher*, *43*(2), 74–84. doi:10.3102/0013189X14523038

Del Blanco, Á., Serrano, Á., Freire, M., Martínez-Ortiz, I., & Fernández-Manjón, B. (2013). E-Learning standards and learning analytics. Can data collection be improved by using standard data models? In *Global Engineering Education Conference (EDUCON)*, 2013 *IEEE* (pp. 1255-1261). IEEE. 10.1109/EduCon.2013.6530268

Demircioğlu, E. & Demircioğlu, İ. H. (2013). Türk Dünyası bilgeleri ve değer eğitimi. *Türk Dünyası Bilgeler Zirvesi: Gönül Sultanları Buluşması*, 26-28.

Demmans Epp, C. (2019). Developing an Adaptive Mobile Tool to Scaffold the Communication and Vocabulary Acquisition of Language Learners. In Y. Zhang & D. Cristol (Eds.), *Handbook of Mobile Teaching and Learning* (2nd ed., pp. 1–26). Springer.

Demmans Epp, C., & Phirangee, K. (2019). Exploring mobile tool integration: Design activities carefully or students may not learn. *Contemporary Educational Psychology*, *59*, 101791. doi:10.1016/j.cedpsych.2019.101791

Demmans Epp, C., Phirangee, K., & Hewitt, J. (2017). Talk with Me: Student Behaviours and Pronoun Use as Indicators of Discourse Health across Facilitation Methods. *Journal of Learning Analytics*, *4*(3), 47–75. doi:10.18608/jla.2017.43.4

Deutsche Forschungsgemeinschaft. (2019). Guidelines for Safeguarding Good Research Practice. Code of Conduct. In (pp. 29). doi:10.5281/zenodo.3923602

Deutsch, G. (2010). *RapidMiner from Rapid-I at CeBIT 2010*. Data Mining Blog.

Dillenbourg, P., Fox, A., Kirchner, C., Mitchel, J., & Wirsing, M. (2014). Massive open online courses: Current state and perspectives. *Proceedings of Dagstuhl Perspectives Workshop*. http://citeseerx.ist.psu.edu/viewdoc/download?doi=10.1.1.657.4811&rep=rep1&type=pdf

Dilmaç, B. (1999). *İlköğretim öğrencilerine insani değerler eğitimi verilmesi ve ahlaki olgunluk ölçeği ile eğitimin sınanması* (Unpublished Master's Thesis). Marmara University, İstanbul.

Divya, K., Bhargavi, P., & Singaraju, J. (2018). Machine Learning Algorithms in Big data Analytics. *International Journal on Computer Science and Engineering*, *6*, 63–70.

Doğanay, A. (2009). *Değerler eğitimi, hayat bilgisi ve sosyal bilgiler öğretimi yapılandırmacı bir yaklaşım* (C. Öztürk, Ed.). Pegem-A Yayıncılık.

Drachsler, H., & Greller, W. (2016). Privacy and analytics. *Proceedings of the Sixth International Conference on Learning Analytics & Knowledge - LAK '16*. 10.1145/2883851.2883893

Drachsler, H., Hoel, T., Scheffel, M., Kismihók, G., Berg, A., Ferguson, R., ... Manderveld, J. (2015, March). Ethical and privacy issues in the application of learning analytics. In *Proceedings of the Fifth International Conference on Learning Analytics and Knowledge* (pp. 390-391). 10.1145/2723576.2723642

Drachsler, H., & Kalz, M. (2016). The MOOC and learning analytics innovation cycle (MOLAC): A reflective summary of ongoing research and its challenges. *Journal of Computer Assisted Learning*, *32*(3), 281–290. doi:10.1111/jcal.12135

Dringus, L. P., & Ellis, T. (2005). Using data mining as a strategy for assessing asynchronous discussion forums. *Computers & Education*, *45*(1), 141–160. doi:10.1016/j.compedu.2004.05.003

Dutt, A., Ismail, M. A., & Herawan, T. (2017). A Systematic Review on Educational Data Mining. *IEEE Access: Practical Innovations, Open Solutions*, *5*, 15991–16005. doi:10.1109/ACCESS.2017.2654247

Dyckhoff, A., Zielke, D., Bültmann, M., Chatti, M., & Schroeder, U. (2012). Design and Implementation of a Learning Analytics Toolkit for Teachers. *Journal of Educational Technology & Society*, 15.

Ebner, M., & Maurer, H. (2008). *Can Microblogs and Weblogs change traditional scientific writing?* Paper presented at the E-Learn: World Conference on E-Learning in Corporate, Government, Healthcare, and Higher Education 2008, Las Vegas, NV.

EDUCAUSE Learning Initiative. (2011). *7 Things you should know about learning analytics*. Washingon, DC: EDUCAUSE Learning Initiative. https://www.educause.edu/eli

Educause Publications. (2020). *2020 Educause horizon report (teaching and learning edition)*. Author.

Einhardt, L., Tavares, T., & Cechinel, C. (2016). Moodle analytics dashboard: a learning analytics tool to visualize users interactions in moodle. *Proceedings - 2016 11th Latin American Conference on Learning Objects and Technology*, 1–6. 10.1109/LACLO.2016.7751805

Ekşi, H. (2003). Temel insani değerlerin kazandırılmasında bir yaklaşım: Karakter eğitimi programları. *Değerler Eğitimi Dergisi*, *1*(1), 79–96.

ElAtia, S., & Ipperciel, D. (2011). *Advancing educational research through a Knowledge Discovery in Data (KDD) model*. Paper presented at the American Educational Research Association annual convention, New Orleans, LA.

ElAtia,S., Ipperciel, D., Bakhshinategh, B., Zaiane, O.R. & Thibaudeau, P. (2020). Graduate Attribute Assessment Program. *The International Journal of Information and Learning Technology*, *38*(3), 25-45.

ElAtia, S., & Ipperciel, D. (2015). At the Intersection of Computer Sciences and Online Education: Fundamental Consideration in MOOCs Education. *Educational Letter*, *11*(2), 2–7.

ElAtia, S., Ipperciel, D., & Hammad, A. (2012). Implications and challenges to using data mining in educational research in the Canadian context. *Canadian Journal of Education, 35*(2), 101–119.

ElAtia, S., Ipperciel, D., & Zaiane, O. R. (2016). *Data Mining and Learning Analytics: Applications in Educational Research*. Wiley & Sons. doi:10.1002/9781118998205

Engeström, Y. (2015). *Learning by expanding: An activity-theoretical approach to developmental research* (2nd ed.). Cambridge University Press. (Original work published 1987)

Ertmer, P. A., & Newby, T. J. (1993). Behaviorism, cognitivism, constructivism: Comparing critical features from an instructional design perspective. *Performance Improvement Quarterly, 6*(4), 50–72. doi:10.1111/j.1937-8327.1993.tb00605.x

Escudeiro, P. (2007). X-TEC Model and QEF Model: A Case Study. In T. Bastiaens & S. Carliner (Eds.), *Proceedings of E-Learn 2007--World Conference on E-Learning in Corporate, Government, Healthcare, and Higher Education* (pp. 258-265). Quebec City, Canada: Association for the Advancement of Computing in Education (AACE).

European Commission. (2014). *Background Document. Public Consultation 'Science 2.0': Science in Transition*. Author.

European Commission. (2016). *H2020 Programme. Guidelines on FAIR Data Management in Horizon 2020*. European Commission.

Fayyad, U., Piatetsky-Shapiro, G., & Smyth, P. (1996). From data mining to knowledge discovery in databases. *AI Magazine, 17*(3), 37.

Fayyad, U., Piatetsky-Shapiro, G., & Smyth, P. (1996). The kdd process for extracting useful knowledge from volumes of data. *Communications of the ACM, 39*(11), 27–34. doi:10.1145/240455.240464

Fecher, B., & Friesike, S. (2014). Open Science: One Term, Five Schools of Thought. In S. Bartling & S. Friesike (Eds.), *Opening Science. The Evolving Guide on How the Internet is Changing Research, Collaboration and Scholarly Publishing*. Springer Open. doi:10.1007/978-3-319-00026-8_2

Ferguson, R., & Clow, D. (2017, March). Where is the evidence? A call to action for learning analytics. In *Proceedings of the Seventh International Conference on Learning Analytics & Knowledge (LAK' 17)*. Society for Learning Analytics Research.

Ferguson, R. (2012). Learning analytics: Drivers, developments and challenges. *International Journal of Technology Enhanced Learning, 4*(5-6), 304–317. doi:10.1504/IJTEL.2012.051816

Ferguson, R. (2019). Ethical Challenges for Learning Analytics. *Journal of Learning Analytics, 6*(3), 25–30. doi:10.18608/jla.2019.63.5

Ferguson, R., Hoel, T., Scheffel, M., & Drachsler, H. (2016). Guest editorial: Ethics and privacy in learning analytics. *Journal of Learning Analytics, 3*(1), 5–15. doi:10.18608/jla.2016.31.2

Field, J. (2007). Looking outwards, not inwards. *ELT Journal*, *61*(1), 30–38. doi:10.1093/elt/ccl042

Flanagan, B., Majumdar, R., Akçapınar, G., Wang, J., & Ogata, H. (2019). Knowledge map creation for modeling learning behaviors in digital learning environments. In *Proceedings of the Ninth International Conference on Learning Analytics & Knowledge (LAK' 19)*. Society for Learning Analytics Research.

Flanagan, J. C., Shanner, W. M., Brudner, H. J., & Marker, R. W. (1975). An individualized instructional system: PLAN. *Systems of Individualized Education*, 136-167.

Fung, F. M., Choo, W. Y., Ardisara, A., Zimmermann, C. D., Watts, S., Koscielniak, T., Blanc, E., Coumoul, X., & Dumke, R. (2019). Applying a virtual reality platform in environmental chemistry education to conduct a field trip to an overseas site. *Journal of Chemical Education*, *96*(2), 382–386. doi:10.1021/acs.jchemed.8b00728

Gari, A., Mylonas, K., & Karagianni, D. (2005). Political and religious group membership, value priorities and educational values. *Journal of Beliefs & Values*, *26*(3), 301–310. doi:10.1080/13617670500371917

Gasevic, D., Dawson, S., & Jovanovic, J. (2016). Ethics and privacy as enablers of learning analytics. *Journal of Learning Analytics*, *3*(1), 1–4. doi:10.18608/jla.2016.31.1

Gašević, D., Dawson, S., & Siemens, G. (2015). Let's not forget: Learning analytics are about learning. *TechTrends*, *59*(1), 64–71. doi:10.100711528-014-0822-x

Gatti, B. A. (2016). Formação de professores: Condições e problemas atuais. *Revista Internacional de Formação de Professores*, *1*(2), 161–171. https://periodicos.itp.ifsp.edu.br/index.php/RIFP/article/view/347

Gavilanes-Sagnay, F., Loza-Aguirre, E., Riofrío-Luzcando, D., & Segura-Morales, M. (2019) Improving the Use of Virtual Worlds in Education Through Learning Analytics: A State of Art. In *Proceedings of the Future Technologies Conference (FTC) 2018. FTC 2018. Advances in Intelligent Systems and Computing* (vol. 880). Springer. 10.1007/978-3-030-02686-8_83

Gavison, R. (1980). Privacy and the limits of law. *The Yale Law Journal*, *89*(3), 421–471. doi:10.2307/795891

Geller, E. S. (2005). Behavior-based safety and occupational risk management. *Behavior Modification*, *29*(3), 539–561. doi:10.1177/0145445504273287 PMID:15784754

Gentil-Beccot, A., Mele, S., & Brooks, T. C. (2009). *Citing and Reading Behaviours in High-Energy Physics. How a Community Stopped Worrying about Journals and Learned to Love Repositories*. https://arxiv.org/abs/0906.5418

George, S. (2019). Games, Simulations, Immersive Environments, and Emerging Technologies. In A. Tatnall (Ed.), *Encyclopedia of Education and Information Technologies*. Springer. doi:10.1007/978-3-319-60013-0_36-1

Géron, A. (2017). Training Models in Hands-on Machine Learning with Scikit-Learn & TensorFlow. O'Reilly Media.

Géron, A. (2017). *Support Vector Machines in Hands-on Machine Learning with Scikit-Learn & TensorFlow. O'Reilly Media.*

Gezelter, D. (2011). *An informal definition of Open Science*. Retrieved from http://openscience.org/an-informal-definition-of-openscience

Gill, P., Arlitt, M., Li, Z., & Mahanti, A. (2007). YouTube traffic characterization: a view from the edge. In *Proceedings of the 7th ACM SIGCOMM conference on Internet measurement* (pp. 15-28). 10.1145/1298306.1298310

Gleditsch, N. P., Metelits, C., & Strand, H. v. (2003). Symposium on Replication in International Studies Research. *International Studies Perspectives*, *4*(1), 89–97.

Graf, S. (2010). A Flexible Mechanism for Providing Adaptivity Based on Learning Styles in Learning Management Systems. *Adv. Learn. Technol.*, 30-34.

Greller, W., & Drachsler, H. (2012). Translating learning into numbers: A generic framework for learning analytics. *Journal of Educational Technology & Society*, *15*(3), 42–57.

Griffiths, D. (2020). The Ethical Issues of Learning Analytics in Their Historical Context. In *Radical Solutions and Open Science* (pp. 39–55). Springer. doi:10.1007/978-981-15-4276-3_3

Grolinger, K. (2014). Challenges for MapReduce in Big Data. *2014 IEEE 10th World Congress on Services, 1*, 182-183.

Gron, O., & Hervik, S. (2007). *Einstein's General Theory of Relativity*. Springer. doi:10.1007/978-0-387-69200-5

Gros, B. (2016). The design of smart educational environments. *Smart Learn. Environ.*, *3*(15), 1–11.

Güler, A., Halıcıoğlu, M. B. & Taşğın, S. (2013). Sosyal bilimlerde nitel araştırma yöntemleri. Ankara: Seçkin Yayıncılık.

Gyamfi, N. (2017). *Big Data Analytics: Survey Paper*. Academic Press.

Hammad, A. M. (2009). *An integrated framework for managing labour resources data in industrial construction projects: A Knowledge Discovery in Data (KDD) approach* (Unpublished doctoral dissertation). University of Alberta, Canada.

Han, J., & Kamber, M. (2006). *Data mining: Concepts and techniques*. Morgan Kaufmann.

Harguess, J., Barngrover, C., & Rahimi, A. (2017, May). An analysis of optical flow on real and simulated data with degradations. In *Geospatial Informatics, Fusion, and Motion Video Analytics VII* (Vol. 10199, p. 1019905). International Society for Optics and Photonics. doi:10.1117/12.2265850

Haridakis, P., & Hanson, G. (2009). Social interaction and co-viewing with YouTube: Blending mass communication reception and social connection. *Journal of Broadcasting & Electronic Media, 53*(2), 317–335. doi:10.1080/08838150902908270

HartmannT. (2019). *Rechtsfragen. Institutioneller Rahmen und Handlungsopitonen für universtiäres FDM*. Frankfurt (Oder): Europa-Universität Viadrina Frankfurt (Oder). doi:10.5281/zenodo.2654306

Hasan, R., Palaniappan, S., Mahmood, S., Abbas, A., Sarker, K. U., & Sattar, M. U. (2020). Predicting Student Performance in Higher Educational Institutions Using Video Learning Analytics and Data Mining Techniques. *Applied Sciences (Basel, Switzerland), 10*(11), 3894. doi:10.3390/app10113894

Hasnine, M. N., Ogata, H., Akcapinar, G., Mouri, K., & Uosaki, N. (2019). Learning analytics to share and reuse authentic learning experiences in a seamless learning environment. In *Proceedings of the Ninth International Conference on Learning Analytics & Knowledge (LAK' 19)*. Society for Learning Analytics Research.

Hershkovitz A., & Nachmias, R. (2008). Developing a log-based motivation measuring tool. *EDM*, 226–233.

Hilliard, A. (2019). Developing an English learner corpus for materials creation and evaluation. In *Proceedings of the Ninth International Conference on Learning Analytics & Knowledge (LAK' 19)*. Society for Learning Analytics Research.

Hodge, V. J., & Austin, J. (2004). A survey of outlier detection methodologies. *Artificial Intelligence Review, 22*(2), 85–126. doi:10.1023/B:AIRE.0000045502.10941.a9

Hoel, T., & Chen, W. (2018). Privacy and data protection in learning analytics should be motivated by an educational maxim-towards a proposal. *Research and Practice in Technology Enhanced Learning, 13*(1), 20. doi:10.118641039-018-0086-8 PMID:30595748

Hollands, F. M. (2014). Why do institutions offer MOOCs? *Online Learning, 18*(3), 1–20. https://eric.ed.gov/?id=EJ1043160

Holmes, G., & Donkin, A. (1994). Weka: A Machine Learning Workbench. *Proc Second Australia and New Zealand Conference on Intelligent Information Systems.*

Hoppenbrouwers, N., Broos, T., & Laet, T. D. (2019). Less (context) is more? Evaluation of a positioning test feedback dashboard for aspiring students. In *Proceedings of the Ninth International Conference on Learning Analytics & Knowledge (LAK' 19)*. Society for Learning Analytics Research.

Hoßfeld, T., Seufert, M., Hirth, M., Zinner, T., Tran-Gia, P., & Schatz, R. (2011). Quantification of YouTube QoE via crowdsourcing. In *2011 IEEE International Symposium on Multimedia* (pp. 494-499). IEEE. 10.1109/ISM.2011.87

Hou, Y., Zhou, P., Xu, J., & Wu, D. O. (2018). Course recommendation of MOOC with big data support: A contextual online learning approach. *IEEE INFOCOM 2018 - IEEE Conference on Computer Communications Workshops (INFOCOM WKSHPS)*, 106–111.

Hou, M., & Fidopiastis, C. (2017). A generic framework of intelligent adaptive learning systems: From learning effectiveness to training transfer. *Theoretical Issues in Ergonomics Science*, *18*(2), 167–183. doi:10.1080/1463922X.2016.1166405

House of Commons Science and Technology Committee. (2011). *Science and Technology Committee – Eighth Report. Peer review in scientific publications.* Retrieved from https://www.publications.parliament.uk/pa/cm201012/cmselect/cmsctech/856/85602.htm

Houtkoop, B. L., Chambers, C., Macleod, M., Bishop, D. V. M., Nichols, T. E., & Wagenmakers, E.-J. (2018). Data Sharing in Psychology: A Survey on Barriers and Preconditions. *APS, 1*(1), 70-85. doi:10.1177/2515245917751886

Hu, H. (2014). Toward Scalable Systems for Big Data Analytics: A Technology Tutorial. *Toward Scalable Systems for Big Data Analytics: A Technology Tutorial, 1*, 658-659, 665.

Huang, R. H., Liu, D. J., Guo, J., Yang, J. F., Zhao, J. H., Wei, X. F., Knyazeva, S., Li, M., Zhuang, R. X., Looi, C. K., & Chang, T. W. (2020). *Guidance on flexible learning during campus closures: Ensuring course quality of higher education in COVID-19 outbreak.* Smart Learning Institute of Beijing Normal University. https://iite.unesco.org/wp-content/uploads/2020/05/Guidance-on-Flexible-Learning-during-Campus-Closures-in-COVID-19-outbreak-SLIBNU-V1.2_0508.pdf

Huang, R. H., Liu, D. J., Tlili, A., Yang, J. F., & Wang, H. H. (2020). *Handbook on facilitating flexible learning during educational disruption: The Chinese experience in maintaining undisrupted learning in COVID-19 outbreak.* Smart Learning Institute of Beijing Normal University. https://iite.unesco.org/wp-content/uploads/2020/03/Handbook-on-Facilitating-Flexible-Learning-in-COVID-19-Outbreak-SLIBNU_V2.0_20200324.pdf

Huebner, R. A. (2013). A survey of educational data-mining research. *Journal of Research In Higher Education.* Retrieved on February 20, 2013 from http://www.aabri.com/manuscripts/121328. pdf

Hu, R. (2016). Key Technology for Big Visual Data Analysis in Security Space and Its Applications. *International Conference on Advanced Cloud and Big Data (CBD)*, 333-333. 10.1109/CBD.2016.065

IBM Big Data & Analytics Hub. (2014). *The Four V's of Big Data.* Author.

IBM100 - The IBM Punched Card. (2015). *The IBM Punched Card.* Author.

Ifenthaler, D., & Schumacher, C. (2016). Student perceptions of privacy principles for learning analytics. *Educational Technology Research and Development*, *64*(5), 923–938. doi:10.100711423-016-9477-y

Ifenthaler, D., & Widanapathirana, C. (2014). Development and validation of a learning analytics framework: Two case studies using support vector machines. *Technology. Knowledge & Learning*, *19*(1-2), 221–240. doi:10.100710758-014-9226-4

Ince, D. (2011). The Duke University scandal - what can be done? *Significance*, 3. doi:10.1111/j.1740-9713.2011.00505.x

Ipperciel, D., & ElAtia, S. (2015). Towards a 21st Century Competency-Based Model of Higher Education: The pragmatics of Accountability. *International Journal of Advances in Education*, *1*(1), 5–12.

Irwin, A. (1995). *Citizen Science: A Study of People, Expertise and Development (Environment and Society)*. Routledge.

Jaakonmäki, R., vom Brocke, J., Dietze, S., Drachsler, H., Fortenbacher, A., Helbig, R., & Yun, H. (2020). Responsible Cooking with Learning Analytics. In *Learning Analytics Cookbook* (pp. 15–30). Springer. doi:10.1007/978-3-030-43377-2_3

Jaffar, A. A. (2012). YouTube: An emerging tool in anatomy education. *Anatomical Sciences Education*, *5*(3), 158–164. doi:10.1002/ase.1268 PMID:22383096

Jeong H., & Biswas, G. (2008). Mining student behavior models in learning by teaching environments. *EDM*, 127–136.

Jindal, R., & Borah, M. D. (2013). A Survey on Educational Data Mining and Research Trends. *International Journal of Database Management Systems*, *5*(3), 53–73. doi:10.5121/ijdms.2013.5304

JISC. (2015). *Code of practice for learning analytics*. https://www.jisc.ac.uk/guides/code-of-practice-for-learning-analytics#

Johnson, M. J., Schwab, R. L., & Foa, L. (1999). Technology as a change agent for the teaching process. *Theory into Practice*, *38*(1), 24–30. doi:10.1080/00405849909543827

Jonassen, D. H. (2010). *Learning to solve problems: A handbook for designing problem-solving learning environments*. Routledge. doi:10.4324/9780203847527

Jones, L., Grant, R., & Hrynaszkiewicz, I. (2019). Implementing publisher policies that inform, support and encourage authors to share data: two case studies. *Insights the UKSG Journal, 32*, 11. doi:10.1629/uksg.463

Jones, K. M. L. (2019). "Just Because You Can Doesn't Mean You Should": Practitioner Perceptions of Learning Analytics Ethics. portal. *Portal (Baltimore, Md.)*, *19*(3), 407–428. doi:10.1353/pla.2019.0025

Jones, S., & Grootveld, M. (2017). *How FAIR are your data?* (2nd ed.)., doi:10.5281/zenodo.1065990

Jones, T., & Cuthrell, K. (2011). YouTube: Educational potentials and pitfalls. *Computers in the Schools*, *28*(1), 75–85. doi:10.1080/07380569.2011.553149

Joyes, G. (2006). An activity theory approach to the exploration of tutors' perceptions of effective online pedagogy. In *Proceedings of the 23rd Annual Conference of the Australasian Society for Computers in Learning in Tertiary Education (Ascilite): Who's learning? Whose technology.* Sydney University Press.

Karasel, N., Altınay, F., Dagli, G., & Altınay, Z. (2018). An investigation of universal values and disability awareness in course books. *Quality & Quantity*, *52*(2), 1235–1243. doi:10.100711135-018-0693-x

Kaur, H. (2015). A Review of Applications of Data Mining in the Field of Education. *International Journal of Advanced Research in Computer and Communication Engineering*, *4*(4), 409–412.

Kaw, A., Clark, R., Delgado, E., & Abate, N. (2019). Analyzing the use of adaptive learning in a flipped classroom for preclass learning. *Computer Applications in Engineering Education*, *27*(3), 663–678. doi:10.1002/cae.22106

Kay, J., Maisonneuve, N., Yacef, K., & Reimann, P. (2006). The big five and visualisations of team work activity. *Intelligent tutoring systems*, 197–206.

Keelan, J., Pavri-Garcia, V., Tomlinson, G., & Wilson, K. (2007). YouTube as a source of information on immunization: a content analysis. *JAMA, 298*(21), 2482-2484.

Keller, F. S. (1968). Good-bye, teacher.... *Journal of Applied Behavior Analysis*, *1*(1), 79–89. doi:10.1901/jaba.1968.1-79 PMID:16795164

Kemmis, S., McTaggart, R. & Nixon, R. (2014). Introducing critical participatory action research. In The action research planner (pp. 1-31). Springer.

Kennedy-Clark, S., & Thompson, K. (2013). Collaborative Process Analysis Coding Scheme (CPACS): Examining the macro-and micro-level of students' discourse in a virtual world. *International Journal of Virtual and Personal Learning Environments*, *4*(2), 19–49. doi:10.4018/jvple.2013040102

Khachan, A. M., & Özmen, A. (2019). IMSSAP: After-school interactive mobile learning student support application. *Computer Applications in Engineering Education*, *27*(3), 543–552. doi:10.1002/cae.22096

Khalil, M. (2017). *Learning analytics in massive open online courses* [Doctoral thesis]. Universidad Carlos III de Madrid.

Khalil, M. (2018). *Learning Analytics in Massive Open Online Courses. Ph.D These.* Graz University of Technology.

Khan, M. L. (2017). Social media engagement: What motivates user participation and consumption on YouTube? *Computers in Human Behavior*, *66*, 236–247. doi:10.1016/j.chb.2016.09.024

Kim, J. (2019). Overview of disciplinary data sharing practices and promotion of open data in science. *Science Editing*, *6*(1), 3–9. doi:10.6087/kcse.149

Kim, J., Lee, A., & Ryu, H. (2013). Personality and its effects on learning performance: Design guidelines for an adaptive e-learning system based on a user model. *International Journal of Industrial Ergonomics*, *43*(5), 450–461. doi:10.1016/j.ergon.2013.03.001

Kirschenbaum, H. (2000). From values clarification to character education: A personal journey. *The Journal of Humanistic Counseling, Education and Development*, *39*(1), 4–20. doi:10.1002/j.2164-490X.2000.tb00088.x

Koehler, M. J., Mishra, P., & Yahya, K. (2007). Tracing the development of teacher knowledge in a design seminar: Integrating content, pedagogy and technology. *Computers & Education*, *49*(3), 740–762. doi:10.1016/j.compedu.2005.11.012

Koh, E., Shibani, A., Tan, J. P. L., & Hong, H. (2016, April). A pedagogical framework for learning analytics in collaborative inquiry tasks: An example from a teamwork competency awareness program. In *Proceedings of the Sixth International Conference on Learning Analytics & Knowledge (LAK' 16)*. Society for Learning Analytics Research.

Kramer, N. S. (2002). Tarih Sümer'de başlar (Yazılı Tarihteki Otuzdokuz İlk). İstanbul: Kabalcı Yay.

Kratz, J., & Strasser, C. (2014). Data publication consensus and controversies. *F1000 Research*, *3*, 94. doi:10.12688/f1000research.3979.3 PMID:25075301

Križanic. (2020). Educational data mining using cluster analysis and decision tree technique: A case study. *International Journal of Engineering Business Management*, *12*, 1–9.

Küken, G. (2003). *Ilkçağda eğitim felsefesi*. Alfa Yayınları.

Kumar, D., & Duvvuri, B., Kamesh, K., & Umar, S. (2014). *A Study on Big Data and its Importance*. Academic Press.

Kumar, V., & Chadha, A. (2011). An empirical study of the applications of data mining techniques in higher education. *International Journal of Advanced Computer Science and Applications*, *2*(3), 80–84.

LAK. (2011). *1st International Conference on Learning Analytics and Knowledge*. Banff, Alberta: LAK.

Lange, P. G. (2007). Publicly private and privately public: Social networking on YouTube. *Journal of Computer-Mediated Communication*, *13*(1), 361–380. doi:10.1111/j.1083-6101.2007.00400.x

Larivière, V., Sugimoto, C. R., Macaluso, B., Milojević, S. a., Cronin, B., & Thelwall, M. (2013). *arXiv e-prints and the journal of record: An analysis of roles and relationships*. https://arxiv.org/abs/1306.3261

Li, B., Ming, X., & Li, G. (2017). Big data analytics platform for flight safety monitoring. *2017 IEEE 2nd International Conference on Big Data Analysis (ICBDA)*, 350-353.

Liao, C., Lei, Y., Liou, K., Lin, J., & Yeh, H. (2015). Using Big Data for Profiling Heavy Users in Top Video Apps. *2015 IEEE International Congress on Big Data*, 381-385. 10.1109/BigDataCongress.2015.63

Lim, L., Gentili, S., Pardo, A., Dawson, S., & Gašević, D. (2018). Combining technology and human intelligence to provide feedback and learning support using OnTask. In *Proceedings of the Eighth International Conference on Learning Analytics & Knowledge (LAK' 18)*. Society for Learning Analytics Research.

Liñán, C., & Pérez, J. (2015). Educational Data Mining and Learning Analytics: Differences, similarities, and time evolution. RUSC. *Universities and Knowledge Society Journal*, *12*(3), 98–112. doi:10.7238/rusc.v12i3.2515

Li, T. M. H., Chau, M., Wong, P. W. C., Lai, E. S. Y., & Yip, P. S. F. (2013). Evaluation of a web-based social network electronic game in enhancing mental health literacy for young people. *Journal of Medical Internet Research*, *15*(5), e80. doi:10.2196/jmir.2316 PMID:23676714

Liu, B. (2007). *Web data mining: exploring hyperlinks, contents, and usage data.* Science & Business Media.

Li, X., Jiang, W., Jiang, Y., & Zou, Q. (2012). Hadoop Applications in Bioinformatics. *Open Cirrus Summit*, *7*, 48–52.

Long, P., & Siemens, G. (2011). Penetrating the Fog: Analytics in Learning and Education. *EDUCAUSE Review*.

Lothian, D., Akcayir, G., & Demmans Epp, C. (2019). Accommodating Indigenous People When Using Technology to Learn Their Ancestral Language. In O. (Adewoyin) Olakanmi, O. Ishola, G. McCalla, I. Adaji, & F. J. Gutierrez (Eds.), *International Workshop on Supporting Lifelong Learning co-located with the 20th International Conference on Artificial Intelligence in Education.* Academic Press.

Loughran, J. (2013). Pedagogy: Making sense of the complex relationship between teaching and learning. *Curriculum Inquiry*, *43*(1), 118–141. doi:10.1111/curi.12003

Lucas, C., Gibson, A., & Shum, S. B. (2019). Pharmacy students' utilization of an online tool for immediate formative feedback on reflective writing tasks. *American Journal of Pharmaceutical Education*, *83*(6), 6800. doi:10.5688/ajpe6800 PMID:31507274

LucraftM.AllinK.BaynesG.SakellaropoulouR. (2019). Challenges and Opportunities for Data Sharing in China. In (Journal contribution ed.): figshare. doi:10.6084/m9.figshare.7718441.v1

Lukarov, V., Chatti, M. A., Ths, H. F., Kia, S., Muslim, A., Greven, C., & Schroeder, U. (2014). Data models in learning analytics. CEUR Workshops, 1227, 88-95.

Macfadyen, L. P., Dawson, S., Pardo, A., & Gaševic, D. (2014). Embracing big data in complex educational systems: The learning analytics imperative and the policy challenge. *Research & Practice in Assessment*, *9*, 17–28.

Madathil, K. C., Rivera-Rodriguez, A. J., Greenstein, J. S., & Gramopadhye, A. K. (2015). Healthcare information on YouTube: A systematic review. *Health Informatics Journal, 21*(3), 173–194. doi:10.1177/1460458213512220 PMID:24670899

Madhuri, J. V. (March 2013). Significance of data warehousing and data mining in business applications. *International Journal of Soft Computing and Engineering, 3*(1).

Mah, D. K. (2016). Learning analytics and digital badges: Potential impact on student retention in higher education. *Technology. Knowledge and Learning, 21*(3), 285–305. doi:10.100710758-016-9286-8

Mampadi, F., Chen, S. Y., Ghinea, G., & Chen, M. P. (2011). Design of adaptive hypermedia learning systems: A cognitive style approach. *Computers & Education, 56*(4), 1003–1011. doi:10.1016/j.compedu.2010.11.018

Marshall, S. (2014). Exploring the ethical implications of MOOCs. *Distance Education, 35*(2), 250-262. doi:10.1080/01587919.2014.917706

Mazzardo, M. D., Nobre, A. M. D. J. F., & Mallmann, E. M. (2017). Small open online course e recursos educacionais abertos na formação continuada de professores do ensino médio no Brasil. *Indagatio Didactica, 9*(2), 175–194. https://repositorioaberto.uab.pt/bitstream/10400.2/6901/1/Small Open Online Course e Recursos Educacionais Abertos.pdf

McHugh, J., Cuddihy, P., Williams, J., Aggour, K., Kumar, V., & Mulwad, V. (2017). Integrated access to big data polystores through a knowledge-driven framework. *2017 IEEE International Conference on Big Data (Big Data),* 1494-1503.

McKenna, K., Folkestad, J. E., & Moraes, M. C. (2019). Reflections of visual form learning analytics: spaced retrieval practice activity. In *Proceedings of the Ninth International Conference on Learning Analytics & Knowledge (LAK' 19).* Society for Learning Analytics Research.

Meegahapola, L. G., & Thilakarathne, C. (2019). Dynamic learner-assisted interactive learning tools for power systems engineering courses. *Institute of Electrical and Electronics Engineers (IEEE) Transactions on Education, 62*(2), 149–156. doi:10.1109/TE.2018.2889621

Memiş, A., & Gedik, E. G. (2010). *Sınıf öğretmenlerinin değer yönelimleri.* http://dergipark.gov.tr/download/article-file/302478

Meng, L., Zhang, M., Zhang, W., & Shi, X. (2019). Personalized learning path recommendation based on knowledge structure. In *Proceedings of the Ninth International Conference on Learning Analytics & Knowledge (LAK' 19).* Society for Learning Analytics Research.

Merceron, A., & Yacef, K. (2008). Interestingness measures for associations rules in educational data. *EDM, 8*, 57–66.

Meyer, M. N. (2018). Practical Tips for Ethical Data Sharing. *Association for Psychological Science, 1*(1), 131–144.

Miles, H. B., & Huberman, A. M. (1994). *Qualitative data analysis: An expanded sourcebook.* Sage.

Mio, C., Ventura-Medina, E., & João, E. (2019). Scenario-based eLearning to promote active learning in large cohorts: Students' perspective. *Computer Applications in Engineering Education, 27*(4), 894–909. doi:10.1002/cae.22123

Misfeldt, M., Allsopp, B. B., Dreyøe, J., & Tamborg, A. L. (2019). Learning objectives and curriculum standards as multimodal analytics in learning platforms. In *Proceedings of the Ninth International Conference on Learning Analytics & Knowledge (LAK' 19)*. Society for Learning Analytics Research.

Mittelmeier, J., Rienties, B., Tempelaar, D., Hillaire, G., & Whitelock, D. (2018). The influence of internationalised versus local content on online intercultural collaboration in groups: A randomised control trial study in a statistics course. *Computers & Education, 118*, 82–95. doi:10.1016/j.compedu.2017.11.003

Mödritscher, F., Garcia-Barrios, V. M., & Gütl, C. (2004). The Past, the Present and the Future of adaptive E-Learning. *Proceedings of ICL 2004.*

Moissa, B., Gasparini, I., & Kemczinski, A. (2014). Learning analytics: um mapeamento sistemático. *Proceedings of XIX Conferência Internacional sobre Informática na Educação.* http://www.tise.cl/volumen10/TISE2014/tise2014_submission_262.pdf

Moor, P. J., Heuvelman, A., & Verleur, R. (2010). Flaming on YouTube. *Computers in Human Behavior, 26*(6), 1536–1546. doi:10.1016/j.chb.2010.05.023

Morgan, D. L. (1996). Focus groups. *Annual Review of Sociology, 22*(1), 129–152. doi:10.1146/annurev.soc.22.1.129

Morgan, D. L., Ataie, J., Carder, P., & Hoffman, K. (2013). Introducing dyadic interviews as a method for collecting qualitative data. *Qualitative Health Research, 23*(9), 1276–1284. doi:10.1177/1049732313501889 PMID:23925406

Muehlenbrock, M. (2005). Automatic action analysis in an interactive learning environment. *Proceedings of the 12th International Conference on Artificial Intelligence in Education*, 73–80.

Müller, A., & Guido, S. (2016). *Supervised Learning in Introduction to Machine Learning with Python. O'Reilly Media.*

Müller, A., & Guido, S. (2016). *Unsupervised Learning and Preprocessing in Introduction to Machine Learning with Python. O'Reilly Media.*

Mulwa, C., Lawless, S., Sharp, M., Arnedillo-Sanchez, I., & Wade, V. (2010, October). Adaptive educational hypermedia systems in technology enhanced learning: a literature review. In *Proceedings of the 2010 ACM conference on Information technology education* (pp. 73-84). 10.1145/1867651.1867672

Naveh, G., Tubin, D., & Pliskin, N. (2012). Student satisfaction with learning management systems: A lens of critical success factors. *Technology, Pedagogy and Education, 21*(3), 337–350. doi:10.1080/1475939X.2012.720413

New Media Consortium (NMC). (2011). *The 2011 Horizon Report*. Author.

Nielsen, M. (2012). *Reinventing Discovery. The New Era of Networked Science*. Princeton University Press.

Olivier, J. (2020). Research Ethics Guidelines for Personalized Learning and Teaching Through Big Data. In *Radical Solutions and Learning Analytics* (pp. 37–55). Springer. doi:10.1007/978-981-15-4526-9_3

Open Knowledge Foundation (Producer). (2019). *Open Data Handbook*. Retrieved from http://opendatahandbook.org

Open Knowledge Foundation. (2015). *Open Definition 2.1*. Retrieved from http://opendefinition.org/

Open Science and Research Intitiative. (2014). *The Open Science and Research Handbook*. Retrieved from https://www.fosteropenscience.eu/content/open-science-and-research-handbook

Ostendorff, P., & Linke, D. (2019). Best-Practices im Umgang mit rechtlichen Fragestellungen zum Forschungsdatenmanagement (FDM). *Bibliotheksdienst*, *53*(10-11), 717–723. doi:10.1515/bd-2019-0098

Oxford, R. L., Tomlinson, S., Barcelos, A., Harrington, C., Lavine, R. Z., Saleh, A., & Longhini, A. (1998). Clashing metaphors about classroom teachers: Toward a systematic typology for the language teaching field. *System*, *26*(1), 3–50. doi:10.1016/S0346-251X(97)00071-7

Özgüven, İ.E. (1994). Psikolojik Testler. Ankara: Psikolojik Danısma, Rehberlik Egitim Merkezi (PEDREM).

Padgett, S. (2014). *Profiling The Fraudster: Removing the Mask to Prevent and Detect Fraud*. . doi:10.1002/9781118929773

Papamitsiou, Z., & Economides, A. (2014). Learning analytics and educational data mining in practice: A systematic literature review of empirical evidence. *Journal of Educational Technology & Society*, *17*(4), 49–64.

Papamitsiou, Z., & Economides, A. A. (2014). Learning Analytics and Educatinal Data Mining in Practice: A Systematic Literature Review of Empirical Evidence. *Journal of Educational Technology & Society*, *17*(4), 49–64.

Pardo, A., & Dawson, S. (2016). *Learning Analytics: How Can Data Be Used to Improve Learning Practice?* Academic Press.

Pardo, A., & Siemens, G. (2014). Ethical and privacy principles for learning analytics. *British Journal of Educational Technology*, *45*(3), 438–450. doi:10.1111/bjet.12152

Park, K., Nguyen, M. C., & Won, H. (2015). Web-based Collaborative Big Data Analytics on Big Data as a Service Platform. *Web-based Collaborative Big Data Analytics on Big Data as a Service Platform*, *1*, 564–566. doi:10.1109/ICACT.2015.7224859

Parry, M. (2010). The Humanities Go Google. *The Chronicles of Higher Education*. http://chronicle.com/article/The-Humanities-Go-Google/65713/

Patton, M. Q. (2014). *Nitel araştırma ve değerlendirme yöntemleri*. Pegem Akademi.

Peña-Ayala, A. (2014). Educational data mining: A survey and a data mining-based analysis of recent works. *Expert Systems with Applications*, *41*(4), 1432–1462. doi:10.1016/j.eswa.2013.08.042

Peng, R. D. (2011). Reproducible Research in Computational Science. *Science*, *334*(6060), 2. doi:10.1126cience.1213847 PMID:22144613

Persico, D., & Pozzi, F. (2015). Informing learning design with learning analytics to improve teacher inquiry. *British Journal of Educational Technology*, *46*(2), 230–248. doi:10.1111/bjet.12207

Phaneendra, S., & Reddy, E. (2013). Big Datasolutions for RDBMS problems- A survey. *IEEE/IFIP Network Operations & Management Symposium, 2.*

Phillips, R., Maor, D., Preston, G., & Cumming-Potvin, W. (2012). Exploring learning analytics as indicators of study behaviour. In *World conference on educational multimedia, hypermedia and telecommunications* (pp. 2861–2867). Denver, CO: EDMEDIA.

Phua, J. Y. C., Yeo, E. M. Y., & Ng, S. J. Y. (2019). Understanding teaching and learning practices of online adaptive mathematics tutoring platform. In *Proceedings of the Ninth International Conference on Learning Analytics & Knowledge (LAK' 19)*. Society for Learning Analytics Research.

Pienta, A. M., Alter, G., & Lyle, J. (2010). The Enduring Value of Social Science Research: The Use and Reuse of Primary Research Data. In Inter-university Consortium for Political and Social Research. Institute for Social Research, University of Michigan. http://hdl.handle.net/2027.42/78307

Piwowar, H. A., & Vision, T. J. (2013). Data reuse and the open data citation advantage. *PeerJ*, (1), 25. doi:10.7717/peerj.175

Piwowar, H. A. (2011). Who shares? Who doesn't? Factors associated with openly archiving raw research data. *PLoS One*, *6*(7), e18657. doi:10.1371/journal.pone.0018657 PMID:21765886

Polyzou, A., Nikolakopoulos, A. N., & Karypis, G. (2019). Scholars Walk: a markov chain framework for course recommendation. In *Proceedings of the Twelfth International Conference on Educational Data Mining (EDM' 19)*. International Educational Data Mining Society.

Pontika, N., Knoth, P., Cancellieri, M., & Pearce, S. (2015). Fostering open science to research using a taxonomy and an eLearning portal. *Proceedings of the 15th International Conference on Knowledge Technologies and Data-driven Business - i-KNOW '15*. 10.1145/2809563.2809571

Poonsirivong, K., & Jittawiriaynukoon, C. (2018, March). Big data analytics using association rules in eLearning. In *2018 IEEE 3rd International Conference on Big Data Analysis (ICBDA)* (pp. 14-18). IEEE. 10.1109/ICBDA.2018.8367643

Priem, J., Taraborelli, D., Groth, P., & Neylon, C. (2010). *Altmetrics: A manifesto*. Retrieved from http://altmetrics.org/manifesto

Prince, A. E. R., & Schwarcz, D. (2020, March). Proxy Discrimination in the Age of Artificial Intelligence and Big Data. *Iowa Law Review*, *105*(3), 1257.

Prinsloo, P., & Slade, S. (2017a, March). An elephant in the learning analytics room: the obligation to act. In *Proceedings of the seventh international learning analytics & knowledge conference* (pp. 46-55). 10.1145/3027385.3027406

Prinsloo, P., & Slade, S. (2017b). Ethics and Learning Analytics: Charting the (Un)Charted. In Handbook of Learning Analytics. SOLAR.

Prinsloo, P. (2019). Learning analytics: Mapping a critique and agenda. *Journal of Learning Analytics*, *6*(3), 20–24.

Prinsloo, P., & Slade, S. (2015). Student privacy self-management: implications for learning analytics. *Proceedings of the Fifth International Conference on Learning Analytics and Knowledge*, 83–92. 10.1145/2723576.2723585

Prinsloo, P., & Slade, S. (2017c). Big Data, Higher Education and Learning Analytics: Beyond Justice, Towards an Ethics of Care. In B. Kei Daniel (Ed.), *Big Data and Learning Analytics in Higher Education*. Springer. doi:10.1007/978-3-319-06520-5_8

Prinsloo, P., & Slade, S. (2018). Student Consent in Learning Analytics: The Devil in the Details? In J. Lester, C. Klein, H. Rangwala, & A. Johri (Eds.), *Learning analytics in higher education: Current innovations, future potential, and practical applications* (pp. 118–139). Routledge. doi:10.4324/9780203731864-6

Puyun, B., & Miao, L. (2016). Research on analysis system of city price based on big data. *2016 IEEE International Conference on Big Data Analysis (ICBDA)*, 1-4. 10.1109/ICBDA.2016.7509819

QS World University Rankings. (2020). *QS World University Rankings 2021*. https://www.topuniversities.com/university-rankings/world-university-rankings/2021

Quigley, D. (2018). A learning analytics approach to scaffolding scientific modeling in the classroom. In *Proceedings of the Eighth International Conference on Learning Analytics & Knowledge (LAK' 18)*. Society for Learning Analytics Research.

Ramos, M. N., & Filgueiras, T. (2014). *Formação continuada de professores no Brasil: Acelerando o desenvolvimento dos nossos educadores*. Instituto Ayrton Senna. https://www.observatoriodopne.org.br/_uploads/_posts/46.pdf?1140547125

RapidMinder. (n.d.a). *Information about*. https://pt.wikipedia.org/wiki/RapidMiner

RapidMinder. (n.d.b). *More Information about*. https://www.capterra.com.br/software/148220/rapidminer

Redavid, D., Corizzo, R., & Malerba, D. (2018). An OWL Ontology for Supporting Semantic Services in Big Data Platforms. *2018 IEEE International Congress on Big Data (BigData Congress),* 228-231.

Reddi, K., & Indira, D. (2013). Different Technique to Transfer Big Data: Survey. *IEEE Transactions, 3*, 708–711.

Reich, J. (2020). *Failure to Disrupt. Why Technology Alone Can't Transform Education*. Harvard University Press. doi:10.4159/9780674249684

Reis, R. & Escudeiro, P. & Escudeiro, N. (2012). Comparing Social Virtual Worlds for Educational Purposes. *Education, 1,* 21-26. doi:10.5923/j.edu.20110101.04

Reis, R. & Fonseca, B. & Escudeiro, P. (2013). *A Structured Approach to Evaluate Collaborative Educational Virtual Environments*. . doi:10.2991/iccnce.2013.54

Reis, R., Marques, B. P., & Sampaio, I. (2020) Learning Analytics Framework for Improving Performance to Students through Educational Virtual Worlds. *International Journal of Education and Information Technologies, 14*, 8-13. Doi:10.46300/9109.2020.14.2

Reisoğlu, İ., Topu, F., Yilmaz, R., Karakus Yılmaz, T., & Goktas, Y. (2017). 3D virtual learning environments in education: a meta-review. *Asia Pacific Education Review, 18*. doi:10.100712564-016-9467-0

Rentier, B. (2016). Open science: A revolution in sight? *Interlending & Document Supply, 44*(4), 155–160. doi:10.1108/ILDS-06-2016-0020

Reyes, P., & Tchounikine, P. (2005). Mining learning groups' activities in forum-type tools. *Proceedings of the 2005 conference on Computer support for collaborative learning: learning 2005: the next 10 years!* 509–513.

Richard, G. T., & Giri, S. (2019). Digital and physical fabrication as multimodal learning: Understanding youth computational thinking when making integrated systems through bidirectionally responsive design. *ACM Transactions on Computing Education, 19*(3), 1–35. doi:10.1145/3243138

Richterich, A. (2018). *The Big Data Agenda : Data Ethics and Critical Data Studies*. University of Westminster Press. doi:10.2307/j.ctv5vddsw

Riding, R., & Rayner, S. (1998). *Cognitive styles and learning strategies: Understanding style differences in learning and behavior*. Routledge.

Rienties, B., Boroowa, A., Cross, S., Kubiak, C., Mayles, K., & Murphy, S. (2016). Analytics4Action Evaluation Framework: A Review of Evidence-Based Learning Analytics Interventions at the Open University UK. *Journal of Interactive Media in Education, 2016*(1).

Ritzema, T., & Harris, B. (2008). The use of Second Life for distance education. *Journal of Computing Sciences in Colleges, 23*(6).

Roberts, L. D., Howell, J. A., Seaman, K., & Gibson, D. C. (2016). Student attitudes toward learning analytics in higher education: "The fitbit version of the learning world. *Frontiers in Psychology, 7*, 1959. doi:10.3389/fpsyg.2016.01959 PMID:28066285

Roberts, L., Chang, V., & Gibson, D. (2016). Ethical considerations in adopting a university- and system-wide approach to data and learning analytics. In B. Kei Daniel (Ed.), *Big Data and Learning Analytics in Higher Education* (pp. 89–108). Springer.

Romanelli, F., Cain, J., & McNamara, P. J. (2014). Should TED talks be teaching us something? *American Journal of Pharmaceutical Education, 78*(6), 113. doi:10.5688/ajpe786113 PMID:25147385

Romero, C., & Ventura, S. (2010). Educational data mining: A review of the state of the art. *Systems, Man, and Cybernetics, Part C: Applications and Reviews, IEEE Transactions on, 40*(6), 601-618.

Romero, C., Ventura, S., Espejo, P. G., & Herv´as, C. (2008). Data mining algorithms to classify students. *EDM*, 8–17.

Romero, C., Ventura, S., Pechenizkiy, M., & Baker, R. S. (2010). *Handbook of educational data mining*. CRC Press. doi:10.1201/b10274

Rosen, Y., Lopez, G., Rushkin, I., Ang, A., Tingley, D., Munson, L., Rubin, R., & Weber, G. (2019). The effects of adaptive learning in a Massive Open Online Course on learners' skill development. In *Proceedings of the Ninth International Conference on Learning Analytics & Knowledge (LAK' 19)*. Society for Learning Analytics Research.

Roussos, M., Johnson, A., Moher, T., Leigh, J., Vasilakis, C., & Barnes, C. (1999). Learning and Building Together in an Immersive Virtual World. Presence, 8(3), 247-263. doi:10.1162/105474699566215

Rubel, A., & Jones, K. M. (2016). Student privacy in learning analytics: An information ethics perspective. *The Information Society, 32*(2), 143–159. doi:10.1080/01972243.2016.1130502

Šašinka, Č., Stachoň, Z., Sedlák, M., Chmelík, J., Herman, L., Kubíček, P., Šašinková, A., Doležal, M., Tejkl, H., Urbánek, T., Svatoňová, H., Ugwitz, P., & Juřík, V. (2019). Collaborative Immersive Virtual Environments for Education in Geography. *Int. ISPRS. J. Geo-Inf., 8*, 3.

Scheffel, M., Drachsler, H., Stoyanov, S., & Specht, M. (2014). Quality Indicators for Learning Analytics. *International Forum of Educational Technology & Society, 17*(4), 117-132. Retrieved from https://www.jstor.org/stable/10.2307/jeductechsoci.17.4.117

Schmidt, B., Gemeinholzer, B., & Treloar, A. (2016). Open Data in Global Environmental Research: The Belmont Forum's Open Data Survey. *PLoS One, 11*(1), e0146695. doi:10.1371/journal.pone.0146695 PMID:26771577

Schneider, J., Di Mitri, D., Limbu, B., & Drachsler, H. (2018, September). Multimodal learning hub: A tool for capturing customizable multimodal learning experiences. In *European Conference on Technology Enhanced Learning* (pp. 45-58). Springer. 10.1007/978-3-319-98572-5_4

Schofield, P. N., Bubela, T., Weaver, T., Portilla, L., Brown, S. D., Hancock, J. M., David, E., Tocchini-Valentini, G., Hrabe de Angelis, M., & Rosenthal, N. (2009). Post-publication sharing of data and tools. *Nature*, *461*(10), 171–173. doi:10.1038/461171a PMID:19741686

Scholes, V. (2016). The ethics of using learning analytics to categorize students on risk. *Educational Technology Research and Development*, *64*(5), 939–955. doi:10.100711423-016-9458-1

Schumacher, C., & Ifenthaler, D. (2018). Features students really expect from learning analytics. *Computers in Human Behavior*, *78*, 397–407. doi:10.1016/j.chb.2017.06.030

Schunk, D. H. (1991). *Learning Theories: An Educational Perspective*. Merrill.

Sclater, N. (2014a). Code of practice for learning analytics: A literature review of the ethical and legal issues. *JISC*. Available online: https://analytics.jiscinvolve.org/wp/2014/12/04/jisc-releases-report-on-ethical-and-legal-challenges-of-learning-analytics/

Sclater, N. (2014b). Snooping professor or friendly don? The ethics of university learning analytics. *The Conversation*. https://theconversation.com/snooping-professor-or-friendly-don-the-ethics-of-university-learning-analytics-23636

Scott, J. (2011). Social network analysis: Developments, advances, and prospects. *SOCNET*, *1*(1), 21–26. doi:10.100713278-010-0012-6

Selwyn, N. (2015). Data entry: Towards the critical study of digital data and education. *Learning, Media and Technology*, *40*(1), 64–82. doi:10.1080/17439884.2014.921628

Selwyn, N. (2019). What's the problem with Learning Analytics? *Journal of Learning Analytics*, *6*(3), 11–19. doi:10.18608/jla.2019.63.3

Selwyn, N. (2020). Re-imagining 'Learning Analytics'… a case for starting again? *The Internet and Higher Education*, *46*, 100745. doi:10.1016/j.iheduc.2020.100745

Selywn, N. (2009). The digital native- myth and reality. *Aslib Proceedings*, *61*(4), 364–379. doi:10.1108/00012530910973776

Sen, A., Patel, P., Rau, M. A., Mason, B., Nowak, R., Rogers, T. T., & Zhu, X. (2018). Machine beats human at sequencing visuals for perceptual-fluency practice. In *Proceedings of the Eleventh International Conference on Educational Data Mining (EDM' 18)*. International Educational Data Mining Society.

Sharma, S., & Sharma, A. (2017). An adaptive approach for Decomposition of Space Variant Blur and It's Restoration using Blind Deconvolution. *International Journal for Research & Development in Technology*, *7*, 492–496.

Shifman, L. (2012). An anatomy of a YouTube meme. *New Media & Society*, *14*(2), 187–203. doi:10.1177/1461444811412160

Shulman, L. (1987). Knowledge and teaching: Foundations of the new reform. *Harvard Educational Review*, *57*(1), 1–23. doi:10.17763/haer.57.1.j463w79r56455411

Shum, S. B., & Ferguson, R. (2012). Learning and Knowledge Analytics. *Journal of Educational Technology & Society, 15*(3), 3–26.

Siemens, G. (2005). Connectivism: A Learning Theory for the Digital Age. *International Journal of Instructional Technology and Distance Learning, 2.* http://www.itdl.org/Journal/Jan_05/article01.htm

Siemens, G. (2011). Learning and academic analytics. *Learning and Knowledge Analytics, 5.*

Siemens, G. (2013). Massive open online courses: innovation in education? In R. Mcgreal, W. Kinuthia, & S. Marshall (Org.), *Open educational resources: Innovation, research and practice* (pp. 5–15). Athabasca University. https://oerknowledgecloud.org/sites/oerknowledgecloud.org/files/pub_PS_OER-IRP_web.pdf#page=31

Siemens, G. (2013). Learning analytics: The emergence of a discipline. *The American Behavioral Scientist, 57*(10), 1380–1400. doi:10.1177/0002764213498851

Siemens, G., & Baker, R. (2012). Learning analytics and educational data mining: Towards communication and collaboration. *Proceedings of the 2nd International Conference on Learning Analytics and Knowledge*, 252-254. 10.1145/2330601.2330661

Siemens, G., & Gasevic, D. (2012). Guest editorial-learning and knowledge analytics. *Journal of Educational Technology & Society, 15*(3), 1–2.

Siemens, G., & Long, P. (2011). Penetrating the fog: Analytics in learning and education. *EDUCAUSE Review, 46*(5), 30.

Silva, T. (2015). *Ferramentas Gratuitas para Desenvolvimento de Soluções de Business Intelligence. Master Tese Degree*. Escola Superior de Tecnologia e Gestão de Viseu. Instituto Politécnico de Viseu.

Šimko, M., Barla, M., & Bieliková, M. (2010, September). ALEF: A framework for adaptive web-based learning 2.0. In *IFIP International Conference on Key Competencies in the Knowledge Society* (pp. 367-378). Springer. 10.1007/978-3-642-15378-5_36

Sin, K., & Muthu, L. (2015). Application of Big Data in Education Data Mining and Learning Analytics – A Literature Review. *ICTACT Journal on Soft Computing,* 1035-1049.

Skinner, B. F. (1958). Teaching machines. *Science, 128*(3330), 969–977. doi:10.1126cience.128.3330.969 PMID:13592277

Slade, P., & Prinsloo, P. (2014). *Student perspectives on the use of their data: between intrusion, surveillance and care.* Paper presented at 8th EDEN Research Workshop, Oxford, UK.

Slade, S., & Tait, A. (2019). *Global guidelines: Ethics in learning analytics.* Retrieved September 6, 2020 from https://www.learntechlib.org/p/208251/

Slade, S., & Prinsloo, P. (2013). Learning analytics: Ethical issues and dilemmas. *The American Behavioral Scientist, 57*(10), 1510–1529. doi:10.1177/0002764213479366

Slade, S., Prinsloo, P., & Khalil, M. (2019, March). Learning analytics at the intersections of student trust, disclosure and benefit. In *Proceedings of the 9th International Conference on learning analytics & knowledge* (pp. 235-244). 10.1145/3303772.3303796

Slater, S., Joksimović, S., Kovanovic, V., Baker, R. S., & Gasevic, D. (2017). Tools for Educational Data Mining: A Review. *Journal of Educational and Behavioral Statistics, 42*(1), 85–106. doi:10.3102/1076998616666808

Snelson, C. (2011). YouTube across the disciplines: A review of the literature. *Journal of Online Learning and Teaching.*

Snickars, P., & Vonderau, P. (2009). *The YouTube reader.* Kungliga biblioteket.

Society for Learning Analytics Research. (2020). *What is Learning Analytics*? https://www.solaresearch.org/about/what-is-learning-analytics

Somyürek, S. (2009). Student modeling: Recognizing the individual needs of users in e-learning environments. *Journal of Human Sciences, 6*(2), 429–450.

Southgate, E., Blackmore, K., Pieschl, S., Grimes, S., McGuire, J., & Smithers, K. (2018). *Artificial intelligence and emerging technologies (virtual, augmented and mixed reality) in schools: A research report.* University of Newcastle, Australia.

Sriramoju, S. (2017). Review on Big Data and Mining Algorithm. *International Journal for Research in Applied Science and Engineering Technology, 5*(XI), 1238–1243. doi:10.22214/ijraset.2017.11181

Stevenson, I. (2008). Tool, tutor, environment or resource: Exploring metaphors for digital technology and pedagogy using activity theory. *Computers & Education, 51*(2), 836–853. doi:10.1016/j.compedu.2007.09.001

Stringer, E. T. (2004). *Action research in education.* Pearson/ Merrill/ Prentice Hall.

Sunahase, T., Baba, Y., & Kashima, H. (2019). Probabilistic modeling of peer correction and peer assessment. In *Proceedings of the Twelfth International Conference on Educational Data Mining (EDM' 19).* International Educational Data Mining Society.

Susarla, A., Oh, J. H., & Tan, Y. (2012). Social networks and the diffusion of user-generated content: Evidence from YouTube. *Information Systems Research, 23*(1), 23–41. doi:10.1287/isre.1100.0339

Tableau. (n.d.). *Information about.* https://en.wikipedia.org/wiki/Tableau_Software

Taibi, D., Chawla, S., Dietze, S., Marenzi, I., & Fetahu, B. (2015). Exploring TED talks as linked data for education. *British Journal of Educational Technology, 46*(5), 1092–1096. doi:10.1111/bjet.12283

Tane, J., Schmitz, C., & Stumme, G. (2004). Semantic resource management for the web: an e- learning application. *Proceedings of the 13th international World Wide Web conference on Alternate Track Papers & Posters*, 1–10.

Tang, C., Lau, R. W., Li, Q., Yin, H., Li, T., & Kilis, D. (2000). Personalized courseware construction based on web data mining. *Web Information Systems Engineering, 2000. Proceedings of the First International Conference on, 2,* 204–211.

Tanimoto, S. L. (2007). Improving the prospects for educational data mining. *Track on Educational Data Mining, at the Workshop on Data Mining for User Modeling, at the 11th International Conference on User Modeling*, 1–6.

Tan, J. P. L., & Koh, E. (2017). Situating learning analytics pedagogically: Towards an ecological lens. *Learning: Research and Practice*, *3*(1), 1–11. doi:10.1080/23735082.2017.1305661

Tan, M., & Wu, M. (2018). An Association Rule Model of Course Recommendation in MOOCs: Based on edX Platform. *European Scientific Journal*, *14*(25), 284. doi:10.19044/esj.2018.v14n25p284

Tardif, M. (2000). Saberes profissionais dos professores e conhecimentos universitários: Elementos para uma epistemologia da prática profissional dos professores e suas conseqüências em relação à formação para o magistério. *Revista Brasileira de Educação*, *13*, 5–24. http://anped.tempsite.ws/novo_portal/rbe/rbedigital/RBDE13/RBDE13_05_MAURICE_TARDIF.pdf

Taşçı, D. & Koç, U. (2007). Örgütsel vatandaşlık davranışı-örgütsel öğrenme değerleri ilişkisi: Akademisyenler üzerinde görgül bir araştırma. *Anadolu Üniversitesi Eğitim Fakültesi Dergisi*, *7*(2), 373–382.

Tashiro, J.S., & Dunlap, D., (2007). The impact of realism on learning engagement in educational games. *Proceedings of Future Play 2007.*

Taylor, S. (2016). Big Data: Understanding. *Big Data.*

TED. (2020). *TED. Our Mission: Spread ideas.* Retrieved from https://www.ted.com/about/our-organization

Tempelaar, D. T., Rienties, B., & Giesbers, B. (2015). In search for the most informative data for feedback generation: Learning analytics in a data-rich context. *Computers in Human Behavior*, *47*, 157–167. doi:10.1016/j.chb.2014.05.038

The Storage Engine. (2015). *1951*: *Tape unit developed for data storage.* Author.

Thompson, C. (2011). How Khan Academy is changing the rules of education. *Wired Magazine*, *126*, 1–5.

Todolí-Signes, A. (2019). Algorithms, artificial intelligence and automated decisions concerning workers and the risks of discrimination: The necessary collective governance of data protection. *Transfer: European Review of Labour and Research*, *25*(4), 465–481. doi:10.1177/1024258919876416

Todos Pela Educação. (2014). *Inovações tecnológicas na educação: Contribuições para gestores públicos*. Inspirare Instituto. https://porvir.org/wp-content/uploads/2014/08/Inova%C3%A7%C3%B5es-Tecnol%C3%B3gicas-na-Educa%C3%A7%C3%A3o_Constribui%C3%A7%C3%B5es-para-gestores-p%C3%BAblicos-1.pdf

Tokel, A., Dagli, G., Altinay, Z., & Altinay, F. (2019). The role of learning management in agile management for consensus culture. *The International Journal of Information and Learning Technology, 36*(4), 364–372. doi:10.1108/IJILT-02-2019-0017

Tran, K.-N., Lau, J. H., Contractor, D., Gupta, U., Sengupta, B., Butler, C. J., & Mohania, M. (2018). Document chunking and learning objective generation for instruction design. In *Proceedings of the Eleventh International Conference on Educational Data Mining (EDM' 18)*. International Educational Data Mining Society.

Tranberg, P., Hasselbalch, G., Olsen, B. K., & Byrne, C. S. (2018). *Data Ethics. Principles and Guidelines for Companies, Authorities & Organisations*. DataEthics.eu. The Independent Thinktank.

Truong, N. B., Lee, G. M., & Ghamri-Doudane, Y. (2015, May). Software defined networking-based vehicular adhoc network with fog computing. In *2015 IFIP/IEEE International Symposium on Integrated Network Management (IM)* (pp. 1202-1207). IEEE. 10.1109/INM.2015.7140467

Tsai, Y. S., Perrotta, C., & Gašević, D. (2020). Empowering learners with personalised learning approaches? Agency, equity and transparency in the context of learning analytics. *Assessment & Evaluation in Higher Education, 45*(4), 554–567. doi:10.1080/02602938.2019.1676396

Tsai, Y. S., Rates, D., Moreno-Marcos, P. M., Muñoz-Merino, P. J., Jivet, I., Scheffel, M., Drachsler, H., Delgado Kloos, C., & Gašević, D. (2020). Learning analytics in European higher education–trends and barriers. *Computers & Education, 155*, 103933. doi:10.1016/j.compedu.2020.103933

Tsai, Y. S., Whitelock-Wainwright, A., & Gašević, D. (2020, March). The privacy paradox and its implications for learning analytics. In *Proceedings of the Tenth International Conference on Learning Analytics & Knowledge* (pp. 230-239). 10.1145/3375462.3375536

Tseng, W., Liou, H., & Chu, H. (2020). Vocabulary learning in virtual environments: Learner autonomy and collaboration. *System, 88*. doi:10.1016/j.system.2019.102190

Tufekci, Z. (2018). YouTube, the great radicalizer. *The New York Times, 10*.

Tuna, G., & Öztürk, A. (2015). Zeki ve uyarlanabilir e-öğrenme ortamları. In *International Distance Education Conference* (pp. 2-4). Academic Press.

Tzelepi, M. (2014, July). Personalizing learning analytics to support collaborative learning design and community building. In *2014 IEEE 14th International Conference on Advanced Learning Technologies* (pp. 771-773). IEEE. 10.1109/ICALT.2014.226

Ueno, M. (2004). Data mining and text mining technologies for collaborative learning in an ILMS "ssamurai". *Advanced Learning Technologies, 2004.Proceedings. IEEE International Conference on*, 1052–1053.

United Nations Educational, Scientific and Cultural Organization. (2016). *Making sense of MOOCs: A guide for policy-makers in developing cauntries.* United Nations Educational, Scientific and Cultural Organization (UNESCO). https://unesdoc.unesco.org/ark:/48223/pf0000245122

Universidade Federal de Pernambuco. (2020). *UFPE em números.* https://www.ufpe.br/institucional/ufpe-em-numeros

Universities, U. K. (2013). *Massive open online courses: Higher education's digital moment?* https://www.universitiesuk.ac.uk/policy-and-analysis/reports/Documents/2013/massive-open-online-courses.pdf

Vainas, O., Ben-David, Y., Gilad-Bachrach, R., Ronen, M., Bar-Ilan, O., & Shillo, R. (2019). Staying in the zone: sequencing content in classrooms based on the zone of proximal development. In *Proceedings of the Twelfth International Conference on Educational Data Mining (EDM' 19).* International Educational Data Mining Society.

Valstar, S., Sih, C., Krause-Levy, S., Porter, L., & Griswold, W. G. (2020). A Quantitative Study of Faculty Views on the Goals of an Undergraduate CS Program and Preparing Students for Industry. *Proceedings of the 2020 ACM Conference on International Computing Education Research*, 113–123.

Valus Education Study Final Report (VES). (2003). *Australian Government, Department of Education, Science and Training.* http://www.curriculum.edu.au/verve/resources/VES_Final_Report14Nov.pdf

Van den EyndenV.KnightG.VladA.RadlerB.TenopirC.LeonD.ManistaF.WhitworthJ.CortiL. (2016). Towards Open Research. Practices, experiences, barriers and opportunities: Welcome Trust. doi:10.6084/m9.figshare.4055448

Van Horik, R., Dillo, I., & Doorn, P. (2013). Lies, Damned Lies and Research Data: Can Data Sharing Prevent Data Fraud? *International Journal of Digital Curation*, *8*(1), 229–243. doi:10.2218/ijdc.v8i1.256

Vanpaemel, W., Vermorgen, M., Deriemaecker, L., & Storms, G. (2015). Are We Wasting a Good Crisis? The Availability of Psychological Research Data after the Storm. *Collabra*, *1*(1). Advance online publication. doi:10.1525/collabra.13

Viberg, O., Hatakka, M., Balter, O., & Mavroudi, A. (2018). The current landscape of learning analytics in higher education. *Computers in Human Behavior*, *89*, 98–110. doi:10.1016/j.chb.2018.07.027

Vicente-Saez, R., & Martinez-Fuentes, C. (2018). Open Science now: A systematic literature review for an integrated definition. *Journal of Business Research*, *88*, 428–436. doi:10.1016/j.jbusres.2017.12.043

Vieira, C., Seah, Y. Y., & Magana, A. J. (2018). Students' experimentation strategies in design: Is process data enough. *Computer Applications in Engineering Education*, *26*(5), 1903–1914. doi:10.1002/cae.22025

Vijh, U. P., Verhagen, J., Phillips, W., & An, J. (2019). Empowering tutors with big-data learning analytics. In *Proceedings of the Ninth International Conference on Learning Analytics & Knowledge (LAK' 19)*. Society for Learning Analytics Research.

Vision, T. J. (2010). Open Data and the Social Contract of Scientific Publishing. *Bioscience*, *60*(5), 330–331. doi:10.1525/bio.2010.60.5.2

Wallace, C., Korb, K. B., & Dai, H. (1996). Causal discovery via mml. *ICML*, *96*, 516–524.

Wampfler, R., Klingler, S., Solenthaler, B., Schinazi, V., & Gross, M. (2019). Affective State Prediction in a Mobile Setting using Wearable Biometric Sensors and Stylus. In *Proceedings of the Twelfth International Conference on Educational Data Mining (EDM' 19)*. International Educational Data Mining Society.

Wang, R., & Zaïane, O. R. (2018). Sequence-Based Approaches to Course Recommender Systems. In S. Hartmann, H. Ma, A. Hameurlain, G. Pernul, & R. R. Wagner (Eds.), Database and Expert Systems Applications (Vol. 11029, pp. 35–50). Springer International Publishing. doi:10.1007/978-3-319-98809-2_3

Wang, V. C. (2014). *Handbook of research on education and technology in a changing society*. IGI Global. doi:10.4018/978-1-4666-6046-5

Watkins, J., & Wilkins, M. (2011). Using YouTube in the EFL classroom. *Language Education in Asia*, *2*(1), 113–119. doi:10.5746/LEiA/11/V2/I1/A09/Watkins_Wilkins

Weka. (n.d.). *Information about*. https://pt.wikipedia.org/wiki/Weka

Wenger, R. H. (1987). Cognitive science and algebra learning. *Cognitive Science and Mathematics Education*, 217-251.

West, D., Huijser, H., & Heath, D. (2016). Putting an ethical lens on learning analytics. *Educational Technology Research and Development*, *64*(5), 903–922. doi:10.100711423-016-9464-3

West, D., Luzeckyj, A., Toohey, D., Vanderlelie, J., & Searle, B. (2020). Do academics and university administrators really know better? The ethics of positioning student perspectives in learning analytics. *Australasian Journal of Educational Technology*, *36*(2), 60–70. doi:10.14742/ajet.4653

Whitehill, J., & Movellan, J. (2017). Approximately optimal teaching of approximately optimal learners. *Institute of Electrical and Electronics Engineers (IEEE). Transactions on Learning Technologies*, *11*(2), 152–164. doi:10.1109/TLT.2017.2692761

Whitelock-Wainwright, A., Gašević, D., Tsai, Y. S., Drachsler, H., Scheffel, M., Muñoz-Merino, P. J., Tammets, K., & Delgado Kloos, C. (2020). Assessing the validity of a learning analytics expectation instrument: A multinational study. *Journal of Computer Assisted Learning*, *36*(2), 209–240. doi:10.1111/jcal.12401

Wiley, K. J., Bradford, A., Pardos, Z., & Linn, M. C. (2019). Beyond autoscoring: extracting conceptual connections from essays for classroom instruction. In *Proceedings of the Twelfth International Conference on Educational Data Mining (EDM' 19)*. International Educational Data Mining Society.

Wilkinson, M. D., Dumontier, M., Aalbersberg, I. J., Appleton, G., Axton, M., Baak, A., Blomberg, N., Boiten, J.-W., da Silva Santos, L. B., Bourne, P. E., Bouwman, J., Brookes, A. J., Clark, T., Crosas, M., Dillo, I., Dumon, O., Edmunds, S., Evelo, C. T., Finkers, R., ... Mons, B. (2016). The FAIR Guiding Principles for scientific data management and stewardship. *Scientific Data*, *3*(1), 9. doi:10.1038data.2016.18 PMID:26978244

Wilson, C. (2013). *Alfabetização midiática e informacional: Currículo para formação de professores*. UNESCO, UFTM. https://unesdoc.unesco.org/ark:/48223/pf0000220418

Wilson, A. D., Onwuegbuzie, A. J., & Manning, L. P. (2016). Using paired depth interviews to collect qualitative data. *Qualitative Report*, *21*(9), 1549.

Wise, A. F. (2014, March). Designing pedagogical interventions to support student use of learning analytics. In *Proceedings of the Fourth International Conference on Learning Analytics & Knowledge (LAK' 14)*. Society for Learning Analytics Research.

Wu, B., Du, F., & Hu, Y. (2019). PBL Discourse analysis in ill-constructive field based on ENA – A case study of Chinese medicine education. In *Proceedings of the Ninth International Conference on Learning Analytics & Knowledge (LAK' 19)*. Society for Learning Analytics Research.

Yadav, S., & Sohal, A. (2017). *Review Paper on Big Data Analytics in Cloud Computing*. Academic Press.

Yalar, T., & Yelken, T. Y. (2011). Değerler eğitiminin iyileştirilmesi ile ilgili öğretmen görüşlerinin belirlenmesi ve bir program modülü örneğinin geliştirilmesi. *Elektronik Sosyal Bilimler Dergisi*, *38*(38).

Yaman, E. (2012). *Değerler eğitimi*. Akçağ Yayınları.

Yang, T. C., Hwang, G. J., & Yang, S. J. H. (2013). Development of an adaptive learning system with multiple perspectives based on students' learning styles and cognitive styles. *Journal of Educational Technology & Society*, *16*(4), 185–200.

Yıldırım, A., & Simsek, H. (2018). *Sosyal bilimlerde nitel araştırma yöntemleri*. Seçkin Yayıncılık.

Yıldırım, N., & Turan, S. (2015). Opinions of primary school classroom teachers about distribution process of values in social science course curriculum [Sınıf öğretmenlerinin hayat bilgisi dersi öğretim programındaki değerlerin kazandırılma sürecine yönelik görüşleri]. *Eğitimde Kuram ve Uygulama*, *11*(2), 420–437.

Yılmaz, K., & Oğuz, E. (2011). Nitel bir görüşme yöntemi: Odak grup görüşmesi. *Kuramsal Eğitimbilim Dergisi*, *4*(1), 95–107.

Yoost, D. (2019). Data Ethics: Beyond Legal Compliance. *The RMA Journal, 101*(8), 16–23.

Yousef, A. M. F., Chatti, M. A., Schroeder, U., Wosnitza, M., & Jakobs, H. (2014). MOOCs: A review of the state-of-the-art. *Proceedings of 6th International Conference on Computer Supported Education*, 9–20. https://www.researchgate.net/publication/275823066_MOOCs_a_review_of_the_state-of-the-a

Yuan, L., & Powell, S. (2013). *MOOCS and Open Education: Implications For Higher Education*. Centre for Educational Technology, Interoperability and Standards (CETIS). https://publications.cetis.org.uk/wp-content/uploads/2013/03/MOOCs-and-Open-Education.pdf

Zaiane, O. R., & Yacef, K. (2015). MOOCs are not MOOCs Yet: Requirements for a True MOOC or MOOC 2.0. *Educational Letter*, *11*(2), 17–21.

Zengin, Y. (2017). Investigating the use of the Khan Academy and mathematics software with a flipped classroom approach in mathematics teaching. *Journal of Educational Technology & Society*, *20*(2), 89–100.

Zhou, R., Khemmarat, S., & Gao, L. (2010). The impact of YouTube recommendation system on video views. In *Proceedings of the 10th ACM SIGCOMM conference on Internet measurement* (pp. 404-410). 10.1145/1879141.1879193

About the Contributors

Ana Azevedo is an Integrated member of CEOS.PP research center and was member of its Directive Board. She is a senior lecture in the Information Systems Department, School of Business / Polytechnic of Porto, Porto, Portugal, teaching courses on E-Commerce, Decision Support Systems, Business Intelligence and Introduction to Database Systems. She holds a PhD in Information Systems and Technologies, University of Minho, Portugal. She is member of the Scientific Board of the Master in E-Business, School of Business / Polytechnic of Porto, Porto, Portugal. She published several articles in journals, conferences, and book chapters. She is associate editor of the International Journal of Technology and Human Interaction (IJTHI), and of the of the International Journal of Decision Support System Technology (IJDSST). She is a member of the Editorial Review Board of the International Journal of Business Intelligence Research (IJBIR), of the International Journal of Grid and Utility Computing (IJGUC), of the Electronic Journal of e-Learning (EJEL), and of the International Journal of Systems and Society (IJSS). She is chair of several conferences and special sessions in conferences. She served as editor for several books and special issues in journals. She regularly serves as member of the program committee for several conferences and also serves as a regular reviewer for several journals and conferences. She regularly supervises and is member of juries of master dissertations. Her primary areas of research interests are Business Intelligence, and Analytics, Decision Support Systems, Data mining, E-Business and Digital Transformation. Her research interests also include E-assessment and Gender Issues in Information Systems and STEM.

Jose Manuel Azevedo is a lecturer in the Mathematics Department, ISCAP/ Polytechnic Institute of Porto (P.PORTO), Porto, Portugal, since 1998. He obtain is PhD in Education (Mathematics) at the University of Beira Interior, Covilhã, Portugal. He teaches subjects such as: Mathematics, Applied Mathematics, Statistics and Algebra. His research interests are Mathematics Education, E-assessment, Financial Mathematics, Financial Time Series, Data Mining, Analytics and e-learning. He published several articles in journals and conferences. He is a member of the program committee of several conferences in his areas of research. In addition, he also serves as a reviewer for some journals and conferences. Researcher at CEOS. PP Research Center.

James Onohuome Uhomoibhi is a Chartered Physicist and a member of the Institute of Physics; He is a Chartered IT Professional, a Fellow of BCS, a Fellow of the UK Higher Education Academy and a member of several national and international professional organisations in Physics, Engineering and Education. He lectures and researches electronics, mechatronics, computer science, and entrepreneurship and innovation in engineering. He is a visiting Professor of Physics, Computer Science and IT in three Nigerian Universities. He is also a visiting Professor of Science, Technology and Environmental Studies at the Open University, Tanzania. James Uhomoibhi holds BSc in Physics Education, BPhil in Philosophy, MSc in Optoelectronics and Optical Information Processing, PGCHET in Higher Education Teaching and PhD in Laser Physics. He has published several articles in journals, conferences and book chapters. He has also edited Books and proceedings. He is a member of Editorial Review Board of several international highly esteemed journals. He is an expert in digital education and e-Research. His research interests are in artificial intelligence, digital education and e-research, machine learning, data science, information security, MAV (mixed augmented and virtual) reality computing. James Uhomoibhi is LEADS scholar in Nigeria and the African Laser Centre representative in Europe.

Ebba Ossiannilsson is the V President for the Swedish Association for Distance Education and for the Swedish Association for E-Competence. She is the CEO of her company on Quality in Open Online Learning. She was awarded the EDEN Fellow title in 2014 and she became Open Education Europa (OEE) Fellow in 2015, and an Ambassador for OEE in 2017. Since 2016 she is ambassador for GLOBE the Community of digital learning. She is a researcher reviewer, advisor and consultant within the area of open, online, flexible, and technology enabled teaching and learning (OOFAT) and quality. Since the year 2000, she worked at Lund University, Sweden, as an e-learning, open online learning expert, and advisor with special focus on quality. She is frequently invited as keynote speaker. She is board member in international associations. She is in the ICDE Focal Points of Quality, in the policy committee for the global advocacy of OER and ICDE ON BOLDIC. She has conducted several research studies and national overview reports. Her PhD at Oulu University, Finland in 2012 was on Benchmarking e-learning in higher education. Her dissertation had a large outreach and is often cited. She has over 200 publications.

* * *

Katarzyna Biernacka is a research assistant and doctoral student at the Humboldt-Universität zu Berlin (HU). She holds a Diploma degree in Computer Science from the Humboldt-Universität zu Berlin. Before she joined the HEADT Centre she worked at the Computer and Media Service of the HU and was the project coordinator and research assistant of FDMentor (a Research Data Management project funded by the Federal Ministry of Education and Research). As an advocate of Open Science, Katarzyna offers various workshops on this and related topics. Her strong interest in digital tools and new forms of learning has shaped her research interest. In her PhD studies she investigates the potential conflict between open research data and the issues of privacy, taking into account both differences between disciplines and between cultural perspectives.

Mustafa Şahin Bülbül completed his undergraduate education at Kafkas University, Faculty of Arts and Sciences, The Department of Physics (2002) and his master's degree in the Institute of Science of the same university with his thesis named "Energy Resolution and Linearity of Hf Detectors Used in the CMS Experiment" (2004). He worked as a classroom and physics teacher during his graduate education (2002-2004). He started to work as a Research Assistant at Kafkas University, Faculty of Education, The Department of Secondary Science and Mathematics Education (OFMAE), Physics Education Department in (2005). He started his doctorate education at Middle East Technical University in 2007 and completed his doctoral dissertation on the ability of visually impaired students to learn physics in inclusive classes (2014). He received his Ph.D. in Physics Education from METU in 2014 and his Associate Professor degree in 2017 from the same field. He continues his undergraduate studies in research of philosophy and sociology with an interest in different subjects such as Chaos theory, Accessible Education, Drama, Futurism, Connectivity, Big Data, Artificial Intelligence, Nature of Science, Contextual Learning, and Creativity. He is currently a lecturer in the Department of Primary Education at the Dede Korkut Faculty of Education at Kafkas University and the director of the www.chaotic.blue web site where the theoretical infrastructure of chaotic learning is shared.

Patricia Cavalcante is Associate 4 Professor of undergraduate course of Centre of Education/UFPE, Vice-head of Teaching Methods and Techniques Department of the Centre of Education/UFPE, researcher at Mathematical and Technological Education Postgraduate Program/EDUMATEC, leader of the Study Group on New Technologies and Education - GENTE/CNPq, Adjunct Coordinator of Open University of Brazil/UFPE, General Secretary of the Open and Digital Education Secretariat of UFPE (SPREAD).

Gokmen Dagli is Dean of Faculty of Education, Vice Rector of University of Kyrenia, Chair of Educational Administration Department at Near East University.

Arvind Dhaka is currently working as Assistant Professor at Manipal University Jaipur.

Samira ElAtia is the McCalla Professor of Assessment in Education and Associate Dean of Graduate Studies, at Faculté Saint-Jean of the University of Alberta. She holds a PhD from the University of Illinois at Urbana-Champaign, USA. Her research interest focuses on issues of fairness in assessment, especially in bilingual contexts. She was member of the board of Director of the Center for Canadian Language Benchmarks in Ottawa. She has served as experts on several international testing agencies: Educational Testing Services in the US, Pearson Education In the UK, The International Baccalaureate Organization, Chambre du commerce et de l'industrie of Paris, Centre international des études pédagogiques of the Ministry of Education in France. She is currently president of the Canadian Association of language Assessment.

Zehra Gazi is Vice Director of Graduate School of Educational Sciences, Co Chair of Societal Research and Development Center, Chair of Educational Sciences Department at Faculty of Education, Near East University.

M. Govindarajan is currently an Associate Professor in the Department of Computer Science and Engineering, Annamalai University, Tamil Nadu, India. He received the B.E, M.E and Ph.D Degree in Computer Science and Engineering from Annamalai University, Tamil Nadu, India in 2001, 2005 and 2010 respectively. He did his post-doctoral research in the Department of Computing, Faculty of Engineering and Physical Sciences, University of Surrey, Guildford, Surrey, United Kingdom in 2011 and at CSIR Centre for Mathematical Modelling and Computer Simulation, Bangalore in 2013. He has visited countries like Czech Republic, Austria, Thailand, United Kingdom (twice), Malaysia, U.S.A (twice), and Singapore. He has presented and published more than 100 papers at Conferences and Journals and also received best paper awards. He has delivered invited talks at various national and international conferences. His current research interests include Data Mining and its applications, Web Mining, Text Mining, and Sentiment Mining. He has completed two major projects as principal investigator and has produced four Ph.Ds. He was the recipient of the Achievement Award for the field in the Conference in Bio-Engineering, Computer Science, Knowledge Mining (2006), Prague, Czech Republic. He received Career Award for Young Teachers (2006), All India Council for Technical Education, New Delhi, India and Young Scientist International Travel Award (2012), Department of Science and Technology, Government of India, New Delhi. He is a Young Scientists awardee under Fast Track Scheme (2013), Department of Science and Technology, Government of India, New Delhi and also granted Young Scientist Fellowship (2013), Tamil Nadu State Council for Science and Technology, Government of Tamil Nadu, Chennai. He also received the Senior Scientist International Travel Award (2016), Department of Science and Technology, Government of India. He is an active Member of various professional bodies and Editorial Board Member of various conferences and journals.

Donald Ipperciel is York University's Chief Information Officer, a position he has held since 2018. Donald joined York University as Principal of Glendon College in 2014 from the University of Alberta's Campus Saint-Jean, where he was Professor of Political Philosophy and served in several administrative roles, including Vice-Dean, Associate Dean Research, Associate Dean Information Technology and Innovation, and Director of the Canadian Studies Institute. He has been the Francophone Editor of the Canadian Journal of Learning and Technology from 2010 to 2020. Prof. Ipperciel is a graduate of the Université de Montréal where he earned his BA and MA and received his PhD from Ruprecht-Karls-Universität in Heidelberg. He was a Canada Research Chair between 2002 and 2012 and was made "Chevalier dans l'Ordre des Palmes académiques" in 2017 by the French Republic.

Paul Joseph-Richard is a Lecturer in Human Resource Management (HRM) at Ulster University Business School. His research seeks to extend our understanding of leadership development, programme evaluation, research-informed teaching, entrepreneurial education, learning analytics and qualitative research methods. He is a Senior Fellow of Higher Education Academy and a Chartered Member of CIPD. Paul has published his research in a range of pedagogic journals. Since 2014, he serves as the Track Chair of the British Academy of Management's Special Interest Group in Leadership and Leadership Development. Prior to his academic career, Paul had a successful HRM career in private and public sector organisations where he developed leadership capabilities in individuals and teams.

Hasan Karal is Vice Rector of Trabzon University.

Josiane Machiavelli is a learning experience designer at the Federal University of Pernambuco, responsible for planning, developing, and offering online courses; training human resources to work in face-to-face and online courses; the development of didactic resources and digital technologies to face-to-face and online courses.

Bertil Maria Pires Marques, PhD in Computer Science by FEUP since 2015. She is teacher at in the Computer Engineering Department IPP-ISEP since 1999. Researcher of Research Group GILT - Games Interaction & Learning Technologies since 2007. Her research interests include e-learning principles, MOOCs, Distance learning, Web tools to support online Learning, collaborative learning and Learning analytics. She has several publications in conferences, journals, and book articles. As hobby event organization, preferably using digital tools.

Amita Nandal is currently working as Associate Professor at Manipal University Jaipur.

Rosa Reis teaches at IPP- ISEP in the Computer Engineering Department. She has a PhD on Informatics at the University UTAD-Tras-os-Montes and Alto Douro, Vila Real. She is a researcher at GILT- Games Interaction and Learning Technologies and her area of research is related to the application of techniques of software engineering in the design of educational collaborative virtual environments.

Arpit Kumar Sharma is currently a PhD scholar at Manipal University Jaipur.

Wenting Sun received her MS in education from Tongji University, Shanghai, China in 2019. In 2020 she was hired as a research assistant by Department of Computer Science at Humboldt University zu Berlin and now is also a PhD student of Humboldt University zu Berlin. Her research interests are learning analytics, learning science, computer supported collaborative learning and educational psychology.

Sunita Sunita is currently a student at Arya Institute of Engineering Technology and Management, Jaipur.

Kumar Swasti is a student at Arya Institute of Engineering Technology and Management, Jaipur.

Index

F

H

I

K

L

M

N

O

P

R

S

T

U

V

W

Y

www.ingramcontent.com/pod-product-compliance
Lightning Source LLC
LaVergne TN
LVHW061542290926
849162LV00004B/879